Race, Ethnicity, and Nationality in the United States

Toward the Twenty-First Century

edited by

Paul Wong

Colorado State University

Westview Press
A Member of the Perseus Books Group

Copyright © 1999 by Westview Press, A Member of the Perseus Books Group

Published in 1999 in the United States of America by Westview Press, 5500 Central Avenue, Boulder, Colorado 80301-2877, and in the United Kingdom by Westview Press, 12 Hid's Copse Road, Cumnor Hill, Oxford OX2 9JJ

A CIP catalog record for this book is available from the Library of Congress.
ISBN 0-8133-3477-2 (hc)—ISBN 0-8133-3478-0 (pb)

The paper used in this publication meets the requirements of the American National Standard for Permanence of Paper for Printed Library Materials Z39.48-1984.

10   9   8   7   6   5   4   3   2   1

UNIVERSITY OF
WOLVERHAMPTON

Race, Ethnicity, and Nationality
in the United States

To my mother,
Diana Shook Cheung Lo Wong,
and my wife,
Karen Henschell

Contents

Preface

This book is intended for use in advanced undergraduate and graduate-level courses on race and ethnicity and on diversity in America. It was first conceived as a collective project of the Research and Resident Scholar Program in Comparative Race Relations at Washington State University, which was established in 1994 with support from the Rockefeller Foundation. A number of the participating authors are established scholars in racial/ethnic studies, and several have published award-winning bestsellers. Others are relative newcomers to the field who were invited to join the project because they were doing important work on less well covered topics, such as relations between African Americans and Chicano/Latino Americans.

The volume is multidisciplinary and interdisciplinary: We deliberately selected chapter authors grounded in diverse disciplines (anthropology, ethnic studies, cultural studies, literary studies, sociology, political science, education, psychology, and history) who are receptive to boundary-crossing. The book is thus particularly well suited for use as a text in the growing number of upper-division undergraduate courses in ethnic studies, sociology, American studies, and general education that are aimed at integrating knowledge about race and ethnicity drawn from diverse disciplines.

A number of the book's chapters, while they were yet in manuscript form, were tested as required readings in such courses, with a good deal of success. In my own courses I have supplemented readings from this book with in-class discussions, videos, and additional reading material. I have found that in this context the book provides a good conceptual "bridge" to the twenty-first century, enhancing students' understanding of the historical evolution and the ongoing impact of race and ethnicity in the United States during an era of accelerating social change.

Paul Wong

Acknowledgments

I would like to thank the various people who read and commented on chapters in this volume, especially the graduate students in my spring 1997 seminar on race and ethnic relations at Washington State University (Dennis Bautista, Maria Chavez, Lorna Hanrahan, Darcy James, Rachel Maldonado, Pui Yan Lam, and Susan Rhode). I also would like to thank the following staff members of the Center for Applied Studies in American Ethnicity at Colorado State University for their assistance in word processing and editing (Rosa Garcia, Robert Koehler, Stacy Ann Nitta, and Irma Rodriguez Woollen).

P. W.

Introduction

PAUL WONG

The field of race and ethnic studies is experiencing an extraordinary growth spurt, in part as a result of demographic change throughout the United States. With the dramatic increase in the Asian Pacific, Chicano/Latino, and Native American populations, this field is no longer dominated by the white versus black perspective, in which other nonwhites were usually subsumed under the categories of "black" or "other." The field has begun to move toward a multiracial and multiethnic perspective. In this process, scholars have come to recognize that past research is not adequate in describing or explaining the changing racial/ethnic realities.

The demand for new methodological approaches and theories and for new substantive knowledge about racial and ethnic groups has been fueled especially by the proliferation of courses on race, ethnicity, and diversity in the general education requirements of many colleges in the United States. Instructors for these courses are drawn from diverse disciplines in the humanities and social sciences, including education, ethnic studies, cultural studies, American studies, women studies, human development, and social work. Rather than focusing on the contributions from any single discipline or on a "smorgasbord" description of various racial/ethnic groups, many of these courses attempt to provide thematic integration and synthesis of knowledge about race and ethnicity from various fields. That is also the approach we have adopted in this book.

From a Racial Formation to a Race/Ethnicity/Nationality Formation Perspective

Our book takes as its starting point the racial formation perspective developed by Omi and Winant (1986; 1994). In the 1986 edition of *Racial Formation in the United States*, Omi and Winant presented a theory of racialization and racial formation and applied it to the analysis of race relations in the United States between the 1960s and 1980s. They looked at race not only as the subject of struggle and contest at the level of social structure but also as a

1

contested theme at the level of social signification—that is, the level of the social production of meanings. In an epilogue to the 1994 edition of their book, Omi and Winant extended their analysis to the 1990s.

Our book further extends the racial formation perspective in a number of ways:

1. Several chapter authors have applied the racial formation perspective to analyses of current racial relations (see the chapters by Winant, San Juan, Jr., and Bonilla-Silva). Their essays raise questions as to whether there have been fundamental changes in racial ideologies and racial structures in recent years. We could infer from each essay its author's views about the possible contours and trajectories of racial relations in the coming century. In this sense, the analysis of the "present as history" is useful in understanding the future.

2. The racial formation perspective has been adopted by Chris Friday in his examination of the evolution of interracial relations in the American West between the mid-nineteenth and the mid-twentieth centuries. In this probing historical analysis, considerations of ethnicity, class, gender, and social space ("place") are interwoven with considerations of color.

3. We have attempted to address an important subject that Omi and Winant had neglected in their earlier theory of racial formation: the intersections of ethnicity, class, and race in a historical materialist framework. Whereas studies of ethnicity in the United States prior to the 1970s (Park, 1950; Gordon, 1964) generally were framed in an immigration and assimilationist paradigm based on the experience of white European immigrants, after the mid-1960s the emergence of various panethnic (which overlap with but are not synonymous with racial) formations—Asian/Pacific American, Latino, and American Indian—led to the need to reexamine the intersections of race, class, and ethnicity. Still, much recent scholarship has failed to connect race, ethnicity, and class dynamics in the United States with the transformation in global capitalism. However, in their chapters in this volume, E. San Juan, Jr. has criticized "the bankrupt metaphysics of poststructuralist speculation" and called for the construction of "a historical-materialist mapping of the present U.S. racial order with specific reference to Asians or Pacific Rim people domiciled here"; and Fred Krissman has examined the situation of Mexican farmworkers in the United States in the context of the political economy of transnational agribusiness. Through meticulous fieldwork that he conducted both in Mexico and in the "factories of the field" in California and in Washington state, Fred Krissman has studied the relationship between the Chicano farm labor contrac-

tors, Chicano farmworkers, labor unions, and transnational agribusiness. The questions of class divisions within the Chicano "race" and the impact of those divisions on the labor movement are also addressed in Krissman's essay.

4. Nation and nationality have been largely neglected in research on race and ethnicity in recent decades. For example, Omi and Winant (1986; 1994) viewed the national question primarily from an African American perspective, referring to the literature on black nationalism and internal colonialism and to Marxist debates on the Black Nation thesis. There are several important reasons why nation and nationality should be given greater attention in ethnic studies. First, there are about five hundred Indian nations in the United States, and more than one hundred of them are still seeking federal recognition; thus, it is clear that nation and nationality, including the question of self-determination, will continue to be significant for the Indian peoples in the twenty-first century. Secondly, the legacy of the conquest of the Southwest and the acquisition of Puerto Rico continues to affect the political economic conditions of the people who live in those areas, and the effects cannot be understood fully without taking into account the questions of nationhood and of nationality. Thirdly, changes in immigration policies since the 1960s have resulted in the influx to the United States of millions of new immigrants from third world countries, particularly from Asia and Latin America. The concepts of race and panethnicity mask the heterogeneity among the various nationality groups subsumed under those categories. In the concluding chapter of this book, Wong argues that the new paradigm for the analysis of race and ethnicity in the United States in the twenty-first century must include national origin, along with class and gender, as major explanatory variables.

5. The theory of racial formation attempts to link micro-level analysis—social signification and the construction of meanings as well as identity at the individual level—with macro-level analysis—changes in racial structure at the societal level as a result of the contestation for power. In this context, two chapters in this volume analyze the deep structure and dynamics of racial identity formation. Using qualitative interview data, Marc Pizarro has investigated how the different realms of identity formation—that is, race, class, religion, family, community, and gender—are linked, and how these linkages are reflected in the scholarly discourse and in his personal conversations with informants. Pizarro has postulated that political (racial) identity is linked to discrimination and in turn to gender and even sexuality, depending on the individual, while cultural (ethnic) identity is linked to family, community/class, and religion. He has shown how the complex self-redef-

inition of Chicanas/os may be understood in terms of *rasquachismo*—roughly translated as an underdog perspective rooted in resourcefulness and adaptability yet mindful of stance and style. Using discourse analysis, Kathryn Shanley has focused in her chapter on how American Indians, as cultural communities, have utilized metaphorical constructs to indicate to themselves and others what they really represent. Both of these essays reinforce Omi's analysis (in this volume) on how social identities develop and evolve within racial/ethnic groups.

6. A highly neglected area of race and ethnic studies is the relationship among subordinate groups and their perceptions toward each other (Wong, Lai, Nagasawa, and Lin, 1998). It is only in the past decade or so that the relationship among peoples of color—African Americans, Asian Pacific Americans, Chicanos/Latinos, and Native Americans—began to receive some attention in race and ethnic studies. One of the reasons is that each of these "others" tended previously to be of interest for academic or political reasons *only* in juxtaposition to whites. Although still at an early stage, the changing demographics across the United States, coupled with increasing multiracial interactions in various spheres, is beginning to stimulate the analysis of minority–minority relations. In this volume, Yolanda Flores Niemann has provided an integrative review on the effects of social ecological contexts on Hispanic–black relations and attitudes.

7. Along with the analysis of the evolution in the form and content of racism, it is important to deal with antiracism and strategies of resistance. Recently, B. P. Bowser (1995) edited a volume on racism and antiracism in world perspective. Advances in information technology have opened up new fronts for racist and antiracist propaganda and organization. In this volume, we have included an essay, by Colin Beckles, on the Internet strategies of white supremacist groups and the antiracist virtual web of resistance. In addition, the need to reformulate a strategy of resistance and liberation is underscored in San Juan's essay, in which the author has underscored the importance of connecting single instances of revolt by Chinese, Japanese, Filipino, or Korean immigrants with a revolutionary alliance of forces opposing the system as a whole. In addition, Bonilla-Silva has shown how the shift from mass movement to electoral politics between the 1960s and the 1990s has narrowed the options of antiracist organization. He argues that mass protests against covert and overt racism must be renewed for such political organization to be effective.

8. No effort previously was made to formalize Omi and Winant's "verbal" theory of racial formation. In his chapter, Richard Nagasawa has organized the assumptions (explicit and implicit), concepts, and

logically disconnected set of statements or propositions into a logically coherent system. In formalizing the theory of racial formation, Nagasawa also has shed light on what propositions need to be tested in order to evaluate the empirical adequacy of the theory. At the same time, Nagasawa revealed that Omi and Winant may have developed two separate theories of racial formation—one at the macro level and a second at the micro level—that are logically disconnected. Winant's response and Nagasawa's rejoinder provide important ideas for the further development of racial formation theory.

In the final chapter of this book, Paul Wong has examined the development of race relations theories in the United States from the 1930s to the 1990s. The major paradigms—ethnicity/assimilation, colonial/internal colonial, class, and racial formation (social construction)—are reassessed in the context of racial dynamics in the United States in the transition from the twentieth to the twenty-first century. This essay also critiqued racial formation theory and argued for a broader, social constructionist approach to the analysis of race, ethnicity, and nationality in the United States.

A Preview of Chapters and Major Themes

In Chapter 1, Winant has elaborated on the confusion about what racism is at the end of the twentieth century. Beginning with the premise that not all racial projects are racist, Winant proposes two criteria to determine whether a racial project is racist or not. He defines a racial project as racist if it creates or reproduces *hierarchical* (dominant/subordinate) social structures based on *essentialized* racial categories. In other words, essentialization and subordination are linked. Winant follows Fuss (1989) in defining essentialism as a belief in unchanging human characteristics, impervious to social and historical contexts. Winant asserts that this approach recognizes the importance of locating racism within a fluid and contested history of racially based social structures and discourses. It seems that the first criterion—that the project not produce or reproduce hierarchical social structures—implies that action to redistribute various types of resources (political, economic, social, and so on) in order to achieve equality among racial groups would be considered nonracist. In this sense, Winant has not addressed situations wherein actions to reduce racial inequality and class inequality, or other possible intersections (race, class, and gender, for example), are in conflict. The second criterion holds the premise that racial categories are continuously in flux. From this premise it follows that social action pertaining to race relations must be grounded in concrete historical times and social contexts. A social policy aimed at reducing racial inequality in a particular time and context might not work well in other times and contexts. Also, as the characteristics of racial categories are continuously in flux, it would be racist to essentialize, for example, a racial group or specific members of the group as either omnipotent or devoid of power. An interesting question is whether Winant's criteria for distinguishing racist projects from nonracist ones may be applied to the analysis of both dominant and subordinate groups' discourses and behaviors.

In Chapter 2, Omi has addressed the dynamic and contested character of racial classifications, using the standards for the creation of "compatible, nonduplicated, exchangeable racial and ethnic data by federal agencies" as an example. The intent of the state to establish "objective" racial and ethnic categories that are valid and reliable in terms of conceptualization and measurement is problematized by the "slippery" nature of the indicators used to classify group membership. Omi discusses how racial and ethnic identities are affected by social and political changes in society, coupled with life cycle effects (that is, changes in an individual's self-conception with regard to race/ethnicity) and other variables. Moreover, the categories used by the government to classify racial and ethnic groups might not be meaningful to the very individuals or groups they purport to represent. Consider, for example, that a Mexican American may identify himself/herself as Mexicano/Mexicana, Hispanic or Hispano, Texano/Texana (if the individual came from Texas), Chicano/Chicana, Latino/Latina, and Mexican American—and this is by no means an exhaustive list. Omi's essay raises serious questions about the possible misuses of racial/ethnic data collected by the government. The gap between administrative requirements and popular consciousness, changes in one's self-identity in different periods of life, and the effects of social movements are factors that complicate racial classification in any multiracial, multiethnic society. As we approach the year 2000, the resolution of these questions—to the extent that they can be resolved—has become an important public policy issue.

In Chapter 3, E. San Juan, Jr. has criticized the major paradigms that academic scholars have employed to analyze the situation of Asians in the late capitalist United States. Predictably, he exposes the immigration/assimilation/modernization paradigm as it has been applied to the analysis of the historical experience of Asian immigrants. He argues that "many Asian American artists and intellectuals subscribe to this paradigm in one degree or another even while they acknowledge the 'racial pattern' of discrimination and exclusion defining the U.S. sociopolitical order." At the same time, San Juan opposes what he considers the "postmodernist idealism that has overtaken Asian American scholars," which has resulted in "the nearly unanimous dismissal of the Marxist critique of capitalist society and its associated ideological/political practices" that characterizes "the mind-set of Asian Americans entrenched in the academies of the Empire."

Is there any evidence that a "new racism" has emerged in the past three or four decades? In Chapter 4, Eduardo Bonilla-Silva has taken up the question of whether a transformation has occurred in the racial structure of the United States in recent years. He contends that despite profound changes that occurred in the 1960s, a new racial structure—that is, a new racism—has evolved, which accounts for the persistence of racial inequality. Bonilla-Silva identified five elements constituting this new racial structure: (1) the increasingly *covert* nature of racial discourse and racial practices; (2) the avoidance of racial terminology and the ever growing claim by whites that they experience "reverse discrimination"; (3) the elaboration of a racial agenda over political matters that eschews direct racial references; (4) the invisibility of most mechanisms that reproduce racial inequality; and (5) the rearticulation of racial practices characteristic of the Jim Crow period of race relations. Bonilla-Silva has surveyed the evidence on how black-white inequality is produced and reproduced in the United States in five areas: social, economic, and political life; social control; and ideology. He argues that since the 1960s, racial discourse and racial practices have become increasingly subtle and covert. These practices are, moreover, insulated through institutionalization in the "normal" operations of many organizations. Bonilla-Silva calls for a return to mass protest at the same time as he recognizes the limits of this tactic in an era of election-centered politics. He disagrees with social scientists, such as Sniderman and Piazza (1993), who he believes failed to envisage the rearticulation and fusion of racist thought with so-called "purely political attitudes," as in whites' current opposition to government intervention in education, employment, and welfare. Following Jackson (1984), Bonilla-Silva asserts that racial privilege today is defended by whites with reference to equal opportunity rather than to egalitarianism or equality of results. In this way, "racial ideology in this period has an apparently nonracial character, can hide under egalitarian ideas, and is driven by the notion of individualism." Another factor one might consider is the widening disjuncture between the content of public discourse and private conversation over racial matters, or the difference in racial talk in racially homogeneous versus mixed gatherings. Another strand of the nonracial character of the current racial ideology is the defense of law and order, which appears to be a race-neutral position. In this essay, Bonilla-Silva has focused on blacks or on black-white relations without bringing in the multiracial, multiethnic tensions and issues that have emerged, particularly in urban and suburban areas, since the 1960s. Further research is needed in order to extend this analysis to other racial groups. For example, in social control measures such as arrests, convictions, and sentencing, are there significant disparities between whites and other minority races, similar to those between whites and blacks? For Asian Americans, does the model minority stereotype lead to a lessening of social control against this group? What are the causes and dynamics of black-Asian or black-brown conflicts? (On this subject, see Flores Niemann, in this volume.)

The theory of racial formation was developed by Omi and Winant for the analysis of the United States—first, from the 1960s to the 1980s, and later, encompassing the 1990s. In Chapter 5, historian Chris Friday has moved the clock back and examined race relations in the American West from about the mid-nineteenth century up to the 1960s. In doing this, he joins a number of scholars (such as Tomás Almaguer [1994]) who believe it is important to fill this gap in the history of racial formation in the American West. Friday has complemented his analysis of racialization and racial formation with an engagement of two powerful narratives or themes of "race and place." He contrasts the narratives in which race relations are viewed in terms of black and white and other groups are portrayed only episodically, as localized and exceptional phenomena, with the "New Western" historians' visions of a western region that was highly multiracialized, gendered, and class-conflict-ridden. He includes in the concept of place or space both the physical and social dimensions. For instance, he states that "until the early 1940s, racialized groups, including whites, competed with each other for control of new social spaces, yet access to the state gave whites the upper hand." He uses the concept of social space, with its underlying emphasis on class, culture, and identity, to analyze multiracial relationships in the development of the West. Friday also has brought the intersection between race and gender constructions into his analysis.

He delineates four stages in the development of race relations in the American West. In the first period, extending from the 1880s to the 1920s, whites used their growing control of the land base and labor markets to establish racial hegemony in the region. Beginning in the 1920s and continuing until the 1940s, racialized groups, including whites, competed for social spaces, which resulted in a multiracial society "riddled by overlapping hierarchies and power relationships." The third period, which began in the late 1930s and lasted until the 1960s, was characterized by massive demographic shifts; huge federal investments in the urban, military, and industrial complex; and dramatic changes in the social landscape. Friday posits the bold hypothesis that in this period, as whites attempted to reconstruct or reassert hegemony and as subordinated racialized groups struggled for political position in the new social order, African Americans achieved the premier position among the subordinated. Finally, in the fourth period, beginning in the 1960s, a multiracial struggle erupted as Asian Americans, Mexican Americans, and Native Americans gained positions that began to rival that of African Americans. In this context, Friday employs the concept of hegemony, which he defines as the control of subordinated groups on the basis of those groups' belief that selective movement out of subjugation can occur even though violent, naked force *can* and *might* be used against transgressors individually or in groups. In light of this definition, which is close to that of Gramsci, the most well-known theorist of hegemony (Gramsci, 1971), it is important to consider whether it is valid to characterize the quasimonopoly of Japanese Americans in the produce industry in the 1920s and 1930s as "ethnic hegemony." Friday has borrowed this phrase from Jiobu (1978), and like the latter, he does not distinguish between "ethnic niches" (e.g., Chinese "domination" of the laundry trades or the Chinese restaurant business) and "hegemony" in terms of political power and the use of force or violence.

In contrast to Friday, the work of Michael Omi and Howard Winant has focused on white hegemony in the specific sense of political power. Omi and Winant's *Racial Formation in the United States* has had a considerable impact on how race and ethnic issues are conceptualized and analyzed; to date no attempt has been made to consider their work in terms of formal theory. To the formal theorist, and perhaps also to empirical researchers who are interested in assessing the validity of a theory, it may appear that Omi and Winant's greatest contribution lies in the concepts introduced—racial formation, racialization, racial trajectory, racial projects, and the racialized state—but not in the coherence of its fundamental principles, axioms, and theorems. Formal theorists would define the work as social thought or verbal theory. In Chapter 6, sociologist and logician Richard Nagasawa has embarked on the tasks of clarifying and formalizing Omi and Winant's racial formation theory. Nagasawa qualifies his attempt as "limited in the sense that others might disagree with the decisions I have made in selecting the basic sentences (or axioms) of the formal system." Nevertheless, Nagasawa has made an important contribution in dissecting the underlying logical structure of Omi and Winant's theory of racial formation, paving the way for future theoretical and empirical work toward extending this theory.

Yolanda Flores Niemann's chapter provides a review and critique of the literature on three related topics: (1) black and Hispanic intergroup attitudes and prejudices, intergroup stereotypes, social distance, and conflict/hostility; (2) the social ecological contexts of blacks and Hispanics, including the disparities in housing, education, employment, health, and political power that underlie negative perceptions and relations between the groups; and (3) the projections of future black-brown relations. Flores Niemann's essay fills an important gap in the race relations literature: the relations and interactions among nonwhite groups. Her conclusions, which are drawn from her extensive review of scholarship, have profound implications for multiracial relations in the twenty-first century. For example, she found that the social distance between blacks and Hispanics is greater than that between each of the two minorities and the majority Anglo group. Furthermore, and more generally, minority group members hold values similar to those of the majority, accepting the majority while rejecting the other minority. She has inferred in these findings that one cannot rely on the experience of discrimination to reduce discrimination. Though her essay was not written with attention to racial formation theory, her review of the research on black-brown differences regarding perceptions of social distance, stereotypes, mutual affinity, intergroup conflicts, and racism are useful in understanding the production of racialized meanings and racial relations at the micro level. Flores Niemann considers the ecological contexts, such as housing, employment, school, and politics—contested terrain at the macro level between African Americans and Hispanics—as well as the effects of competition on the relationship between these two groups. Her analysis suggests that the existence of the "middleman" or "model" minorities further complicates multiracial relations.

How the racialized incidents that occur in everyday life influence identity development is explored through ethnographic interviews in Chapter 8. In this chapter, Marc Pizarro examines what he alternately called the sites, realms, or arenas of identity formation among Chicana/o students. These sites include the family, church, school, the Chicano community, and external communities, as well as institutions such as the police. In personal interviews, Pizarro discovered that race was by far the most dominant facet of students' identities. However, the complexities of their racial identity were reflected clearly in their responses to the interviewer's questions. Pizarro observes that "while students bring up a number of other realms of potential identity formation that are involved in their development, many of them are discussed as embedded within the construct of race itself." He found that in most cases, class was consciously or subconsciously deemed a part of being Chicana/o. Specifically, being Chicana/o was seen as being disadvantaged in terms of class position. Another important conceptual contribution of Pizarro's research is the distinction between racial identity and cultural identity. In his in-depth interviews, Pizarro found that racial or political identity was linked to experience of discrimination and in turn to gender and even sexuality, while cultural or ethnic identity was linked to family, community, and religion. Ethnic-cultural identity is local and embedded in Chicana/o family and community experience, while racial-political identity evolved from experiences of discrimination in schools and other arenas. Pizarro links racializing incidents occurring in schools, with the police, and in the interaction between Chicanas/os and whites with the hierarchical structures of race relations. Finally, he elaborates the concept of *rasquachismo* as a worldview or an approach to life that reconceives "lower-class" cultures as powerful by invigorating specific cultural icons with reinterpreted significance. He sees *rasquachismo* as an ideology to be used in the struggle against racial oppression, endowing Chicanas/os with cultural capital, and reconstructing the image of the Chicana/o.

Fred Krissman, in Chapter 9, has examined the divide-and-conquer strategies of agribusinesses in California and Washington in their relationship to farm workers. Krissman's analysis has revealed the importance of interrogating the ideological roots and material basis of racial solidarity versus divisions based on class, gender, nationality, and other factors. Pivotal to this understanding are the historical and contemporary roles of the Chicano farm labor contractor as the "middleman" between agribusiness and Chicano farm workers. The racial formation paradigm tends to concentrate on the relationship between the dominant race, subordinate races, and the racialized state, neglecting racial and other types of divisions within race. In this respect, the racial formation paradigm tends to overemphasize race as the source of social inequalities above other factors.

Kathryn Shanley's essay (Chapter 10) focuses on how cultural communities utilize metaphorical constructs to indicate to themselves and others what they ideally represent. She argues that the linguistic gestures people make toward establishing a sense of nationhood or community find their basis first in concepts of selfhood, and more specifically, in beliefs about the human body. Thus the sense of nationhood or nationality is linked to social conceptions of the physical self. Occasions of textual collaboration between peoples—such as treaties and as-told-to autobiographies—provide material for analyzing such ontological and epistemological differences. At the core of Shanley's project is an exploration of why the "right to be Indian" has historically been under siege in the United States and how American Indians' survival as Indians relates to body-centered discourse and values.

In Chapter 11, Colin Beckles has examined the problem of racial polarization on the Internet. Beginning with the premise that the Internet is a source of social power, he focuses on how the violent, white racist organizations such as the Ku Klux Klan and Skinheads have used the Net in their quest to "reestablish their supreme position within the global racial order." He shows that the strategies of these organizations on the Internet are couched in the language of a war of annihilation, of whites over African Americans, Latinos, Asian Americans, and Native Americans. He then turns to an analysis of how antiracists use the Net to disseminate antiracist educational information, to monitor and censor white supremacists, to organize antiracist protests in the real world, and to form antiracist networks. Beckles's research into racism on the Internet is a good illustration of the immensely accelerated pace of the contestation over the production of racial ideologies due to the advances in communications technology.

In Chapter 12, Paul Wong has examined the historical development of theories of race and ethnicity (including nationality) in the United States. He shows that American theories of race and ethnicity have been enormously influenced by the ideology and politics of the eras during which these theories were developed. In the first half of the twentieth century, when America was concerned particularly with the problem of absorbing the large European white ethnic immigrant groups into the Anglo-Saxon mainstream, assimilation or ethnicity theories predominated. Theories of internal colonialism flourished from about the late 1960s to the end of the 1970s, as scholars attempted to explain the transition of the black civil rights movement to the black power movement. Internal colonialism was used not only to analyze black-white relations but also to explain the relationship between whites and other nonwhite groups in the 1960s and 1970s. Racial formation theory attempted to purge internal colonialism of its "nation-based" and territorial assumptions. Racial formation theory presupposes that race relations at both the macro and the micro levels are continuously changing and that the processes as well as outcomes do not necessarily follow a set course. In that sense, it differs from ethnicity theory, which predicts an orderly progression toward assimilation and internal colonialism, projecting instead a volatile path toward conflict and even revolution. Though the process of racial formation is seen as highly contested at both the macro and the micro levels, the outcomes are not unidirectional but move back and forth between equilibrium and disequilibrium. Racial formation theory was developed in the late 1970s and the 1980s, when radical racial movements had faded and actions for racial justice were reabsorbed into the legislative and other established institutional arenas. Racial formation theory focuses on dominant-subordinate interracial relations and on the actions of the racialized state. In this chapter, Wong examines persistent as well as new issues in race and ethnic relations in America and assesses the gaps in theoretical and empirical research of these issues.

REFERENCES

Almaguer, T. (1994). *Racial Fault Lines: The Historical Origins of White Supremacy in California*. Berkeley: University of California Press.

Bowser, B. P., ed. (1995). *Racism and Anti-Racism in World Perspective*. Thousand Oaks, CA: Sage.

Friday, C. (1993). *Organizing Asian American Labor*. Philadelphia, PA: Temple University Press.

Fuss, D. (1989). *Essentially Speaking: Feminism, Nature, and Difference*. New York: Routledge.

Gordon, M. M. (1964). *Assimilation in American Life*. New York: McGraw Hill.

Gramsci, A. (1971). *Selections from the Prison Notebooks*. New York: International Publishers.

Jackson, M., and Muha, M. J. (1984). "Education and Intergroup Attitudes: Moral Enlightenment, Superficial Democratic Commitment, or Ideological Refinement?" *American Sociological Review* 49 (December), pp. 751–769.

Jiobu, R. (1988). "Ethnic Hegemony and the Japanese of California." *American Sociological Review* 53, pp. 353–367.

Omi, M., and Winant, H. (1986). *Racial Formation in the United States: From the 1960s to the 1980s*. New York: Routledge.

_____. (1994). *Racial Formation in the United States: From the 1960s to the 1990s*. New York: Routledge.

Park, R. E. (1950). *Race and Culture*. Glencoe, IL: Free Press.

San Juan, E., Jr. (1992). *Racial Formations/Critical Transformations*. Atlantic City, NJ: Humanities Press.

Shanley, K. (1997). *"Only an Indian": Reading James Welch*. Lincoln: University of Nebraska Press.

Sniderman, P., and Piazza, T. (1993). *The Scar of Race*. Cambridge, MA: Harvard University Press.

Winant, H. (1994). *Racial Conditions*. Minneapolis: University of Minnesota Press.

Wong, P., Lai, F., Nagasawa, R., and Lin, T. (1998). "Asian Americans As a Model Minority: Self-Perceptions and Perceptions By Other Racial Groups." *Sociological Perspectives* 41, no. 1, pp. 95–118.

one

Racism Today:
Continuity and Change in
the Post–Civil Rights Era

HOWARD WINANT

In the complex crosscurrents of the post–civil rights era, what is racism? Is it the same, or has it changed in response to the changing dynamics of race in the post–civil rights era? To answer such questions, to understand the meaning of racism today, and to take an informed and politically effective stand in such complex crosscurrents is no easy matter.

Before we even tackle the matter of racism, we must first develop a working understanding of what we mean by race. This also is not easy. Today we recognize that the concept of race is problematic, that the meaning of race is socially constructed and politically contested. This is a hard-won recognition, one that has obtained fairly generally only since World War II (Omi and Winant, 1994).

But problematizing race is not enough. We must steer between the Scylla of thinking that race is a mere illusion, mere ideology (in the sense of false consciousness), on the one hand, and the Charybdis of thinking that race is something objective and fixed. Both of these positions have their temptations, and by no means only for those who would deny the significance of race. The former position ("race as illusion") is upheld today not only by neoconservatives but also by radical theorists of race such as Anthony Appiah and Barbara Fields. In the work of these scholars, whatever its other

Previous versions of this chapter were presented in the Working Papers Lecture Series of the Afro-American Studies Program at Princeton University, and in the Rockefeller Lecture Series in Comparative American Cultures at Washington State University. Particular thanks to Eduardo Bonilla-Silva, Wahneema Lubiano, Michelle Lamont, and Paul Wong.

merits, there is little recognition of the autonomy and depth of racialization in the United States. The latter view (race as "objective") is accepted not only by biological determinists and scientific racists but also by many social scientists (including a number who are progressive)—for example, William Julius Wilson, Milton Gordon, or Michael Banton. In the work of these analysts, whatever its other merits, there is little recognition of the socially constructed, politically contested meaning of racial categories, racial identity, and racialized experience.

In contrast to these approaches, Michael Omi and I have proposed the theory of racial formation, which looks at race not only as the subject of struggle and contest at the level of social structure but also as a contested theme at the level of social signification, of the production of meanings. In the first category we include such issues as the racial dimensions of social stratification and distribution, of institutional arrangements, political systems, laws, and so on. The latter category consists of the ways in which race is culturally figured and represented, the manner in which race comes to be meaningful as a descriptor of group or individual identity, social issues, and experience.

We have sought to theorize racial formation as a permanent process in which historically situated projects interact. Human bodies and consciousnesses, as well as social institutions and structures, are represented and organized in the clash and conflict, the accommodation and overlap of these projects. We argue that in any given historical context, racial signification and racial structuration are ineluctably linked. To represent, interpret, or signify race, then, to assign meaning to it, is at least implicitly and often explicitly to locate it in social structural terms.

The linkage between culture and structure, which is at the core of the racial formation process, gives racial projects their cohesiveness. Thus, arguments that the United States is inherently a "white man's country" (as in certain far-right racial discourses), or that race is a spurious anachronism beneath the notice of the state (as in neoconservative positions), or that racial difference is a matter of "self-determination" (as in certain radical racial discourses) are closely succeeded by the consequent patterns of political orientation, economic and social programs, and other structural manifestations.

The reverse is also true: When organizations, institutions, or state agencies advocate or resist a certain racial policy or practice, when they mobilize politically along racial lines, they necessarily engage in racial signification, at least implicitly, and usually explicitly. When the Supreme Court rules that individualism and meritocracy are the only legitimate criteria for employment decisions or university admissions, it inevitably and simultaneously represents race as illusory and spurious. Let me give some other examples. Consider the implications when spokespersons for the Aryan Nation or the Church of the Creator (two fascist groups in the United States) propose setting aside areas of the country for whites only: In this structural initiative, they are simultaneously representing race as a natural, invariant, biological difference. At the opposite pole of the political spectrum, consider what happens when radical democratic organizations, such as the Highlander Center or UNITE—the newly merged needle trades union—engage in community or labor organizing that seeks both to build multiracial organizations and to recognize the relevance of distinct racialized experiences among their constituents. In this effort to mobilize politically, to change the social structure, these organizations necessarily represent race in terms of decenteredness, flexibility, and the relative permanence of difference, embracing the DuBoisian synthesis of full democracy and racial "conservation" (Du Bois, 1897 [1995]).

Keep this idea of racial formation via racial projects on hold while the discussion is refocused on racism; I shall return to the dynamics of racial formation presently. In what follows I shall first discuss the transformations that have affected the concept of racism since the ambiguous triumph of the civil rights "revolution" in the mid-1960s. Next, I shall offer an account of contemporary racism that I believe more adequately addresses present conditions. Finally, in a brief conclusion, I offer some thoughts about the changing link between racial formation and racism on the threshold of the new millennium.

Our Concept of Racism Has Deteriorated

The understanding we have of racism, an understanding that was forged in the 1960s, is now severely deficient. A quarter century of sociopolitical struggle has rendered it inadequate to the demands of the present. At the same time, I would hardly wish to argue (in the manner of neoconservatives) that racism itself has been largely eliminated in the post–civil rights era. But although we are pretty sure that racism continues to exist, indeed flourish, we are less than certain about what it means today.

In fact, since the ambiguous triumph of the civil rights movement in the mid-1960s, clarity about what racism means has been slipping away. The concept entered the lexicon of "common sense" only in the 1960s. Before that, although the term had surfaced occasionally, the problem of racial injustice and inequality was generally understood in a more limited fashion, as a matter of prejudiced attitudes or bigotry on the one hand and of discriminatory actions on the other.

Solutions to this problem, it was believed, would therefore involve two elements: first, the overcoming of prejudiced attitudes through the achievement of tolerance, the acceptance of "brotherhood," and the like; and second, the passage of laws prohibiting discrimination with respect to access to public accommodations, jobs, education, and so on. Social scientific work tended to focus on the origins of prejudiced attitudes (Adorno et al., 1950; Allport, 1954); on the interests served by discrimination (Rose, 1948; Becker,

1957; Thurow, 1969); and on the ways in which prejudice and discrimination combined or conflicted with each other (Merton, 1949).

The early civil rights movement explicitly reflected such views. In its espousal of integration and its quest for a "beloved community" it sought to overcome racial prejudice. In its litigation activities and agitation for civil rights legislation it sought to challenge discriminatory practices.

The later 1960s, however, signaled a sharp break with this vision. The emergence of the slogan "black power" (and soon after, of "brown power," "red power," and "yellow power"); the wave of riots that swept the urban ghettos from 1964 to 1968; and the founding of radical movement organizations of nationalist and Marxist orientation all coincided with the recognition that racial inequality and injustice had much deeper roots. They were not simply the product of prejudice, nor was discrimination only a matter of intentionally informed action. Rather, prejudice was an almost unavoidable outcome of patterns of socialization that were "bred in the bone," affecting not only whites but even minorities themselves. Discrimination, far from manifesting itself only (or even principally) through individual actions or conscious policies, was a structural feature of U.S. society, a product of centuries of systematic exclusion, exploitation, and cultural assault upon racially defined minorities.

This combination of relationships, prejudice, discrimination, and structural inequality (in other words, "institutional racism") defined the concept of racism at the end of the 1960s. Without a doubt, such a synthesis was an advance over previous conceptions. Its very comprehensiveness was better suited to the rising tide of movement activity and critique of white supremacy. Notably, its emphasis on the structural dimensions of racism allowed it to address the intransigence that racial injustice and inequality continued to exhibit even after discrimination had supposedly been outlawed and bigoted expression stigmatized.

But such an approach also had clear limitations. As Robert Miles has argued (1989), it tended to "inflate" the concept of racism to the point where it lost precision. If the "institutional" component of racism were so pervasive and deeply rooted, it would become difficult to recognize what the movement had achieved or what progress civil rights reforms represented. How, under these conditions, could one validate the premises of political action aimed at racial justice and greater substantive social equality? If institutional racism were indeed so ubiquitous, it would become difficult to affirm the existence of any democracy at all where race was concerned. The result was a leveling critique that denied any distinction between the Jim Crow era (or even the whole *longue duree* of racism, beginning with European conquest and leading through racial slavery and Jim Crow) and the present. Similarly, if prejudice were so deeply inbred, it would be difficult to account for the apparent racial hybridity and cultural interpenetration that characterizes civil society in the

United States, as evidenced not only by the shaping of popular mores, values, language, and style, for example, but also by the millions of people, white and black (and neither white nor black), who occupy interstitial and ambiguous racial positions. The result of the "inflation" of the concept of racism was thus a deep pessimism about any efforts to overcome racial barriers in the workplace, the community, or any other sphere of lived experience. An overly comprehensive view of racism, then, potentially served as a self-fulfilling prophecy.

Yet the alternative view, which had surfaced with a vengeance in the 1970s and urged a return to the conception of racism held before the movement's "radical turn," was equally inadequate. This was the neoconservative project, which deliberately restricted its attention to injury done to the individual as opposed to the group and to advocacy of a "color-blind" racial policy. Such an approach reduced race to ethnicity and almost entirely neglected the continuing organization of social inequality and oppression along racial lines. Worse yet, it tended to rationalize racial injustice as a supposedly natural outcome of group attributes in competition (Sowell, 1983).

Thus have we arrived at today's dilemmas. In the post–civil rights era, U.S. society has undergone a substantial modification of the previously far more rigid lines of exclusion and segregation, permitting real mobility for more favored sectors (that is, certain class-based segments) of racially defined minority groups. This period also witnessed the substantial diversification of the North American population in the aftermath of the 1965 reform of immigration laws. Panethnic phenomena have increased among Asians, Latinos, and Native Americans, reconstituting the U.S. racial panorama in a multipolar (as opposed to the former, bipolar) direction. Racial identity has been problematized (at least somewhat) for whites—a fact that has its dangers but also reflects progress—and the movements to which the black struggle gave initial impetus—notably, feminism and gay liberation in their many forms—have developed to the point where a whole range of crosscutting subjectivities and tensions as well as new alliances have been framed.

But the post–civil rights era also has witnessed a significant racial reaction. The racial reaction has rearticulated the demands for equality and justice made by the black movement and its allies in a conservative discourse of individualism, competition, and laissez-faire. We must recognize that it is this "new right" discourse that is hegemonic today, as racism in these terms is rendered invisible and marginalized as an artifact of the past.

Racism Today

Today, then, the absence of a clear, "commonsense" understanding of what racism means has become a significant obstacle to efforts aimed at challenging it. As usual there are different interpretations—different racial projects—

in conflict with one another over the very meaning and structure of racism. It is common to find the view, especially among whites (but also among nonwhites), that we must somehow get "beyond" race in order to overcome racism. For example, I often hear in my classes comments such as "I don't care if someone is black, white, green, or purple; a person's just a person to me." Such statements imply that racism is equivalent to color-consciousness and consequently that nonracism must be a lack of color-consciousness. We should recognize that this idea, however naive, is a true product of the civil rights era, notably the movement's early, "liberal" years.

On the other hand, I hear from other students (from my black and brown students particularly, but by no means only from them), that racism is a "system of power." This statement implies that only whites have power, and thus only whites can be racists. We should also recognize the origins of this idea, which exhibits a different but no less dangerous naïveté—for it is highly problematic to assert that racially defined minorities are powerless in the contemporary U.S.—in the radicalized later years of the civil rights era.[1]

Given this crisis of meaning, and in the absence of any "commonsense" understanding, does the concept of racism retain any validity? If so, what view of racism should we adopt? Is a more coherent theoretical approach possible? I believe it is.

Recall the discussion of racial formation theory, above. Let us recognize that like race, racism has changed over time. It is obvious that the attitudes, practices, and institutions of the epochs of slavery, say, or of Jim Crow, no longer exist today. Employing a similar logic, it is reasonable to question whether concepts of racism that were developed in the early days of the post–civil rights era, when the limitations of both moderate reform and militant racial radicalism of various types had not yet been encountered, could possibly remain adequate to explain circumstances and conflicts a quarter century later.

Racial formation theory also allows us to differentiate between race and racism—two concepts that should not be used interchangeably. I have argued that race has no fixed meaning but is constructed and transformed sociohistorically through competing political projects, through the necessary and ineluctable link between the structural and cultural dimensions of race in the United States. This emphasis on projects allows us to refocus our understanding of racism as well, for racism can now be seen as characterizing some but not all racial projects.

Today, a racial project can be defined as racist *if it creates or reproduces hierarchical social structures based on essentialized racial categories.* This approach recognizes the importance of locating racism within a fluid and contested history of racially based social structures and discourses. It allows us to recognize that there can be no timeless and absolute standard for what constitutes racism, because social structures undergo reform (and reaction) and discourses are always subject to rearticulation. This definition therefore does not invest the concept of racism with any permanent content but instead sees racism as a property of certain political projects that link the representation and organization of race—that engage in the "work" of racial formation. Such an approach focuses on the "work" essentialism does for domination, and the "need" domination displays to essentialize the subordinated.[2]

It is also important to distinguish between racial awareness and racial essentialism. Attribution of merits or faults, allocation of values or resources, and/or representations of individuals or groups on the basis of racial categories should not be considered racist in and of themselves. Such projects may in fact be quite benign. Of course, any of these projects may be considered racist, but only if they meet the criteria I have just outlined: In other words, essentialization and subordination (which are always linked) must be present.

Consider the following examples. First, a discursive one: the statement "Today, many Asian Americans are highly entrepreneurial." Second, a structural one: the organization of an association of, say, black accountants. The first racial project, in my view, signifies or represents a racial category ("Asian Americans"), and locates that representation within the social structure of the contemporary United States (in regard to business, class issues, socialization, and so on). It does not, however, essentialize; it is qualified in time ("today") and in respect to overgeneralization ("many"). The second racial project is organizational or social structural, and therefore must engage in racial signification. Black accountants, the organizers might maintain, have certain common experiences and characteristics and thus can offer each other appropriate support. The effort to organize such a group is not in and of itself antagonistic to other groups; it does not aim at others' subordination but only at members' well-being and uplift.

Neither of these racial projects, then, can fairly be labeled racist. Of course, racial representations may be biased or may misinterpret their subjects, just as racially based organizational efforts may be unfair or unjustifiably exclusive. If such were the case—if, for instance, in our first example the statement in question read "Asian Americans are naturally entrepreneurial"—then this project by my criterion would be racist. Similarly, if the effort to organize black accountants had as its rationale the raiding of clients from nonblack accountants, it would by my criteria be racist as well.

Proceeding with this standard, to allocate values or resources—let us say, academic scholarships to racially defined minority students—is not racist, since no essentializing/subordinating standard is at work here. Scholarships are awarded to Rotarians, children of insurance company employees, and residents of the Pittsburgh metropolitan area. Why then should they not also be offered, in particular cases, to blacks or Chicanos or Native Americans? The latter categories are no more suspect than the former ones.

What if particular scholarships were offered only to whites? Such action would be suspect, not on the grounds of essentialism but on those of domination and subordination, since the logic of such a racial project would be to reproduce an existing racial hierarchy.

Let us take an example that is much on our minds today: the effort to invalidate affirmative action programs on the grounds that they constitute "reverse discrimination." This project would, I think, be vulnerable to criticism under the criteria of racism I am developing here. This is because, as we have learned in the post–civil rights era, it is possible to reproduce racial categories even while ostensibly repudiating them. The preservation of racial hierarchy may operate through an essentializing logic that dissembles or operates subtextually:

> When science apologizes and says there is no such thing, all talk of "race" must cease. Hence "race," as a recently emergent, unifying, and forceful sign of difference in the service of the "Other," is held up to scientific ridicule as, ironically, "unscientific." A proudly emergent sense of ethnic diversity *in the service* of the new world arrangements is disparaged by white male science as the most foolish sort of anachronism. (Baker, 1986, p. 385; the emphasis is in the original)

The familiar "code word" phenomenon—that is, the subtextual signification of race—has much the same effect. Thus, the claim first made in 1896 and recently elevated to nearly hegemonic jurisprudential doctrine, that "our Constitution is color-blind," can in fact be understood in two ways. It can mean, as Justice Harlan evidently intended in his ringing dissent in the Plessy case, and as the early civil rights movement clearly understood, that the power of the state should not be used to enforce invidious racial distinctions. But it can also mean that the power of the state should not be used to uproot those distinctions either. Based on the criteria I have advanced here, I suggest that despite its antiessentialist appearance, the "color-blind" denial of the significance of race is in fact an essentializing representation of race—an erasure of race, so to speak—which in the present-day United States is generally linked to the perpetuation of racial hierarchy. It is, then, a form of racism, a type of racist project (Gotanda, 1995).

In order to identify a social project as racist using the criterion of essentialism, one must demonstrate a link between essentializing representations of race and hierarchical social structures. Such a link might be revealed in efforts to protect dominant interests, framed in racial terms, from democratizing racial initiatives: for example, changing to at-large voting systems when minority voters threaten to achieve significant representation. But such a link might also consist of efforts simply to reverse the roles of the racially dominant and the racially subordinate. In certain theories of racial superiority, such as that of Welsing (1991), or in the racial ontology of the Nation of

Islam with its mad scientist Dr. Yacub, we see racist projects that have a black provenance. Racism is not necessarily white, though in the nature of things, it is more often so. It inheres in those political projects that link racial essentialism and racial hierarchy, wherever and however that link is forged.

Racism and Racial Formation

Although we can conclude that racism is not invariably white, we must also recognize that today, as in the past, there is a hegemonic racial project—that of the "new right"—which in general defends white racial privilege. It employs a particular interpretive schema, a particular logic of racial representation, to justify a hierarchical racial order in which, albeit more imperfectly than in the past, dark skin still correlates with subordination, and subordinate status often, though not always, is still represented in racial terms.

Furthermore, a key problem of racism, today as in the past, is its denial, or flattening, of difference within the categories it represents, in essentialist fashion. Members of racially defined subordinate groups have for a long time faced practices of exclusion, discrimination, and even of outright extermination. Such groups thus have been forced to band together in order to defend their interests (if not, in some instances, their very lives). Following this argument, such "strategic essentialism" cannot be equated with the essentialism practiced in service of hierarchical social structures. Nor would it prevent the interrogation of internal group differences, though these are sometimes overridden by the imperative for group "conservation," to use Du Bois's term.

Obviously, any abstract concept of racism is severely tested by the untidy world of reality. Yet I believe that it is imperative to meet that test at the level of theory, and indeed at the level of practice that ought to flow from theory, just as we must meet the test in our everyday lives.

Today we live in a situation in which "the old is dying and the new cannot be born," in which formerly unquestioned white supremacy is now questioned. An antiracist countertradition in politics and culture has made significant gains; but despite the changes wrought by this antiracist project, this radical democratic initiative that derives from the postwar black movement, it has not been possible to overthrow the deeply rooted belief that the United States is still, as the phrase goes, a "white man's country." It has not been possible fully to transform the social, political, economic, and cultural institutions that afford systematic privileges to whites. It has not been possible significantly to alter the displacement of the burdens and problems of the society (such as unemployment, undereducation, poverty, and disease) onto the shoulders of nonwhites.

Thus the racial dualism that Du Bois identified nearly 100 years ago continues to operate today. Recall that he characterized the black experience as a conflict between "two souls, two thoughts, two unreconciled strivings" (Du Bois, 1903 [1995]). This characterization now applies, albeit in very different ways, to everybody. The full exposition of this point is beyond the scope of this brief chapter, but I have discussed it more fully elsewhere (Winant, 1997; Winant, 1994). Suffice it to say here that as a society and as individuals, we both uphold and resist white supremacy. We experience our particular privilege or subalternity, and to the extent we can, we resist it.

Confronting racism in such a situation is difficult. Racism is a moving target, a contested terrain. Inevitably, as a society, as political movements, and as individuals, we will make many mistakes; we have to see our action and our thought, our praxis, in pragmatic terms. Because racism changes and develops, because it is simultaneously a vast phenomenon framed by epochal historical developments and a moment-to-moment experiential reality, we can never expect fully to capture it theoretically. Nor can we expect that it will ever be fully overcome. That does not mean, however, that we are free to stop trying.

NOTES

1. Bob Blauner has argued that the central point distinguishing the two foregoing positions is the centrality afforded to race in one's worldview. For those to whom race is central, racism remains very present; and for those to whom race is less central, racism is seen as "a peripheral, nonessential reality" (Blauner, 1992).

2. By *essentialism* I mean a belief in unchanging human characteristics, impervious to social and historical context (Fuss, 1989).

REFERENCES

Adorno, T. W., et al. (1950). *The Authoritarian Personality*. New York: Harper and Bros.

Allport, G. W. (1954). *The Nature of Prejudice*. Cambridge, MA: Addison-Wesley.

Baker, H. A., Jr. (1986). "Caliban's Triple Play." In Gates, Henry Louis, Jr., ed., *"Race," Writing, and Difference*. Chicago: University of Chicago Press.

Becker, G. (1957). *The Economics of Discrimination*. Chicago: University of Chicago Press.

Blauner, B. (1992). "Talking Past One Another: Black and White Languages of Race." *The American Prospect* 10.

Du Bois, W.E.B. (1897 [reprint ed. 1995]). "The Conservation of Races." In Lewis, D. L., ed., *W.E.B. Du Bois: A Reader*. New York: Henry Holt.

_____. (1903 [reprint ed. 1995]). "Of Our Spiritual Strivings." In Lewis, D. L., ed., *W.E.B. Du Bois: A Reader*. New York: Henry Holt.

Fuss, D. (1989). *Essentially Speaking: Feminism, Nature, and Difference.* New York: Routledge.

Gotanda, N. (1995). "A Critique of 'Our Constitution Is Color-Blind.'" In Crenshaw, K., et al., eds., *Critical Race Theory: The Key Writings That Formed the Movement.* New York: New Press.

Merton, R. K. (1949). "Discrimination and the American Creed." In MacIver, R. W., ed., *Discrimination and the National Welfare.* New York: Harper and Bros.

Miles, R. (1989). *Racism.* New York: Routledge.

Omi, M., and Winant, H. (1994). *Racial Formation in the United States: From the 1960s to the 1990s.* New York: Routledge.

Rose, A. M. (1948). *The Negro in America.* New York: Harper and Bros.

Sowell, T. (1983). *The Economics and Politics of Race: An International Perspective.* New York: Quill.

Thurow, L. (1969). *Poverty and Discrimination.* Washington, DC: Brookings Institution.

Welsing, F. C. (1991). *The Isis Papers: The Keys to the Colors.* Chicago: Third World Press.

Winant, H. (1994). *Racial Conditions: Politics, Theory, Comparisons.* Minneapolis: University of Minnesota Press.

_____. (1997). "Racial Dualism at Century's End." In Lubiano, W., ed., *The House That Race Built.* New York: Random House.

two

Racial Identity and the State: Contesting the Federal Standards for Classification

MICHAEL OMI

In February 1995, the *Chronicle of Higher Education* carried a feature article on racial classification and the sciences that highlighted an interesting dilemma facing scientists in the United States. On the one hand, they routinely utilize racial categories in their research and regularly make comparisons between the races with respect to health, behavior, and (as the *Bell Curve* controversy reminds us) intelligence. On the other hand, most scientists feel that racial classifications are meaningless and unscientific. In the *Chronicle* article, Kenneth Kennedy of Cornell University is quoted as saying: "In the social sense, race is a reality. In the scientific sense, it is not."

It is the reality of race in the "social sense" that I want to explore by focusing on the racial categories utilized by the federal government and the problems associated with them, highlighting the deeply political character of such categories.

My initial interest in state definitions of race was inspired by a court case in the early 1980s. In 1977, Susie Guillory Phipps, who was then 43 years old, found herself in need of her birth certificate in order to apply for a passport. As she had believed all her life that she was white, you can imagine her surprise when a clerk at the New Orleans Division of Vital Records showed her that she was designated "colored." Quoting Ms. Phipps:

> It shocked me. I was sick for three days. I was brought up white, I married white twice. The problem was a 1970 Louisiana state law which allowed for anyone with more than 1/32nd black blood to be defined as "black." Prior to that a black person was defined as anyone who had "any traceable amount" of

black ancestry. According to the state's genealogical investigation, Ms. Phipps'
great-great-great-great-grandmother was a black woman slave named Mar-
garita. Ms. Phipps was at least 1/32nd black.(Omi and Winant, 1994).

The logic of this racial classification is consistent with what anthropologist Marvin Harris has called the "principle of hypodescent." This descent
rule requires us to classify anyone who is known to have had a black ancestor as black. Ms. Phipps went on to sue the state of Louisiana to change her
racial designation from "colored" to "white." She lost. In 1983, the state
Supreme Court denied her motion and upheld the state's right to classify and
quantify racial identity. In 1986, the U.S. Supreme Court refused to review
the case and thus let the lower court's decision stand.

The designation of racial categories and the determination of racial identity are not simple tasks. During the past several centuries, these tasks have
provoked numerous debates around the country involving matters of natural versus legal rights, such as who should be permitted to become a naturalized citizen, and who should be permitted to marry whom.

State Definitions of Race

Racial and ethnic categories in the U.S. have historically been shaped by the political and social agendas of particular times. The first U.S. census, conducted in
1790, distinguished holders of the franchise (namely, white male property owners) from the general population. Later, the practice of slavery motivated changes
in categorization, including the division of blacks into free and slave populations.

The current census categories were assigned and implemented in response to
the antidiscriminatory and equal opportunity laws of the 1960s and 1970s. Established in 1977, OMB Directive No. 15 fosters the creation of compatible,
nonduplicated, exchangeable racial and ethnic data by federal agencies for three
reporting purposes: statistical, administrative, and civil rights compliance.

Office of Management and Budget (OMB) Statistical Directive No. 15
Race and Ethnic Standards for
Federal Statistics and Administrative Reporting

1. Definitions

The basic racial and ethnic categories for Federal Statistics and program
administrative reporting are defined as follows:

a. American Indian or Alaskan Native. A person having origins in any of
the original peoples of North America, and who maintains cultural identification through tribal affiliation or community recognition.

b. Asian or Pacific Islander. A person having origins in any of the original
peoples of the Far East, Southeast Asia, the Indian subcontinent, or the Pacific Islands. This area includes, for example, China, India, Japan, Korea, the
Philippine Islands, and Samoa.

c. Black. A person having origins in any of the black racial groups of Africa.

d. Hispanic. A person of Mexican, Puerto Rican, Cuban, Central or South American or other Spanish culture or origin, regardless of race.

e. White. A person having origins in any of the original peoples of Europe, North Africa, or the Middle East.

2. Utilization for Recordkeeping and Reporting

To provide flexibility, it is preferable to collect data on race and ethnicity separately. If separate race and ethnic categories are used, the minimum designations are:

a. Race:
- American Indian or Alaskan Native
- Asian or Pacific Islander
- Black
- White

b. Ethnicity:
- Hispanic origin
- Not of Hispanic origin

Note the problems inherent in this categorization. Some of the categories are racial, some geographic, and some cultural.

The Census Bureau and most government agencies use three different sets of questions and concepts to describe and measure race and ethnicity:
- Race (the 1990 Census question included 16 categories of race)
- Ethnicity (designed to ascertain whether a person is of Hispanic origin)
- Ancestry (open-ended, with no precoded categories)

The existing framework is being seriously questioned. In February 1994, I participated in a two-day session convened by the National Research Council at the request of the Office of Management and Budget. The purpose of the meeting was to assess the existing racial and ethnic categories (as defined in OMB Statistical Directive No. 15); to note their limitations; and perhaps to suggest more stable and coherent categories for research and administrative purposes. In my opinion, this session—however well intended—was ill founded: Any attempt to frame such coherent categories immediately confronts a range of contradictory choices and gaps in understanding.

Gaps Between State Definitions and Individual/Group Identities

First, there is the gap between administrative requirements and popular consciousness. The federal, state, and local agencies involved in compiling and analyzing racial and ethnic data do so with the intent to track socioeconomic progress, assess health trends, and determine patterns of discrimination, as well as to measure other important indicators of well-being and life chances. Agencies want relatively static racial and ethnic categories that can be objectively determined—meaning that they must be conceptually valid, exclusive and exhaustive, measurable, and reliable over time.

Such categories, however, would clash with conceptions of race and ethnicity that stress their dynamic nature and the "slippery," subjective indicators of that dynamism, such as self-identity. Administrative definitions, therefore, might not be meaningful to the very individuals or groups they purport to represent.

Clara Rodriguez's studies of Latinos, which reveal a strong group rejection of the dominant mode of conceptualizing racial categories in the United States, provide evidence of precisely such a disjuncture. More than half of Rodriguez's Puerto Rican respondents answered the race/ethnicity question wrong. Rodriguez's findings are supported by other data: The Census Bureau reported that 40 percent of Hispanic respondents in 1980 and 1990 chose no other racial or ethnic identity. It was also estimated that 95 percent of persons reporting in the "other race" category were Hispanic.

Part of the problem lies with differences in conceptualizing race. With respect to new immigrant populations, it is important to examine the shifts in racial self-identity as immigrants move from a society organized around specific concepts of race to a new society with a different mode of conceptualization.

Life Cycle Effects

Given the contextual nature of racial and ethnic identification, it may be difficult to achieve the reliability and consistency in time series data and analysis. You are likely to elicit different responses on racial and ethnic identification in different historical periods. You are also likely to elicit different responses from the same individual at different points in her or his life cycle.

Since 1989, births have been categorized by the race of the mother. Racial classification at death, by contrast, is designated by a third party, either a physician or funeral director. This has led to the overassignment of deaths to black and white categories and an underassignment of deaths to American Indian and Asian categories.

In addition to these problems with existing classifications, there is also the temporal effect of evolving racial and ethnic labels. New labels come into vogue, old groups dissolve through assimilation, and new groups emerge as a result of changes in civil status or patterns of immigration.

FIGURE 2.1   Race and Ethnic Identification and Classification by Life Cycle

Birth:	by mother
Childhood:	by household head for the decennial census
	by self, parents, or administrators for school forms
	by self, parents, or administrators for health forms
Adulthood:	by household head for the decennial census
	by self or administrators for employment forms
	by self or administrators for health forms
	by self or administrators for misc. government and business forms
Death:	by physician or funeral home administrator
	(perhaps in consultation with relatives of deceased)

Changing Self-Identification

A fascinating example of changing self-identification is the dramatic increase in the American Indian population. American Indians increased from 552,000 in 1960 to 1,959,000 in 1990—255 percent in 30 years. This rate of increase is virtually impossible demographically.

Much of the increase is explainable by changes in racial self-identification that are driven by shifts in attitudes toward American Indians, a romanticization of the past, and tangible benefits tied to American Indian identification. There is a very large pool of Americans who claim some degree of American Indian ancestry. In 1980, only 1.4 million chose American Indian as a racial category, whereas 6.8 million noted that they were American Indian on the open-ended ancestry question. In 1990, the number claiming American Indian ancestry increased to 8.8 million.

Panethnicity

The reorganization of old groups and the creation of new groups are features of changing political and social contexts. One dramatic political development in the post–civil rights era is the rise of *panethnic* consciousness and organization. Groups whose previous national or ethnic identities were quite distinct became consolidated into a single racial (or in the case of Latinos, ethnic) category.

Prior to the late 1960s, for example, there were no "Asian Americans." In the wake of the civil rights movement, distinct Asian ethnic groups—primarily Chinese, Japanese, Filipino, and Korean Americans—began to frame and assert their "common identity" as Asian Americans. This political label reflected the similarity of treatment that these groups historically encountered at the hands of state institutions and the dominant culture at large. Different Asian ethnic groups had been subject to exclusionary immigration laws, restrictive naturalization laws, labor market segregation, and patterns of "ghettoization" by a polity and culture that treated all Asians as alike.

The panethnic organization of Asian Americans involved the muting of profound cultural and linguistic differences and significant historical antagonisms that existed among the distinct nationalities and ethnic groups of Asian origin. In spite of diversity and difference, Asian American activists found the political label a crucial rallying point for raising political consciousness about the problems in Asian ethnic communities and for asserting demands on political institutions.

These panethnic formations are not stable. Conflicts often occur over the precise definitions and boundaries of various panethnic groups, and over their adequate representation in census counts, reapportionment debates, and minority aid programs. Panethnic consciousness and organization are, to a large extent, situationally and strategically determined. There are times when it is advantageous to be in a panethnic bloc and times when it is seen as more desirable to mobilize along particular ethnic lines.

However, for researchers and policymakers, lumping various groups together results in a flattening of important distinctions that we might wish to discern and analyze. Specific groups might "all look alike," but they are not homogeneous. How meaningful, for example, is an Asian American category for analysis when both Japanese and Laotian Americans are subsumed under it? Only 28.4 percent of Japanese Americans are foreign born, and only 9 percent do not speak English well. Their median family income is 137 percent of the national average, and their poverty rate is 4.2 percent. By contrast 93.7 percent of Laotians are foreign born, and 69 percent do not speak English well. Their median family income is 26 percent of the national average, and their poverty rate is 67.2 percent. The point is that the conflation of important "differences" is a hazard with the construction and use of particular categories.

The Shifting Meaning of Racial/Ethnic Identification

The meaning of racial/ethnic identification for specific groups and individuals varies enormously. Recent research on white Americans suggest that they do not experience their ethnicity as a definitive aspect of their social identity. Rather, they perceive it dimly and irregularly, picking and choosing among its varied strands, which allows them to exercise, in the words of sociologist Mary Waters (1990), an "ethnic option." Waters found that ethnicity was flexible, symbolic, and voluntary for her white respondents in ways that it was not for nonwhites.

TABLE 2.1   Selected Ancestry Groups: 1980 and 1990 Censuses

Ancestry	Is the Group Listed as an Example?		Population (in thousands)		Percent Change
	1980	1990	1980	1990	
German	Yes	Yes	49,224	57,986	15
English	Yes	No	49,598	32,056	−34
Italian	Yes	Yes	12,184	14,715	21
French	Yes	No	12,892	10,321	−20
Polish	Yes	Yes	8,228	9,366	14
Ukrainian	Yes	Yes	730	741	2
Hungarian	Yes	No	1,777	1,582	−11
Slovak	Yes	Yes	777	1,M	142
Czech*	No	No	1,892	1,G1S	−15
Serbian	No	No	101	117	15
Croatian	No	Yes	233	554	115
French Canadian	No	Yes	780	2,167	178
Cajun	No	Yes	<10	668	>6000
Taiwanese	No	Yes	15	193	1106
Born in Taiwan	–	–	75	244	225

*Includes Czechoslovakian.

A recent analysis (Petersen, 1997, pp. 315–320) of the open-ended question on ancestry or descent that first appeared in the 1980 Census underscores the fluid nature of white ethnicity. The examples given below the question had a dramatic influence on responses.

Multiracial Category

An important emerging issue is the inability of existing state definitions to deal with people of mixed racial descent. A concerted effort has been made by school boards and organizations such as Project RACE (Reclassify All Children Equally) to have the category "multiracial" added to the census form. This change has been opposed by many civil rights organizations, including the Urban League and the National Council of La Raza. Some groups fear a reduction in their numbers and worry that a multiracial category would spur debates regarding the "protected status" of groups and individuals. According to various estimates, from 75 to 90 percent of census respondents who now check off the "black" box could check off "multiracial." This is not to say they would, but only to suggest that complex issues of identity would emerge from the institutionalization of a multiracial category.

Objectifying Race: The Debate's Meaning
for Social Science Research

An important point I want to make is that the state definitions have inordinately shaped the discourse of race in the United States. Originally conceived solely for the use of federal agencies, OMB Directive No. 15 has become the de facto standard for state and local agencies, the private and nonprofit sectors, and the research community. Social scientists use the directive's categories because they are available.

Among scholars, there is a continuous temptation to think of race as an *essence,* as something fixed, concrete, and objective. And there is also an opposite temptation: to imagine race as a mere illusion, a purely ideological construct that masks some other, more fundamental division, such as class.

Much of sociological research, though firmly committed to a social interpretation of race as opposed to a biological one, nevertheless slips into a kind of objectivism about racial identity and racial meaning. There is a marked tendency to treat race as an independent variable and to downplay its variability and historically contingent character. Thus sociologists can correlate race and residential patterns, race and crime, and race and intelligence, without problematizing the concept of race itself.

There is no discussion about the constantly shifting parameters through which race is thought about—how group interests are conceived, status is ascribed, agency is attained, and roles performed. Although abstractly acknowledged to be a sociohistorical construct, race in practice is often treated as an objective fact: One simply *is* one's race.

Sociologists have been debating the validity of race and have been arguing whether to eliminate the concept, scale it back in usage to specific and verifiable applications, or leave it alone. David Decker (1982) argues that a proper sociological protocol should require that

> the use of race be defined explicitly when it is used in research so that it is clear whether the term is being used to refer to a mythical but perceived relationship between superficial anatomical characteristics and specific groups, or pointing to patterns and processes of discrimination, or to the history of the use and abuse of the term in human societies. It should not be used in a haphazard manner to seek correlates between race as a variable and other variables. It should not be used when researchers have not explained how and why the concept has been defined and is being used.

As an example, Decker states that there is little basis for presenting criminal arrest rates by race without explicitly explaining the meaning of race. Is race being used to indicate the inequity of arrest procedures? Is it being used to show how processes of racial discrimination and its socioeconomic consequences have an impact upon the likelihood of criminal involvement? Or is it suggesting that some groups are by genes or culture more predisposed to criminal activity?

That said, a central question continues to haunt policy-oriented research: What is it that we are trying to get at in defining racial and ethnic categories? What do we want to know and why?

The federal government is currently grappling with this question. Many social scientists and statisticians are arguing explicitly for categories that are conceptually valid, exclusive and exhaustive, measurable, and reliable over time. I think that race and ethnicity will continue to defy our best efforts to establish coherent definitions over time. The real world is messy. Nothing demonstrates this better than the social construction of racial and ethnic categories.

The strange and twisted history of the classification of Asian Indians in the United States provides an instructive example. During and after the peak years of immigration, Asian Indians were referred to and classified as "Hindu" though the clear majority of them were Sikh. In the Thind decision (1923), the U.S. Supreme Court held that Thind, as a native of India, was indeed "Caucasian" but not "white," and therefore was ineligible to become a naturalized citizen. "It may be true," the court declared, "that the blond Scandinavian and the brown Hindu have a common ancestor in the dim reaches of antiquity, but the average man knows perfectly well that there are unmistakable and profound differences between them today."

Their status as nonwhite was reversed after World War II, when they became "white" in part as reward for their participation in the Pacific war and as a consequence of the postwar political climate, which was distinctly anticolonial. In the post–civil rights era, Asian Indian leaders sought to change their classification in order to seek "minority" group status. In 1977, the Bureau of the Census agreed to reclassify immigrants from India and their descendants from "White/Caucasian" to "Asian Indian." Currently, Asian Indian students at my campus, the University of California at Berkeley, prefer the term "South Asian" in order foster panethnic identification with students from Pakistan, Bangladesh, and other countries neighboring India.

The point is that because race and ethnic category are often the effects of political interpretation and struggle, the categories in turn have political effects. I believe that this understanding is crucial for the ongoing debates around the federal standards for racial and ethnic classification.

REFERENCES

Decker, D., Schichor, D., and O'Brien, R. M. (1982). *Urban Structure and Victimization.* Lexington, MA: Lexington Books.

Omi, M., and Winant, H. (1994). *Racial Formation in the United States: From the 1960s to the 1990s.* New York: Routledge.

Petersen, W. (1997). *Ethnicity Counts.* New Brunswick, NJ: Transaction Books.

three

From the Immigrant Paradigm to Transformative Critique: Asians in the Late Capitalist United States

E. SAN JUAN, JR.

> Only in this context, which sees the isolated facts of social life as aspects of the historical process and integrates them into a totality, can knowledge of the facts hope to become knowledge of reality.
> —Georg Lukacs, *History and Class Consciousness*

> What "ought to be" is therefore concrete; indeed it is the only realistic and historicist interpretation of reality, it alone is history in the making and philosophy in the making, it alone is politics.
> —Antonio Gramsci, *Prison Notebooks*

On the threshold of the third millennium, many observers have noted a general anxiety in U.S. society concerning demographic changes anticipated in the next fifty years: The white population will decline to 68 percent (in California, to less than 50 percent) and the racialized minorities will increase beyond previous expectations, with Asians becoming nearly 12 percent of the total (Yip, 1997). Some predict that as early as 2015, Americans of European descent will be in a minority. While Latinos generally blend with the white majority (except for the language), Asians in the United States are often resignified as the proto-white "model minority," thus provoking reaction from aggrieved African Americans, Native Americans, and disadvantaged whites. In contrast, *Money* magazine celebrates this "lively ethnic stew" as confirmation of the ethnic settlement myth, immigration as the basis of the nation-state: "The melting pot is bubbling away just as it always has, and will continue to simmer—albeit with more Latin spice—over the next 25 years" (Sivy, 1997, p. 101). Notwithstanding Glazer and Moynihan's (1963) reduction of ethnic presence to group claims or interests, the belief in intermarriage as a prophylaxis to white supremacy is the genetic core of assimilationist thinking. Until biology solves the problem, the majority would continue to maintain the boundaries of an ethnically based hierarchy in order to keep Asians and other people of color in their place.

As the images of armed Korean merchants defending their stores in the 1992 Los Angeles riots slowly dissolve in public memory, two news stories erupted recently to recall to us the inescapable scrutability of what were once regarded as "inscrutable Orientals": first, the Chinagate campaign finance scandal, featuring John Huang and the Bank of China in Beijing (Dawnay, 1997); and second, the Andrew Cunanhan serial killings leading to the death of Italian fashion designer Gianni Versace, among other victims (Thomas, 1997). Stories in the mass media reminded us again and again of the "Asian" background of these protagonists: Huang was born in 1945 in Fujian, China, then fled to Taiwan during the civil war, emigrated to the United States, married a Chinese American, and became a banker specializing in Asian business, in which capacity he made connections with the Chinese-Indonesian Lippo Group and Bill Clinton. Cunanhan at first was mistaken for an Irish immigrant but later correctly identified as the son of a Filipino father and an American mother, the father being an ex-Navy man who fled to the Philippines to escape criminal charges. Cunanhan grew up as a normal child, but his sexual "deviance" pushed him to mimic the expensive lifestyle of rich gay Californians, and later, the dizzying heights of the fashion world. While Huang could be stereotyped easily as the devious and shrewd "Oriental" hustler who easily wormed his way into Washington circles by his native wit, Cunanhan at first defied the commonsensical optic: He could pass for white, although on closer scrutiny his nose and skin betrayed his nonwhite descent. At any rate, he too ended up being psychoanalyzed as an individual case epitomizing the larger group—the "race," in folk wisdom—an approach that apparently was key to unlocking his mystery.

"Asian" is a clear marker of stigmatization. This racial category possesses an ideological resonance validated in eighteenth-century Europe by Linnaeus and Blumenbach (in their equation of "Mongolian" and "yellow") and later, in the nineteenth century, resignified as the "yellow peril" in colonial encounters between Western powers and local Chinese rulers. It was not geography but geopolitical conflict that laid the condition for the pejorative resemanticization of "Oriental" and "Asian." Between the time of the Opium Wars and the Boxer Rebellion, the Chinese in the United States stood for the

"Asian" menace to Anglo-Saxon civilization, and later, to the white American labor unions in California and elsewhere (Dudley, 1997; Takaki, 1993).

In the context of renewed nativism during the economic crisis of the 1870s, the Chinese became the first racial group in the annals of U.S. jurisprudence to be prohibited from entry into U.S. territory. The 1882 Chinese Exclusion Act signaled the beginning of an attempt by the state to sanitize the national space of a contagion presumed to be harmful to the body politic. Together with the 1917 "barred zone" act and the supplementary 1924 act, the 1882 act kept out all Asians—except for Filipinos, who although they were labeled "American nationals" and were denizens of the only U.S. colony in Asia, functioned merely as surrogates or replacements for Chinese and Japanese labor in Hawaii (Chan, 1991).

The Migration Imaginary

The immigration paradigm has functioned as the racializing framework for people from Asia in the official and academic discourse since their entry to the United States after the Civil War and Reconstruction. Refinement in discrimination disaggregated the mass of "Orientals." Entry of Japanese was regulated by the Gentlemen's Agreement of 1917–18, whereas the Filipinos were controlled by the U.S. colonial administration, which treated the natives as a variety of domesticated "Indians." Japanese, Filipinos, and Koreans were recruited by the Hawaiian Sugar Plantation Association initially as indentured and contracted field hands; later, some became sojourners, and eventually, overstaying or illegal aliens. In his survey of U.S. policy toward Asian immigrants, historian Roger Daniels (1993) has focused on the denial of naturalization or eligibility for citizenship in immigration policy toward Asians. Immigration was not the problem; rather, it was the possibility that Asians might settle in the country and claim rights accorded only to citizens and be included in the polity on the same basis as whites.

Whatever the vicissitudes to which Asians were subject between 1882 and 1943, their ordeals (revisited poignantly in Fae Myenne Ng's novel *Bone* [1993]) can be happily ignored: With the help of the liberal white establishment, President Roosevelt saw the light and rewarded China's participation in the war against Japan by repealing the 1882 Exclusion Act. This reversal simultaneously canceled the 1790 statute limiting naturalization to "free white persons," a law that had been abrogated for blacks in the 14th Amendment to the Constitution in 1868 but that still applied to Asians. The Indians and Filipinos became eligible for naturalization only in 1946, the year when Filipinos were granted formal independence.

Ideology and geopolitics once more determined state policy on the entry of peoples into U.S. territory. It took the McCarran-Walter Act of 1952, at the height of the Cold War, to eliminate all restrictions for citizenship eligibility for all Asians. If we punctuate this unfolding narrative with the climax of the 1965 Immigration Act, which finally abolished the "national origins" premise of U.S. policy and led to the unprecedented increase of populations from the Pacific Rim, we get an evolutionary curve that fulfills the traditional vision of America as a land of immigrants. Daniels in fact argues against fellow historians (Hansen, Stephenson) who concluded that the 1924 immigration act put an end to one of the "most fundamental forces in American history" (Higham, 1955, p. 330) by postulating the continuity of immigration as a distinguishing element in the U.S. social formation. He even considers the 1965 act an unprecedented restructuring of the U.S. state and its juridical apparatuses: The U.S. government "had not only ended the blatant discrimination against Asians but also created a new system which could be used by Asians to make themselves the most favoured beneficiaries of the new law" (1993, p. 330). But Daniels doesn't celebrate a success story in the proverbial "melting pot," since he admits that Asian Americans cannot be treated as a homogeneous group—Asian Indians enjoy median incomes higher than whites, whereas a majority of Indochinese refugees live below the poverty line and many Chinese and Filipinos share the same deprivations. Class rather than ethnicity will become more significant in differentiating Asian Americans, Daniels suggests, and adds: "Asian American is essentially a racial term. . . . The conglomerate image of 'Asian Americans' is an illusion. Hmong and Japanese are no more alike than Albanians and Scots. Yet because Asian Americans are not Caucasians, the media, the Census Bureau, and almost everyone else will continue to speak of them as if they were one people" (1993, pp. 331, 334).

Caught in the web of the immigration template, the historian here has edged dangerously close to collapsing the histories of the racialized Asians with that of the ethnic European immigrants and endorsing the Horatio Alger myth. But truth insists on what is embedded in the paradigm of movements in and out of the national space: the still dominant linear narrative of development (e.g., Reimers, 1992). What ultimately legitimates immigration policy based on territorial sovereignty is a Eurocentric plot that aligns the white race on the side of "civilization" and the others on the side of the objects of a "civilizing mission." Immigration implies a movement from what is intolerable to what is promising, from despair to hope, from reality to dream. It misleads us into conspiring with the conquistadors and the imperial benefactors. Literary critic Barbara Harlow exposes the hidden agenda of the NAFTA agreement as a logic of subordination

> that locates necessarily the *terminus ad quem* of progress within the territorial borders and political ideology of the United States, the historical trajectory of participants in and aspirants to that modernization narrative must lead always across those nonetheless well-defended borders. Whether for migrant workers

or political refugees, jobs and freedom are always to be sought "on the other side," in the United States. (1995, p. 512)

Underlying this modernization ethos of NAFTA and the putative rationality of the circulation of bodies around the planet is of course the hegemonic leadership of the United States in the inter-state hierarchy of liberal free-market polities after World War II.

Most histories of Asian communities in the United States operate within the immigration/modernization paradigm that subscribes to the folklore of the United States as the original land of promise, the virgin land for "the free and the brave." The Declaration of Independence and the Constitution enshrined the pristine ideals of Enlightenment learning theorized by John Locke and Adam Smith; the "New World" became the negation of the corrupt and benighted "old world" of monarchic Europe. The fabled social contract enunciated within the Lockean philosophical framework privileged the white male endowed with rational faculties. This became the theoretical foundation for a *Herrenvolk* democracy that prevailed in the antebellum U.S. south and resurfaced in apartheid South Africa (van den Berghe, 1972). Many Asian American artists and intellectuals (a recent example may be found in Min [1995]) subscribe to this paradigm in one degree or another even while they acknowledge the "racial pattern" of discrimination and exclusion defining the U.S. sociopolitical order from the beginning (the genocide of the American Indians and chattel slavery of Africans) to the present. Empirical accounts by historians Sucheng Chan and Ronald Takaki, among others, have exposed the discrepancy between democratic forms and capitalist reality.

Nonetheless, the reason why well-intentioned Asian Americans are compromised by one or more versions of U.S. "exceptionalism" inheres in their failure to inscribe the modernization plot in the larger structure of the growth of the capitalist state founded on a process of alienation and its racializing effects—the separation of the producer from the means of production, of political from economic relations, of labor from needs, and so on. When the U.S. sociopolitical formation is represented as the outgrowth of the normal evolutionary development from tradition to modernity, and therefore as almost natural and necessary, instead of being entailed by the accumulation process and racialized, gendered class violence underlying unequal property relations, then citizenship extended to immigrants becomes an unquestioned "good." The state acquires a life of its own apart from the commingled nationalities. Consequently, historical realities become reified to occlude contradictions and suppress possibilities. This provides the condition of possibility, for example, for the contrived phenomenon of thousands of Chinese workers being rendered invisible when the completion of the transcontinental railroad at Promontory Point, Utah, in 1869 was photographed. This also helps to explain why the dominant majority today accept the position of Asians as protowhites. Such a framework of intelligibility demarcating insiders and outsiders, citizens and aliens, has long been prepared for by the genocide of the natives, slavery of Africans, caste-driven segregation, indentured labor, and the disciplinary regime of immigration.

The observance of the Columbus Quincentennial in 1992 resurrected the notion of the United States as a "postnational" experiment in ethnic diversity. Ironically, this experiment required a foundation myth together with founding people discovering a primordial homeland. The mythic claim of having created a distinctive and exclusive polity that affirms civic republicanism and egalitarian principles coexists uneasily with a body of juridical and social practices premised on material inequality and injustice (Hutchinson, 1994). Such a dilemma belies the claim that "the state no longer organizes and enforces white supremacy" (Winant, 1994, p. 128) with the ascendancy of "metaracism" or cultural racism. I contend that precisely because embattled collective meanings, interpretations, and symbols acquire overdetermined significance in times of transition, the ruling bloc renews its effort to maintain hegemony by realigning subject-positions (Miles, 1989; Blaut, 1992; Deland, 1997). This power bloc revamps the ideological state apparatuses to give concessions and incorporate new subjects, so as to redefine the terms of class war to its advantage. It also reorganizes a new stage of the accumulation process (see Harvey, 1996). Attempts to restructure the system after the Civil War failed—until the civil rights acts, and the 1965 immigration reform, partly rectified the effects of institutional racism. With the neoconservative "passive revolution" of the 1980s, such advances (affirmative action, for example) have been reversed and a marketized, neo–social Darwinism conjoined with Christian fundamentalism now legitimates immigration, citizenship, and a refurbished white supremacist dispensation.

In the context of the neoliberal state renewing the racial order through destruction of the welfare program and the implementation of new coercive measures, a few Asian American academics have downgraded political engagement in favor of cultural activism. Following the vogue of Lyotard, Foucault, Baudrillard, and Butler, they have rejected the Marxist critique of exploitation and alienation in favor of an eclectic and anarchist attitude. The literary critic Lisa Lowe writes: "To the extent that Marx adopts the abstract and universalist propositions of the economic and political spheres, his classic critique of citizenship cannot account for the particular racialized relations of production on which this nation has been founded" (1996, p. 25).

Like the proponents of racial formation theory (Omi and Winant, 1986), the blanket repudiation of a historical-materialist critique opens the gate to bourgeois reformism, naive moralizing, and ultimately hedonistic elitism suited to the marginalized role of academics. Culture then becomes the privileged site of contestation; and discourse or performance, the theater for enacting rites of self-determination. Because the state controls the domain of rights, "the regulatory locus of the citizen-subject," and political representation, it is only through culture, the contemporary repository of memory and history, that alternative forms of subjectivity, collectivity, and public life can be imagined. Lowe believes that "Asian American particularity [whatever that means] returns a differently located dialectical critique of the universality proposed by both the economic and political spheres" (p. 28). This stance, I think, invents a culturalist metaphysics fixated on loss, dispersal, fragmentation—the obsessive iconology of *victimage* and *ressentiment*—that functions as the mirror image of the exclusive and hierarchical ethnic identification of "white power." Since politics and economics are the preserve of the bourgeois state that abstracts from the individual differences, difference thereby constituting the singularity of Asian American and other subaltern identities, therefore those cultures, primordial and untainted, remain the only space from which resistance can be launched. Such figuration of difference, ironically, underwrites dependency and subordination, as Colette Guillaumin (1995) points out. Evacuating the field of politics and economics to the enemy and taking a last-ditch defense in the ramparts of art-forms and tropes seems to me defeatist if not disingenuous opportunism. On the whole, it is a false reading of the historical record and a sectarian put-down of the multifaceted struggles in which militant collectives of Asian Americans, Chicanos, African Americans, and Native Americans have been engaged from the 1960s to the present.

One symptom of the postmodernist idealism that has overtaken Asian American scholars is the almost omnipresent failure to understand the Filipino predicament in the United States. A few reminders may be useful. The early Filipino presence in Hawaii and the U.S. mainland was a consequence of U.S. imperial violence and suppression of the Filipino revolutionary forces in the Filipino-American War of 1898–1902 (Francisco, 1973; Nearing and Freeman, 1969). Subjugation by the U.S. racializing sovereignty ruled out any claim by Filipinos to U.S. citizenship. This was not the case with Chinese (Europe and the United States shared the task of destabilizing the warlord territories), Japanese, Korean, or Indian immigrants. Up to 1946, the Filipinos may be likened to the Vietnamese refugees—displaced by U.S. colonial underdevelopment of the homeland, converted into anonymous scapegoats or nomadic surrogates for "wild" Indians domesticated on reservations and for blacks running from lynchers. Pursued as communists in the era of Bulosan and as deviants in the era of Cunanhan, Filipinos have eluded the honorific mantle of "model minority." Philip Vera Cruz's autobiography stands as a scrupulous response to the "strategic essentialism" that seeks to unify differences by selective omission. What happened to the imperial *Realpolitik* that supported Marcos for almost two decades? Who ever remembers and includes Silme Domingo and Gene Viernes (Churchill, 1995) in the chronicle of Asian American cultural transgression and opposition?

The nearly unanimous dismissal of the Marxist critique of capitalist society and its associated ideological/political practices characterizes the mind-set of Asian Americans entrenched in the academies of the Empire. They have wholly equated any radical critique of the regnant socioeconomic order with economic determinism, with dogmatic class-reductionism oblivious of race and gender, and even with totalitarianism. On the other hand, they quote Gramsci, Althusser, Walter Benjamin, Adorno, Lukacs, and Brecht, with of course heavy qualifications and reservations following the dicta of post-Marxists like Chantal Mouffe and Ernesto Laclau. Lacking a historical-materialist view of the mediated, dynamic relations between the political, ideological, and economic realms in bourgeois society, they have replicated the positivistic and empiricist method of mainstream sociology that tends to divorce institutions from the historical processes and structural conditions that brought them about. This reinforces the alienation and reification that reproduce the narrowly restricted concepts of state, citizenship, rights, and so on that have all been surrendered to the utilitarian imperatives of the ruling bloc. From the culturalist point of view, "race" is a signifier devoid of any connection with human needs, purposes, and everyday practices.

I propose that we move from the bankrupt metaphysics of poststructuralist speculation to a historical-materialist mapping of the present U.S. racial order with specific reference to Asians or Pacific Rim people domiciled here. This requires a shift of focus from immigration to a critique of the capitalist state and the transnational political economy of commodification in order to frame our understanding of culture within the process of hegemonic struggle defined by Italian communist theorist Antonio Gramsci. This will lay the foundation for reinscribing culture within the overdetermined conjuncture of the U.S. racial order. This foundation recognizes economics and politics as constitutive elements in the field of signification involving the production of meaning and contexts and the interpellation of subjects.

Return to the Gramscian Matrix

From the perspective of a radical social ontology derived from Marx, Gramsci described bourgeois society as one where the representation of social relations is determined by the historically specific mediation of social relations and nature through the production of commodities. Based on the separation between the producer/worker and the means of production (now privately owned by capitalists), such human social products—both commodities and superstructures—are abstracted from the actual process of creation and endowed with an autonomy and power over social life. Labor power and its products (including social relations) are estranged from humans, with the worker's intellectual and spiritual energies embodied in objects outside of human control. In this fetishism of commodities, humans yield their social power of objectification—the appropriation of nature for human needs and the naturalization of humans—and submit to the "violence of things" (Marx and Engels, 1970, p. 84). Social life, culture included, becomes mystified and alienated. As Mark Rupert stressed, "Under the *specific historical conditions* [emphasis added] of capitalism, the ontologically central process of objectification takes the form of alienation" (1993, p. 70). By exploiting alienated labor, the capitalist accumulates wealth and reproduces the capital/labor relation to which workers are subordinated. What needs emphasis is the contradiction between historical actuality and possibility at the heart of this process of objectification (mediation between social beings and nature) and the reality of alienation (Meszaros, 1995). Given the historical conditions that produced alienation, in particular the seemingly natural "impersonal forces of the market," the overcoming of alienation can be achieved if the oppressed classes can analyze the totality of relations of forces and on that basis craft a strategy for a long-term counterhegemonic politics.

What is crucial in explaining the possibilities of abolishing alienation is the relation between the state and civil society. The modern state is based on a system of class rule in which property belongs to the private sphere of civil society, the area of individual self-interests (Jessop, 1982; Ollman, 1993). In capitalist society, property ownership is an individual right exempt from questioning by persons in the public sphere, and class relations disappear because all citizens are formally equal. Bourgeois property assumes, then, the separation of politics and economics, guaranteed by the state. Removed from communal and political oversight, the private powers of capital reside in the fold of civil society and influence the public sphere by making it a self-limiting form of community, a false universality. Marx and Engels clarify the linkage between these two spheres: "Through the emancipation of private property from the community, the state has become a separate entity, beside and outside civil society; but it is nothing more than the form of organization which the bourgeoisie necessarily adopt both for internal and external purposes, for the mutual guarantee of their property and interests" (1970, p. 80).

The capitalist state thus embodies alienation. It is the political expression of the estrangement of individuals from their social powers. While the state can aggregate individual preferences and interests, it cannot go beyond them; it functions as the instrument of a particular interest, unable to resolve the atomistic isolation of individuals in civil society (Miliband, 1969). The capitalist state therefore guarantees the estrangement of community and communal powers from daily life. Politics in effect is detached from the entire process of social reproduction (in culture, economic activity, and so on). Alienation embraces the whole complex of social relations of production and reproduction. This constellation of forces is distinguished by the social division of labor as well as by the formal separation of public and private, politics and economics, state and society, brought about in the process of humans' objectifying their collective powers. Alienation thus conditions the "superstructure," including cultural production and artistic practices, laws, religion, media, and so on. Marx's critique, however, shows that alienation harbors contradictory impulses, revealing the precondition and possibility for their transcendence.

Approaching this problematic of alienation pervading capitalist society, Gramsci deploys a dual perspective in his philosophy of praxis. In Gramsci's radical social ontology patterned after Marx and Engels, humans constitute themselves in the act of consciously transforming their internal relations with their social and natural environments. Reality, then, is a historical creation born from the application of human will to social lives and to nature, with humans potentially able to self-consciously guide their collective activity and chart the trajectory of their *becoming* (Gramsci, 1971, pp. 351–357; 445–446). Politics concerns historically concrete struggles to determine "effective reality" as "a relation of forces in continuous motion and shift of equilibrium" (1971, p. 172). This implies that reality as an unceasing conflict of forces can convert economic, political, and ideological aspects of society into terrains of struggle for hegemony, domination (coercion), and direction (consent). Whereas the state monopolizes the means of coercion, in the Weberian construal, civil society serves as the site of cultural institutions and practices in which the hegemony of a class in a historic bloc can be built or destroyed. Contrary to the liberal view, civil society and state are internally sutured: Civil society affords the cultural/ideological linkage between class relations in the economy and the political function of the state (Sassoon, 1980; Buci-Glucksmann, 1980). Together, they comprise the extended or integral state—the domain in which the bourgeoisie has established its rule as "hegemony protected by the armour of coercion" (1971, p. 263). The state then can be grasped as "the entire complex of practical and theoretical activities with which the ruling class not only justifies and maintains its dominance, but manages to win the active consent of those over whom it rules" (1971, pp. 244, 257–263). Culture is deeply embedded in this legitimizing and signifying process.

What Gramsci aims at is a praxis of transformative critique. He seeks to integrate theory and practice to overcome the division of the capitalist order into rulers and ruled, dominant and subaltern, state and society—a series of dichotomies enabled by the prime opposition of manual and mental labor. The goal of a socialist project is to transform a capitalist economy, but this project is not caused or limited by economic variables. It is in fact bourgeois ideology that absolutizes the economic. Socialism involves the comprehensive transformation of society through the shaping of an alternative worldview and a new social order in which the participation of the masses is the key integral element. The aim, in short, is a qualitatively new form of the integral state, a "self-determining community" (Rupert, 1993, p. 79) opposed to the abstract, alienated universalism of the capitalist state. Socialism is opposed to economism, statolatry, and the reformism of social democracy and the welfare state. In this vision of revolutionary praxis, the entire society becomes a terrain of struggle in which subordinate groups can challenge bourgeois hegemony by discovering possibilities suppressed or obscured by the system.

Central to this project of fashioning a new hegemony by actualizing possibilities immanent in the alienated present is the building of a historic bloc of forces under the leadership of the class-conscious working masses that would articulate the most advanced and all-encompassing worldview. This bloc is the prerequisite for the exercise of hegemony. Gramsci writes: "Structures and superstructures form an 'historic bloc.' That is to say the complex contradictory and discordant *ensemble* of the superstructures is the reflection of the *ensemble* of the social relations of production" (1971, p. 366). What is involved is a dialectical transaction: not only domination of the enemy but also direction, the intellectual and moral leadership of the subaltern masses allied to the proletariat (Cox, 1993). State-society relations need to be reconstructed through organic changes in the political, economic, and cultural levels. Leadership of the historic bloc will give coherence to a wide range of disparate practices sanctioned by the bourgeois separation of state and civil society; it will articulate a unifying program and ideology as universal totality because it has the consent and participation of subordinate groups to which concrete concessions are made. But it is not just piecemeal concessions that will dissolve the contradiction between leaders and led and ultimately resolve the antinomies between politics and economics, state and society. It is the whole revolutionary process through which the masses participate directly in the reconstruction of the integral state, their collective destiny—a state of affairs in which the "social powers of self-production are commonly and consensually regulated" (Rupert, 1993, p. 81). Hegemony is finally attained by a class or fraction leading the bloc when narrow economic or corporatist (ethnic) interests are superseded by a more universal vision—in effect, a complex and dynamic ensemble of social practices rooted in historically specific sociopolitical conditions and production relations (Bocock, 1986; Sassoon, 1980).

Within this radical social ontology, Gramsci envisages a wide-ranging cultural politics immune from charges of economism, positivism, and empiricist one-sidedness. In the program of the revolutionary bloc, we find class forces, political agencies, and historical objectives synthesized to mobilize the whole society in actualizing historic possibilities blocked by alienated and reified conditions, specifically by the capitalist organization of production and reproduction of social life centered on profit and commodity-fetishism.

Where does the emancipatory project of Asian America (taking this, for the moment, as a hypothetical component of a revolutionary historic bloc in the making) fit into this Gramscian scheme of critique and transformative praxis?

Uncanny Strategy

Asians in the United States need to commit "ethnic suicide," to put it somewhat melodramatically, so as to transcend the Scylla of model-minoritism and the Charybdis of "the alien within." This can occur in the act of participating in a social bloc whose counterhegemonic advance proceeds through a stage called "catharsis." "Catharsis" is Gramsci's pregnant term for the passage from the economic-corporative sphere to the "complex superstructures" (Gramsci, 1971, pp. 366–367). By the latter term, he means not just culture but a constellation of practices, institutions, *habitus* (Bourdieu's term), codes, and norms linking the economic, political, and ideological instances of sociality. Immigration is one of the institutions in this constellation whose valence is dictated by other variables.

Given the condition of alienation pervading the market-centered polity of the United States, it is necessary to undertake an inventory of inequalities in the distribution of material resources so as to calculate which priorities need to be addressed. It will soon be discovered that particular situations of marginalization and denial are connected to juridical positions and legal rights, indexing the relations of power in civil society to the disposition of forces in the bureaucracy and state ideological apparatuses (Althusser, 1971), as well as the alignment of institutions such as the church, family, education, media, and so on. Citizenship figures here as a mode of configuring membership in civil society mediated by politics: congressional legislation, court trials, and so on.

In the horizon of thought about civic nationalism, the elements of a universalist and secular interpretation of citizenship are articulated with the normative ideals of cultural pluralism or tolerance of ethnic diversity. This produces a contradictory ensemble of positions associated with various interest groups, political parties, ethnic assemblages, and so on. This conjuncture approximates a "historic bloc"—except that here the exclusion of Asians from citizenship noted earlier confirms the observation that alienation defining capitalist relations of production can legitimate the racializing of segments of the labor force and their exclusion from the exercise of constitutional rights. This should not be a puzzle anymore. The deployment of exclusionary laws is a constitutive part of the U.S. bourgeoisie's attempt to reinforce its hegemony over ethnic European immigrants (non-Anglo Saxons) by conceding their advance in the ethnic status hierarchy over the "half-breeds": Chinese, Japanese, the colonized indigenes like the Native Americans, Filipinos, Mexicans, and so on. What is needed is a counterhegemonic movement to critique the alienated nature of capitalist production relations from the viewpoint of alienated labor (gendered and racialized) and to build a historic bloc energized by a universal vision of autonomy and equality against the hierarchizing, differential schemes of imperial *Realpolitik*.

Alienation and reification underlie the failure of American civic nationalism to neutralize or expunge the racializing drive of capital. Racialization, the categorization of groups on the grounds of sociocultural competence (not genetics) to deny them access to resources, complements the revitalization of ethnicity. The sociologist Daniel Bell (1975) expressed the mainstream sociological view in the 1970s that the salience of ethnic identification can be explained by several factors: First, the desire for primordial anchorage of identity (attenuated or diffused by a syncretistic culture and a more bureaucratic social organization) occurs in the context of the breakup of traditional authority structures. Secondly, "the politicization of the decisions that affect the communal lives of persons makes the need for group organization more necessary, and ethnic grouping becomes a ready means of demanding group rights or providing defense against other groups." Thirdly, the ethnic option is not a need for primordial attachment but a "strategic choice by individuals" to gain power and privilege. Bell urges a functionalist interpretation: "It is the *salience* not the *persona* which has to be the axial line for explanation. And because salience may be the decisive variable, the attachment to ethnicity may flush or fade very quickly depending on political and economic circumstances" (1975, p. 171). Ethnicity as identity via group attachment thus functions as a means for political-economic struggle in a milieu of alienation, where class solidarity is inchoate or has been weakened by the state's destruction of the political resources available to the dominated masses.

Absent "ethnic suicide," we are left with identity politics in a milieu of ludic indeterminacy, lost in the plethora of undecidable hybridities, contingencies, and syncretisms. The salience of Asian American panethnicity can be explained in this light as a reformist strategy to win more concessions from the bourgeois state: legislative representation, bilingual education, funding for mental health clinics, and so on. This is understandable as the route of the assimilationist petite-bourgeoisie, the middle strata of immigrants who seek to negate their ethnic genealogy and assume a new persona as American entrepreneurs.

The sociologist John Rex argues the Durkheimian functionality of ethnicity: First, in a situation of anomie (the accepted jargon for alienation/reification), individuals need moral and emotional support from an intermediate group between the family and the state. Second, "individuals need the networks and cultural ideals which their group offers if they are to have the solidarity which is necessary in their fight for equal rights" (1996, p. 244); ethnic mobilization is what generates that solidarity for claiming entitlements. Third, the utilitarian argument urges that new cultures may have some objective validity the recognition of which might contribute to the larger social good. Obscuring the centrality of the appropriation of surplus value, Rex endorses a moral principle in favor of egalitarian multiculturalism: The organic solidarity of various groups in any society must have a moral basis in the unity of consciences through the pursuit of justice in the public sphere. He quotes Durkheim's repudiation of Spencer's view of economic exchange: "The image of the one who completes us becomes inseparable from ours. . . . It thus becomes an integral and permanent part of our conscience" (Rex, 1996, p. 245). Rex's view of integration as moral, social, and psychological dialogue or interdependency brackets the problem of alienation and reification in the capitalist order. Espousal of such liberal ideals, although instructive for some, cannot resolve the disjunctions of state and civil society, public and private, egoistic individualism and community, manual and intellectual labor, that underpin capital accumulation. Ethnicity then becomes instrumental in the preservation of alienation even as it affords a means for solidarity and survival among the oppressed.

The Asian American claim to a vanguard role in cultural reformism, in my opinion, can be reinscribed into this sociological modality of valorizing ethnicity divorced from any revolutionary politics of counterhegemony. It chooses the parameter of an alienated social field where the cultural and aesthetic exist apart from the political and economic, the latter being regions corrupted by a homogenizing, canonical standard of intelligibility. However, Asian American cultural activists cannot so peremptorily abandon the Marxist critique of alienation, self-estrangement, and dehumanization without becoming knowing accomplices—or perhaps more accurately, accessories—to their own subordination. To abandon the critique is to commit the mistake of essentialism that they are trying to avoid. Isn't the notion of self-determination an Enlightenment idea associated with Locke's themes of private property and ego-centered appropriation? If Asian American narratives draw from ancestral roots more than from encounters with the dominant American milieu, in what way can they provide directive agency to those invoking unique ethnic sources of their own? The only way out of this impasse, I suggest, is the radical social ontology of Marx and Gramsci.

What Is Our Responsibility?

From the perspective of a materialist critique that uncovers the determinant conditions of possibility for transformative praxis (Zavarzadeh and Morton, 1991), the domain of culture in capitalist society becomes a multilayered and mutable site where narratives of citizenship and political emancipation intermesh with immigrant acts of dissidence and refusal. There can be no single instance of revolt by Chinese, Japanese, Filipino, or Korean "immigrants" without reference to a larger enabling narrative of collective emancipation from the bonds of archaic, feudal, and kinship modes of production. The inadequacy of postulating the agency of Asian Americans (the homogeneous rubric immediately begs the question) as differential locution or discourse becomes manifest as a symptom of the social fragmentation and disintegration alluded to earlier. Each single act of revolt lacks the dialectical and synergizing quality needed to convert it into a counterhegemonic leitmotif that will precipitate "catharsis," that is, the dissolution of ethnicity into a revolutionary alliance of forces opposing the system as a whole. This lack stems from the rejection of the historical-materialist theory of alienation that explains precisely the condition of possibility for both the abstract citizenship of U.S. national culture and the Asian American discourse of ethnic vanguardism.

Both forms of primordial and situational ethnicity arise from, and reproduce, the liberal pluralist hegemony of capital. Despite the presence of oppositional approaches to power relations in a market democracy, the prevailing consensus on ethnic and race relations in the United States still deploys a psychological-cum-group interest paradigm (Talcott Parsons plus Erik Erikson) to explain the acquiescence of the ruled (Gleason, 1996). With the general crisis of U.S. capital in the late 1970s and 1980s, the strategy for maintaining the active consent of the ruled has centered on revitalizing the slogans of freedom, self-discipline, and individual choice identified with the market and with private enterprise as against the ideals of equality and social justice.

This amplified cathexis of the ideological terrain has led some observers to consider identity politics, the articulation of subject-positions in "new social movements," as the most valuable stake in the political arena, a shift of the trajectory that eclipses the "war of maneuver" against the state (Laclau and Mouffe, 1985; Hall, 1996). While identity politics called attention to human agency and organized consciousness, aspects ignored by the kind of technological determinism prevalent in the Soviet Union and its satellites, the cognitive grasp of the totality of social relations disappeared (Sears and Mooers, 1995). Dialectics was displaced by an idealist voluntarism that privileged the ideological over the economic and political.

This error has been analyzed by Gramsci as one that conflates directly the organic crisis of capitalism and its extended duration with the conjunctural events in shorter periods, in which the underlying conflicts in the social relations of production are fought out in terms of ideological and political contestation. By eliding the dialectical interaction among economics, politics, and ideology, one succumbs to "an exaggeration of the voluntarist and individual element" (Gramsci, 1971, pp. 177–178). Voluntarism vitiates the postmodern ideologism of Asian American academics who abandon a historical-materialist critique for ludic pragmatism. Political "trench warfare," or the war of position (as Gramsci originally envisaged it), becomes fetishized, one-sidedly detached from a war of maneuver on the capitalist state. Celebrating the virtues of Asian American cultural practices without comprehending the alienation and fragmentation of experience and connecting that with the overarching power structures that rest on status hierarchy and class divisions can only be an exercise in reaffirming one's complicity with the oppressors.

It is now public knowledge how influential the "model minority" orthodoxy has grown since its inaugural propagation in the sixties as an antidote to the burgeoning civil rights movement. Even the orthodox left is not immune from the virus. Victor Perlo, the theoretician of the U.S. Communist Party, concludes, on the basis of the presence of Asians in the ranks of high corporate executives and investors in transnational business, that " it is no longer appropriate to regard Asian people as a whole as an oppressed minority economically, although a relatively small section can be so categorized" (1996, p. 46). Despite certain qualifications, this judgment of economic parity or even slight superiority of Asians over whites leads Perlo, and others with a similar economistic bent, to align Asians with the ruling capitalist bloc. This idea may be substantiated by Omatsu's perceptive diagnosis of stratification in the Asian American community in the 1980s and 1990s, a fact that explodes the myth of that community's monolithic panethnicity.

In a recent survey, the sociologist Yen Le Espiritu noted how among post-1965 Filipino immigrants, regional disparities aggravated by class divisions block the spontaneous acquisition of group consciousness. Despite her narrow focus on internal differentiation, Espiritu concludes: "Because of the position of the Philippines within the global racial order and the social location of Filipinos in the United States, Filipino immigrants, regardless of their class status and familiarity with US culture, will continue to be defined as 'non-white' and face the attendant consequences of being so labelled" (1996a, p. 43; see also Chan, 1991; Rose, 1997). The allusion to the persistence of a global racial order and the survival of an archaic racism inflected with sociocultural criteria that affects not only Filipinos but all post-1965 Asian immigrants, especially the refugees from Vietnam, Laos, and Cambodia, undermines the hypothesis of a plural, ambivalent panethnicity that would be both inclusive and unitary (Espiritu, 1996b). Ethnic manipulation of diacritical cultural markers cannot help immigrants escape the racializing gaze of the establishment, whose supremacy needs these "others" for legitimacy and self-regeneration.

Panethnicity is the last gasp of flexible globalized pluralism and its cult of laissez-faire multiculturalism. Its appeal as the magic refuge of an idea of community proclaimed to be fluid, open-ended, and congenial to heterogeneous mores and life-forms obversely mirrors the mentality of beleaguered "white power" militias and evangelical cults that cannot endure the regime of anomie and alienation existing between the state and the nuclear family. The post–Cold War epoch has ushered in a new zone of indeterminacy that has problematized the ambition of the ideologues of panethnicity. The novelist Frank Chin comments on the post-1965 cohorts of "unredeemed Chinese Chinese" immigrants: "In Chinese-America, it is the new immigrants threatening our relationship with the whites, not the blacks" (quoted in Terkel, 1992, p. 314). The historian Arif Dirlik interprets the problem as neither cultural nor regional but one belonging to the stage of global postmodernity:

> What is specific to Asian America is its relationship to new centers of global economic power in the Pacific and, to a lesser extent, South Asia, that have been responsible for bringing the Pacific to the forefront of global consciousness, in the process challenging Eurocentric conceptions of modernity that were themselves empowered by the apparently unchallengeable supremacy of Euro-American capitalism. What this challenge implies remains to be seen; but in an immediate sense, the emergence of Pacific Asian economies as key players in the global economy has had a transformative effect on the Asian American self-image, as well as on the perceptions of Asian Americans in the society at large (1996, pp. 2–3).

While Dirlik posits the conflict between capitalist developmentalism and community identity (local welfare) as the crucial arena where Asian Americans are compelled to choose sides—a matter not of ethnic predestiny but of political choice—I think the dialectic of contradictions has been short-circuited. Asian Americans must discriminate in a larger space than that of internal relations in the United States, in which panethnicity may be grounded in trans-Pacific solidarity or not; we must choose between transnational corporate power that uses the modern state apparatus-cum-military of the hegemonic nation-states (including Japan), and the peoples of the Pacific Rim—Koreans, Filipinos, Chinese, Japanese, Malaysians, Indonesians, and so on—who are exploited in multiple ways (by race, class, gender, nationality, and so on) and who are mounting various forms of opposition and resistance.

In conclusion, I want to stress the armed and legal struggles raging in the Philippines as signs of transformative praxis in a weak link in the imperial hegemonic chain. Placed in this context, the more than 6 million Filipinos in the diaspora carry into the heart of the empire the stigma of uneven development to disrupt the hubris of the "civilizing mission." In various books (San Juan, 1996; 1997a; 1997b), I have argued that Filipinos in the United States cannot be classified simply as another immigrant ethnic cohort on the way to acculturation and assimilation. The Philippines, in the first place, was the only direct U.S. colony in southeast Asia that suffered incalculable violence from the U.S. military and other coercive agencies of the state, foreshadowing what happened in Vietnam fifty years later (Francisco, 1973). The long and durable history of Filipino resistance against U.S. colonialism since its advent in 1898, the unmitigated peasant and worker insurrections from the turn of the century to the granting of formal independence in 1946, and the current "people's war" against U.S. neocolonial control through local clients all continue to exert a powerful if sometimes submerged influence on the Filipino "amalgamated" consciousness across class and regional boundaries

(San Juan, 1992). During the long period of the Marcos dictatorship (1972–1986), Filipinos in the United States, specifically the children of those who became citizens before and after World War II, went through a profound experience of politicization and group mobilization that established a point of reference and of departure for succeeding generations.

Filipinos in the diaspora don't need Cunanhan or the adventurous Manilamen of the Louisiana bayous to respond to antifoundationalism with myths of origin and ethnic distinctiveness. We need only attend to what is going on today in the battlefronts of the transnational corporate empire. Although burdened with the perennial "colonial mentality" so endemic to all "third world" subalterns, recent Filipino immigrants cannot be oblivious to the raging fires of "people's war" in the homeland—hitherto the only potentially serious challenge to U.S. domination in southeast Asia and throughout the Pacific Rim. While the Filipino "Manongs," the farmworkers of Hawaii and the West Coast, can be credited with acts of intransigent revolt against racism and exploitation (celebrated by Carlos Bulosan and Philip Vera Cruz in their writings) from the first decades up to the McCarthy period, it is the anti-imperialist work of activists like Silme Domingo and Gene Viernes, martyrs of the fight against the Marcos regime, that meaningfully connects the peoples of the Pacific Rim, their memories and aspirations, to the multi-ethnic communities here.

History is always contemporary. Not the economic miracles of the "Asian tigers" but the contemporary struggles of workers and peasants—Chinese, Filipinos, Koreans, Indonesians, Thais, and Malaysians from all walks of life—are what we need to attend to in forging an emancipatory cultural politics that counters the alienation and fragmentation of mass consumer society. We witness in the daily strivings of millions of people in the Pacific Rim the birth of initiatives and intellectual forces destined to reconfigure the knowledge paradigms we have about Asians in the United States.

To understand the new alignment of forces in the transnational project of reconquering global hegemony outlined above, I think we need to transvalue the immigrant paradigm and sublate it within a framework of radical critique based on the insight that global capitalism, notwithstanding its retooling and adaptation to a new, technologically refined environment, continues to depend on the surplus value produced by the labor of racialized populations residing in core territories and in peripheral provinces, enabling the contradictions outside to produce effects inside and unsettling the ethnic boundaries that once sheltered bodies and souls from the ravages of capital accumulation (James, 1995). From those ethnic havens and shelters, bodies transported from the Pacific Rim to the "belly of the beast" (to use Jose Marti's permanently relevant epithet), now have to confront the realities of exploitation and oppression, no longer consoled by the alibis of cultural mystifications and pacified by ludic illusions of incommensurable difference.

REFERENCES

Althusser, L. (1971). *Lenin and Philosophy*. New York: Monthly Review.

Blaut, J. M. (1992). "The Theory of Cultural Racism." *Antipode* 24, no. 4, pp. 289–299.

Bocock, R. (1986). *Hegemony*. London: Tavistock Publications.

Buci-Glucksmann, C. (1980). *Gramsci and the State*. London: Lawrence and Wishart.

Chan, S. (1991). *Asian Americans: An Interpretive History*. Boston: Twayne.

Churchill, T. (1995). *Triumph Over Marcos*. Seattle: Open Hand.

Cox, R. (1993). "Gramsci, hegemony and international relations: an essay in method." In Gill, S., ed., *Gramsci, Historical Materialism and International Relations*. Cambridge: Cambridge University Press.

Daniels, R. (1993). "United States policy towards Asian immigrants: contemporary developments in historical perspective." *International Journal* 48 (Spring), pp. 310–334.

Dawnay, I. (1997). "Silent Huang keeps 'Chinagate' inquiry guessing." *Sunday Telegraph* (July 13), p. 27.

Deland, M. (1997). "The Cultural Racism of Sweden." *Race and Class* 39, no. 1 (July–Sept. 1997), pp. 51–59.

Dirlik, A. (1996). "Asians on the Rim: Transnational Capital and Local Community in the Making of Contemporary Asian America." *Amerasia Journal* 22, no. 3, pp. 1–24.

Dudley, W., ed. (1997). *Asian Americans: Opposing Viewpoints*. San Diego, CA: Greenhaven Press.

Espiritu, Y. L. (1996a). "Colonial oppression, labour importation, and group formation: Filipinos in the United States." *Ethnic and Racial Studies* 19, no. 1, pp. 29–43.

_____. (1996b). "Crossroads and Possibilities: Asian Americans on the Eve of the Twenty-First Century." *Amerasia Journal* 22, pp. vii-xii.

Francisco, L. (1973). "The First Vietnam." In *The Philippines: End of an Illusion*. London: AREAS and *Journal of Contemporary Asia*.

Glazer, N., and Moynihan, D. P. (1963). *Beyond the Melting Pot*. Cambridge, MA.: MIT Press.

Gleason, P. (1996). "Identifying Identity: A Semantic History (1983)." In Sollors, W., ed., *Theories of Ethnicity: A Classical Reader*. New York: New York University Press.

Gramsci, A. (1971). *Selections from the Prison Notebooks*. New York: International Publishers.

Guillaumin, C. (1995). *Racism, Sexism, Power and Ideology*. New York: Routledge.

Hall, S. (1996). *Stuart Hall: Critical Dialogues in Cultural Studies*. New York: Routledge.

Harlow, B. (1995). "Negotiating Treaties: Maastricht and NAFTA." Pp. 506–517 in Callari, A., Cullenberg, S., and Biewener, C., eds., *Marxism in the Postmodern Age*. New York: Guilford Press.

Harvey, D. (1996). *Justice, Nature and the Geography of Difference*. Cambridge, MA: Blackwell.

Higham, J. (1971 [1955]). *Strangers in the Land*. New York: Atheneum.

Hutchinson, J. (1994). *Modern Nationalism*. London: Fontana Press.

James, J. (1995). "Racism, Genocide and Resistance: The Politics of Language and International Law." In Callari, A., Cullenberg, S., and Biewener, C., eds., *Marxism in the Postmodern Age*. New York: Guilford Press.

Jessop, B. (1982). *The Capitalist State*. New York: New York University Press.

Laclau, E., and Mouffe, C. (1985). *Hegemony and Socialist Strategy*. London: Verso.

Lowe, L. (1996). *Immigrant Acts*. Durham, NC: Duke University Press.

Marx, K., and Engels, F. (1970). In Arthur, C. J., *The German Ideology*. New York: International Publishers.

Meszaros, I. (1995). *Beyond Capital*. New York: Monthly Review Press.

Miles, R. (1989). *Racism*. New York: Routledge.

Miliband, R. (1969). *The State in Capitalist Society*. London: Weidenfeld and Nicolson.

Min, P. G., ed. (1995). *Asian Americans: Contemporary Trends and Issues*. Thousand Oaks, CA: Sage.

Nearing, S., and Freeman, J. (1969). *Dollar Diplomacy: A Study in American Imperialism*. New York: Monthly Review Press.

Ollman, B. (1993). *Dialectical Investigations*. New York: Routledge.

Omatsu, G. (1994). "The 'Four Prisons' and the Movements of Liberation: Asian American Activism from the 1960s to the 1990s." In Aguilar-San Juan, K., ed., *In the State of Asian America*. Boston: South End Press.

Omi, M., and Winant, H. (1986). *Racial Formation in the United States from the 1960s to the 1980s*. New York: Routledge.

Perlo, V. (1996). *Economics of Racism II*. New York: International Publishers.

Reimers, D. M. (1992). *Still the Golden Door: The Third World Comes to America*. New York: Columbia University Press.

Rex, J. (1996). "Multiculturalism in Europe." In Hutchinson, J., and Smith, A., eds., *Ethnicity*. New York: Oxford University Press.

Rose, P. (1997). *They and We: Racial and Ethnic Relations in the United States*. 5th ed. New York: McGraw-Hill.

Rupert, M. (1993). "Alienation, Capitalism and the Inter-State System: Toward a Marxian/Gramscian Critique." In Gill, S., ed., *Gramsci, Historical Materialism and International Relations*. Cambridge: Cambridge University Press.

San Juan, E. (1992). *Racial Formations/Critical Transformations*. Atlantic City, NJ: Humanities International Press.

_____. (1996). *The Philippine Temptation*. Philadelphia: Temple University Press.

_____. (1997a). *Beyond Postcolonial Theory*. New York: St. Martin's Press.

_____. (1997b). *From Exile to Diaspora: Versions of the Filipino Experience in the United States*. Boulder: Westview Press.

Sassoon, A. S. (1980). *Gramsci's Politics*. New York: St. Martin's Press.

Sassoon, A. S., ed. (1980). *Approaches to Gramsci*. London: Writers and Readers.

Sears, A., and Mooers, C. (1995). "The Politics of Hegemony: Democracy, Class and Social Movements." In Zavarzadeh, M., Ebert, T., and Morton, D., eds., *Post-ality: Marxism and Postmodernism*. Washington, DC: Maisonneuve Press.

Sivy, M. (1997). "What America Will Look Like in 25 Years." *Money* 26, no. 10 (October), pp. 98–106.

Takaki, R. (1993). *A Different Mirror*. Boston: Little, Brown.

Terkel, S. (1992). *Race*. New York: New Press.

Thomas, E. (1997). "Facing Death." *Newsweek* (July 28), pp. 20–30.

Van den Berghe, P. (1972). *Race and Racism*. New York: John Wiley.

Winant, H. (1994). *Racial Conditions*. Minneapolis: University of Minnesota Press.

Yip, A. (1997). "The Big Picture." *AsiaWeek* (January 3), pp. 12–13.

Zavarzadeh, M., and Morton, D. (1991). *Theory (Post)modernity Opposition*. Washington, DC: Maisonneuve Press.

four

The New Racism: Racial Structure in the United States, 1960s–1990s

EDUARDO BONILLA-SILVA

Introduction

Some analysts claim that race and racism have decreased in importance in contemporary America (Wilson, 1987 [1978]). This view is consistent with survey data on white attitudes since the early 1960s (Hyman and Sheatsley, 1964; Greeley and Sheatsley, 1971; Schuman, Steeh, and Bobo, 1985; Sniderman and Piazza, 1993) as well as with many demographic and economic studies comparing the status of whites and blacks in terms of income, occupation, health, and education, which suggest that a remarkable reduction in racial inequality has occurred in America (Duncan, 1968; Palmore and Whittington, 1970; Farley and Hermalin, 1972; Freeman, 1978 [1973]; Farley, 1993 [1984]; Farley and Allen, 1987; Smith and Welch, 1986).

A smaller number of social scientists believe that race continues to play a role similar to the one it played in the past (Pinkney, 1984; Fusfeld and Bates, 1984; Willie, 1989; Bell, 1992). For these authors, little has changed in America in terms of racism, and there is a general pessimism about the prospect of changing the racial status of minorities. Although this is a minority viewpoint in academia, it represents the perception of many members of minority communities, especially of the black community.

These opinions about the changing significance of race and racism in the United States are based on a narrowly defined notion of racism. For these analysts, racism is fundamentally an ideological or attitudinal phenomenon.

The author would like to thank Amanda Lewis for her assistance in the preparation of this chapter.

In contrast, we regard racism as a *structure*, that is, as a network of social relations at social, political, economic, and ideological levels that shapes the life
chances of the various races.[1] What social scientists define as racism is conceptualized in this framework as racial ideology. Racism (racial ideology)
helps to glue together and to organize the nature and character of race relations in a society (Bonilla-Silva, 1994). From this vantage point, rather than
arguing about whether the significance of race has declined, increased, or not
changed at all, the real issue is assessing whether a transformation has occurred in the *racial structure* of the United States. It is our contention that
despite the profound changes that occurred in the 1960s, a new racial structure—the New Racism, for short—is operating, which accounts for the persistence of racial inequality.

The elements that make up this new racial structure are: (1) the increasingly covert nature of racial discourse and racial practices; (2) the avoidance
of racial terminology and the ever growing claim by whites that they experience "reverse racism"; (3) the elaboration of a racial agenda over political
matters that eschews direct racial references; (4) the invisibility of most
mechanisms to reproduce racial inequality; and finally, (5) the rearticulation
of a number of racial practices characteristic of the Jim Crow period of race
relations.

This paper begins with a brief description of how the New Racism came
about. Against this backdrop, we survey the evidence of how black-white
racial inequality is produced and reproduced in the United States in five areas: social, economic, political, social control (criminal justice system, arrest
rates, and the like), and ideological. The evidence is perused from 1960 until
the present with the goal of examining the mechanisms that keep minorities
"in their place." We conclude the paper with a discussion of social, political,
and legal repercussions of this new racial structure in America.

The Emergence of a New Racial
Structure in the 1960s

Blacks were kept in a subordinate position during the Jim Crow period of
race relations through a variety of bluntly racist practices. At the economic
level, blacks were restricted to menial jobs by the joint effort of planters,
corporations, and unions. In the south, they were mostly tenant farmers.
Their occupational confinement was accomplished through vagrancy and
apprenticeship laws, restrictions on the right of blacks to buy land and to
work in certain occupations, imprisonment due to debt, and the convict
lease system (Greene and Woodson, 1930; Fredrickson, 1981; Norton et al.,
1990). In the North, the exclusionary practices of managers and unions kept
blacks in unskilled occupations with very little chance for occupational mobility (Myrdal, 1944; Spero and Harris 1974; Higgs, 1977; Foner, 1981;

Marable, 1983). Spero and Harris characterized the jobs of blacks in the following fashion: "The jobs into which the Negroes went were usually those which native Americans and Americanized foreign-born white labor did not want. This largely accounts for the almost spectacular increase in the proportion of Negroes in the iron and steel foundries where the work is dirty, hot, and unpleasant" (Spero and Harris, 1974, pp. 155–156).

At the social level, the rules of the new racial order emerged slowly, given that the Civil War and the Reconstruction period (1865–1877) shook the rules of racial engagement and challenged the place of blacks in society (Woodward, 1966; Fredrickson, 1981). By the late 1880s, segregationist laws and practices had emerged that separated whites and nonwhites in public accommodations, housing, schools, and in the workplace. C. Vann Woodward describes the extent of these laws in the following manner:

> The extremes to which caste penalties and separation were carried in parts of the South could hardly find a counterpart short of the latitudes of India and south Africa. . . . Curfew . . . separate phone booths . . . separate books and storage of books in public schools . . . South Carolina separated the mulatto caste . . . separation of prostitutes, and even "Ray Stannard Baker found Jim Crow Bibles for Negro witnesses in Atlanta and Jim Crow elevators for Negro passengers in Atlanta buildings" (Woodward, 1966, p. 102).

Politically, blacks were virtually disenfranchised in the South and were almost totally dependent on white politicians in the North. In the South, poll taxes, literacy tests, and outright coercive strategies constrained blacks' political options (Walton, 1972; Marable, 1983). In the North, black politicians were subordinate to white ethnic political machineries and did not obtain many gains for black communities (Patterson, 1974).

In terms of social control, blacks in the South were regulated by the actions of individual whites, violent racist organizations such as the Ku Klux Klan, mob violence in the form of lynching, and the lack of enforcement of the laws of the land by state agencies (Marable, 1983). In the North, blacks suffered less from these practices largely because they were extremely residentially segregated and thus did not pose a "threat" to whites. However, whenever blacks "crossed the line," whites erupted in violence—as happened during the race riots of the late 1910s (Tuttle, 1970).

Finally, in consonance with the above practices, racial ideology during the Jim Crow period of race relations was explicitly racist. Without question, most whites believed that minorities were intellectually and morally inferior, that they should be kept apart, and that whites should not mix with any of them (Gossett, 1963).

The apartheid that blacks experienced in the United States was predicated on (1) keeping blacks in rural areas, mostly in the South, (2) maintaining them as agricultural workers, and (3) excluding them from the political process. However, as blacks successfully challenged their socioeconomic position by migrating initially from rural to urban areas in the South and later to the North and West (Henri, 1975; Harrison, 1991); by pushing themselves into nonagricultural occupations through strike-breaking and other means (Tuttle, 1970; Foner, 1981; Leiman, 1992); and by developing political organizations and movements like Garveyism, the National Association for the Advancement of Colored People, the National Urban League, and the Southern Regional Council (Woodward, 1966; McAdam, 1982; Morris, 1984), the infrastructure of apartheid began to crumble.

Among the other factors leading to the abolition of the segregationist order, the most significant were the participation of blacks in World Wars I and II, which patently underscored the contradiction between fighting for freedom abroad and lacking it at home (Dalfiume, 1969; Foner, 1974; Wynn, 1993); the Cold War, which made it a necessity to eliminate overt discrimination at home in order to sell the United States as the champion of democracy; and a number of judicial decisions, legislative acts, and presidential decrees that were enacted after the 1940s (Woodward, 1966; Burkey, 1971).

The aforementioned political, social, and economic processes occurred in a fast-changing U.S. political economy. From 1920 until 1940, the North expanded its industrialization process at a furious pace. After World War II the South industrialized at an even more dramatic pace. Many northern industries moved southward during this time, in search of lower production costs (Reich, 1981; Leiman, 1992), and have continued to do so (Harrison and Bluestone, 1988). Today, more than 70 percent of the southern labor force is engaged in nonagricultural pursuits (Leiman, 1992, p. 90). This industrialization process provided the pull factor for blacks to move from the rural south, which, coupled with the push factor of escaping the violence of Jim Crow (Tolnay and Beck, 1991) and with the demise in agricultural jobs (Marshall, 1965; Christian and Pepelasis, 1978), created optimal conditions for the "great migration." Although the 1.8 million blacks (Davis, 1991) who migrated between 1910 and 1940 from the South to the North and West faced severe discrimination and economic constraints from white workers, labor unions, and whites in general (Tuttle, 1970; Foner, 1981; Marks, 1991), the North provided them expanded opportunities in all realms of life (Leiman, 1992). For that reason the great migration continued between 1940 and 1970, when 4.4 million more blacks left the South (Davis, 1991).

The impact of this migration was enormous on the overall condition of blacks. By 1970 blacks were geographically diffused throughout the United States. Eighty percent were urban dwellers and had achieved a higher rate of urbanization than whites. Blacks had increased their levels of education, and a small but thriving black middle class had emerged. Social and political organizations flourished and became training grounds for many black leaders; by virtue of their new geographic dispersion, blacks increasingly became a national group and were able to develop a new consciousness, new attitudes, and a new view on how to deal with racial discrimination—characterized by Gunnar Myrdal as the "protest motive" (Myrdal, 1944; Henri, 1975; Davis, 1991).

Even in the South, the social, political, and cultural condition of blacks improved somewhat with the early process of industrialization (Myrdal, 1944, pp. 998–999). And after the 1960s, even their economic condition changed as the top business elite abandoned all-out discrimination because of the adverse economic effects created by violence and protest demonstrations (Christian and Pepelasis, 1978). This pattern was reinforced by the penetration of northern industrial capital into the South, making the "southern system of brutality, social discrimination, and legalized (or extra-legalized) persecution . . . more and more economically and politically dysfunctional" (Leiman, 1992, p. 174).

To be clear, neither urbanization nor industrialization was intrinsically nonracial, "rational," or progressive. Both northern and southern capitalists accommodated racial discrimination in their hiring practices, company policies, and daily practices. In the case of southern capitalists, industrialization became a necessity with the deepening decline of the South's agricultural economy. Although southern capitalists were able to maintain Jim Crow policies alongside industrialization for more than fifty years (from the 1890s to the 1950s), by the mid-1950s it had become clear that the two could not coexist peacefully. Blacks in the North had acquired enough political muscle to push the federal government to do something about their civil rights. After the *Brown* decision of 1954 and its rejection by most of the South, instability and protests spread throughout the South. Such instability was anathema for attracting capital, and hence the southern business elite, reluctantly and gradually, developed an accommodation with the new policies.[2] In the North, the accommodation began much earlier—in the 1920s, 1930s, and particularly after World War II[3]—and involved the subordinate incorporation of blacks into industry. This accommodation, although progressive, maintained the view that blacks were inferior workers and kept them in the bottom of the occupational hierarchy. The views of northern managers were typified by a "progressive" manager who in the fifties commented: "Negroes, basically and as a group, with only rare exceptions, are not as well trained for higher skills and jobs as whites. They appear to be excellent for work, usually unskilled, that requires stamina and brawn—and little else. They are unreliable and cannot adjust to the demands of the factory" (Morrow, 1957, p. 69). Views like this have continued to plague American capitalists in the post-1960 period (Perlo, 1975; Kirschenman and Neckerman, 1994). Industrialization and urbanization provided a new context that made the Jim Crow system impossible to maintain in the face of black opposition.

These demographic, social, political, and economic factors, as well as the actions of blacks, made change almost inevitable. But ripe conditions are not enough to change any structural order. Hence, the racial order had to be *directly* challenged if it was to be effectively transformed. That was the role fulfilled by the civil rights movement and the other forms of mass protest by blacks (so-called race riots) that took place in the 1950s, 1960s, and early 1970s. Organized and spontaneous challenges were the catalysts that brought down overt segregation.

Yet the demise of Jim Crow did not end racial discrimination in America. Many analysts (Caditz, 1976; Wellman, 1977; Kinder and Sears, 1981; Sears, 1988; Pettigrew, 1994) have argued that "racism" (as usually defined) and race relations have acquired a new character since the 1960s. They point out the increasingly covert nature of racial discourse and racial practices; the avoidance of racial terminology in racial conflicts by whites; and the elaboration of a racial agenda over political matters (state intervention, individual rights, responsibility, and so on) that eschews any direct racial reference. In the following sections we detail the discriminatory practices of the post–civil rights era and assess their character.

Interracial Social Interaction

In all areas of social life, blacks and whites remain mostly separate and disturbingly unequal. A close examination of research in the areas of housing, education, and everyday social interaction reveals startlingly little progress since the 1960s.

Residential Segregation

Residential segregation in the United States peaked in the 1950s and 1960s, and since then, only modest changes have occurred (Farley and Allen, 1987). Today blacks are more segregated than any other racial or ethnic group; have experienced segregation longer than any other group; and are segregated at every income level. In their book *American Apartheid,* Massey and Denton (1993) measure the block-level indices of residential segregation of thirty metropolitan areas between 1940 and 1980. The index of residential segregation for the North is around 80 and for the South around 70 (an index of 100 indicates total segregation, and one of 0, no segregation at all).

The costs to blacks of residential segregation are high: They are likely to pay more for housing in a limited market and to have lower quality housing; less likely to own their housing; likely to live in areas where employment is difficult to find; and likely to have to contend with prematurely depreciated housing (Baron, 1969; Franklin and Resnick, 1973; King and Mieszkowski, 1973; Galster, 1977; Yinger, 1978; Jackman and Jackman, 1980; Struyk and

Turner, 1986; Kain, 1986; Farley and Allen, 1987; Turner, Struyk, and Yinger, 1991). The big difference is in how segregation is accomplished today. In the Jim Crow era the housing industry used overtly discriminatory practices. Real estate agents often refused outright to rent or sell properties to black customers. Others employed various methods of subterfuge to discourage blacks from seeking housing in certain areas. Federal redlining policies, overtly discriminatory insurance and lending practices, and racially restrictive covenants on housing deeds also contributed to the maintenance of segregated communities (Tauber and Tauber, 1965; Tabb, 1970; Massey and Denton, 1993). In the post–civil rights era, covert behaviors have replaced these practices, with the same outcome—separate communities.

Many studies have detailed the obstacles that minorities face from government agencies, real estate agents, money lenders, and white residents, which continue to limit their housing options (Galster, 1990a; Turner, Struyk, and Yinger, 1991; Kaestner and Fleisher, 1992; Massey and Denton, 1993; Cloud and Galster, 1993). Housing audits everywhere suggest that blacks are denied available housing from 35 to 75 percent of the time, depending on the city in question (Smith, 1995, p. 64). Turner, Struyk, and Yinger (1991), in reporting the results of the Department of Housing and Urban Development's *Housing Discrimination Study,* found that blacks and Hispanics were discriminated against in approximately *half* of their efforts to rent or buy housing. These housing studies have shown that when paired with similar white counterparts, blacks are likely to be shown fewer apartments, to be quoted higher rents or offered worse conditions, and to be steered to specific neighborhoods (Yinger, 1986; Galster, 1990b; Turner, Struyk, and Yinger, 1991).

In a study of lending practices conducted by the Kentucky Human Rights Commission (Center for Community Changes 1989), black and white testers with similar characteristics requested conventional mortgages for the same housing from ten of the top lending institutions in Louisville. Although discrimination against some was apparent (for example, some blacks had trouble getting appointments), in the 85 visits made to inquire about loans, none of the black testers save one knew they were being discriminated against. Blacks were given less information, less encouragement to return and apply for the loan, fewer helpful hints as to how to successfully obtain a loan, and differential treatment in prequalifying. Some were told they would not qualify for a loan, whereas whites of the same profile were told that they would. Similar studies done in Chicago and New York revealed discrimination in seven out of ten lending institutions in Chicago and in the one institution studied in New York City (Cloud and Galster, 1993). New national data from the Home Mortgage Disclosure Act show that black applicants are denied mortgages at least twice as frequently as whites of the same income and gender regardless of their income (Smith, 1995, p. 67).[4] Finally, a study by the Federal Reserve Bank of Boston found that controlling for a number of variables, blacks on average are denied loans 60 percent more times than whites (Oliver and Shapiro, 1989).

In terms of real estate agents, George Galster's review of several fair housing audits found that blacks were systematically steered to different neighborhoods in more than half of the audited transactions. He concludes: "The evidence was fully consistent with only one hypothesis about why real estate agents steer. They steer so as to perpetuate two segregated housing markets buffered by a zone of racially transitional neighborhoods" (Galster, 1990b, p. 39).

Education

The history of black-white education in this country is one of substantive inequities maintained through public institutions. Today many of the traditional barriers to black advancement have been outlawed, yet the situation of blacks is by no means one of equity with whites. Although scholars have documented the narrowing of the gap in the quantity of education attained by blacks and whites (Farley, 1984; Farley and Allen, 1987; Jaynes and Williams, 1989), little has been said about the persisting gap in the *quality* of education received. Persistent (and in some cases worsening) high levels of *de facto* segregation are at least partly to blame for the gap in quality (Rivken, 1994). Tracking, differential assignment to special education, and other informal school practices are other important factors.

More than 30 percent of black students attend schools that are 95 percent or more nonwhite, and more than 30 percent of white students attend schools that are less than 95 percent white (Booker, Krueger, and Wolkon, 1992; Orfield, 1993).[5] Despite modest progress made during the period immediately after 1964, the level of school segregation for black students remains relatively high in all regions and has deteriorated in the Northeast and Midwest (Orfield and Monfort, 1992). As Gary Orfield has noted, "Segregated schools are still profoundly unequal" (Orfield, 1993, p. 235). Inner-city minority schools, in sharp contrast to white suburban schools, lack decent buildings, are overcrowded, have outdated equipment—if they have equipment at all—do not have enough textbooks for their students, lack library resources, are technologically behind, and pay their teaching and administrative staff less, which produces, despite exceptions, a low level of morale. These "savage inequalities" (Kozol, 1991) have been directly related to lower reading achievement and learning attained by black students (Dreeben and Gamoran, 1986) and to their limited computer skills (Booker, Krueger, and Wolkon, 1992).

In integrated schools, blacks still have to contend with discriminatory practices. Oakes and her coauthors (1992) have found clear evidence of discriminatory practices in tracking within schools. Whites (and Asians) are considerably (and statistically speaking, significantly) more likely to be placed in the academic track than comparably achieving African American and Latino students (Oakes et al., 1992). The implication of not being placed in the academic track are less preparedness for college work and lower test scores. No wonder black students tend to score lower on the SAT than white students.

Other Areas of Social Life

A brief survey of research in other areas of social life reveals persistent discrimination, unequal treatment, and in some cases, exclusion. In terms of intermarriage, blacks are less likely than any other racial or ethnic group to intermarry (Lieberson and Watters, 1988). This is one of the few areas where whites still openly express reservations in surveys (Schuman, Steeh, and Bobo, 1985). In 1980, less than two percent of all marriages were black-white unions (Tucker and Mitchell-Kernan, 1990). In 1993, only 0.4 percent of all new marriages were black-white unions (Otis-Graham, 1995). In addition to whites' negative attitudes toward interracial relationships, the high level of residential segregation and the limited friendships between blacks and whites contribute to this low rate of intermarriage. Research by Jackman and Crane (1986) showed that only 9.4 percent of whites could name one good black friend. This led them to conclude that very few whites "could rightly claim that some of their best friends are black" (Jackman and Crane 1986, p. 460).

In the realm of everyday life, several recent works have attempted to examine the daily experiences blacks have with racism (Collins, 1989; Essed, 1990; Cose, 1993; Feagin and Sikes, 1994; Otis-Graham, 1995). In his interviews of middle-class blacks who have supposedly "made it," Ellis Cose (1993) repeatedly discovered a sense among these "successful blacks" that they were being continually blocked and constrained in ways that make it impossible to hold anyone accountable. Black executives, lawyers, and bankers repeatedly reported a feeling of being second class, of having a constant, nagging sense that they were being treated differently although they did everything they were supposed to do. In one series of examples Cose reports experiences of job tracking in which blacks were only given those jobs that dealt with "minority concerns" and that were seen as either unimportant or undesirable. Cose quotes many of his interviewees discussing the feeling of being susceptible to being "stripped of status at a moment's notice" by a store clerk, a cab driver, the waiter at a restaurant, a security guard, etc. (Cose, 1993).

In 1981 Howard Schuman and his coauthors replicated a 1950 study of restaurants in New York's Upper East side and found a substantial amount of discrimination remained. Similar to the housing audits, the discrimination was of a subtle nature. Lawrence Otis-Graham reports in his recent book *Member of the Club* that when he and his friends visited ten of New York's best restaurants, in most of the establishments they were stared at, mistaken for restaurant workers, seated in terrible spots, and buffered so as to avoid proximity to whites. Actually, Otis-Graham (1995) reports that they were treated reasonably well in only two of the ten restaurants, one Russian and the other French. The suits recently filed against Denny's, Shoney's, and the International House of Pancakes seem to suggest that discrimination in restaurants is experienced by blacks of all class backgrounds (Feagin and Sikes, 1994).

Joe R. Feagin and Melvin P. Sikes also document the dense network of discriminatory practices confronted by middle-class blacks in everyday life. Although they correctly point out that blacks face discriminatory practices that range from overt and violent to covert and gentle, the latter seem prevalent. In public spaces the discriminatory behavior described by black interviewees included poor service, special requirements applied only to them, surveillance in stores, being ignored at retail stores selling expensive items, receiving the worst accommodations in restaurants or hotels, being confused constantly with menial workers, along with the usual but seemingly less frequent epithets and overtly racist behavior (see chapter 2 in Feagin and Sikes, 1994).

The Political Structure of the New Racial Order

Almost all commentators on black politics recognize that blacks became serious participants in "legitimate" politics very recently (Knowles and Prewitt, 1969; Stone, 1972b; Walton, 1972; Patterson, 1974; Marable, 1991 [1983]). But since 1965, as blacks were able to register and vote, their representation in local and national political structures has increased dramatically. The data on this point are fairly clear. Whereas in 1970 there were only 1,460 black elected officials at all levels of the U.S. political system, by 1989 the total had increased to 7,226, and in the early 1990s their number reached 8,000 (Chambliss, 1992, p. 55; Lusane, 1994). Moreover, by 1990 "blacks held elective positions in every state except Idaho, Montana, and North Dakota" (Pinkney, 1993, p. 97). In Congress there has been an increase in the number of African American elected officials from ten, or 1.9 percent of the members of Congress in 1970, to twenty-six, or 5.8 percent of the total in 1991 (Chambliss, 1992, pp. 55–57). Furthermore, whereas in 1970 only 48 cities, two with populations of 50,000 or more, had black mayors, by 1989 the number had mushroomed to 299, with 26 black mayors having been elected in large cities.

Overall, the changes in this area give the impression of substantial progress and the beginning of a truly pluralist America (for a critique of this view, see Jennings, 1992). The new political space that blacks have gained has without question provided them with some benefits. Today blacks have direct—although small—influence on policies; have sensitized white politicians about the needs of blacks not only through their policy suggestions but simply by their presence; and have established a direct link between government and citizenship (Cole, 1975). In terms of the cities where blacks have been elected as mayors, some commentators have pointed out that "African American–owned businesses expand, the rate of small business failure declines, and there are significant increases in both the number and proportions of African Americans employed in city government" (Chambliss, 1992, p. 67; see also Browning, Marshall, and Tabb, 1990; Perry, 1990). But despite these accomplishments, blacks remain a subordinate group in the political system. What follows is a discussion of the current limitations that blacks face in the political system.

Structural Barriers to the Election of Black Politicians

Racial gerrymandering, multimember legislative districts, election runoffs, annexation of predominantly white areas, at-large district elections, and anti-single-shot devices (disallowing concentrating votes in one or two candidates in cities using at-large elections) have become standard practices to disenfranchise blacks since 1965 (Knowles and Prewitt, 1969; Parker, 1992; Moss et al., 1993). All of these tactics attempt to either minimize the number of majority-black election districts or neutralize their electoral impact by diluting the black vote (Parker, 1992). Except for gerrymandering (drawing districts so that minority coalitions waste their votes), the mechanisms have the facade of expanding democracy and being race-neutral. For instance, at-large districts were initially developed to weaken political machines by diluting the ethnic vote, but in recent times have become a way of diluting the black vote in cities (Dorn, 1979). All these procedures are effective because black representation is still dependent upon the existence of black districts (Berg, 1994).

Furthermore, the very structure of Congress and the rules of the game impose limits on what blacks can accomplish there even in the best of all possible scenarios (Welch, 1990). As John C. Berg has argued:

> Congress has an internal structure, and positions in this structure give an advantage to those who hold them, but this advantage is biased; it is not equally available to the powerless and the powerful. Throughout America's brief history, when representatives of oppressed groups have used the accommodationist strategy, that strategy has failed. They have climbed patiently up the ladder of congressional seniority and committee position, only to find that they could not use their new power to effect the changes most needed by their constituents (Berg, 1994, p. 137).

Underrepresentation Among Elected and Appointed Officials

The best proof that there are still structural barriers to the election of blacks is the fact that despite burgeoning rates of black voter registration and participation since 1965, only between 1 and 2 percent of all elected officials are black (Wilhelm, 1983; Henry, 1987; Pinkney, 1993; Parker, 1992). Even more significant, blacks are substantially underrepresented even in places where they constitute 30 percent or more of the entire population (Walton, 1972; Smith, 1992). Black appointees tend to be concentrated in the civil rights and social welfare bureaucracies; those that occupy offices in other government sectors are often "sanitized" blacks like Justice Thomas or General Colin Powell.[6]

Why are blacks so underrepresented? Because of the historical tendency of whites to vote for or to appoint only white candidates (Walton, 1972; Henry, 1987; Parker, 1992; Berg, 1994). Thus the election and appointment of blacks seem to be circumscribed to locales in which blacks constitute a substantial segment of the population (40 percent plus) or to black candidates who "mainstream" or show "moderation" (Gomes and Williams, 1992).

The Limited Possibilities of Elected and Appointed Officials

What is the overall impact of black elected officials and appointees for the black community at large? In Congress, because of their relatively small numbers, blacks have a very limited role in creating policy. At best, they can shape aspects of legislation to soften the impact on poor minority communities; and so far, they have succeeded in curtailing anti–civil rights legislation (Stone, 1972a; Smith, 1992). The record of black appointees—and they have been historically few (Stone, 1972a)—suggests that they tend to have an even more limited role in shaping policy. In addition, there is a disturbing trend of appointing antiblack blacks (a trend begun by President Carter) that fits well into our new racism argument (Smith, 1992). By appointing conservative blacks to certain positions, the political system symbolically integrates while maintaining policies and politics that keep blacks "in their place."

The Limited Impact of Elected Black Mayors

Elected black mayors are in a political quandary because of the decline of political machines. This decline reduces significantly the power of the mayoral position, since political machines allowed mayors in the past to dispense resources to their constituencies. Given that these political machines have been replaced by nonpartisan bureaucratic political structures, the likelihood of a black mayor being able to use his/her position to redistribute resources has been seriously eroded (Knowles and Prewitt, 1969; Franklin and Resnick, 1973; Nelson and Meranto, 1977; Nelson, 1990; Moss et al., 1993). Moreover, the financial crisis of cities limits drastically the projects that mayors can carry out, as well as their overall independence from the dominant elite (Franklin and Resnick, 1973).

Furthermore, since cities are controlled by the interests of white business elites (Patterson, 1974; Wilhelm, 1983), elected black mayors are increasingly captive to pro-growth policies based on making cities conducive to business investments. These policies usually imply neglecting the most pressing needs of racial minorities and the poor (Nelson, 1987; Jennings, 1992). Moreover, despite the progressive impact that many have noted in the black community (in the appointment of blacks to various city positions, the increase in the ratio of black municipal employees, higher responsiveness to the needs of the poor, and so on), most of the resultant benefits have not accrued to blacks. More importantly, the election of black mayors, unlike those from white ethnic groups in the past, has not led to the institutionalization of "black control in the realms of public and private decision making" (Nelson, 1990, p. 193). Thus black mayors become "political managers" of cities in which the present economic, social, and political arrangements still benefit whites in general, and the elite in particular (Jennings, 1992).

Electoral Participation as Entrapment

The subordinate incorporation of blacks into electoral politics has reduced their options to effect meaningful social change. Historically, blacks have advanced in this country through overt protest politics (Hamilton, 1973; Newman, 1978; Piven and Cloward, 1979; Button, 1989; Bell, 1992; Berg, 1994). Hence the extension of universal suffrage to blacks has been a double-edged sword. On the one hand, it is one of the most enduring victories of the civil rights movement; but on the other hand, it is progressively becoming an obstacle for further black progress. Because the number of blacks in significant decisionmaking bodies (such as the House and the Senate) is minuscule; because whites still vote largely for white candidates; and because blacks do not have enough economic and social resources to utilize formal political rights as effectively as whites, electoral politics is restricting the political options of blacks in the United States.

An example of how electoral politics restricts the options of blacks is the current political impasse experienced by blacks. They cannot vote Republican since that party has become increasingly a pro-white party (Edsall and Edsall, 1992); they cannot fully trust the Democratic party because it has shown in recent times a tremendous degree of ambivalence in its commitment to blacks, as evidenced in the racialized discourse of many leaders on welfare, crime, government spending, and affirmative action; and the third party option, advocated by many Progressives, is still a far-fetched idea with a very limited impact among black urban voters. The way out of this impasse seems to be through a return to mass protest; but it is precisely that type of political activity that is incompatible with electoral politics. Hence, what blacks need is what electoral participation limits.

Racial Ideology and the New Racism

In the post–civil rights era, it has become increasingly difficult to assess with precision the meaning of the attitudes of whites. Since the 1960s, whites have distanced themselves from the old racist views but at the same time have maintained a degree of ambivalence (Dovidio and Gaertner, 1991), or paradoxical views (Schuman, Steeh, and Bobo, 1985), that puzzles many social scientists. The commitment of the majority of whites to nonracist views was noted for the first time by Herbert Hyman and Paul B. Sheatsley, who wrote a widely influential article on the matter, which was published in *Scientific American* in 1964. The authors rated the changes in white attitudes as "revolutionary" (Hyman and Sheatsley, 1964; see also chapter 9 in Brink and Harris, 1963). Although in later work Sheatsley was very careful in parsing the data and analyzing how regional, class, educational, and religious affiliation affected the racial views of whites, he concluded in a heroic tone:

> The mass of white Americans have shown in many ways that they will not follow a racist government and that they will not follow racist leaders. Rather, they are engaged in the painful task of adjusting to an integrated society. It will not be easy for most, but one cannot at this late date doubt the basic commitment. In their hearts they know that the American Negro is right (Sheatsley, 1966, p. 323).

The pattern of white racial attitudes noted by Sheatsley (1966) continued through the 1970s, 1980s, and 1990s. For example, noted social psychologists Campbell and Schuman, in their report to the National Advisory Commission on Civil Disorders, found a willingness of whites to support integration, and more importantly, to support strong government intervention to bring about changes to improve blacks' socioeconomic status (Brink and Harris, 1967 [1963]; Campbell and Schuman, 1970). Although this last has stagnated and even declined in recent years, overall the positive trend on racial views of whites has continued (Schuman, Steeh, and Bobo, 1985; Sniderman and Hagen, 1985; Firebaugh and Davis, 1988; Sniderman and Piazza, 1993). John Dovidio and Samuel Gaertner summarized the post-1960 trend in whites' racial attitudes as follows:

> In summary, across a variety of surveys concerning personal characterizations and social and political issues, approximately 80 percent of white Americans

consistently respond in a nonprejudiced and egalitarian manner. Only a minority of whites, 20 percent, seem to exhibit the old-fashioned, direct, and traditional form of racial prejudice (Dovidio and Gaertner, 1991, pp. 124–125).

But they also immediately added, "We believe, however, that racial bias is not confined to this 20 percent of the white population but may also characterize the attitudes of many people who appear tolerant using traditional survey methods" (Dovidio and Gaertner, 1991, p. 125).

In fact, no in-depth studies have been done exploring whether the 80 percent who express support for egalitarian principles live according to those principles. We do know that America is still highly segregated (Massey and Denton, 1993); that minorities still face myriad discriminatory practices in various settings (Jaynes and Williams, 1989; Feagin and Sikes, 1994; Feagin and Vera, 1995); and that whites, when pressed with real rather than hypothetical racial issues, respond differently than we would expect based on their recent expressions of attitude.

This apparent contradiction between expressed positive racial attitudes of whites and their behavior should not surprise anyone. There is fairly strong evidence suggesting that whites underreport their "racism" particularly when the questions are simple, clear, and straightforward (Crosby, Bromley, and Saxe, 1980). The few studies that have probed more deeply into whites' racial attitudes (Blauner, 1989; Terkel, 1992; Rubin, 1994) have shown that whites still believe many of the stereotypes about blacks and harbor hostility toward them. In interview after interview, whites explicitly say that they are not racist and that they believe in the idea of equal opportunity; but almost immediately they engage in a highly racist diatribe against blacks. One example is the moderate white woman interviewed by Studs Terkel, who in the 1960s claimed that she was in "sympathy with Negroes" (Terkel, 1992, p. 42), but in the 1990s said things like "[blacks] *seem* like they're all involved with the negative part of living: cheating, lying, stealing, dope, that type of thing" (Terkel, 1992, p. 43). Another example is the working-class white man who said: "If I'm dealing with them one on one, I'm not a bigot in the least. But if I thought that, as a whole, they're comin' into my neighborhood, I would have my feelings" (Terkel, 1992, p. 143).

Survey researchers also have noted this ambivalence in the racial attitudes of whites. Whites show widespread support on questions dealing with the *principles* of integration, equal opportunity, and affirmative action, but at the same time exhibit significant resistance on questions dealing with the *implementation* of policies designed to guarantee racial equality (Caditz, 1976; Schuman, Steeh, and Bobo, 1985; Gaertner and Dovidio, 1986; Jackman and Crane, 1986; Dovidio and Gaertner, 1991; Carmines and Merriman, 1993; Bobo and Smith, 1994). The ambivalence of whites is also shown in the fact that many still subscribe to stereotypical views of blacks[7] and reduce their level of commitment to egalitarian principles when the questions involve personal choices.[8] Finally—and of extreme importance for our theoretical claim—is the finding that even the few whites who interact on a regular basis with blacks (the 9.4 percent of whites who can name a "good friend" who is black) do not support programs designed to ameliorate racial inequality in the United States (Jackman and Crane, 1986).

One group of researchers has explained this ambivalence in white attitudes by suggesting that there is a new type of racism, which they alternately label "symbolic racism," "modern racism," or "aversive racism."[9] The argument, initially developed by David Sears and his associates (Sears and Kinder, 1971; see also Gaertner and Dovidio, 1986; and McConahay, 1986), is that a new, more subtle and less direct kind of racial attitude has replaced the more overt, "redneck" racism in the United States. In contrast with old-fashioned racism "composed of derogations of an antagonism toward blacks *per se,* or of support for formal inequality" (Sears, 1988), symbolic racism is:

> a blend of antiblack affect and the kind of traditional American moral values embodied in the Protestant ethic, . . . a form of resistance to change in the racial status quo based on moral feelings that blacks violate such traditional American values as individualism and self-reliance, the work ethic, obedience, and discipline (Kinder and Sears, 1981, p. 416).

Although this interpretation opens new ground for analyzing the racial attitudes of whites, it is limited by its reliance on the traditional *individualist* concept of prejudice (for critiques see Wellman, 1977; Bonilla-Silva, 1994; Jackman, 1994). By failing to develop an analysis of prejudice that is connected to the larger racial structure of the United States, authors in this tradition fail to explain why these new attitudes emerged, their relation to continuing racial inequality in the United States, and their relevance to the racial attitudes of whites toward other minority groups.

These limitations have been addressed by social psychologists following Herbert Blumer's (1958) understanding of prejudice as sense of group position (Jackman and Muha, 1984; Bobo, 1988; Bobo and Smith, 1994; Jackman, 1994). Bobo argues that racial ideologies are connected to larger socioeconomic and political structures and thus contends that if there is a new ideology in America it must "reflect a group-interested ideology tailored to new circumstances" (Bobo, 1988, p. 107). In a more recent work (1994), Bobo refines somewhat his earlier argument. He now claims that "we have witnessed the virtual disappearance of overt bigotry, demands for strict segregation, advocacy of government enforced discrimination and adherence to the belief that blacks are categorical intellectual inferiors of whites" (Bobo and Smith, 1994, p. 7).

Bobo and Smith (1994, p. 48) contend that the change in the geographic and economic position of blacks in the twentieth century, the increase in indigenous resources of blacks, and the defeat of the planter class were the reasons why the "Jim Crow social order, quite naturally, began to atrophy and wither under a steady assault by blacks and their white allies." Bobo's analysis is consonant with that of Mary Jackman and her coauthors. Jackman and Muha (1984) argue that racial ideology in the United States changed from overt during the period of paternalistic race relations before the 1960s to covert since the late 1960s, as race relations became openly antagonistic and reflected distal rather than intimate racial relations. Specifically, they contend that as blacks made their claims in a more vocal manner, whites' justification for their privilege shifted from one based on group differences to one based on individualism. When racial inequality is explained as the outcome of individual processes, "the rights of *groups* are thus rendered illegitimate and unreasonable" (Jackman and Muha, 1984, p. 760). Furthermore, Jackman argues that racial privilege is also defended by whites today through a staunch defense of equal opportunity rather than egalitarianism (Jackman, 1994, pp. 87–90). Jackman documents in her book how little interaction there is between whites and blacks, the comprehensive role of segregation, the avoidance of hostility in racial conflict that Jackman labels "muted hostility," and the systematic rift in the prescriptions about how active the federal government should be in pursuing policies to ameliorate racial inequality.

In sum, whites today exhibit a very different racial ideology than whites during the apartheid period of race relations. The new ideology of whites, characteristic of the distal and antagonistic post–civil rights race relations (Jackman, 1994), avoid direct hostility toward minority groups and affirm the principles of equal opportunity and egalitarianism but at the same time reject programs that attempt to ameliorate racial inequality in reality rather than in theory (Carmines and Merriman, 1993). Generally speaking, contemporary white ideology denies the fact that race imposes a number of constraints upon minorities and proclaims that we are all individual actors with similar opportunities in the market (Kluegel and Bobo, 1993; Jackman, 1994). Since racial privilege in the contemporary period depends less on the individual actions of whites and more on the normal racialized operation of institutions (Knowles and Prewitt, 1969; Franklin and Resnick, 1973; Chester, 1976; Wellman, 1977; Omi and Winant, 1986), the emphasis on individualism and equal opportunity is the modern Trojan horse for maintaining racial inequality. The emphasis on individualism denies the structural character of racial inequality (Kluegel and Bobo, 1993; Jackman, 1994), and that on equal opportunity denies group differences in material resources, thus legitimating unequal outcomes. Moreover, because inequality is reproduced mostly through institutional channels, whites do not have to develop a defensive, elaborate racial posture as in the previous period. As Mary Jackman contends:

The institutionalization of inequality releases the individual members of the dominant group from any sense of personal complicity. As they seek to interpret the happy situation in which they find themselves, they have no reason to feel personally defensive—after all, they have personally taken no steps to extract from others the benefits that regularly come their way (Jackman, 1994, p. 65).

This is why racial ideology today has an apparently nonracial character, can hide under egalitarian ideas, and is driven by the notion of individualism. In the popular consciousness of whites, the main threads of this ideology have been articulated under the notion of "reverse racism." The argument is simple: America has banished discrimination since the 1960s, and therefore, if blacks and other minorities are behind, it is their own fault. Programs that attempt to equate outcomes—affirmative action programs—are viewed as discriminatory against whites. Individual effort and merit, so the argument goes, should be the only criteria used to allocate positions in society. And this popular argument, as simple and ahistorical as it is, has been adopted by liberals and conservatives alike.[10] Currently the notion of reverse discrimination has become one of the linchpins and political assets of the Republican party (Edsall and Edsall, 1992), as evidenced by the fact that all of that party's top leaders embrace the notion; and Democrats, although a bit more cautious, are also talking about "mending" affirmative action by eliminating "quotas" and other forms of "preferential treatment" (Omi and Winant, 1993).

"Keeping Them in Their Place": The Social Control of Blacks Since the 1960s

All domination is ultimately maintained through social control strategies. For example, during slavery, whites used the whip, overseers, night patrols, and other highly repressive practices along with a number of paternalistic ones to keep blacks "in their place" (Stampp, 1956; Genovese, 1974). After slavery was abolished, whites felt threatened by free blacks, hence very strict written and unwritten rules of racial contact (the Jim Crow laws) were developed to specify "the place" of blacks in the new environment of "freedom." And, as "insurance," lynching and other terroristic forms of social control were used to guarantee white supremacy. In contrast, as the Jim Crow practices have subsided, the control of blacks has been chiefly attained through state agencies (police, criminal court system, FBI) (Marable, 1983). Manning Marable describes the new system of control as follows:

> The informal, vigilante-inspired techniques to suppress Blacks were no longer practical. Therefore, beginning with the Great Depression, and especially after 1945, white racists began to rely almost exclusively on the state apparatus to carry out the battle for white supremacy. Blacks charged with crimes would receive longer sentences than whites convicted of similar crimes. The police forces

of municipal and metropolitan areas received a *carte blanche* in their daily acts of brutality against Blacks. The Federal and state government carefully monitored Blacks who advocated any kind of social change. Most important, capital punishment was used as a weapon against Blacks charged and convicted of major crimes. The criminal justice system, in short, became a modern instrument to perpetuate white hegemony. Extralegal lynchings were replaced by "legal lynchings" and capital punishment (Marable, 1983, pp. 120–121).

In the following sections of this chapter, we have reviewed the available data to see how well it fits Marable's interpretation of the contemporary system of control.

The State as Enforcer of Racial Order

Data on arrest rates show that the contrast between black and white arrest rates since 1950 has been striking (Jaynes and Williams, 1989). The black rate increased throughout this period, reaching almost 100 per 1,000 by 1978, compared to 35 for whites (Jaynes and Williams, 1989, pp. 457–459). The 1989 data suggest that the arrest rate for blacks has stabilized at around 80 to 90 per 1,000 (Garwood, 1991, p. 204). In terms of how many blacks are incarcerated, we found a pattern similar to their arrest rates. Although blacks have always been overrepresented in the inmate population, this overrepresentation has skyrocketed since the late 1940s. In 1950, blacks were 29 percent of the prison population (Jaynes and Williams, 1989; Garwood, 1991). Ten years later, their proportion reached 38 percent. By 1980, the incarceration rate of blacks was 47 percent, six times that of whites (Williams-Myers, 1995). *Today the incarceration rate of blacks has "stabilized" at around 50 percent.*

This dramatic increase in black incarceration has been attributed to legislative changes in the penal codes and the "get tough" attitude in law enforcement fueled by white fear of black crime (Marable, 1983; Hagan and Peterson, 1995; Williams-Myers, 1995). Furthermore, the fact that blacks are disproportionately convicted and receive longer sentences than whites for similar crimes contributes to their overrepresentation among the penal population (Chideya, 1995). For example, "according to the Federal Judicial Center, in 1990 the average sentences for blacks on weapons and drug charges were 49 percent longer than those for whites who had committed and been convicted of the same crimes—and that disparity has been rising over time" (Chideya, 1995, p. 195).

Official State Brutality Against Blacks

Police departments grew exponentially after the 1960s, particularly in large metropolitan areas with large concentrations of blacks (Jacobs, 1979; Jackson and Carroll, 1981; Jackson, 1989). This growth has been related by various studies to black urban mobilization and rebellion in the 1960s (Jackson and Carroll, 1981; Liska et al., 1981). Another way of measuring the impact of police departments on the life of blacks is surveying how blacks and whites rate police performance. Rosentraub and Harlow (1984), in an article reviewing surveys on the attitudes of blacks and whites toward the police from 1960 through 1981, found that blacks consistently viewed the police in a much more negative light than did whites. Despite attempts in the 1970s and 1980s to reduce the friction between black communities and police departments by hiring more black police officers, and in some cases, even hiring black chiefs of police, there has been little change in the attitudes of blacks toward the police, especially when the attitudes of black respondents are compared to those of white respondents" (Rosentraub and Harlow, 1984, p. 119).

The level of police force used with blacks has always been excessive (Marable, 1983). In 1975, 46 percent of all people killed by the police in official action were black (Sherman, 1980, p. 95). That situation has not changed much since. Robert Smith (1995) reported recently that of the people killed by the police, over half have been black, and that the police usually claimed that when they killed blacks it was "accidental" because they thought that the victim was armed although in fact the victims were unarmed in 75 percent of such cases. Smith also reported an increase in the 1980s in the use of deadly force by the police, and asserted that the only ameliorating factor was the presence of a sensitive mayor in a city. In the aftermath of the King verdict, 87 percent of civilian victims of police brutality reported in the newspapers of fifteen major American cities were black, and 93 percent of the officers involved were white (Smith, 1995, pp. 47–48).

Capital Punishment as a Modern Form of Lynching

The raw statistics on capital punishment seem to indicate racial bias *prima facie:* "Of 3984 people lawfully executed since 1930 [until 1980], 2113 were black, over half of the total, almost five times the proportion of blacks in the population as a whole" (Gross and Mauro, 1989). However, social scientific research on racial sentencing has produced mixed results. A number of authors have found a bias in sentencing (Spohn, Gruhl, and Welch, 1981–1982; Petersilia, 1983; Zatz, 1984), but some have claimed that as legal factors are taken into account, the bias disappears (Klein, Petersilia, and Turner, 1990; Kleck, 1981; Pruitt and Wilson, 1983; Myers and Talarico, 1987). Yet recent research has suggested that "discrimination has not declined or disappeared but simply has become more subtle and difficult to detect" (Spohn, 1994).[11] In a review of recent social scientific literature Spohn contends that "race affects sentence severity indirectly through its effect on variables such as bail status or type of attorney or that race interacts with other variables and affects sentence severity only in particular types of cases or for particular defendants" (1994, p. 249). Others have pointed out that the discrimination experienced by blacks may occur at earlier stages. For instance, research by Radelet and Pierce (1985) suggests that homicides with white victims and black suspects are more likely to be defined by prosecutors in terms of charges bearing the most serious penalties. Thus, straightforward regression models (additive and linear) will likely miss the effect of race (Spohn 1994).

There is a substantial body of research showing that blacks charged of murdering whites are more likely to be sentenced to death than any other victim-offender dyad (Spohn 1994). Similarly, blacks charged with raping white women also have received the death sentence at a much higher rate (Walsh, 1987; LaFree, 1989 [1980]). The two tendencies were confirmed by Spohn in a 1994 article using data for Detroit in 1977 and 1978: "Blacks who sexually assaulted whites faced a greater risk of incarceration than either blacks or whites who sexually assaulted blacks, or whites who sexually assaulted whites; similarly, blacks who murdered whites received longer sentences than did offenders in the other two categories" (Spohn, 1994, p. 264).

The most respected study on race and death penalty, carried out by David C. Baldus to support the claim of Warren McClesky, a black man convicted of murdering a white police officer in 1978, found that there was a huge disparity in the imposition of the death penalty in Georgia (Baldus, Pulaski, and Woodworth, 1986). The study found that in cases involving white victims and black defendants the death penalty was imposed 22 percent of the time, whereas in the white-black dyad, the death penalty was imposed in only 1 percent of cases. *Even after controlling for a number of variables, blacks were 4.3 times as likely as whites to receive a death sentence* (Bell, 1992, p. 332). In a 1990 review of 28 studies on death penalty sentencing, Bell reported that 23 of these studies found that the fact that victims are white "influences the likelihood that the defendant will be charged with a capital crime or that death penalty will be imposed" (Bell, 1992, pp. 332–333).

It should not surprise anyone that in a racist society, court decisions on cases involving the death penalty exhibit a race effect. Research on juries suggests that they tend to be older, more affluent, more educated, more prone to convict, and more white than the average person in a particular community (Alker, Hosticka, and Mitchell, 1976; Nemeth, 1981; Benokratis, 1982). Moreover, research on the process of selecting jurors for death penalty cases suggests that the voir dire process (questioning of prospective jurors by the judge to determine their suitability) in such cases produces juries that are biased toward the death penalty (Blunk and Sales, 1977; Haney, 1984b [1984a]). This particular bias has been found to have a racial effect. Gregory D. Russell, in his *The Death Penalty and Racial Bias: Overturning Supreme Court Assumptions* (1994), found indirect data (exhibited via surrogate measures) of racial bias among death-qualified jurors.[12] This finding adds to our understanding of why there is a differential conviction rate for blacks and whites in cases involving the death penalty. As Russell explains:

> The evidence developed did suggest that juries composed of death-qualified jurors are more likely to be white, punitive, and authoritarian. Hence, they are more likely, on this evidence, to exhibit a tendency toward racially biased decisions. Will every juror or jury act in this manner? Of course not. The evidence simply suggests the probability that juries so composed are more likely than not to be more predisposed to racially biased determinations than other juries, though the appearance of racial bias is quite idiosyncratic (Russell, 1994, p. 128).

High Propensity to Arrest Blacks

Blacks complain that police officers mistreat them, disrespect them, assume that they are criminals, violate their rights on a consistent basis, and are more violent when dealing with them (Blackwell, 1991). Blacks and other minorities are stopped and frisked by police in "alarmingly disproportionate numbers" (Bell, 1992, p. 340). Why is it that minorities receive "special treatment" from the police? Studies on police attitudes and their socialization suggest that police officers live in a "cops' world" and develop a cop mentality (Bayley and Mendelsohn, 1972; Cooper, 1980). And that cops' world is a highly racialized one; minorities are viewed as dangerous, prone to crime, violent, and disrespectful. Various studies have noted that the racist attitudes that police officers exhibit have an impact on their behavior toward minorities (Skolnick, 1972). Furthermore, other studies have suggested that police discretion and demographic bias contribute to the overarrest of blacks. Extralegal subjective characteristics such as demeanor, appearance, and race have been found to influence the decisions of police officers to arrest individuals (Chambliss and Nagasawa, 1969; Black, 1976; Lizote, 1978). In terms of demographic bias, research suggests that because black communities are overpatrolled, officers patrolling these areas develop a stereotypical view of residents as more likely to commit criminal acts and are more likely to "see" criminal behavior than in white communities (Geis, 1972; Blumestein, 1982; Clayton, 1983).

Thus, it is not surprising that blacks are disproportionately arrested compared to whites. It is possible to gauge the level of overarrest endured by blacks by comparing the proportion of times that they are described by victims as the perpetrators with their arrest rates. Using this procedure, Farai Chideya contended:

> For virtually every type of crime, African-American criminals are arrested at rates above their commission of the acts. For example, victimization reports in-

dicated that 33 percent of women who were raped said that their attacker was black; however, black rape suspects made up fully 43 percent of those arrested. The disproportionate arrest rate adds to the public perception that rape is a "black" crime (Chideya, 1995, p. 194).

Using these numbers, the rate of overarrest for blacks in cases of rape is 30 percent. As shocking as this may be, the rate for cases where the victim is white is even higher. Smith, Visher, and Davidson (1984) found that whereas the probability of arrest for cases in which the victim was white and the suspect black was 33.6 percent, for cases of white suspects and black victims the probability dropped to 10.7 percent.

Repression of Black Leaders and the Civil Rights Movement

Leaders of the black movement, such as Elijah Muhammad, Malcolm X, Stokely Carmichael, Louis Farrakhan, Huey P. Newton, Bobby Seale, Ron Karenga, and Martin Luther King, Jr., and organizations such as SNCC, NAACP, SCLC, Black Panthers, RAM,[13] and MOVE, have been monitored by the FBI. Of particular significance was the six-year investigation (from 1962 to 1968) launched by the FBI against Martin Luther King, Jr.—especially given that King, unlike other black leaders of his time, was not advocating change through radical means. As David Garrow points out, "It is quite apparent that no other black leader came in for the intensive and hostile attention that Dr. King was subjected to in the mid-1960s" (Garrow, 1983, pp. 154–155). Although initially the FBI claimed that the surveillance of King and the SCLC was motivated by the fact that communists were involved in the organization, the FBI's investigation soon delved into purely private matters of King's life with the explicit intent of discrediting him (Garrow, 1983; Friedly and Gallen, 1993). Although many theories have been advanced for why King was singled out (J. Edgar Hoover's racism, racism in the Bureau, Hoover's reaction to King's public criticism of the Bureau in 1961, the conservatism of the Bureau, and Hoover's and top FBI agents' fascination with sexuality), the bottom line was that King, the most important black leader of this century, was carefully monitored by the FBI until his assassination in 1968.

The FBI's persecution of leaders such as Elijah Muhammad and Malcolm X and their organization, the Nation of Islam, was less hostile and consistent than that of King and the SCLC because they were not mobilizing the black masses as King was. Only after Malcolm began making overtures to civil rights leaders and advocating militant political involvement did the FBI begin paying serious attention to him (Carson, 1991). After Malcolm's assassination in 1965—a crime in which the FBI was apparently involved[14]—the

FBI launched a special offensive to curb the spread of black nationalism by any means necessary (Smith, 1974; Churchill and Vander Wall, 1988). By 1967, the FBI had over 3,000 informants in black communities as part of this program and was conducting surveillance and playing "dirty tricks"[15] on SNCC leader Stokely Carmichael and on the Black Panthers (Carson, 1991, pp. 46–47). The FBI through a smear campaign and other techniques neutralized Stokely Carmichael, H. Rap Brown, Reverend Charles Koen of the Cairo United Front, and activist-comedian Dick Gregory (Churchill and Vander Wall, 1988, p. 58). Even seemingly less threatening groups such as black student unions on campuses around the nation were infiltrated by the FBI (Churchill and Vander Wall, 1988, p. 59; Berry, 1994). By the time the COINTELPRO became known to the American people in 1971, radical black organizations had been all but dismantled.

Post–Civil Rights Social Control and the New Racism

The mechanisms by which blacks experience social control in the contemporary period are not overwhelmingly covert. Yet they share with the previous mechanisms discussed in this chapter their invisibility. The mechanisms to keep blacks in "their place," are rendered invisible in three ways. First, because the enforcement of the racial order from the 1960s onward has been institutionalized, individual whites can express a detachment from the *racialized* way in which social control agencies operate in America. Second, because these agencies are legally charged with defending order in society, their actions are deemed neutral and necessary. Thus, it is no surprise that whites consistently support the police in surveys (Rosentraub and Harlow, 1984). Finally, incidents that seem to indicate racial bias in the criminal justice system are depicted by white-dominated media as isolated cases (Chideya, 1995). For example, cases that presumably expose the racial character of social control agencies (e.g., the police beating of Rodney King, the police killing of Malice Green, and the acquittals or lenient sentences received by officers accused in other cases of police brutality) are viewed as uncharacteristic and are separated from the larger social context in which they transpire.

The Continuing Racial Economic Inequality

The economic life of blacks has always been influenced by structured racial inequality. A substantial body of literature on white-black employment differences has documented the influence of labor market discrimination, wage differentials, occupational segmentation, and income and wealth inequalities in explaining racially differential economic outcomes (Knowles and Prewitt, 1969; Franklin and Resnick, 1973; Perlo, 1975; Allen and Farley, 1985; Jaynes and Williams, 1989). Despite the well-documented disparities between blacks and whites, many social scientists have focused their attention on the growth of the black middle class (Wattenberg and Scammon, 1973; Freeman, 1978; Wilson, 1978; Sowell, 1984). Some of them have projected the "success" of this segment to the entire community, creating an image of general economic progress. To be sure, African Americans have experienced significant progress in several areas of their economic life during the past three decades (for example, in the economic standing of black women vis-à-vis white women, the opening of jobs that previously were reserved for whites, the development of a significant black middle class, and the like). Yet the overall situation of blacks relative to whites has not advanced much (Darity, Cotton, and Hill, 1993). The following sections of this chapter highlight the economic status of blacks and the mechanisms that structure racial inequality at the economic level in the post–civil rights period.

Income and Earnings Differentials

Studies analyzing the differences in median income between blacks and whites have revealed some convergence (Hirschman and Wang, 1984; Smith and Welch, 1986; Farley and Allen, 1987; Farley, 1993), much of which has been attributed to the rising levels of educational attainment of African Americans, in particular among younger cohorts (Smith and Welch, 1986) as well as affirmative action policies (Bound and Freeman, 1987; Leonard, 1990; Heckman and Payner, 1992). However, the empirical evidence regarding racial convergence in income is mixed. Several social scientists have found that the family incomes of African Americans began rapidly to converge with those of whites after World War II; but during the recession of the early 1970s, African Americans' income levels began to stagnate and the racial convergence ceased (Jaynes and Williams, 1989; Jaynes, 1990). In fact, by 1990 a substantial black-white earnings gap had reemerged as the black-white family income ratio reached 0.56, a ratio hardly larger than the 0.55 of 1960 (Pinkney, 1993). Interestingly, the decline in African Americans' income vis-à-vis whites has been attributed to the decline in enforcement of antidiscrimination laws and affirmative action policies by the federal government in the 1980s (Bound and Freeman, 1989; Leonard, 1990).[16] Thus, while African Americans made marked advancement from World War II to the early 1970s, they have experienced more recently—in the 1980s and 1990s—a substantial deterioration in their incomes relative to whites (Bradbury and Browne, 1986; Jaynes and Williams, 1989).

Furthermore, analysts who focus on income convergence tend to mask serious trends affecting the African American population—like unemployment and underemployment, and the decrease in the rate of labor force participation—by making their comparisons based on full-time workers. Darity and Myers (1980) astutely observe that the exclusion of African Americans with zero income (the unemployed and the jobless) from social scientists' assessment of income differences between African Americans and whites masks the persistent racial fault line in economic life (see also Darity et al., 1993; Badgett, 1994). The gap in unemployment between blacks and whites increased during the 1970s and the 1980s—the same period in which African Americans' incomes ceased converging with those of whites (Cotton, 1989; Farley, 1984). Income differences reflect to a large extent the different earning potential of blacks and whites in America. Blacks earn today around 60 percent as much as whites. This vast difference is attributed to blacks' lesser educational attainment, lesser rates of return for their education and their labor market experience, and their concentration in the South, all directly related to the racial dynamics in this country (Farley and Allen, 1987; Hacker, 1992; Ashraf, 1994). Does the difference in earnings disappear when the comparison is between blacks and whites with similar characteristics? The answer is no. Farley and Allen (1987) carried out such a comparison for 1980 and found the gap for black men to be 14 percent. Although this gap, known in the literature as the "cost of being black," was better than the 19 percent gap of 1960, the fact that the gap grew to 16 percent in 1985 does not give much hope.

Occupational Mobility and Segmentation

One of the primary reasons why blacks' economic standing is much worse than whites' is because of occupational race-typing (Boston, 1988). Although recent occupational data show that African Americans have made substantial progress in obtaining employment in occupational categories from which they previously were, for all practical purposes, excluded (Hout, 1984; Farley, 1984; Farley and Allen, 1987; O'Hare, Pollard, Mann, and Kent, 1991), they are still overrepresented among unskilled workers and underrepresented in higher-paying white-collar jobs. In 1960, whereas 60.4 percent of white men worked in blue-collar jobs, a whopping 76.7 percent of blacks did so (Farley and Allen, 1987). In 1990, as the economy shifted away from the industrial to the service sector, the proportion of both blacks and whites in blue-collar jobs decreased significantly. However, 52.5 percent of black men worked in blue-collar occupations, compared to 43.2 percent of whites (Pinkney, 1993). More significantly, whereas white men worked primarily as managers and professionals (27.3 percent), black men were more likely to be employed as operators, fabricators, and laborers (33.4 percent).

Two other factors point to the segmentation experienced by blacks in America. First, despite the increase in the proportion of blacks in managerial and professional occupations, those employed in these occupations have lower earnings than their white counterparts (Cotton, 1990). Second, their occupational mobility is less frequent and more restricted than that of whites

(Pomer, 1986; Waddoups, 1991). Some mainstream analysts have attributed the racial differences in earnings to the existing educational gap between blacks and whites (Featherman and Hauser, 1976; Hout, 1984; Smith and Welch, 1986). However, an examination of returns from education challenges what may be an oversimple assessment. Cotton (1990) found that racial differences among those employed in the managerial and professional occupations could not be explained by educational differences. This is not surprising, since research has consistently shown that blacks earn less than whites in almost all occupations. For instance, Farley and Allen's (1987) analysis of 1979 data for full-time workers with the same educational attainment and of similar age revealed that black men earned less than white men in all occupations. For instance, black doctors between the ages of 25 and 34 earned $3.39 less per hour than their white counterparts, and janitors earned $1.33 less per hour than their counterparts (Farley and Allen, 1987, p. 318).

On the second point, studies since the 1960s have suggested that for the most part, Jim Crow discrimination has been replaced by a new web of practices that limits the mobility of blacks and affects their everyday performance (Norgren and Hill, 1964; Morgan and Van Dyke, 1970; Kovarsky and Albrecht, 1970; Fernandez, 1982; Landry, 1988; Dudley, 1988; Collins, 1989; Brooks, 1990; Travis, 1991; Cose, 1993; Graham, 1995). One of the most pervasive of these practices is pigeonholing blacks in specific positions, a practice reminiscent of typecasting blacks for "nigger jobs" during the Jim Crow era (Cose, 1993). For instance, Collins (1989) finds that many African American executives fill affirmative action, community relations, minority affairs, or public relations positions created during the 1960s and 1970s to respond to civil rights demands—positions that do not provide much mobility.

Labor Market Discrimination

Since the early 1960s, social scientists have acknowledged that labor market discrimination is an important causal factor in explaining the differential employment outcomes of blacks and whites (Samuels, 1969; Becker, 1971; Oaxaca, 1973; Thurow, 1975 [1969]; Garfinkel, Haveman, and Betson, 1977). Yet until recently, studies on labor market discrimination assessed discrimination as the unexplained residual in black and white earnings after controlling for a number of variables. Although this measurement is useful, it tends to underestimate the real impact of discrimination by eliminating differences—for example, in education and occupational status—that are themselves the product of discrimination (Perlo, 1975; Alexis, 1976; Boston, 1988).

During the 1990s, analysts have developed a research strategy to *directly* assess the impact of discrimination. The technique used to examine labor market discrimination is called an "employment audit," and consists of sending subjects matched in most characteristics except their race to find jobs (Cross et al., 1990; Bendick et al., 1991; McRae, 1991; Turner et al., 1991). By adopting this approach, analysts have been able to estimate the *extent* as well as the *form* of discrimination that minorities endure in the labor market. Culp and Dunson (1986) conducted the first employment audits and reported that black males were not (1) addressed as "Mr."; (2) offered a seat; (3) offered a handshake; or (4) engaged in conversation. In addition, Culp and Dunson found two clear signs of discrimination in that several employers in the sample did not tell the black males about employment opportunities and quoted lower wages to black male applicants.

Probably the most famous of these studies was that carried out by the Urban Institute in 1991. It was conducted on randomly selected employers in San Diego, Chicago, and Washington, D.C., and found that on average, white testers were significantly favored over black testers (Turner et al., 1991). For example, in 20 percent of the audits, blacks were denied job opportunities, and in 31 percent of the audits, Latinos were denied job opportunities.

Finally, research by Braddock and McPartland (1987) indicates that blacks are discriminated against at all levels of the job process. In the search process, they are left behind because most employers rely on informal social networks to advertise their jobs. And since blacks are not part of those networks, they are left out in the cold (Cherry, 1989). At the job entry level, in addition to the practices mentioned before, blacks are screened out by tests and the requirement of a high school diploma. These two practices were developed in the late 1950s and early 1960s as substitutes for outright exclusion from jobs and were mentioned in the 1964 Civil Rights Act as practices that could have exclusionary results (Norgren and Hill, 1964; Kovarsky and Albrecht, 1970). They are discriminatory because the diploma and the tests are not usually essential to job performance. Finally, in terms of job promotion, blacks face a glass ceiling because (1) they are pigeonholed in dead-end jobs (Spratlen, 1976; Landry, 1987; Dudley, 1988; Collins, 1989; Brooks, 1990; Travis, 1991; Cose, 1993; Graham, 1995); (2) employers seek people for promotion informally and blacks are less likely to be part of the "good old boys' network"; and (3) seniority rules favor whites when promotion time comes around (Powell, 1969).

Wealth

There is very little data on the wealth differentials between blacks and whites in the United States. Yet the available data indicate that the disparities in this important area are greater than in any other economic area. One of the earliest studies, using data for 1967, showed that blacks on average had 18.8 percent the net wealth of whites (Alexis, 1976). Although the wealth gap decreased with education and income, it never topped 47 percent. This study also showed that whereas whites had a more diversified portfolio of assets

(30 percent liquid and 70 percent nonliquid), blacks had almost all their assets in nonliquid forms (equity in homes, cars, and so on). Data for 1984 indicated no change in this area. For instance, the black-white net worth[17] averaged 9 percent for all households; and although the gap decreased at higher levels of income, it never topped 46 percent.

The most recent study on wealth indicated that the black-white ratio in net worth for 1988 was 8 percent and that blacks did not own any financial assets (Oliver and Shapiro, 1989). The implications of this last point were startling. According to Oliver and Shapiro, 61 percent of blacks, compared with 25 percent of whites, do not have liquid assets to survive at the *poverty level* in case of unemployment or a family crisis. If you include in the figure of those who cannot survive for more than three months, the proportion reaches 79 percent for blacks and 38 percent for whites. As in previous studies, the wealth fragility of blacks was evidenced in all groups. For instance, the net financial assets of the black middle class, whether indexed by income, occupation, or education, did not surpass $290.

In addition to the historical effects of discrimination, Oliver and Shapiro uncovered a number of practices that contribute to the current wealth disparity. Among the institutional factors that they discuss are the higher denial of loans for blacks (60 percent higher than for whites), the higher interest rates that banks charge them (1 percent higher), and the lower appreciation of their houses.

Managerial Views on Blacks

Recent research suggests that the views of white managers on blacks have not changed dramatically since the 1960s. Earlier studies were optimistic in predicting that managers would assume their social responsibilities toward blacks after years of exclusion (Strauss, 1967; Northrup, 1967). A study sponsored in the 1960s by the American Management Association, in which black white-collar workers were interviewed, revealed that 60 percent thought white managers were condescending to them (Morgan and Van Dyke, 1970). Another study concluded that employers were paying lip service to Title VII of the 1964 Civil Rights Act and that they were placing the brunt of the blame for employment problems with blacks on blacks themselves (Levine, 1972). In the 1970s, Fernandez (1975) found in his survey of eight firms in California that a significant proportion of managers held old-fashioned racist views and believed that blacks were pushing too hard. Furthermore, on open-ended questions managers who had scored relatively well in other parts of the survey were more likely to express antiblack views. All in all, only 10 percent of black managers and 17 percent of whites said that they were not aware of any negative attitude toward blacks. The results of these studies were confirmed by more recent surveys of blacks in corporate

America. Blacks have complained that they are bypassed by white managers for promotion, that they are not treated as equals, and that they endure a subtle hostility from their fellow workers and supervisors (Collins, 1989; Travis, 1991; Cose, 1993; Graham, 1995).

White employers and managers hiring for unskilled positions generally hold views that are more openly racist. In their interviews with Chicago and Cook county employers, Kirschenman and Neckerman (1991) found that blacks were viewed as having a bad work ethic, as creating tensions in the workplace, as lazy and unreliable, lacking leadership, and having a bad attitude. Many of these views were captured by a suburban drugstore manager, who said:

> It's unfortunate, but in my business I think overall [black men] tend to be known as dishonest. I think that's too bad but that's the image they have. (Interviewer: so you think it's an image problem?) Yeah, a dishonest, an image problem of being dishonest, mean and lazy. They are known to be lazy. They are [laughs]. I hate to tell you, but. It's all an image though. Whether they are or not, I don't know, but it's an image that is perceived. (Interviewer: I see. How do you think that image was developed?) Go look in the jails [laughs]. (Kirschenman and Neckerman, 1994).

Concluding Remarks

As the United States entered a profound crisis of accumulation in the 1970s, poor and working-class whites began blaming minorities for the crisis (Marable, 1983). Hence, hate crimes typical of the apartheid period of race relations have resurfaced in America since the late 1970s (Marable, 1983; Blackwell, 1991; Levin and McDevitt, 1993). Organized hate groups such as the Ku Klux Klan grew in membership from 5,000 in 1973 to 20,000 by 1990. Levin and McDevitt estimate that the total number of people involved in organized hate groups today is between 20,000 and 50,000 (1993, p. 109).

Yet despite this upsurge in racial attacks in the United States and the increase in the membership of the Klan and Klan-like groups, their membership today pales against the 5 million members they had in the 1920s. Moreover, extralegal violence today, as sensational and symbolic as it is, is not the primary method used to keep blacks in check. As we argued in this paper, new racial practices, characterized by covertness and subtlety, explicit avoidance of traditional racist discourse, and insulation through institutionalization in the "normal" operations of many organizations, have replaced Jim Crow practices.

The changes in racial dynamics at all levels seem to amount to a reorganization—still incomplete—of the racial structure of this country. This reorganization is incomplete because (1) not all the mechanisms and practices have settled, that is, have become institutionalized; and (2) we still have many legacies of the previous period affecting the life chances of blacks. On the first point, discrimination in the realm of education, for example, has not taken a definite institutional pattern in the contemporary period. Instead, there are various means (resegregation through white flight to the suburbs and to private schools, segregation within schools, tracking, and so on) to guarantee white advantages. On the second point, we still have old-fashioned racists, extralegal violence, and an undeclared apartheid in the housing arena. Although many of these practices are manifestations of the legacies of slavery and the Jim Crow era (Winant, 1994), the evidence reviewed here suggests that blacks and other minorities should fear less the angry men with white hoods and their traditional discriminatory practices than the men in business suits and their "smiling discrimination" (Brooks, 1990).

We agree with Pettigrew and Martin when they claim: "The greater subtlety of these new forms [of racial discrimination] poses new problems of remedy. They act at both the structural-institutional level focused on by sociologists, and the face-to-face situational level focused on by social psychologists" (Pettigrew and Martin, 1987, p. 42). The obstacles to remedy are many.

(1) Proving racial discrimination is extremely difficult for the party being discriminated against. Thus, is not surprising that many progressive whites do not take seriously many claims of discrimination. As Pettigrew and Martin point out:

> Often the black is the only person in a position to draw the conclusion that prejudice is operating in the work situation. Whites have usually observed only a subset of the incidents, any one of which can be explained away by a nonracial account. Consequently, many whites remain unconvinced of the reality of subtle prejudice and discrimination, and come to think of their black co-workers as "terribly touchy," and "overly sensitive," to the issue. For such reasons, the modern forms of prejudice frequently remain invisible even to its perpetrators (Pettigrew and Martin, 1987, p. 50).

(2) The standards that the Supreme Court enacted recently on discrimination cases (plaintiffs carrying the burden of proof in discrimination cases and the denial of statistical evidence as valid proof of discrimination) help to preserve intact the contemporary forms for reproducing racial inequality in America (Gross and Mauro, 1989; Bell, 1992). Unless the court becomes cognizant of the new character of racial discrimination and changes its current practice of requiring the "smoking gun" in discrimination cases, the Court itself will be participating in covering up the far-reaching effects of racism in America.

(3) Minority leaders who continue to focus on the "old racism" will miss the most important ways in which racial inequality is being reproduced in

America. It is vital that studies documenting the pervasive and comprehensive character of the new racism be systematically conducted.

(4) Research that is still focused on the old racism will invariably find a decline in the significance of race. Research on racial practices has to become as sophisticated as the new racism. The studies carried out by the Urban Institute and by the federal department of Housing and Urban Development (HUD) in which testers are sent out to various settings and organizations are an example of what can be done. Unfortunately, that type of research is not viewed as "scientific" in many quarters and has even been deemed "unethical."

(5) On the policy front, there are at least two major hurdles: First, because many civil rights regulations were based on the struggle against Jim Crow racism, they are not very effective tools for fighting contemporary discrimination. Second, the call for replacing race-based policies with class-based ones (Wilson, 1987), despite its intellectual appeal, must be rejected. Since racial discrimination is alive and well, eliminating current race-specific policies without first putting racially based alternatives in place is nonsensical.

The web of discriminatory practices in the contemporary period has not yet become cemented. It is still possible to mount an offensive that will change its course. However, at the present time, the prospects for such an offensive look bleak. Today, many of the achievements of the civil rights movement (affirmative action, the real possibility of bringing claims against organizations for discrimination, and efforts to desegregate schools) are being rapidly eroded and the civil rights movement and many of its organizations are in disarray. At the same time, there is a serious crisis in leadership in minority communities (Marable, 1983 [1983]; Lusane, 1994), and many traditional allies have moved to the right. For example, during summer 1995, the U.S. Supreme Court imposed "formidable standards" for government-sponsored affirmative action programs (Greenhouse, 1995) and the Board of Regents of the University of California system decided to eliminate its affirmative action programs; yet organizations representing minorities have offered no significant resistance. Progressives and civil rights groups have not been able to challenge the subtle racialization of the current political discourse on crime, taxes, and welfare that is being pursued by both major political parties. Unless this situation is reversed, the new racial practices will become entrenched, and much harder to dislodge, in the years to come.

NOTES

1. For a full elaboration of this structural framework, see author (1994).

2. For a superb collection of articles dealing with the attitudes for various southern elites in this period, see Jacoway and Colburn, *Southern Businessmen and Desegregation* (1982).

3. The incorporation of blacks became almost a necessity with the tremendous manpower needs of World War I, World War II, the Korean War and the economic boom during the *Pax Americana* (1994–1960s). This process was slow and marred by opposition and posturing from northern capitalists and pressure from local states and the federal government as well as civil rights organizations. For an account of the racial attitudes of northern business people and of the protracted process of acceptance of blacks in industry, see Steven M. Gelber, *Black Men and Businessmen: The Growing Awareness of a Social Responsibility* (1974).

4. This rate was confirmed in a recent article in *The Wall Street Journal* about a study done by the Federal Reserve Bank of Chicago (Wilke, 1995). Although that study did not find that minority borrowers with good credit histories experience discrimination, it did find that those with poor credit histories have an approval rate of 16 percent compared to 69 percent for whites in the same category.

5. These numbers include only those students attending public schools; since a greater proportion of white students than blacks attend private schools (Blackwell, 1991), it is likely that these numbers underestimate the real extent of segregation experienced by blacks.

6. Manning Marable terms the politics of this group of black politicians "post Black." By that he means that they are "elected officials, recruited from the professional classes, who are racially and ethnically 'Black' but who favor programs with little kinship in the traditional agendas of the civil rights movement. . . . [They] generally favor the death penalty, oppose new taxes, and support corporate interests" (Marable, 1990, p. 20).

7. For recent data on white views on blacks, see Sniderman and Piazza (1993), chapter 2.

8. For instance, whites tend to agree (66 percent) with the idea that there should not be laws prohibiting intermarriage, but do not approve of intermarriages (60 percent). Likewise, on the matter of school integration, when the question deals with sending their children to schools where there are few blacks, half of the children are black, or most of the children are blacks, commitment to racial equality declines substantially. On these matters, see in Schuman, Steeh, and Bobo (1985), chapter 3, and Jackman (1994), chapter 6.

9. There is a significant debate among social psychologists about whether a new set of racial attitudes is operating in American society. Although the proponents of this view (McConahay and Hough, 1976; Kinder and Sears, 1981; Gaertner and Dovidio, 1986; McConahay, 1986; Sears, 1988) have slightly different conceptions of the context and meaning of the new racial attitudes, they all agree that it includes a "subtler cluster of racial attitudes consisting of a combination of anti-Black and traditional American values" (Sidanius, Devereux, and Pratto, 1992). Opposing these views is a group of authors who argue that we still have the "old racism" (Weigel and Howes, 1985; Sniderman and Tetlock, 1986; Sniderman and Piazza, 1993) and that the "new racism" proponents are conflating opposition to government intervention (a political matter) with racial matters (Schuman, Steeh, and Bobo, 1985; Sniderman and Piazza, 1993). Many of those who oppose the "new racism" argument seem to hold a purely ideological notion about American traditional values (e.g., Sniderman and Piazza, 1993), to conceive of racial ideology as static, and not to envisage how racist thinking can be *rearticulated* and fused with what they define as purely "political" attitudes.

10. Scholars on the conservative side, such as Nathan Glazer (1975) and Charles Murray (1984), have endorsed the notion of reverse racism; and scholars and authors on the liberal side, such as Christopher Jencks (1992) and Thomas and Mary Edsall (1992) also have subscribed to this idea. The Edsalls' case is interesting because, in their otherwise superb book *Chain Reaction* (1992), where they explain how race has been articulated by Republicans since the 1970s to win over the white electorate, they slide into believing that reverse racism is a *real* phenomenon.

11. Chapter 2 in Samuel R. Gross and Robert Mauro, *Death and Discrimination,* provides excellent examples of how race may affect the outcome of cases involving the death penalty before the trial begins. In the authors' opinion, discrimination of a particular type at an early stage of the criminal justice process may conceal, or partially conceal, discrimination of the same type at a later stage (1989, p. 25).

12. In the selection of jurors for cases involving the death penalty, the jurors must be death-qualified—that is, they must be capable, in the opinion of the trial judge, of sentencing the accused to death if they believe that he or she is guilty.

13. This was the Revolutionary Action Movement, organized by Maxwell Stanford in Philadelphia in 1967 (Churchill and Vander Wall, 1988).

14. Malcolm X told Alex Haley one day before his assassination, "The more I keep thinking about this thing, the things that have been happening lately, I'm not at all sure it's the Muslims—I know what they can do, and what they can't, and they can't do some of the stuff recently going on" (Carson, 1991, p. 83). For an elaboration on the thesis that the FBI was involved in Malcolm's assassination, see George Breitman, Herman Porter, and Baxter Smith, *The Assassination of Malcolm X* (1976).

15. The dirty tricks used by the FBI were eavesdropping, bogus mail, false black propaganda, disinformation, harassment arrests, infiltration of organizations, planting *agents provocateurs,* spreading rumors, fabricating evidence, and assassinations (Churchill and Vander Wall, 1988).

16. Conservative and some liberal social scientists attribute contemporary differences in family income to differences in family structure between whites and blacks. But, as Steven Shulman has rightly pointed out, these differences are related to the socioeconomic conditions experienced by poor blacks—conditions that are shaped by racial discrimination (Shulman, 1989).

17. The net worth, unlike the net wealth index, subtracts from the total wealth the debts that people have. Hence the difference in the figures for 1967 and 1984.

REFERENCES

Alexis, M. (1976). "Black and White Wealth: A Comparative Analysis." Pp. 191–206 in Barnett, M. R., and Hefner, J. A., eds., *Public Policy for the Black Community: Strategies and Perspectives.* New York: Alfred Publishing.

Alker, H. R., Jr., Hosticka, C., and Mitchell, M. (1976). "Jury Selection as a Biased Social Process." *Law and Society* 11 (Fall), pp. 9–41.

Ashraf, J. (1994). "Differences in Returns to Education: An Analysis By Race." *American Journal of Economics and Sociology* 53, no. 3, pp. 281–290.

Badgett, M.V.L. (1994). "Rising Black Unemployment: Changes in Job Stability or in Employability." *Review of Black Political Economy* 22 (Winter), pp. 55–75.

Baldus, D. C., Pulaski, C. A., Jr., and Woodworth, G. (1983). "Comparative Review of Death Sentences: An Empirical Study of the Georgia Experience." *Journal of Criminal Law and Criminology* 74, no. 3, pp. 661–753.

———. (1986). "Arbitrariness and Discrimination in the Administration of the Death Penalty: A Challenge to State Supreme Courts." *Stetson Law Review* 15, no. 2, pp. 133–261.

Baron, H. (1969). "The Web of Urban Racism." Pp. 134–176 in Knowles, L. L., and Prewitt, K., eds., *Institutional Racism in America*. Newark, NJ: Prentice-Hall.

Bayley, D. H., and Mendelsohn, H. (1972). "The Policemen's World." Pp. 206–218 in Rason, C. E., and Kuykendall, J. L., eds., *Race, Crime, and Justice*. Pacific Palisades, CA: Goodyear Publishing.

Becker, G. S. (1971). *The Economics of Discrimination*. Chicago: University of Chicago Press.

Bell, D. (1992). *Race, Racism and American Law*. Boston: Little, Brown.

Bendick, M., Jackson, S., Reinoso, V., and Hodges, L. (1991). "Discrimination Against Latino Job Applicants: A Controlled Experiment." *Human Resource Management* 30, no. 4, pp. 469–484.

Benokratis, N. (1982). "Racial Exclusion in Juries." *Journal of Applied Behavioral Science* 18, no. 1, pp. 29–47.

Berg, C. J. (1994). *Class, Gender, Race, and Power in the U.S. Congress*. Boulder: Westview Press.

Berry, M. F. (1994). *Black Resistance, White Law: A History of Constitutional Racism in America*. London: Allen Lane/Penguin Press.

Black, D. (1976). "The Social Organization of Arrest." *Stanford Law Review* 23, pp. 1087–1111.

Blackwell, T. A. (1991). *The Black Community: Diversity and Unity*. New York: Harper and Collins.

Blauner, R. (1989). *Black Lives, White Lives: Three Decades of Race Relations in America*. Berkeley: University of California Press.

Blumer, H. (1958). "Race Prejudice as a Sense of Group Position." *Pacific Sociological Review* 1, pp. 3–7.

Blumestein, A. (1982). "On the Racial Disproportionality of U.S. Prison Populations." *Journal of Criminal Law and Criminology* 73, pp. 1259–1281.

Blunk, R. A., and Sales, B. D. (1977). "Persuasion During the *Voir Dire*." In Sales, B. D., ed., *Psychology in the Legal Process*. New York: Spectrum.

Bobo, L. (1988). "Group Conflict, Prejudice, and the Paradox of Contemporary Racial Attitudes. Pp. 85–114 in Katz, P. A., and Taylor, D. A., eds., *Eliminating Racism: Profiles in Controversy*. New York: Plenum Press.

Bobo, L., and Smith, R. (1994). "From Jim Crow Racism to *Laissez-Faire* Racism: An Essay on the Transformation of Racial Attitudes in America." Paper presented at the annual meeting of the American Sociological Association, Los Angeles, August 26, 1994.

Booker, M. A., Krueger, A. B., and Wolkon, S. (1992). "Race and School Quality Since *Brown v. Board of Education*." Brookings Papers on Economic Activity: Microeconomics. Washington, DC: Brookings Institution.

Boston, T. D. (1988). *Race, Class, and Conservatism*. Boston: Unwin Hyman.

Bound, J., and Freeman, R. B. (1987). "Black Economic Progress: Erosion of the Post-1965 Gains in the 1980s." Pp. 32–49 in Shulman, S., and Darity, W., eds., *The Question of Discrimination: Racial Inequality in the U.S. Labor Market*. Middletown, CT: Wesleyan University Press.

Bradbury, K. L., and Browne, L. E. (1986). "Black Men in the Labor Market." *New England Economic Review*, March-April, pp. 32–42.

Braddock, J. H., and McPartland, J. M. (1987). "How Minorities Continue to Be Excluded from Equal Employment Opportunities: Research on Labor Market and Institutional Barriers." *Journal of Social Issues* 43, no. 1, pp. 5–39.

Breitman, G., Porter, H., and Smith, B. (1976). *The Assassination of Malcolm X*. New York: Pathfinder Press.

Brink, W., and Harris, L. (1963). *The Negro Revolution in America*. New York: Simon and Schuster.

———. (1967). *Black and White: A Study of U.S. Racial Attitudes Today*. New York: Simon and Schuster.

Brooks, R. L. (1990). *Rethinking the American Race Problem*. Berkeley: University of California Press.

Browning, R. P., Marshall, D. R., and Tabb, D. H. (1990). "Minority Mobilization in Ten Cities: Failures and Successes." Pp. 8–32 in Browning, R. P., Marshall, D. R., and Tabb, D. H., eds., *Racial Politics in American Cities*. New York: Longman.

Burkey, R. M. (1971). *Racial Discrimination and Public Policy in the United States*. Lexington, MA: Heath Lexington Books.

Button, J. W. (1989). *Blacks and Social Change: Impact of the Civil Rights Movement in Southern Communities*. Princeton: Princeton University Press.

Caditz, J. (1976). *White Liberals in Transition: Current Dilemmas of Ethnic Integration*. New York: Spectrum.

Campbell, A., and Schuman, H. (1970). "Black Views of Racial Issues." Pp. 346–365 in Goldschmid, M. L., eds., *Black Americans and White Racism: Theory and Research*. New York: Holt, Rinehart, and Winston.

Carmines, E. G., and Merriman, W. R., Jr. (1993). "The Changing American Dilemma: Liberal Values and Racial Policies." In Sniderman, P. M., Tetlock, P. E., and Carmines, E. G., eds., *Prejudice, Politics, and the American Dilemma*. Stanford: Stanford University Press.

Carson, C. (1991). *Malcolm X: The FBI File*. New York: Carroll and Graf.

Center for Community Change. (1989). *Mortgage Lending Discrimination Testing Project*. Washington, DC: CCC/U.S. Department of Housing and Urban Development.

Chambliss, T. (1992). "The Growth and Significance of African American Elected Officials." Pp. 53–70 in Gomes, R. C., and Williams, L. F., eds., *From Exclusion to Inclusion: The Long Struggle for African American Political Power*. New York: Greenwood Press.

Chambliss, W., and Nagasawa, R. H. (1969). "On the Validity of Official Statistics: A Comparative Study of White, Black and Japanese School Boys." *Journal of Research on Crime and Delinquency* 6, pp. 71–77.

Cherry, R. (1989). *Discrimination: Its Impact on Blacks, Women, and Jews*. Lexington, MA: Lexington Books.

Chester, M. (1976). "Contemporary Sociological Theories of Racism." In Katz, P. A., ed., *Towards the Elimination of Racism*. New York: Pergamon Press.

Chideya, F. (1995). *Don't Believe the Hype: Fighting Cultural Misinformation About African-Americans.* New York: Penguin Books.

Christian, V., and Pepelasis, A. (1978). "Rural Problems." In Christian, V., and Pepelasis, A., *Employment of Blacks in the South.* Austin: University of Texas Press.

Churchill, W., and VanderWall, J. (1988). *Agents of Repression: The FBI's Secret Wars Against the Black Panther Party and the American Indian Movement.* Boston: South End Press.

Clayton, O. (1983). "A Reconsideration of the Effects of Race in Criminal Sentencing." *Criminal Justice Review* 8, pp. 15–20.

Cloud, C., and Galster, G. (1993). "What Do We Know About Racial Discrimination in Mortgage Markets?" *Review of Black Political Economy* 21, pp. 101–120.

Cole, L. A. (1975). *Blacks in Power: A Comparative Study of Black and White Elected Officials.* Princeton: Princeton University Press.

Collins, S. M. (1989). "The Marginalization of Black Executives." *Social Problems* 36, pp. 317–331.

Cooper, J. L. (1980). *The Police and the Ghetto.* Port Washington, NY: Kennikat Press.

Cose, E. (1993). *The Rage of a Privileged Class: Why Are Middle Class Blacks Angry? Why Should America Care?* New York: HarperCollins.

Cotton, J. (1989). "Opening the Gap: The Decline in Black Economic Indicators in the 1980s." *Social Science Quarterly* 70, pp. 803–819.

———. (1990). "The Gap at the Top: Relative Occupational Earnings Disadvantages of the Black Middle Class." *Review of Black Political Economy,* Winter.

Crosby, F., Bromley, S., and Saxe, L. (1980). "Recent Unobtrusive Studies of Black and White Discrimination and Prejudice: A Literature Review." *Psychological Bulletin* 87, pp. 546–563.

Cross, H., Kenney, G., Mell, J., and Zimmermann, W. (1990). *Employer Hiring Practices.* Washington, DC: Urban Institute Press.

Culp, J., and Dunson, B. H. (1986). "Brother of a Different Color: A Preliminary Look at Employer Treatment of White and Black Youth." Pp. 233–260 in Freeman, R., and Holzer, H. J., eds., *The Black Youth Employment Crisis.* Chicago: University of Chicago Press.

Dalfiume, R. M. (1969). *Desegregation in the Armed Forces: Fighting on Two Fronts, 1939–1953.* Columbia: University of Missouri Press.

Darity, W., Jr., Cotton, J., and Hill, H. (1993). "Race and Inequality in the Managerial Age." Pp. 33–80 in Reed, W. L., ed., *African Americans: Essential Perspectives.* Westport, CT: Auburn House.

Darity, W. A., Jr., and Myers, S. L. (1980). "Changes in the Black-White Income Inequality, 1968–1978: A Decade of Progress?" *Review of Black Political Economy* 10 (Summer), pp. 365–392.

Davis, D. (1991). "Toward a Socio-Historical and Demographic Portrait of Twentieth-Century African Americans." Pp. 1–19 in Harrison, A., ed., *Black Exodus: The Great Migration from the American South.* Jackson: University Press of Mississippi.

Dorn, E. (1979). *Rules and Racial Equality.* New Haven: Yale University Press.

Dovidio, J. F., and Gaertner, S. L. (1991). "Changes in the Expression and Assessment of Racial Prejudice." In Knopke, H. T., ed., *Opening Doors: Perspectives on Race Relations in Contemporary America.*

Dreeben, R., and Gamoran, A. (1986). "Race, Instruction, and Learning." *American Sociological Review* 51, pp. 660–669.

Dudley, R. G. (1988). "Blacks in Policy-Making Positions." Pp. 15–26 in Corner-Edwards, A. F., and Spurlock, J., eds., *Black Families in Crisis: The Middle Class.* New York: Bruinner/Mazel.

Duncan, O. (1968). "Patterns of Occupational Mobility Among Negro Men." *Demography* 5, pp. 11–22.

Edsall, T. B., and Edsall, M. D. (1992). *Chain Reaction: The Impact of Race, Rights, and Taxes on American Politics.* New York: W. W. Norton.

Essed, P. (1991). *Understanding Everyday Racism: An Interdisciplinary Approach.* London: Sage.

Farley, R. (1984). *Blacks and Whites: Narrowing the Gap?* Cambridge: Harvard University Press.

———. (1993). "The Common Destiny of Blacks and Whites: Observations About the Social and Economic Status of the Races." In Hill, H., and Jones, J. E., Jr., eds., *Race in America: The Struggle for Equality.* Madison: University of Wisconsin Press.

Farley, R., and Allen, W. R. (1987). *The Color Line and the Quality of Life in America.* New York: Russell Sage Foundation.

Farley, R., and Hermalin, A. (1972). "The 1960s: A Decade of Progress for Blacks?" *Demography* 9, pp. 353–370.

Feagin, J. R., and Sikes, M. P. (1994). *Living with Racism: The Black Middle Class Experience.* Boston: Beacon Press.

Feagin, J. R., and Vera, H. (1995). *White Racism: The Basics.* New York: Routledge.

Featherman, D. L., and Hauser, R. M. (1976). "Prestige or Socioeconomic Scales in the Study of Occupational Achievement." *Sociological Methods and Research* 4, no. 4 (May), pp. 403–422.

Fernandez, J. P. (1975). *Black Managers in White Corporations.* New York: John Wiley and Sons.

———. (1982). *Racism and Sexism in Corporate Life: Changing Values in American Business.* Lexington, MA: Heath.

Firebaugh, G., and Davis, K. E. (1988). "Trends in Antiblack Prejudice, 1972–1984: Region and Cohort Effects." *American Sociological Review* 94, pp. 251–272.

Foner, J. D. (1974). *Blacks in the Military in American History: A New Perspective.* New York: Praeger.

Foner, S. P. (1981). *Organized Labor and the Black Worker, 1619–1981.* New York: International Publishers.

Franklin, R. S., and Resnick, S. (1973). *The Political Economy of Racism.* New York: Holt, Rinehart and Winston.

Fredrickson, G. (1981). *White Supremacy: A Comparative Study in American and South African History.* New York: Oxford University Press.

Freeman, R. B. (1973). "Black Economic Progress Since 1964." *The Public Interest,* Summer.

———. (1978). "Decline in Labor Market Discrimination and Economic Analysis." *American Economic Review* 63, May, pp. 280–286.

Friedly, M., and Gallen, D. (1993). *Martin Luther King, Jr.: The FBI File.* New York: Carroll and Graf.

Fusfeld, D. R., and Bates, T. (1984). *The Political Economy of the Urban Ghetto*. Carbondale: Southern Illinois University Press.

Gaertner, S. L., and Dovidio, J. F. (1986). "The Aversive Form of Racism." Pp. 61–89 in Dovidio, J. F., and Gaertner, S. L., eds., *Prejudice, Discrimination, and Racism*. New York: Academic Press.

Galster, G. C. (1977). "A-Bid Rent Analysis of Housing Market Discrimination." *American Economic Review* 67, pp. 144–155.

———. (1990a). "Racial Steering by Real Estate Agents: Mechanisms and Motives." *Review of Black Political Economy*, Spring, pp. 39–61.

———. (1990b). "Racial Steering in Urban Housing Markets: A Review of the Audit Evidence." *Review of Black Political Economy*, pp. 105–129.

Garfinkel, I., Haveman, R. H., and Betson, D. (1977). *Earnings Capacity, Poverty, and Inequality*. New York: Academic Press.

Garrow, D. J. (1983). *The FBI and Martin Luther King*. New York: Penguin Books.

Garwood, A. N. (1991). *Black Americans: A Statistical Sourcebook*. Boulder: Numbers and Concepts.

Geis, G. (1972). "Statistics Concerning Race and Crime." Pp. 61–78 in Reasons, C., and Kuykendall, J. L., eds., *Race, Crime, and Justice*. Pacific Palisades, CA: Goodyear.

Gelber, S. M. (1974). *Black Men and Businessmen: The Growing Awareness of a Social Responsibility*. Port Washington, NY: National University Publications, Kennikat Press.

Genovese, E. D. (1974). *Roll, Jordan, Roll: The World Slaves Made*. New York: Pantheon.

Glazer, N. (1975). *Affirmative Discrimination: Ethnic Inequality and Public Policy*. Cambridge: Harvard University Press.

Gomes, R. C., and Williams, L. F. (1992). "Coalition Politics: Past, Present, and Future." Pp. 129–160 in Gomes, R. C., and Williams, L. F., eds., *From Exclusion to Inclusion: The Long Struggle for African American Political Power*. New York: Greenwood Press.

Gossett, T. (1963). *Race: The History of an Idea in America*. Dallas: Southern Methodist University Press.

Graham, L. O. (1995). *Member of the Club: Reflections on Life in a Racially Polarized World*. New York: HarperCollins.

Greeley, A. M., and Sheatsley, P. B. (1971). "Attitudes Toward Racial Integration." *Scientific American* 225, pp. 13–19.

Greene, L., and Woodson, C. G. (1930). *The Negro Wage Earner*. New York: Association for the Study of Negro Life and History.

Greenhouse, L. (1995). "Ruling Elite: A Big Shift." *The New York Times*, June 13.

Gross, S. R., and Mauro, R. (1989). *Death and Discrimination: Racial Disparities in Capital Sentencing*. Boston: Northeastern University Press.

Hacker, A. (1992). *Two Nations: Black and White, Separate, Hostile, Unequal*. New York: Ballantine Books.

Hagan, J., and Peterson, R. D. (1995). "Criminal Inequality in America: Patterns and Consequences." Pp. 14–36 in Hagan, J., and Peterson, R. D., eds., *Crime and Inequality*. . Stanford: Stanford University Press.

Hamilton, C. (1973). *The Black Political Experience in America*. New York: Capricorn Books.

Haney, C. (1984a). "On the Selection of Capital Juries: The Biasing of the Death Qualification Process." *Law and Human Behavior* 8, nos. 1 and 2, pp. 121–132.

_____. (1984b). "Examining Death Qualification: Further Analysis of the Process Effect." *Law and Human Behavior* 8, nos. 1 and 2, pp. 133–151.

Harrison, A. (1991). *Black Exodus: The Great Migration from the American South*. Jackson: University Press of Mississippi.

Harrison, B., and Bluestone, B. (1988). *The Great U-Turn: Corporate Restructuring and the Polarizing of America*. New York: Basic Books.

Heckman, J. J., and Payner, B. S. (1992). "Determining the Impact of the Federal Antidiscrimination Policy on the Economic Status of Blacks: A Study of South Carolina." *American Economic Review* 79, no. 1, pp. 138–172.

Henri, F. (1975). *Black Migration: Movement North, 1900–1920*. New York: Anchor Press/Doubleday.

Henry, C. P. (1987). "Racial Factors in the 1982 Gubernatorial Campaign: Why Bradley Lost." In Preston, M. B., Henderson, L. J., Jr., and Puryear, P. L., eds., *The New Black Politics: The Search for Political Power*. New York: Longman.

Higgs, R. (1977). *Competition and Coercion: Blacks in the American Economy, 1865–1914*. Cambridge: Cambridge University Press.

Hirschman, C., and Wong, M. G. (1984). "Socioeconomic Gains of Asian Americans, Blacks, and Hispanics: 1960–1976." *American Journal of Sociology* 90, pp. 584–607.

Hout, M. (1984). "Occupational Mobility of Black Men: 1962–1973." *American Sociological Review* 49 (June), pp. 308–322.

Hyman, H. H., and Sheatsley, P. B. (1964). "Attitudes Toward Desegregation." *Scientific American* 211 (July), pp. 16–23.

Jackman, M. (1994). *Velvet Glove: Paternalism and Conflict in Gender, Class, and Race Relations*. Berkeley: University of California Press.

Jackman, M., and Jackman, R. (1980). "Racial Inequality in Home Ownership." *Social Forces* 58, pp. 1221–1254.

Jackman, M., Jackman, R., and Crane, M. (1986). "'Some of My Best Friends Are Black . . .': Interracial Friendship and Whites' Racial Attitudes." *Public Opinion Quarterly* 50, pp. 459–486.

Jackman, M., and Muha, M. J. (1984). "Education and Intergroup Attitudes: Moral Enlightenment, Superficial Democratic Commitment, or Ideological Refinement?" *American Sociological Review* 49 (December), pp. 751–769.

Jackson, P. J. (1989). *Minority Group Threat, Crime, and Policing*. New York: Praeger.

Jackson, P. J., and Carroll, L. (1981). "Race and the War on Crime: The Non-Southern U.S. Cities." *American Sociological Review* 46 (June), pp. 290–305.

Jacobs, D. (1979). "Inequality and Police Strength: Conflict and Coercive Control in Metropolitan Areas." *American Sociological Review* 44 (December), pp. 913–925.

Jacoway, E., and Colburn, D. R., eds. (1982). *Southern Businessmen and Desegration*. Baton Rouge: Louisiana State University Press.

Jaynes, G. (1990). "The Labor Market Status of Black Americans: 1939–1985." *Journal of Economic Perspectives* 4, pp. 9–24.

Jaynes, G. D., and Williams, R. M., eds. (1989). *A Common Destiny: Blacks and American Society.* Washington, DC: National Academy Press.

Jencks, C. (1992). *Rethinking Social Policy: Race, Poverty, and the Underclass.* New York: HarperCollins.

Jennings, J. (1992). *The Politics of Black Empowerment: The Transformation of Black Activism in Urban America.* Detroit: Wayne State University Press.

Kaestner, R., and Fleischer, W. (1992). "Income Inequality as an Indicator of Discrimination in Housing Markets." *Review of Black Political Economy* 20, pp. 55–77.

Kain, J. (1986). "The Influence of Race and Income on Racial Segregation and Housing Policy." In Goering, J., ed., *Housing Desegregation and Federal Policy.* Chapel Hill: University of North Carolina Press.

Kinder, D. R., and Sears, D. O. (1981). "Prejudice and Politics: Symbolic Racism Versus Racial Threats to the Good Life." *Journal of Personality and Social Psychology* 40, pp. 414–431.

King, T. A., and Mieszkowski, P. (1973). "Racial Discrimination, Segregation, and the Price of Housing." *Journal of Political Economy* 81, pp. 590–606.

Kirschenman, J., and Neckerman, K. M. (1994). "'We'd Love To Hire Them, But . . . ': The Meaning of Race for Employers." In Pincus, F. L., and Erlich, H. J., eds., *Race and Ethnic Conflict.* Boulder: Westview Press.

Kleck, G. C. (1981). "Racial Discrimination in Sentencing: A Critical Evaluation of the Evidence with Additional Evidence on Death Penalty." *American Sociological Review* 43, pp. 783–805.

Klein, S., Petersilia, J., and Turner, S. (1990). "Race and Imprisonment Decisions in California." *Science* 247, pp. 812–816.

Kluegel, T. R., and Bobo, L. (1993). "Dimensions of Whites' Beliefs About the Black-White Socioeconomic Gap." Pp. 127–147 in Sniderman, P. M., Tetlock, P. E., and Carmines, E.G., eds., *Prejudice, Politics, and the American Dilemma.* Stanford: Stanford University Press.

Knowles, L. L., and Prewitt, K. (1969). *Institutional Racism in America.* Englewood Cliffs, NJ: Prentice-Hall.

Kovarsky, I., and Albrecht, W. (1970). *Black Employment: The Impact of Religion, Economic Theory, Politics, and Law.* Ames: Iowa State University Press.

Kozol, J. (1991). *Savage Inequalities: Children in America's Schools.* New York: HarperCollins.

LaFree, G. D. (1980). "The Effect of Sexual Stratification By Race on Official Reactions to Rape." *American Sociological Review* 45, pp. 842–854.

_____. (1989). *Rape and Criminal Justice: The Social Construction of Sexual Assault.* Belmont, CA: Wadsworth.

Landry, B. (1987). *The New Black Middle Class.* Berkeley: University of California Press.

Leiman, M. M. (1992). *Political Economy of Racism.* London: Pluto Press.

Leonard, J. (1985). "The Effectiveness of Equal Employment Law and Affirmative Action Regulation." Report to the Subcommittee on Employment Opportunities of the Education and Labor Committee and the Subcommittee on Civil and Constitutional Rights of the Judiciary Committee, U.S. Congress. School of Business Administration, University of California, Berkeley.

Leonard, J. S. (1990). "The Impact of Affirmative Action Regulation and Equal Employment Law on Black Employment." *Journal of Economic Perspectives* 4 (Fall), pp. 47–63.

Levin, J., and McDevitt, J. (1993). *Hate Crimes: The Rising Tide of Bigotry and Bloodshed.* New York: Plenum Press.

Levine, M. (1972). *The Untapped Human Resources: The Urban Negro Employment Equality.* Morristown, NJ: General Learning Press.

Lieberson, S., and Watters, M. C. (1988). *From Many Strands: Ethnic and Racial Groups in Contemporary America.* New York: Russell Sage Foundation.

Liska, A. E., Lawrence, J. J., and Benson, M. (1981). "Perspectives on the Legal Order: The Capacity for Social Control." *American Journal of Sociology* 87 (September), pp. 413–426.

Lizote, A. J. (1978). "Extra-Legal Factors in Chicago's Criminal Courts: Testing the Conflict Model of Criminal Justice." *Social Problems* 25, pp. 564–580.

Lusane, C. (1994). *African Americans at the Crossroads: The Restructuring of Black Leadership and the 1992 Elections.* Boston: South End Press.

Marable, M. (1983). *How Capitalism Underdeveloped Black America.* Boston: South End Press.

_____. (1990). "A New Black Politics." *The Progressive,* August, pp. 20–21.

_____. (1991). *Race, Rebellion, and Reform: The Second Reconstruction in Black America, 1945–1990.* Jackson: University Press of Mississippi.

_____. (1992). *The Crisis of Color and Democracy: Essays on Race, Class, and Power.* Monroe, ME: Common Courage Press.

Marks, C. (1991). "The Social and Economic Life of Southern Blacks During the Migration." Pp. 36–50 in Harrison, A., ed., *Black Exodus: The Great Migration from the American South.* Jackson: University Press of Mississippi.

Marshall, R. (1965). "Industrialisation and Race Relations in the Southern United States." Pp. 61–96 in Hunter, G., ed., *Industrialisation and Race Relations: A Symposium.* London: Oxford University Press.

Massey, D., and Denton, N. (1993). *American Apartheid: Segregation and the Making of the American Underclass.* Cambridge: Harvard University Press.

McAdam, D. (1982). *Political Process and the Development of Black Insurgency, 1930–1970.* Chicago: University of Chicago Press.

McConahay, J. B. (1986). "Modern Racism, Ambivalence and the Modern Racism Scale." Pp. 91–125 in Dovidio, J. R., and Gaertner, S. L., eds., *Prejudice, Discrimination, and Racism.* Orlando, FL: Academic Press.

McConahay, J. B., and Hough, J. C., Jr. (1976). "Symbolic Racism." *Journal of Social Issues* 32, pp. 23–45.

McRae, M. (1991). "Sex and Race Bias in Employment Decisions: Black Women Considered." *Journal of Employment Counseling* 28, pp. 91–98.

Morgan, J. S., and Van Dyke, R. L. (1970). *White-Collar Blacks: A Breakthrough?* Washington, DC: American Management Association.

Morris, A. (1984). *The Origins of the Civil Rights Movement: Black Communities Organizing for Change.* New York: Free Press.

Morrow, J. J. (1957). "American Negroes: A Wasted Resource." *Harvard Business Review* (January-February), pp. 65–74.

Moss, Y. E., et al. (1993). "Black Political Participation: The Search for Power." Pp. 81–118 in Reed, W. L., ed., *African Americans: Essential Perspectives*. Westport, CT: Auburn House.

Murray, C. (1984). *Losing Ground: American Social Policy, 1950–1980*. New York: Basic Books.

Myers, M. A., and Talarico, S. M. (1987). *The Social Contexts of Criminal Sentencing*. New York: Springer-Verlag.

Myrdal, G., et al. (1944; reprint ed. 1964). *An American Dilemma*. New York: McGraw-Hill.

Nelson, W. E. (1987). "Cleveland: The Evolution of Black Political Power." In Preston, M. B., ed., *The New Black Politics*. New York: Longman.

_____. (1990). "Black Mayoral Leadership: A Twenty-Year Perspective." Pp. 188–195 in Barker, L., ed., *Black Electoral Politics*. New Brunswick, NJ: Transaction Publishers.

Nelson, W. E., and Meranto, P. J. (1977). *Electing Black Mayors: Political Action in the Black Community*. Columbus: Ohio State University Press.

Nemeth, C. J. (1981). "Jury Trials: Psychology and the Law." In Berkowitz, L., *Advances in Experimental Psychology*, vol. 14. New York: Academic Press.

Newman, D. K., et al. (1978). *Protest, Politics, and Prosperity: Black Americans and White Institutions, 1940–1975*. New York: Pantheon.

Northrup, H. R. (1967). "Industry's Racial Employment Policies." Pp. 290–307 in Ross, A. M., and Hill, H., eds., *Employment, Race, and Poverty*. New York: Harcourt, Brace, and World.

Norton, M. B., et al. (1990). *A People and a Nation: A History of the U.S.* 3d ed. Boston: Houghton Mifflin.

Oakes, J., Selvin, M., Karoly, L., and Guiton, G. (1992). *Educational Matchmaking: Academic and Vocational Tracking in Comprehensive High Schools*. Santa Monica, CA: RAND.

Oaxaca, R. (1973). "Male-Female Wage Differentials in Urban Labor Markets." *International Economic Review* 14, no. 3, pp. 693–709.

O'Hare, W., Pollard, K., Mann, T., and Kent, M. (1991). "African Americans in the 1990s." *Population Bulletin* 46, no. 1.

Oliver, M., and Shapiro, T. M. (1989). "Race and Wealth." *Review of Black Political Economy*, Spring.

Omi, M., and Winant, H. (1986). *Racial Formation in the United States: From the 1960s to the 1980s*. New York: Routledge.

_____. (1993). "The L.A. Riot and U.S. Politics." Pp. 97–114 in Gooding-Williams, R., ed., *Reading Rodney King, Reading Urban Uprising*. New York: Routledge.

Orfield, G. (1993). "School Desegregation After Two Generations: Race, Schools and Opportunity in Urban Society." In Hill, H., and Jones, J. E., eds., *Race in America*. Madison: University of Wisconsin Press.

Orfield, G., and Monfort, F. (1992). *Status of School Desegregation: The Next Generation*. Alexandria, VA: National School Boards Association.

Otis-Graham, L. (1995). *Member of the Club: Reflections on Life in a Racially Polarized World*. New York: HarperCollins.

Palmore, E., and Whittington, F. T. (1970). "Differential Trends Towards Equality Between Whites and Nonwhites." *Social Forces* 49, pp. 108–117.

Parker, F. R. (1992). "Eradicating the Continuing Barriers to Effective Minority Voter Participation." In Gomes, R. C., and Williams, L. F., eds., *From Exclusion to Inclusion: The Long Struggle for African American Political Power*. New York: Greenwood Press.

Patterson, E. (1974). *City Politics*. New York: Dodd, Mead.

Perlo, V. (1975). *Economics of Racism in the USA: Roots of Black Equality*. New York: International Publishers.

Perry, H. L. (1990). "The Evolution and Impact of Biracial Coalitions and Black Mayors in Birmingham and New Orleans." Pp. 140–154 in Browning, R. P., Marshall, D. R., and Tabb, D. H., eds., *Racial Politics in American Cities*. New York: Longman.

Petersilia, J. (1983). *Racial Disparities in the Criminal Justice System*. Santa Monica, CA: RAND.

Pettigrew, T. F. (1994). "New Patterns of Prejudice: The Different Worlds of 1984 and 1964." In Pincus, F. L., and Erlich, H. J., eds., *Race and Ethnic Conflict*. Boulder: Westview Press.

Pettigrew, T. F., and Martin, J. (1987). "Shaping the Organizational Context for Black American Inclusion." *Journal of Social Issues* 43, no. 1, pp. 41–78.

Pinkney, A. (1984). *The Myth of Black Progress*. Cambridge, UK: Cambridge University Press.

_____. (1993). *Black Americans*. 4th ed. Englewood Cliffs, NJ: Prentice-Hall.

Piven, F. F., and Cloward, R. (1979). *Poor People's Movements: Why They Succeed, How They Fail*. New York: Pantheon.

Pomer, Marshall. (1986). "Labor Market Structure, Intragenerational Mobility, and Discrimination: Black Male Advancement Out of Low-Paying Occupations, 1962–1973." *American Sociological Review* 51, pp. 650–659.

Powell, R. M. (1969). *Race, Religion, and Promotion of the American Executive*. Columbus: Ohio State University, College of Administrative Science.

Pruitt, C. R., and Wilson, J. Q. (1983). "A Longitudinal Study of the Effect of Race in Sentencing." *Law and Society Review* 7, pp. 613–635.

Radelet, M. L., and Pierce, G. L. (1985). "Race and Prosecutorial Discretion in Homicide." *Law and Society Review* 19.

Reich, M. (1981). *Racial Inequality: A Political-Economic Analysis*. Princeton: Princeton University Press.

Rivken, S. (1994). "Residential Segregation and School Integration." *Sociology of Education* 67, pp. 279–292.

Rosentraub, M. S., and Harlow, K. (1984). "Police Policies and the Black Community: Attitudes Toward the Police." Pp. 107–121 in Rice, M. F., and Jones, W., Jr., eds., *Contemporary Public Policy Perspectives and Black Americans*. Westport, CT: Greenwood Press.

Rubin, L. (1994). *Families on the Fault Line: America's Working Class Speaks About the Family, the Economy, Race, and Ethnicity*. New York: HarperCollins.

Russell, G. D. (1994). *The Death Penalty and Racial Bias: Overturning Supreme Court Assumptions*. Westport, CT: Greenwood Press.

Samuels, H. J. (1969). "Prejudice in the Marketplace." Pp. 150–168 in Glock, C. Y., and Siegelman, E., eds., *Prejudice U.S.A.*. New York: Praeger.

Schuman, H., Singer, E., Donovan, R., and Sellitz, C. (1983). "Discriminatory Behavior in New York Restaurants." *Social Indicators Research* 13, pp. 69–83.

Schuman, H., Steeh, C., and Bobo, L. (1985). *Racial Attitudes in America: Trends and Interpretations.* Cambridge: Harvard University Press.

Sears, D. O., and Kinder, D. R. (1971). "Racial Tensions and Voting in Los Angeles." In Hirsch, W. Z., ed., *Los Angeles: Viability and Prospects for Metropolitan Leadership.* New York: Praeger.

Sheatsley, P. B. (1966). "White Attitudes Toward the Negro." Pp. 303–324 in Parsons, T., and Clark, K. B., eds., *The Negro American.* Boston: Beacon Press.

Sherman, L. W. (1980). "Execution Without Trial: Police Homicide and the Constitution." *Vanderbilt Law Review* 33, pp. 71–100.

Shulman, S. (1989). "A Critique of the Declining Discrimination Hypothesis." Pp. 126–152 in Shulman, S., and Darity, W., eds., *The Question of Discrimination: Racial Inequality in the U.S. Labor Market.* Middletown, CT: Wesleyan University Press.

Sidanius, J. E., Devereux, E., and Pratto, F. (1992). "A Comparison of Symbolic Racism Theory and Social Dominance Theory as Explanations for Racial Policy Attitudes." *Journal of Social Psychology* 131, pp. 377–395.

Skolnick, J. H. (1972). "The Police and the Urban Ghetto." Pp. 236–258 in Reasons, C. E., and Kuykendall, J. L., eds., *Race, Crime, and Justice.* Pacific Palisades, CA: Goodyear.

Smith, B. (1974). *Secret Documents Exposed: FBI Plot Against the Black Movement.* New York: Pathfinder Press.

Smith, D., Visher, C. A., and Davidson, L. (1984). "Equity and Discretionary Justice: The Influence of Race on Police Arrest Decisions." *Journal Of Criminal Law and Criminology* 75, pp. 234–249.

Smith, J. P., and Welch, F. R. (1986). *Closing the Gap: Forty Years of Economic Progress for Blacks.* Santa Monica, CA: RAND.

Smith, R. C. (1992). "Politics Is Not Enough: The Institutionalization of the African American Freedom Movement." Pp. 97–126 in Gomes, R. C., and Williams, L. F., eds., *From Exclusion to Inclusion: The Long Struggle for African American Political Power.* New York: Greenwood Press.

————. (1995). *Racism in the Post–Civil Rights Era: Now You See It, Now You Don't.* New York: State University of New York Press.

Sniderman, P., and Hagen, M. G. (1985). *Race and Inequality: A Study in American Values.* Chatham, NJ: Chatham House.

Sniderman, P., and Piazza, T. (1993). *The Scar of Race.* Cambridge: Harvard University Press.

Sniderman, P., and Tetlock, P. E. (1986). "Symbolic Racism: Problems of Motive Attribution in Political Analysis." *Journal of Social Issues* 42, pp. 129–150.

Sowell, T. (1984). *Civil Rights: Rhetoric or Reality?* New York: Morrow.

Spero, S. D., and Harris, A. L. (1974). *The Black Worker: The Negro and the Labor Movement.* New York: Atheneum.

Spohn, C. (1994). "Crime and the Social Control of Blacks: Offender/Victim Race and the Sentencing of Violent Offenders." Pp. 249–268 in Bridges, G. S., and Myers, M. A., eds., *Inequality, Crime, and Social Control.* Boulder: Westview Press.

Spohn, C., Gruhl, J., and Welch, S. (1981–1982). "The Effect of Race on Sentencing: A Re-Examination of an Unsettled Question." *Law and Society Review* 16, pp. 72–88.

Spratlen, T. H. (1976). "Blacks in the American Economy: Problems, Policies, and Prospects." Pp. 207–236 in Barnett, M. R., and Hefner, J. A., eds., *Public Policy for the Black Community: Strategies and Perspectives*. New York: Alfred Publishing.

Stampp, K. M. (1956). *The Peculiar Institution: Slaver in the Ante-Bellum South*. New York: Alfred A. Knopf.

Stone, C. (1972a). "Measuring Black Political Power." Pp. 227–252 in Henderson, L. J., Jr., ed., *Black Political Life in the United States*. San Francisco: Chandler Publishing.

_____. (1972b). "Up from Slavery: From Reconstruction to the Sixties." Pp. 35–51 in Henderson, L. J., Jr., ed., *Black Political Life in the United States*. San Francisco: Chandler Publishing.

Strauss, G. (1967). "How Management Views Its Race Relations Responsibilities." Pp. 261–289 in Ross, A. M., and Hill, H., eds., *Employment, Race, and Poverty*. New York: Harcourt, Brace, and World.

Struyk, R. J., and Turner, M. A. (1986). "Exploring the Effects of Preferences on Urban Housing Markets." *Journal of Urban Economics* 119 (March), pp. 131–147.

Tabb, W. K. (1970). *The Political Economy of the Black Ghetto*. New York: W. W. Norton.

Tauber, K. E., and Tauber, A. E. (1965). *Negroes in Cities*. Chicago: Aldine.

Terkel, S. (1992). *Race*. New York: New Press.

Thurow, L.C. (1969). *Poverty and Discrimination*. Washington, DC: Brookings Institution.

_____. (1975). *Generating Inequality*. New York: Basic Books.

Tolnay, S., and Beck, E. M. (1991). "Rethinking the Role of Racial Violence in the Great Migration." Pp. 20–35 in Harrison, A., ed., *Black Exodus: The Great Migration from the American South*. Jackson: University Press of Mississippi.

Travis, D. J. (1991). *Racism American Style: A Corporate Gift*. Chicago: Urban Research Press.

Turner, M. A., Struyk, R., and Yinger, J. (1991). *The Housing Discrimination Study*. Washington, DC: Urban Institute.

Turner, M. B., and Mitchell-Kernen, C. (1990). "New Trends in Black American Interracial Marriage: The Social Structural Context." *Journal of Marriage and the Family* 52, pp. 209–218.

Tuttle, W. M., Jr. (1970). "Labor Conflict and Racial Violence: The Black Worker in Chicago, 1894–1919." Pp. 86–110 in Cantor, M., ed., *Black Labor in America*. Westport, CT: Negro Universities Press.

Waddoups, J. (1991). "Racial Differences in Intersegment Mobility." *Review of Black Political Economy* (Fall), pp. 23–43.

Walsh, A. (1987). "The Sexual Stratification Hypothesis and Sexual Assault in Light of the Changing Conceptions of Race." *Criminology* 25, pp. 153–173.

Walton, H. (1972). *Black Politics: A Theoretical and Structural Analysis*. Philadelphia: J.B. Lippincott.

Wattenberg, B., and Scammon, R. (1973). "Black Progress and Liberal Rhetoric." *Commentary* (April), pp. 35–44.

Weigel, R. H., and Howes, P. (1985). "Conceptions of Racial Prejudice: Symbolic Racism Reconsidered." *Journal of Social Issues* 1, pp. 117–138.

Welch, S. (1990). "Critique of Chapter 5, 'Black Political Participation'." Pp. 7–12 in Reed, W. L.,ed., *Critiques of the NRC Study "A Common Destiny": Blacks and American Society*. Boston: University of Massachusetts, William Monroe Trotter Institute.

Wellman, D. T. (1977). *Portraits of White Racism*. New York: Cambridge University Press.

Wilhelm, S. (1983). *Black in a White America*. Cambridge, MA: Schenkman.

Wilke, J. (1995). "Race Is a Factor in Some Loan Denials." *The Wall Street Journal,* July 13.

Williams-Myers, A. J. (1995). *Destructive Impulses, An Examination of an American Secret in Race Relations: White Violence*. Lanham, MD: University Press of America.

Willie, C. V. (1989). *Caste and Class Controversy on Race and Poverty: Round Two of the Willie/Wilson Debate*. New York: General Hall.

Wilson, W. J. (1978). *The Declining Significance of Race*. Chicago: University of Chicago Press.

_____. (1987). *The Truly Disadvantaged*. Chicago: University of Chicago Press.

Winant, H. (1994). *Racial Conditions: Politics, Theory, Comparisons*. Minneapolis: University of Minnesota Press.

Woodward, C. V. (1966). *The Strange Career of Jim Crow*. Second Revised Edition. New York: Oxford University Press.

Wynn, N. A. (1993). *The Afro-American and the Second World War*. Revised ed. New York: Holmes and Meier.

Yinger, J. (1978). "The Black-White Price Differential in Housing: Some Further Evidence." *Land Economics* 54, pp. 188–208.

_____. (1986). "Measuring Discrimination with Fair Housing Audits: Caught in the Act." *American Economic Review* 76 (December), pp. 881–893.

Zatz, M. S. (1984). "Race, Ethnicity, and Determinate Sentencing: A New Dimension to an Old Controversy." *Criminology* 22, pp. 146–171.

five

"In Due Time": Narratives of Race and Place in the Western United States

CHRIS FRIDAY

"A new focus of racial difficulty [has] appear[ed] on the West Coast involving Latin-Americans, Orientals and Negroes," ran the 1943 report in the first issue of the new monthly magazine *Race Relations*. "Here," the editors continued, "the pattern of racial adjustment has been broken by the evacuation of the Japanese, the new international importance of Mexico, and the unprecedented increase in the number of folk Negroes from Louisiana and Texas in California and Washington" (Aug. 1943, p. 2).[1] Five months later, the magazine carried the news of the formation of the Inter-racial Council in Stockton, California, by a variety of African American organizations ranging from the National Association for the Advancement of Colored People (NAACP), the Negro Elks Club, the Negro Women's Club of San Francisco, and Stockton's African American churches. The Council also drew members from the Chinese Association and the Mexican Association as well as from local Filipino and Mexican churches. Although Stockton also had Greek, Jewish, and Asian Indian populations, the Council was to contain no members of those groups. According to its director, the Council's "primary work will be on Negro-white racial relations but . . . there are existing tensions involving the Mexicans and the Chinese which must be dealt with in due time" (Dec. 1943, p. 18).[2]

These two news reports hint at five critical aspects of understanding race relations in the western United States in the twentieth century. First, they reveal that the region was multiracial in its demographic reality as well as in the manner in which the various racialized groups contested for position beneath white hegemony. Second, in spite of the contestations, prior to World

War II a pattern of "racial adjustment" could be observed between racialized peoples, and an unmarked but still racialized white population had reached some level of stasis. Third, wartime migrations caused jarring transformations in race relations. Fourth, international events impinged on racial formations. Finally, the text of the latter news item apocryphally predicted that in the postwar era black-and-white constructions of race relations would take precedence, demand immediate attention, and dominate the discussion, whereas those of all other racialized peoples would be addressed "in due time" and even then in a descending order that placed far too many at the back of the line.

A focus on race relations in the western United States[3] engages two powerful narratives of race and place in American society. The common story of American race relations is one of black and white with other groups portrayed episodically, as some localized and exceptional phenomena, or only in binary opposition to whites (Almaguer, 1994; Gutierrez, 1995; Okihiro, 1994; Omi and Winant, 1994).[4] Even the most cursory glance at college-level texts, for example, is revealing (Limerick, 1992a, 1992b, 1995).[5] Native Americans appear in early Atlantic seaboard contact with European settlers and on the Great Plains in the late nineteenth century, with little attention being given to their lives or the role they might play on the national level during any other period. Similarly, Asian Americans appear as victims of the Chinese Exclusion Act, of Japanese American internment, and as model minorities since the 1960s, but they are not credited as shaping national history or the discourse on race in any lasting way. They, like Mexican Americans, are constructed as sojourners, disengaged from life in the United States.

Textbook authors have also made these racialized groups into localized, regional entities. "Real Indians" live in the West. Asian Americans reside in Pacific Coast states, especially California and Hawaii, and to a lesser degree, Washington. Mexican Americans live only in California and the Southwest. Significant interaction between any of the racialized groups is not considered. Such common constructs are belied not only by demographics but also by the historical presence and activities of these racialized peoples in the United States. These textbooks are reflective of a broader popular narrative of race in the United States, a narrative that is binary—that places only whites and blacks in the national story—rather than possessing multiple points of racialization.

At times as powerful and limiting as the narrative of race, that of place has gripped the national imagination. In addition to the South and the North, two imaginary regions that have dominated the national narrative, the idea of the western "frontier" has had immense influence. In spite of its repeated falls from grace, the notion of a frontier in the American West has shown amazing recuperative and regenerative powers.[6] One of the strengths of the older frontier thesis was the seductive argument that the West was integral to the creation of a national character, that it was at the very center of American history. In the process, that story privileged whites and characterized the "conquered" peoples as savage and uncivilized.

In contrast, the more recent "New Western" historians, whose visions of the West vary tremendously, have created a highly racialized, gendered, and class-ridden conflictual model of the West as a region. It is, in the words of one historian, "a longer, grimmer, but more interesting story" (West, 1991, pp. 103–111). Yet one tendency has been to focus on exceptional relationships in a place or places that has had the unintended effect of withdrawing what happened in the region from national history.[7] Like the narrative of race, that of place in national history has thus remained polarized in a North-South paradigm. The two "stories"—black and white, North and South—are tightly linked and mutually reinforcing, leaving little room for a West with ambiguous, shifting multiracialism.

In this chapter, therefore, I have sought to historicize the discussion of race relations in the West, to undermine the salience of biracial and biregional narratives so prevalent in the scholarly literature and the popular imagination (Almaguer, 1994; Chan, Daniels, Garcia, and Wilson, 1994; Deutsch, 1992; Deutsch, Sanchez, and Okihiro, 1992; Pascoe, 1991; White, 1986).[8] It outlines the ways in which race has been constructed in the West and reveals a series of transformations that break into four larger historical periods. In the first period, between the 1880s and the 1920s, whites used their growing control of the land base and labor markets to establish a racial hegemony in the region. By the 1920s, the cumulative economic shifts had created large urban centers and had drawn many people to the region; yet older, commercial agricultural interests remained powerful forces. In the second period, lasting until the early 1940s, racialized groups including whites competed with each other for control of new social spaces, yet their access to the state gave whites the upper hand. The result was not pluralism but a multiracial society riddled by overlapping hierarchies and power relationships.

Beginning in the late 1930s and continuing until the 1960s, massive demographic shifts and huge federal investments in the urban, military, and industrial complex created dramatic changes in the social landscape of the West that seemed to many whites to threaten the racial order. As whites attempted to reconstruct or reassert hegemony, subordinated racialized groups struggled for political position in the new social order. African Americans achieved the premier position among the subordinated. This reordered the discussion of Western race relations along a largely black-white axis, at least on the levels of policy formulation and media representation. The result was the "nationalization" or polarization of racial constructs in the region that pitted a dichotomized vision against a fragmented reality.

Not until the 1960s did Asian Americans, Mexican Americans, and Native Americans achieve positions that began to rival that of African Americans. A new struggle over positions has ensued. Racialized groups vie for federal largesse, or at least for whatever crumbs are left. They also wrestle with the conflicting interests of building multiracial coalitions and focusing on narrower cultural nationalist programs. Rather than declining in significance, then, race has emerged as the predominant question in the late twentieth century, not only for the western United States but for the nation as a whole.[9] Understanding how these racial formations occurred, their complexities, and their transformations is necessary to achieve an understanding of the present and future formations. This essay focuses on the first three periods—the establishment of hegemony, racial maneuvering, and the reassertion of hegemony—and leaves the fourth stage for other authors in this volume to explore in greater depth. What follows is necessarily brief and suggestive rather than exhaustive and definitive. It is meant as a challenge to rethink race and region.[10]

Establishing Hegemony

Hegemony is the control of subordinated groups that rests on the belief that selective movement out of subjugation can occur. Control depends upon the threat that violent, naked force *can* and *might* be used against transgressors individually or in groups. Hegemonic control, though, seeks not to use that force, or at least masks it; for overt violent control begets overt violent revolts (Przeworski, 1980).[11] In the western United States, up to about 1880, the unmasked violence was part and parcel of the "war of incorporation" (Brown, 1994).[12] The formal war ended at different times in different places: as early as 1848 in the Southwest, 1858 in the Mormon empire of Deseret, the late 1870s in the Pacific Northwest, or perhaps even as late as 1890 on the Great Plains (Cornell, 1990; Limerick, 1987; Montejano, 1987; Trafzer and Scheuerman, 1986; Utley, 1982). Although those conquests represent significant historical and sociological moments, what followed was even more significant.

Sociologist David Montejano's analysis of nineteenth-century Texas points to a fruitful interpretive path. U.S. annexation and incorporation of the area, Montejano argues, brought with it "pogroms, expulsions, and subjugation of Mexicans." Yet the functioning "accommodative arrangement between the leaders of the victors and those of the defeated" created a "peace structure" that gave the subjugated some degree of power and diffused outright rebellion. It also allowed the Anglo elite to control the political economy without frequent, overt force (1987, p. 8).

That process began earlier in Texas than in most of the rest of the West, took quite some time to develop, and depended upon the widespread capitalist transformation of the region. Capitalist penetrations into the region prior to the 1880s, though they all had significant environmental and social effects, paled in comparison to what followed. At one end of the spectrum, those early activities included extensive, widespread enterprises like the ranches in Texas. At the other end were highly mobile, intensive silver mining in California, and the subsequent gold rushes. Positioned between those two extremes, the fur trade and even early logging in the Pacific Northwest were at once extensive and intensive enterprises (Cornell, 1990, pp. 380–382; Gibson, 1992; Johnson, 1993; Montejano, 1987; Montoya, 1993; Van Kirk, 1980). During the 1880s, the full-scale arrival of transcontinental railroads throughout the West created a new stage of capitalist development and social relations that extended the "accommodative arrangements" or "peace structure" to a broader region. The railroads marked the significant and widespread beginnings of the establishment of "white" hegemony, as opposed to direct racial conflict.

Hegemony was not possible without state action; but in the West, the latter category need not be construed as exclusively military efforts to subdue indigenous peoples. The U.S. government's substantial investments in the basic communications and transportation infrastructure did as much, or more, to transform the region. Government subsidies for the building of military wagon roads in the 1850s started the trend toward linking disparate subregions together and the similar financing of most railroads expanding westward made a qualitative difference in the ability of investors to profit from the lands and waters of the region. By the mid-1880s, not just one, but five major transcontinental railroad lines spanned the country with multiple spurs, roads, rivers, and trails reaching far into the most remote areas (Beck and Hasse, 1989).[13]

Not only did these rail lines make large-scale extraction[14] possible, they also acted as conduits for the rapid demographic transformation of the West. In 1860, the population of the region amounted to only 619,000 people. Although it was still relatively isolated in 1870, the area's population grew by 60 percent, more than twice the national rate (26.6 percent), to 991,000. Over the next decade the population grew by 82 percent, to 1,801,000 in 1880, and then by 74 percent in the following decade, to reach 3,134,000 in 1890. During those two decades, the western growth rate stood at levels three times greater than the national average. In the 1890s, national and regional financial crises slowed the rate of population increase in the region to only 37 percent, two and a half times the national average. As of 1900, the West's population was 4,309,000, which still represented nearly a sixfold increase in the region's population since 1860 (U.S. Department of Commerce, 1975, pp. 8, 22–23).

The completion of the major railroad links across the continent redistributed people in the region. Prior to the coming of the railroads in 1860, the coastal states of Washington, Oregon, and California contained 72 percent of the West's occupants. By 1870, the coastal states claimed 68 percent of the region's population. More significant declines came between 1880 and 1900, when the proportion of western residents living in those three states dropped from 62 percent to 56 percent. The inordinate growth of the region and the redistribution of the population away from coastal entrepôts reflected the thoroughgoing capitalist penetration of the West (U.S. Department of Commerce, 1975, pp. 22–23, 25, 33, 36).

The process of "settlement" was by no means benign.[15] Control of the land base helped assure white hegemony, but the seizure was neither immediate nor uniform. Prior to 1880, Native Americans and Mexican Americans lost control of huge tracts of land through coerced treaty negotiations and courtroom battles, sales and seizures, federal policies, or intermarriages with "Anglo" elites (Hoxie, 1984; Montejano, 1987; Montoya, 1993; Washburn, 1975).[16] From the 1880s on, although Native Americans and Mexican Americans continued to hold some of the land base, the two groups were severely disadvantaged by white dominance of the legal systems; by the measurement and commodification of the landscape in units of economic value by the cadastral surveys; and by the threat of force.

On Indian reservations, whites leased lands from Native Americans, and traders took produce, resources, and art as in-kind payments. On Southwest ranchos, the Anglo elite intermarried and established paternalistic relations with many of their Mexican American workers. In both settings, hegemony rested on an "accommodative agreement" that placed whites in power but that demanded that they engage in a constant negotiation (Fowler, 1987; Montejano, 1987; Montoya, 1993; Friday, 1993–1996). It is beyond the scope of this essay to demonstrate the extent to which racialized peoples exerted power and acted on their own choices, but we must acknowledge that the relationships between whites and racialized groups in the West were often ambiguous and inconsistent. Yet paradoxically, the variations in the power balance between the groups in various contexts helped to sustain white hegemony. Because they had the upper hand over the land base, whites were able to assert that Mexican Americans were foreigners in the land of their birth and that Native Americans were vanishing. The "alienation" and "marginalization" of indigenous groups provided the foundation on which whites' assumptions about "free" and open lands in the West were based.

The "opening" of the Western land base to commercial agricultural interests did not inevitably result in white ownership and control. Instead, a series of contestations, often racial as well as economic in nature, continued. Outside of those waged by Native Americans and Mexican Americans, Chinese American entrepreneurs established small plots of land near urban or industrial areas where they raised truck crops, chickens, and hogs for local retail markets. Some even became major landholders. Chinese market gardeners faced early restrictions as white townspeople began to demand the removal of gardens to the more remote countryside based on arguments about sanitation. The impetus for these demands came from the growth of household production by white women who sought to market their produce in competition with the Chinese and from townspeople who wanted to control the urban environment and who defined control in racial terms (Chan, 1986, pp. 86–88; Friday, 1994, p. 59).

Restrictions on Chinese gardens were dwarfed by the alien (primarily anti-Japanese) land laws established in California and ten other states during the first several decades of the twentieth century. But racialized peoples negotiated and circumvented those laws, for many whites wished to continue to sell or lease lands rather than risk their labor and capital in the ventures. Through the alien land laws, as in the case of city ordinances against Chinese gardens, whites allocated space on the basis of race (Jiobu, 1988, pp. 353–367; Kim, 1994, pp. 126–131).

Attempts by African Americans to gain access to lands in the West yielded similar results. In some sections of the West, such as Oregon, African Americans faced formal Black Codes that restricted their rights to enter the territories much less hold land titles. While a few, like George Washington Bush, found enough social space to purchase land in places like Washington Territory and even became influential local figures, the experiences of Exodusters in their migrations to Kansas, Nebraska, and Oklahoma are more representative. On lands recently seized from Native Americans, blacks in the Reconstruction era hoped to break into the ranks of landholders and commercial farmers. However, restrictive legal systems and unsupportive, unsympathetic financial institutions frustrated black attempts to become either first-class farmers or citizens. Although landholding and black towns provided a sense of worth, they offered only small gains in dollars and cents. White hegemony rested upon the contradictions between opportunity and suppression. So long as the repressions could be negotiated, most whites could continue to benefit from their "whiteness" and racialized peoples would continue to strive for opportunity even though they remained subordinate (Mumford, 1989, pp. 79–81; White, 1986, p. 198).[17]

While disputes over the land base persisted, the arena of confrontation for most racialized peoples increasingly shifted from disputes over land to disputes over labor. Between the 1880s and the 1920s, segmented labor markets emerged and became entrenched in the West. In the process, racialized peoples found themselves virtually trapped in poorly paid, highly unstable sectors of the western economy, which was generally characterized by tremendous boom and bust cycles. European Americans also struggled in the same lower tier of jobs; yet through the use of state policies that favored white men and to a lesser degree white women (such as the franchise), unionization, and assertions of racial superiority, enough European Americans achieved a measure of upward mobility to lend credence to the myth that the "frontier" (and indeed "America") was the land of opportunity. This same perception of mobility also fueled the growing notion of "whiteness." In the West's expanding economy, Italian, Irish, and other European American ethnics realized the "wages of whiteness" by separating themselves from racialized peoples. Differentness thus was structured into the economy (Roediger, 1994; White, 1986).[18]

The capitalist penetration of relatively isolated parts of the West linked by the railroads catalyzed labor conflict. Racialized peoples struggled to negotiate from within the context of their own cultures and sensibilities. They acted on assumptions about wage work and the gendered allocation of tasks that sometimes supported capitalism and sometimes undermined it. The decisions at which they arrived through these negotiations ultimately "manufactured" a larger "consent" to capitalism (Burawoy, 1979; Przeworski, 1980).

In the Southwest between the 1880s and the 1920s, "regional labor markets" emerged as Mexican American control of the land base eroded. When combined with Mexican American and Anglo assumptions about gender roles, those transformations encouraged Mexican American men to engage in seasonal labor migrations. Women remained behind in the small towns and were forced to expand their activities to include the daily maintenance of the household with localized economic and political activities. Those responsibilities transformed gender relations within the family and Mexican American culture. Nonetheless, Anglos controlled most of the region's political economy (Deutsch, 1987; White, 1986, p. 324).

Native Americans similarly participated in wage-labor markets. For several decades, seasonal subsistence practices allowed many to enter and exit the labor market; but by the 1920s, wage work in seasonal jobs brought more dependence than independence (Boxberger, 1989; Harmon, 1995; White, 1983, pp. 241–249; Wyatt, 1987). As with Mexican Americans, gender and place affected how Native Americans approached wage work. In the "pastoral" reaches of the West, many Native American (as well as Mexican American and African American) men moved to jobs in the livestock industries, becoming "cowboys" and herdsmen (Iverson, 1994; White, 1994; Worster, 1987).

In areas of intensive extractive enterprises, Native American men often engaged in seasonal labor as railroad section workers, fishers, loggers, mill hands, and longshoremen. Women, girls, and boys found work in commercial agriculture, harvesting crops such as berries and hops. Salmon canneries, especially in British Columbia and Alaska, hired Native American women to supplement the "regular" crews made up of Chinese laborers in the nineteenth century, and of Japanese, Filipinos, and others in the twentieth century. Native American men fished for the same companies, often in competition with company-imported fishers of Italian, Greek, Finnish, Norwegian, or Swedish ancestry (Friday, 1994; Harmon, 1995; Philpott, 1963).

Scholars who have claimed that Native American labor was not necessary or essential to the regional economy have misread the situation (Cornell, 1990, pp. 380–383). True, Native Americans seldom made up a majority of

the workforce, but they gave employers a flexibility the latter might otherwise not have had. A Native American presence in the labor market lessened
the need for overt force to be used to coerce laborers recruited from "outside" to meet production demands. At the same time, access to wage work
sustained Native American communities and engaged them just enough in
the growing consumer-oriented marketplace to prevent wholesale rebellion.

For Chinese Americans, the establishment of "white" hegemony took
forms as broad as those directed against Native Americans, Mexican Americans, and African Americans in the West. These suppressions ranged from
bottom-tier jobs in the labor market and marginalized entrepreneurial activities to tight controls on the very physical space that Chinese immigrants occupied. Unlike Native Americans and Mexican Americans, who had once
controlled the land base, or many African Americans, whose post–Civil War
agenda included the acquisition of land as part of first-class citizenship, the
vast proportion of Chinese immigrants to the western United States made si-
multaneous entrances to the region and to its labor markets. From their earliest arrival in significant numbers during the 1850s and 1860s, Chinese immigrants found themselves in the most marginal sectors of the western
economy. They sifted through mine "tailings" that other prospectors had
left behind. They took up "women's" work, cooking and washing for white
workers—activities that reveal the intersection between race and gender
constructions in the largely male western population. In rural sectors, Chinese worked on rail lines, in agricultural harvests and field maintenance, or
in salmon canneries. In a few urban locations they held positions in light industry, wrapping cigars, sewing leather for harnesses or shoes, or manufacturing clothing and other textiles. These and other jobs for Chinese were
highly competitive and unstable, often being strictly seasonal. In the West's
dual wage labor market, Chinese and other peoples of color occupied the
bottommost rungs, with few opportunities for movement up or out of that
position (Chinn, Choy, and Lai, 1969; Lippin, 1994).

In the 1870s, increasing anti-Chinese sentiment and violence culminated
in national legislation designed to prevent Chinese immigration to the
United States. The 1882 Chinese Exclusion Act, which went through a series
of renewals and revisions until its 1904 revision, which extended exclusion
indefinitely, represented what is often called the first immigration restriction
based on race (Chan, 1991). In the late 1870s and early 1880s, California's
white working class used Chinese exclusion as a glue to cement its political
unity. During the economic slump of the mid-1880s, the series of violent
race riots against Chinese throughout the West gave notice that legal bans on
immigration were too limited for many whites (Saxon, 1971; Schwantes,
1979; Tsai, 1986).

Chinese responded to immigration laws by fighting them in the courts[19]
and to incidents of violence by returning to China or moving to relatively

safe havens in San Francisco's Chinatown or to smaller Chinatowns in areas like the San Joaquin river delta or Astoria, Oregon, where the economy was too dependent on Chinese labor to permit of such violence. They also migrated to places like Phoenix, Arizona, where the rapid growth of the economy promised many jobs and where the more numerous Mexican Americans and Native Americans bore the brunt of discrimination (Friday, 1994, pp. 57–58).

The new urbanization of the Chinese prompted whites to draw even more distinct racial lines around them. Under the guise of urban hygiene reforms, white residents and officials of large and small cities expanded on the earlier bans on urban gardens and created cubic air laws designed to restrict the number of Chinese living in a particular building. There were great ironies, for these restrictions came as Chinese migrated to cities to escape rural violence directed at them and as white city dwellers tried to limit the expansion of Chinese residences. At first the restrictions were informal. As early as 1879, for example, European Americans in Astoria, Oregon, expressed an intense desire "to colonize the Chinese in . . . one place in the city . . . if possible" (Friday, 1994, p. 57). From Vancouver, British Columbia, to Los Angeles, whites acted to control Chinese residential patterns. In 1892, San Francisco whites went one step further and began to codify residential patterns through some of the West's earliest restrictive covenants in property deeds. In 1895, in Phoenix, white merchants purchased a section of the Chinese quarter and razed the buildings. They believed that this early version of "urban renewal" enhanced their business possibilities by literally removing "race" from those city blocks (*The Crisis*, 1946, p. 138; Anderson, 1991; Luckingham, 1988, p. 92).

Another instructive case is that of the Mexican American barrio in Phoenix in the 1870s. Although its urban history is much different than that of older Southwest towns like Santa Fe, Albuquerque, and El Paso, Phoenix is an archetypical western city. It was one of the West's many "instant cities," emerging because of its centrality to rail lines that connected it to the various mining districts, and because of its location in a productive agricultural region. Barely a hamlet in the 1870s, with Mexican Americans making up nearly half its population, Phoenix grew quickly in size and Anglo domination. The new Anglo migrants brought economic and political power with them and the new Mexican American migrants entered the city through segmented labor markets and specialized economic niches. As the town grew, Anglos tried to lock Mexican American settlement into specific districts. In their sections of town, whites symbolically eschewed adobe buildings because they appeared "too Mexican" and instead built wood-frame and brick houses. Not content with physical and symbolic separation, whites attempted to establish the primacy of what they considered "their" culture over that of Mexican Americans. In the public schools, Anglos insisted that teachers adopt English-only practices, and even resisted the printing of political materials in Spanish (Luckingham, 1994, pp. 18–36, 48–49, 65).

Particularly in the political arena, Phoenix's history illustrates the ways in which Anglos denied Mexican Americans (as well as Native Americans, Chinese Americans, and African Americans) access to power. In the 1870s and 1880s, Mexican Americans voted and ran for office. The ensuing resistance against Spanish-language political materials in the 1890s only proved to be a warm-up for full-fledged disenfranchisement at the height of the "Progressive" era. During the second decade of the twentieth century, white reformers abolished the city's political system, consisting of a mayor and city council with members elected from various wards. This arrangement, they argued, allowed for too much favoritism, corruption, and bossism. In its stead, they instituted a city manager—a "trained" professional—and city commissioners elected "at large." That switch pitted a much larger bloc of Anglo voters against Mexican Americans. To make matters worse, in 1913 the state legislature approved a literacy test for voters. The at-large elections persisted until 1983, and the literacy tests, until 1972 (Luckingham, 1994).

Simultaneously with the implementation of those political limitations on Mexican Americans, state legislators in 1914 required proprietors to employ at least 80 percent citizens in their businesses. After the Ninth Circuit Court declared the law unconstitutional the following year, the law's proponents tried to find other ways to achieve the same end—barring Mexican Americans from jobs—through another English-only bill. The bill did not pass, but the state and city forced "Americanization" through the school systems; and well-intentioned reformers set up Friendly House to carry out like-minded efforts for Mexican Americans in the city. As in the rest of the Southwest, the latter programs were largely aimed at Mexican American women, whom the reformers believed to be the most effective tool for transforming the home. Such efforts proved too inconsistent and failed to address the most pressing concerns of Mexican Americans. Nonetheless, like Chinese Americans, Mexican Americans confronted residential segregation, disenfranchisement, and legal and social assaults on their economic and cultural pursuits (Luckingham, 1994; Sanchez, 1994).

From the 1880s on, the solidification of barriers around racialized peoples accelerated the creation of ethnic enclaves,[20] whether Chinatowns, barrios, or reservations. These enclaves were essentially residential. Most people in them had to find work outside, in white neighborhoods or through seasonal or periodic migration to more distant jobs. An "ethnic economy"—the provision of goods and services largely to coethnics within the enclave—provided entrepreneurial or professional positions for a few people. Frequently these same individuals, often merchants in urban centers, played multiple roles as labor contractors and as "culture brokers" in local politics, much like compradores negotiating between the colonizers and the colonized. It is neither helpful nor appropriate to pin unitary labels such as "progressive," "acculturationist," "assimilationist," or "sellout" on these complex individuals. Our understandings of their "multipositionality," or the ways in which they interacted with different groups of people—from working class to social elite, from coethnics to whites and people from other racialized groups, and from men to women and children—reveals just how complicated their lives and positions were (Friday, 1994; Lewis, 1990; Lewis, 1993; Sanchez, 1993).

It is just as erroneous to think of these ethnic enclaves as wholly belonging to one group as it is to assume that the residents' lives did not carry them outside the enclaves, for at least four reasons. First, the "ethnic" enclaves were made up of vastly different peoples. "Chinatowns" contained emigrants from several ethnic groups as well as from various district and clan associations. Mexican Americans similarly divided themselves on the basis of emigrant district origins in addition to claims of "European" rather than "Indian" heritage, or timing of their migration. Federal policies of lumping together several tribes or bands on Native American reservations further exacerbated clan and family divisions as well as intergroup rivalries. Chinese American, Mexican American, and Native American (or even white) identities have been long in developing and will never be complete except in the eyes of outsiders who seek to lump people into racialized groups. The relative worth of each group has been measured against yardsticks that have changed dramatically over time (Cornell, 1990; Espiritu, 1992).

Second, ethnic enclaves often contained or at least were contiguous to populations of different racialized peoples that included working-class whites. In public places such as streets and parks, in restaurants, taverns, stores, and theaters, and in their places of work, racialized peoples came into regular contact with each other. While anecdotal evidence suggests some segregation, urban social landscapes forced interaction (Johnson, 1993, pp. 25–29). Even in rural settings such as reservations, social relations were never wholly contained within the supposed ethnic enclaves. People traveled great distances for work, school, or church affairs and made broader contacts. Leasing of reservation lands opened up interactions with a host of European American "ethnics" as well as with Asian immigrants and Asian Americans who sought to lease reservation land to escape state bans on alien landholding and leasing (U.S. House of Representatives, 1930; Nomura, 1987).[21]

Third, ethnic enclaves often became the imagined as well as real sites of white exotic and erotic tourism, contributing to the creation of what David Roediger has called a "mulatto culture" in another context (1994). Reservations became the imagined place of premodern society preserved. Beginning about the turn of the century, Boy Scout troops and other Indian hobbyists recreated what they believed to be "authentic" ceremonies and performed in costume. Hobbyists and other cultural "tourists" looted cultural sites during Indian arrowhead–hunting trips. By the 1920s, those activities transferred into a market for Indians of crafts and curios. While the exchange of goods by native peoples with "outsiders" was an old practice, that exchange in the early twentieth century symbolized a growing Native American dependence on the cash economy and a ritual consumption by whites of premodern culture. Women's participation in the production of curios often fit with earlier seasonal patterns of mixed subsistence and wage work at the same time that many established men's activities were circumscribed. The degree to which this reinforced or remade gender relations depended upon the particular culture of the Native American groups and the local economy. Nonetheless, the commercialization of Indian art had important consequences among Native Americans (Powers, 1988, pp. 557–561).

Chinatowns and barrios, although they were located within the urban context, had a much higher incidence of this type of tourism. Perhaps because whites tended to see them as antimodern places, they were viewed as "vice districts." The sale of bodies for sex, access to illegal and quasilegal drugs, and gambling were all a part of the exchange. Whites imagined the degradation of young girls and women and the fall of young men and married men in these enclaves, which justified their attack on the very victims of the segregated worlds. The white world could be maintained as good and pure only by its separation from the other, racialized world, which many whites identified as bad and impure. For their part, a great many residents of ethnic enclaves had little to do with the world whites imagined. When they did become involved in vice, they did so with two primary motives. One was to earn money: Few options other than poorly paid work existed for most racialized people, and participation in vice economies held at least the illusory promise of a way out of poverty. Another was to defy the definitions imposed by the oppressors' culture: The performance of "bad" roles became an act of resistance against the imagery of the oppressor. The blade cut both ways, though, for that performance confirmed the differentness of the racialized actor for many whites (Light, 1974; Lyman 1974; Sanchez, 1994; Wong, 1995).

Finally, just at the historical moment of their creation, these ethnic enclaves were beginning to break down as singular ethnogeographic entities. As urban centers in the West grew and expanded, some members of racialized groups began to live outside these segregated districts. Chinese and Japanese American entrepreneurs set up small service enterprises throughout urban areas and lived in or near their places of business, while their working-class, largely "bachelor" coethnics still lived in residential hotels and boarding houses on a seasonal basis in the older, segregated districts. Those districts continued to offer an important social nexus for the "ethnic" community, but urban growth mitigated their separative powers (Toll, 1996).[22]

Problematic as their construction might have been, between the 1880s and the 1920s Chinese Americans, Mexican Americans, and Native Americans found their lives increasingly circumscribed by ethnic enclaves. Yet the relatively few African American migrants and the comparatively recent Japanese immigrants faced significantly different circumstances. In urban settings, African Americans tried to carve out a social space between Mexican Americans, Asian Americans, and Native Americans. Some African Americans drew on notions of "backward," "Catholic Mexicans" as well as of "heathen Chinese" to differentiate themselves from those groups. In so doing, they played up their Protestant practices and their rights to citizenship. Yet while black city dwellers in Seattle, Portland, San Francisco, Los Angeles, Phoenix, and elsewhere faced tremendous economic discrimination and lived in increasingly segregated areas, they confronted outright, life-threatening physical violence less often than in the South. Amid the slim economic pickings, many western African Americans aspired to and attained a kind of middle-class life and community. Porters, janitors, religious leaders, and local newspaper publishers alike did their best to be "Victorian." The presence of other racialized peoples in much greater numbers made for economic competition and encouraged African Americans to leverage themselves against Asian Americans and Mexican Americans by claiming citizenship as their birthright. Thus, membership in a racialized community did not automatically create coalitions of "color" (Broussard, 1993; Daniels, 1980; Melcher, 1991; Taylor, 1994).

Japanese immigrants, most of whom entered the United States in the first two decades of the twentieth century, found a West of a much different character than had the Chinese before them. The Japanese entered almost directly into well-established, highly segmented labor markets. There they found themselves in intense competition for jobs with other racialized peoples and with recent European immigrants to the region. The Japanese responded by taking jobs at the extremely low pay offered by commercial farmers for harvest labor over the short run, just to get the work. In short order, though, they attempted to bring their wages up, sometimes through strikes, labor organization, and short-lived multiracial alliances. They also took jobs, sometimes in relatively new fields or particularly harsh work. Isolated railroad section handwork and sugar beet labor were two such examples (Almaguer, 1994; Ichioka, 1988; Marchak, 1987).

Japanese immigrants, partly because of timing which meant that other racialized groups often controlled the economies of the older segregated districts, led the way in the dispersal of the ethnic enclave. Japanese Americans did settle in certain districts, but those areas tended to be dominated by residential hotels whose patrons came from many groups and businesses in the "ethnic" or service economies. In Los Angeles, for example, the Nihonmachi (Japanese town) was more a collection of these hotels and businesses than it was an enclosed community. Other, smaller settlements dotted the Los Angeles basin, and many small, family-run businesses, especially stores, laundries, and restaurants, spread throughout a variety of neighborhoods. The pattern was much the same in Seattle, Portland, and other western cities. Rather than increased residential segregation in one "ghetto," the trend was toward dispersal (Warren 1986–1987).

In the first two decades of the twentieth century, a great many Japanese immigrants made the occupational transition from laborer to small-scale entrepreneur, which contributed to the pattern of residential dispersal throughout urban centers. Perhaps as many as one-fifth of all Japanese male immigrants also drew on family labor by bringing a wife, by various means, to the United States. Japanese men used this strategy to lessen the time they spent on "reproductive" labor, and the paid labor of women and children brought extra cash to the family. Particularly those family units among Japanese immigrants helped them move from wage laborers to farmers and small-scale entrepreneurs. The farm families sometimes gained small plots of land as an exchange for clearing larger tracts for European American farmers and other times through combined savings amassed by extended families or other immigrant networks. These strategies were so successful that they provided the very ammunition with which whites attacked Japanese. Whites complained that Japanese were too aggressive at driving wages down, or conversely, too active in striking and organizing. Their use of family labor and the fact that many immigrants upon marriage immediately began to have children caused an uproar among whites about high birthrates and unfair competition. Erroneous statistics and images of animal-like reproductive rates got paraded about as proof of a Japanese "takeover." National restrictions on Japanese male immigration, and later, on "picture brides," were the results. These were accompanied by state statutes barring Japanese and other "aliens" from holding land (Glenn, 1986; Matsumoto, 1993; Park et al., 1925; Tamura, 1993).

By the 1910s and 1920s, the West's capitalist transformation was well under way, with few locales left untouched. The "conquest" involved an ongoing struggle over control in which "whites" increasingly saw themselves in a unified position vis-à-vis people of color. Of course, white unity was problematic. In 1869, white women's achievement of suffrage in Wyoming—the first state in the nation to give women the vote—was gained through the unity of whites who feared the misdirection of newly enfranchised blacks, the encroachment of Chinese, and the unwillingness of Native Americans to cede lands and power. In granting white women the vote, the male political elite of the territory believed that white women would surely wish to protect themselves from the ravages of "race" and their votes would give Democrats the balance of power and end radical Republican influences. They were sorely disappointed when white women split along the same lines as white men (Scharff, 1995). The unity of whiteness was an elusive goal.

Ethnicity among European Americans remained a powerful dividing force. Much of the resistance to the anti-Chinese movement drew upon the strength of anti-Irish and anti-Catholic sentiments. Mormons in the West suffered tremendous resentment and even physical attacks for their beliefs and practices. Similarly, at the end of the nineteenth and the beginning of the twentieth centuries, it was not inevitable that Italian or Greek immigrants would join the ranks of whites any more than it was certain that Mexican Americans who identified themselves as Spanish would be typecast as Mexican (Leonardo, 1987; Limerick, 1992a; Peck, 1993; Smith, 1943). That one's entrance into the white camp assured greater privilege, assured that "human capital" investments might bring rewards, was an essential part of establishing hegemony. But as theorist Adam Przeworski has argued, hegemony rests on the consent of the exploited, who temporarily accept exploitation because of the real though slim likelihood that they can get ahead. Yet hegemony also depends on the unspoken power the dominant group holds: the threat of physical force, of outright coercion in order to maintain control (Przeworski, 1980). The less force is used, the more hegemonic is the control.

In the case of the West and its race relations, the multiplicity of racialized groups that could be divided against each other meant that whites could exert hegemony over this or that group even while using brute force against another group. The uneven and inconsistent application of force bolstered white hegemony. By the 1920s, though, an odd balance or "equilibrium" had been reached (Hoare and Smith, 1971).[23] The lands had long since been wrested from earlier inhabitants and their labors had been subsumed in a racially segmented capitalist economy. Immigration laws and barriers to citizenship and land ownership limited Asian American abilities to gain much political power within the United States. African Americans, few in number and relieved to achieve even the few advances available, were perhaps the most consenting of the groups as they struggled to carve out a space between whites and Asians Americans, Native Americans, and Mexican Americans. For the next two decades, white hegemony overlaid a site of intense racial competition as these various groups struggled with each other and with whites. Each group fought to improve its "position" whether or not that came at another group's expense.

"Wars of Maneuver," Racial Contestation, and Racial Suppressions

Borrowing Antonio Gramsci's language of class relations, Michael Omi and Howard Winant posit a stage in racial formations that they call a "war of maneuver" (Hoare 1994, pp. 80–81; Hoare and Smith, 1971, pp. 206–209). In the original argument, Gramsci explains that a war of maneuver takes place when the subordinate class (the proletariat) can only make frontal attacks on the dominant class (the bourgeoisie) because no mechanism exists for it to have a political influence. The subordinate class has to use "a kind of commando tactics . . . with great circumspection" to affect the political economy, but even then may meet with state repression. In more democratic moments, this gives way to a "war of position," when the subordinate class gains access to the political system of the dominant group and uses that access to effect change (Hoare and Smith 1971, pp. 230, 239).

In their work, Omi and Winant focus on racialized groups rather than classes. Prior to World War II, they argue, those groups were "banned from the political system and relegated to what was supposed to be a permanently inferior sociocultural status." The maneuvering came as they tried to "preserve and extend a definite territory, to ward off violent assault, and to develop an internal society as an alternative to the repressive social system they confront[ed]." In the postwar era, they hold that a war of position emerged in which racialized groups "sought to transform dominant racial ideology in the U.S." through political struggle that confronted the "racial state" (1994, pp. 80–81).

In their analysis, Omi and Winant give much more attention to the postwar positioning than they do the prewar maneuvers. Thinking in terms of maneuvering is useful for the prewar period, though one cannot stretch it back indefinitely. These wars of maneuver (the plural form better reflects the multiplicity of groups involved) certainly took place before the 1920s in the western United States, and indeed, were not unique to the West. Yet the series of state-sanctioned limitations on citizenship, redefinitions of those eligible for immigration, and controls on economic pursuits of the 1920s marked the culmination of programs against racialized peoples that until then had been piecemeal. Western variations of those programs were highly racialized in more complicated and ambiguous ways than those in other sections of the country.

In the West, the 1920s brought new levels of white hegemony and a new stage in race relations. Mexican, Filipino, and somewhat earlier, Japanese immigrants entered the region in greater numbers than ever before. To complicate matters, the racial competition their entrance engendered only intensified as time passed. Furthermore, the Depression and then World War II piqued white anxieties, unmasking the social controls inherent in hegemonic relations. During those years, whites condoned overt racial suppression rather than implicit coercion in their attempts to stabilize the social order in an unstable era. From the 1920s to the end of World War II, different racialized groups in particular locales at specific times managed to exert enough influence to at least gain a predominance over other racialized peoples as well as to exert some counterhegemonic pressures against whites.

Among the newer arrivals to the West, Japanese Americans rapidly carved out a sphere of considerable influence. Japanese immigrants began arriving in considerable numbers in the West in the late 1890s, first as a largely male, working-class migration, but then increasingly supplemented by the migration of men and women in the first two decades of the twentieth century. By the time of the 1924 Immigration Act, which banned further Asian immigration, including that of family members, as much as a fifth of Japanese immigrants had taken up some form of agriculture, from small truck farms to orchards of various sizes and large mono-crop agribusinesses. In concert with those enterprises in some locales, especially in Los Angeles and Seattle, Japanese Americans held a near monopoly on certain crops and their supporting enterprises, from their production (farm management and farm labor) to their distribution and marketing, and even the maintenance and supply of goods and services to those enterprises. Japanese Americans' resulting control over virtually every aspect of those economic pursuits afforded them a measure of achievement within that segment of the economy, protected the group as a whole from competition and discrimination in that context, and allowed them to resist white domination (Jiobu, 1988, pp. 353–367).

Robert M. Jiobu characterizes this degree of control and lack of a clear geographic enclave as "ethnic hegemony." Jiobu is primarily concerned with "how well an ethnic minority establishes an *economic niche* within a host society" in "ghettoized [ethnic enclaves] and non-ghettoized" situations. He distinguishes an ethnic hegemony from an ethnic enclave primarily on the basis of the former's lack of any tightly defined spatial components. In addition, the former need not be renewed by continued immigration, nor is human capital investment necessarily rewarded within the group context.[24]

The idea that a subordinated ethnic or racial group can exercise hegemony may be troubling for some.[25] The historical and contemporary evidence makes clear that an ethnic group, particularly one that has been racialized, never attains political or economic influence equal to that of whites. If the model is expanded beyond the creation of an economic niche, however, to embrace the fluid, shifting grounds of social conflicts, it holds greater promise. It goes beyond "ethnic enclave" theories or "social solidarity," for it incorporates how class, culture, and identity interact to create a group, and then how that group may use its internal, "spontaneous consent" to leverage itself against other racialized groups and offer opposition to the dominant group (Hoare and Smith, 1971, p. 12). (This is, in fact, what historian Kerby Miller has done in an examination of the formation of Irish American identity. [1990].) It asks, rather than assumes, how, why, and when identity formations occur but also attempts to discuss the broadly political ramifications of the assertion of ethnic hegemony for the particular "ethnic" group and for those with which it competes. The key question becomes how one group's ethnic hegemony acts as a counterhegemonic force while it effectively exercises relative power over other groups and within the group. Nonetheless, the concept should not be confused with the much stronger hegemony exercised by whites and must be applied with a continual eye to it.

A broader conceptualization of ethnic hegemony in the western United States in the 1920s and 1930s helps to illuminate race relations there. During this period, "new" groups of racialized immigrants entered the region, resulting in heightened levels of multiracial conflicts and cooperation. How particular racialized groups in particular locales established ethnic hegemonies and negotiated with whites for various political, economic, and social concessions forms the central focus of this section of the chapter. How whites responded and when they exercised racial suppression also will enter into discussion.

Jiobu's brief description of Japanese in California's agriculture is illustrative. Nearly half of all Issei and Nisei in California between 1920 and 1940 were engaged in some aspect of specialized agricultural production, supply, and marketing. The unity of ethnic enterprise protected the economic position of Japanese Americans; and although Jiobu does not elaborate on this point, as a result of this unity, Japanese held positions of power vis-à-vis other racialized people and whites. In relationships with the former, Japanese Americans occupied important segments of the agricultural labor force. Many were foremen and contractors, many had ties of mutual obligation with the farmers that ranged from the relatively weak, generic "ethnic" variety to direct ties of kinship. Japanese farm laborers were just as likely to line up against fellow Mexican, Filipino, Chinese, or white field workers as they were to stand up with them in labor disputes. In relationship to whites as a whole, a more or less unified presence allowed Japanese Americans to play white small farmers who wished to sell or lease marginal lands to Japanese Americans against whites who wished to restrict Japanese access to farmland for political and economic reasons. The result was the circumvention of alien land laws through the creation of a temporary arena of common interest between Japanese Americans and at least some whites (Jiobu, 1988).

The assertion of this type of ethnic hegemony by Japanese Americans brought similar, if fleeting moments of relative power so long as the group retained virtual or substantial control over a specific sector of the local economy.[26] In labor, for example, Japanese Americans exerted significant influence in the 1903 Oxnard sugar beet strike and the 1907 Rock Springs coal workers' strike; and on a more continual basis, on Hawaiian plantations and in Alaskan salmon canneries (Almaguer, 1994; Beechert, 1985; Friday, 1994; Ichioka, 1988; Takaki, 1983).

In many cases, however, the exertion of ethnic hegemony came at the expense of another group. This is not to forward a "zero sum" thesis suggesting that ethnic hegemony and class hegemony are mutually exclusive. Instead, I would suggest that the assertion of ethnic hegemony can have its own discriminatory and repressive consequences, even if unintended, because it involves the exercise of power. In urban Seattle before World War II, Japanese Americans ran a great many of the city's hotels and boarding houses for working-class people. (They depended heavily on the use of unpaid family labor, exploiting the labors of women and children.) Their group control of the hotels and a number of restaurants, barbershops, and mercantile stores meant that they garnered an inordinate proportion of working-class wages spent on room and board. (In this sense, the Japanese American businesses were much like their counterparts in the "Chinatowns" along the Sacramento River and San Joaquin River deltas, which have been described as "parasitic" in their relationship to the scores of Filipinos and Mexican Americans, as well as Chinese, who toiled in the region's agricultural harvests.) In Seattle, the Japanese Americans' strength in service-related fields forced the city's Central Labor Council to agree to an uneasy detente between its member unions and Japanese ethnic organizations. In certain cases it even involved official American Federation of Labor chartering of segregated local chapters for Japanese workers. As much competition as cooperation grew out of these segregated ethnic charters (Chu, 1970; Frank, 1994; Lukes and Okihiro, 1985; Miyamoto, 1984; Sone, 1979).

Japanese competition was not with whites but with other racialized groups, in settings like the Pacific Coast salmon canning industry. Prior to the unionization during the mid-1930s, the Chinese, the Japanese, and a couple of Filipino labor contractors controlled the bulk of the industry's labor markets. These contractors informally divided up the canneries among themselves and awarded special privilege to coethnic laborers although they always had the possibility of employing people from other ethnic groups to use as a coercive threat. Beginning in the 1930s, though, Filipinos used their numeric dominance in the industry, their status as U.S. nationals, and the "new" rules of New Deal agencies that interjected the government between labor and management to form the first unions. For Filipinos, early unionization was an attempt to wrest control of the labor market from Chinese and Japanese contractors—to break their respective ethnic hegemonies and to assert a new one (Friday, 1994, pp. 125–171).

Historical circumstances forced Filipinos to reconstruct an ethnic hegemony different from that held earlier by Chinese and Japanese. The passage of the 1934 Tydings-McDuffie Act, which declared Filipinos aliens and allowed only fifty of them per year to immigrate to the United States, while promising Philippine independence within twelve years, weakened the impetus for an ethnically exclusive Filipino labor organization. Filipinos could not effectively counter Japanese American strengths in the labor market, even though the latter amounted to roughly a quarter of all workers in agricultural industry. Instead of ethnically segregated locals, a vision of multiracial organizing won out, and the union that emerged represented all workers. Still, under the new union Filipinos managed to leverage themselves into central positions, largely taking control of former "Chinese" dominated canneries, while Japanese Americans maintained their representation at various canning locations until internment left Filipinos largely in control of the union (Friday, 1994).

For all of the relative power Filipinos exerted, the ability of the U.S. government to transform their status as nationals into that of "aliens" with the Tydings-McDuffie Act was a severe handicap. Filipinos had long used a two-pronged argument about shared Christian and progressive cultures in the U.S. and the Philippines. When they became foreigners in the legal sense, Filipinos tried to argue that their intermarriage with women who held American citizenship, that their raising of children with U.S. citizenship, and that their long stay in the U.S. entitled them to the rights of citizens—but all for naught. Politicians castigated Filipinos for their efforts to "step up" to a level equal to whites rather than "down" to the level of other racialized peoples, cast Filipinos as "oversexed," looked with disdain at miscegenation, and increasingly pushed Filipinos into a legal position that matched the popular perception of them as the latest "yellow" (or brown) peril (U.S. House of Representatives, Dec. 1937–Jan. 1938; and 1930).

In many respects, the circumstances Mexican Americans faced were similar to those confronted by Filipinos. Throughout the Southwest, Mexican Americans dominated certain segments of the labor market—especially in agriculture, mining, and urban service occupations. Yet Mexican Americans were not confined to the Southwest, nor were they trapped in agricultural or mine labor. Many migrated northward, first to agricultural harvests in the upper Midwest, and from there to industrial jobs in Chicago, Detroit, and other urban centers. San Francisco labor contractors hired hundreds for salmon cannery work in Alaska. By the 1930s and early 1940s, many also found work in Northwest agriculture (Friday, 1994, pp. 150–151; Gamboa, 1990; Vargas, 1993).

In the interwar years, middle-class voluntary associations pursued an assimilationist agenda in order to gain political and economic benefits in the United States. Yet up to the 1940s, those middle-class groups represented far less than a majority of Mexican Americans and were not always fully united behind attempts at Americanization. Instead, large proportions of Mexican Americans and Mexican immigrants, especially those of the working class, considered themselves resident aliens and took pride in maintaining and recreating a distinctive culture. Much more than some nostalgic grasping at the past, this transborder culture, though it did have its divisions and conflicts, provided some measure of power and effectiveness. Mexican Americans and Mexican immigrants drawing on family, friendship, and community ties joined *mutualistas* (mutual aid societies) and built alliances with labor unions on both sides of the border as well as with the Mexican government to assert power in the Southwest. To a degree, they were successful (Barrera, 1985; Bustamante, 1995; Gutierrez, 1995; Sanchez, 1993; Weber, 1994; Zamora, 1993).[27]

By looking across the border, however, Mexican Americans inadvertently fed their construction by whites as "aliens." Among whites, this construction was quite powerful. Even union leaders fell prey to it. In 1939, legislative representative for the American Federation of Labor Paul Scharrenberg explained that in places like the copper mining districts of the Southwest, "a great many aliens, principally Mexicans, [are] employed" and that "aliens predominate in some of our unions." He made these claims in spite of official counts that placed the foreign-born Mexican population of those mining districts at less than a thousand out of a total Mexican and Mexican American population of about 63,000 (Bustamante, 1995; p. 81; U.S. Senate, 1940, p. 15).

Yet outside the mining districts, the 25,000 or so Mexican immigrants who entered the United States each year during the 1920s contributed to the alien image and created tensions between the immigrants and longtime U.S. residents and their U.S.-born children, in large part because Anglos lumped them all together indiscriminately. Like Filipinos, Mexican Americans held a desire to define self-worth in their own culturally specific ways, and believed that their many years of work and residence in the United States should stand as the basis for fair treatment and basic political and economic rights. As with Filipinos, federal, state, and local governments refused to recognize these claims. In the 1940s and 1950s, contradictory federal activities like the Bracero Program and Operation Wetback only added to state policies that reinforced Anglo images of Mexican Americans as "aliens" (Gutierrez, 1995).[28]

An ironic and significant difference emerges in the comparison of Filipinos and Mexican Americans to African Americans in the region. Nationally and in the West, African Americans had available to them a broad spectrum of voluntary associations that ran the political gamut, from programs endorsed by Booker T. Washington, W.E.B. DuBois, and A. Philip Randolph to Father Divine and Marcus Garvey. Historian Quintard Taylor has suggested that involvement in these voluntary associations had even deeper meaning for African Americans in the West than for those in the North or the South. Each association had to fulfill multiple social roles, in part because pre–World War II western black populations were too small to support extensive, multiple social organizations. In particular, Garveyism—though it may seem at odds with urban western black aspirations for a "Victorian" lifestyle—was especially attractive, for it catered to the establishment of black enterprises and offered an immersion in, or at least a connection to, an African American cultural core otherwise largely absent in the West (Broussard, 1993; Taylor, 1994; Tolbert, 1994). In this sense, Garveyites openly celebrated the cultural, political, and economic consequences of being black, just as Mexican Americans or Filipinos celebrated their respective cultures. Yet whites had much more difficulty remaking African Americans into legal "aliens." Much the same held for Native Americans. The result was that two large racialized groupings emerged in the interwar West—one of "foreigners," the other of "Americans." Their legal status notwithstanding, American-born Asian Americans and Mexican Americans got lumped together with immigrants in the former category.

Even within those two larger groups, separate racializations brought with them different racial suppressions. The federal government never levied racially restrictive immigration and citizenship laws against Mexican Americans to the degree that it did against Asian Americans. Instead, up to the 1950s, most racial suppressions of Mexican Americans came through state and local actions, many of them extralegal. Among the more visible of these were the "repatriations" of the Depression, which sent an average of almost 80,000 people to Mexico annually under varying degrees of coercion. (These were not official deportations, which would have entailed either extensive individual hearings or some clear executive or legislative action, as was the case with Japanese American internment.) Only the Emergency Farm Labor Program, the Bracero Program, Operation Wetback, the 1950 Internal Security Act, and the 1952 McCarren-Walter Immigration Act had direct federal implications for Mexican Americans. The first three were federal programs directed specifically at "Mexicans," whereas the provisions of the last two were not clearly aimed at either Mexican immigrants or Mexican Americans (Gutierrez, 1995, pp. 170–174). Ultimately, though, politicians sensitive to the power of white voters directed those laws also against Mexican Americans.

With the onset of the Great Depression, though, the "repatriation" of Mexican Americans had the effect of reducing the population as well as symbolizing the power of Anglos over Mexican Americans. The fact that Mexican Americans looked to the Mexican consulate to bring influence to bear in repatriation, the Zoot Suit riots, and labor relations only reinforced the image of Mexican Americans as "outsiders." Recent work on the Fair Employment Practices Committee in the Southwest, for example, demonstrates that racial discrimination against Mexican Americans was treated as a local problem *and* as a matter for the State Department rather than as a manifestation of larger patterns of historical, racial discrimination (Daniels, 1991). Wartime labor recruitment and the Cold War extension of the "good neighbor policy" contributed to this construction of the "Mexican problem." According to historian David Gutierrez, this overlap of Mexican American and Mexican immigrant issues created a "twilight zone" that made it "virtually impossible for them to collectively engage in effective political or social action in American society" (Gutierrez, 1995). Kith and kin networks, community organizations, labor unions, and the like did deal with Mexican American civil rights, but accomplished more at the local level than the national level. Not until the social movements of the 1960s began to address Mexican American and Mexican immigrant issues as a whole were Mexican Americans able to begin to impress upon whites that the problems they faced were part and parcel of racism within the United States rather than necessarily a matter of immigration and foreign affairs (Barrera, 1985, pp. 12–18; *Race Relations,* Jan. 1947, pp. 175–177; and April 1947, pp. 298 and 325; Schorr, 1946, pp. 412–413).

Even Native Americans during this period exercised some measure of ethnic hegemony, labored under ethnic competition, and suffered racial suppressions. In southeast Alaska, Tlingit, Haida, and Tsimshian peoples joined together in 1913 to form the Alaska Native Brotherhood (ANB), and in 1915, the Alaska Native Sisterhood (ANS). At first the two groups were interested most in inculcating Christianity among their members, but in the 1920s the ANB and ANS shifted their focus to civil rights. ANB and ANS members successfully fought for the franchise before the 1924 federal act that granted U.S. citizenship to Native Americans. With their voting bloc, ANB and ANS members found political representation in the Territorial government. In the late 1920s, they used their clout to desegregate public schools in Southeast Alaska. In the mid-1930s, they began legal suits that formed the basis for the 1971 Alaska Native Claims Settlement Act, and in the late 1930s, used the Wheeler-Howard Act and the Wagner Act to argue that the ANB and ANS had the legitimate right to act as a labor union to represent the interests of fishers and cannery hands. All of these represented assertions of ethnic hegemony, and some—such as the ANB-led labor union effort—were attempts to exercise power over other racialized groups—in this case, the same Asian American (particularly Filipino) unionists who had just gained control of the labor market by breaking independent Chinese and Japanese contractors and establishing a broad multiethnic union under the charter of the Congress of Industrial Organizations. ANB unionists found that they had much in common with white resident Alaskans against the "outsider" Asian American unionists; yet even so, ANB forces split over the choice between independent organization or affiliation with the American Federation of Labor, which also sought to unite whites and Native Alaskans (Friday, 1994).

As was the case in Alaska, throughout the West the establishment of tribal governments under the Indian Reorganization Act (IRA), which had been intended as an assimilationist device, quickly developed into vehicles for the political pursuit of sovereignty. Legal challenges to treaty violations and new assertions of treaty rights accelerated and pitted IRA tribal governments against the various western states. Suppression of these assertions of power followed in short order. The states mounted substantial resistance to legal challenges, and the cases have dragged on for more than a half century with no definitive end in sight. Opponents of Native American sovereignty designed and supported federal programs to force the disappearance of Native American tribes and individuals. Federal urban relocation programs during World War II were one such effort, and the "termination" of federal recognition that followed in the 1950s was another. Even the Indian Claims Commission (ICC), well-intentioned as it might have been, ultimately represented an attempt to end all negotiations by paying off Native Americans for treaty violations. Originally intended to last only several years, the ICC persisted for a quarter century.[29]

The efforts to assimilate Native Americans, to repatriate Mexican Americans, and to make Filipinos aliens were suppressions of racialized groups' attempts to assert power. In this sense, the internment of West Coast Japanese Americans was also a statement of white supremacy. After internment, Japanese Americans remained understandably cautious about open assertions of power for nearly two decades. The circumstances of one young Nisei are illustrative of the pernicious nature of this suppression. Fascinated by music, this boy took into the internment camp several of his favorite jazz records and his trombone. The records he nearly wore out, and one can guess that his trombone playing must have nearly done the same to his neighbors in the thin-walled camp setting. Upon his release from camp, he began touring with jazz bands made up largely of African American musicians. Fearful of the discrimination he might suffer as a Japanese American, he passed himself off as Harry Lee, a Chinese American. Not until some time later did this man finally enroll at Berkeley under his real name—Harry Kitano. Through it all, Kitano still harbored some measure of pride in being Japanese; but he did not publicly express this sentiment until decades later (Kitano, 1993, pp. 52, 70, 164–165).[30]

Kitano's efforts to pass as Chinese are particularly poignant because some Chinese attempted to profit from U.S. hostilities with Japan in the 1930s and 1940s in order to strengthen their own position in the United States and to cement their Chinese American identity. During the Pacific War (1937–1945), Chinese Americans in the West (as well as in New York City) openly celebrated their Chinese heritage, openly raised funds to "save China," formed militia units and women's drum corps, and joined the U.S. military— in the belief that they could "save" themselves as Chinese Americans in the process.

To some degree, though, their linkage of their status in the United States to the fate of China contributed to continued views of Chinese Americans as "foreigners." Their testimony before congressional committees earned American-born Chinese the epithet of "pseudo-Americans." When Congress debated rescinding Chinese exclusion in 1943 largely as a wartime propaganda tool, Representative William P. Elmer of Missouri complained that the bill promised to bring "millions of aliens" into the United States and pointedly asked: "Since when did the Chinese devils become Chinese saints?" (Spivak, 1943, pp. 740–741). Many white workers were no more enthusiastic. One member of Seattle's Building Services Employees Industrial Union complained to Senator Warren G. Magnuson, a sponsor of the effort to end Chinese exclusion: "Those who favor its repeal should remember that while the Chinese are good Allies now, they are still Orientals in thought and action" (McKinney, Sept. 17, 1943). The construction of Chinese as inscrutable Orientals, whether abroad or in the United States, clearly persisted despite changes in legislation.

Although racialized groups in the West pursued significant political organization, particularly in the realms of labor and voluntary ethnic associations, they were unable to gain access to the political system and to effect meaningful change. Racial contestations met with racial suppressions. Efforts to exert ethnic hegemony accomplished short-term goals but did not place racialized groups on a par with whites either in political power or in social status. In short, racialized groups could only engage in "wars of maneuver." It is ironic that Robert Park, Paul S. Taylor, and Carey McWilliams, some of the foremost authorities on race of their day, all made forceful arguments that race relations in the western states were an essential part of the national story.[31] Nonetheless, the social crises generated by depression, war, and generational shifts created tensions and forced a reordering of power relationships that began in the 1940s and muted those earlier sociological observations (Conzen, Gerber, Morawska, and Pozzetta, 1989). It took a quarter of a century or more for those notions to be rediscovered.

Reconstructing Hegemony:
Privileging the Subordinate Racialized Position

In the context of the marginalization of Asian Americans, Mexican Americans, and Native Americans, African Americans in the West began to attract and assert new levels of attention. On December 23, 1943, *Business Week* featured an article about the "Negro problem" in the West. New black and white migrants to the region found themselves in competition for jobs and at odds not only with previous white residents but also with earlier African American migrants to the region. The strife was no worse than in other regions. The major issue was that the large "new" migration of African Americans presented "a challenge to existing power alignments" in the region (Burgess, 1949, pp. 10–11; Lemert and Rosberg, 1946, p. 136). As historian Marilynn Johnson argues, wartime black migration to the West "provoked fears of social unrest and a disintegration of established racial boundaries . . . [that] would become the most troublesome legacy of the War" (Johnson, 1993, pp. 4–5). Shifts in the political economy of the West, resulting demographic changes, and the political potential that African Americans brought to the region aided them in establishing an ethnic hegemony over other racialized people, although African Americans also continued to suffer under white oppression.

The newly established military-industrial (and urban) complex of the wartime and Cold War West funneled millions of dollars into the region's cities, causing massive demographic changes. In World War II, nearly 10 percent of total federal expenditures went to California alone and a third of that to the "metropolitan-military" complex in San Francisco (Johnson, 1993, pp. 8, 31).[32] Between 1940 and 1950, the region's population increased by 40 percent in spite of a brief postwar slump in growth—the highest increase since the first decade of the century. Especially California boomed during the 1940s, when the already populous state witnessed a 53.3 percent increase in the number of its residents. The African American presence in the West increased even more dramatically. In California, which had the highest concentration of African Americans in the West, the black population rose from 124,000 in 1940 to 462,000 in 1950. In Washington, another important site of federal investments, the state's African American residents increased in number from 7,000 to 31,000 in that same decade. Even apparently bucolic Oregon, despite the loss of the shipyards at Vanport to postwar layoffs and the 1948 flood, registered an overall increase in black population from 3,000 to 12,000, as many who had been in the shipyards chose to remain in the Portland area (Taylor, 1977, pp. 211–215; U.S. Department of Commerce, 1975).

In contrast to those increases, census figures for other "nonwhites" suggest much less of a boom. In California, that category increased from 186,000 to 209,000 in 1950. Although the numbers indicate a 12.4 percent jump over 1940, it was more than four times less the growth rate for the state as a whole and many times less than the stunning increase of nearly 275 percent in the African American population. With most Filipinos and Chinese still barred from entry by immigration restrictions, relatively high male to female ratios in those same populations, and miscegenation laws in place in California, little growth was seen by way of "natural" population increases, intermarriage, and immigration. Federal recruitment of Mexicans brought many "aliens" into the region, but not as permanent residents. The internment and subsequent release of Japanese Americans did not return as many to California as had been there before the war. As a result, longtime western residents, white and nonwhite, suddenly saw concentrations of African Americans where few blacks had been before. Similarly, the new migrants to the region carried with them their own notions of race relations and found those patterns all too easy to act upon in the new setting.

In spite of the popular imagery that black and white racial conflict was imported to the region by newly arriving southern whites and blacks, the evidence is contradictory. The source of negative imagery surrounding southern whites came from the 1920s and 1930s migrations of "Okies" that generated so much class anxiety in California. This was easily transferred to new wartime migrants in general even with the selective dispersal of southern white migrants. Many new arrivals to central California came from the South, but they amounted to no more than a quarter of all newcomers. In other regions, such as the Pacific Northwest, most of the migrants came from the upper and central Midwest states. Southern California, especially

Los Angeles, was the most "cosmopolitan," drawing migrants fairly evenly from across the country (Johnson, 1993, pp. 41–59). The new arrivals, although they certainly brought their own "racial baggage" with them, were not solely responsible for its promulgation. Quintard Taylor notes that longtime residents of the region, especially white unionists, struggled to maintain a type of segregation that had existed for some time (Burgess, 1949, pp. 71–80, 88; Schmid, June 1946, pp. 128–132, and March 1945, pp. 14–15; Taylor, 1977, pp. 210–211; Wiley, 1949, p. 97).

The debate over the origins of prejudice matters much less than the context in which those notions were acted upon. As David Montejano has noted, for Mexican Americans in Texas the midcentury shift from agricultural production to urban, industrial, and service economies intensified racial competition. In the West a tremendous rural to urban shift took place under the guise of wartime migration. In locales of specific wartime industries, nearly two-thirds of the newcomers were likely to come from rural settings (Reuss, 1944, p. 25). When these new immigrants entered the urban economy, they found themselves in competition for jobs as they had not in more segregated rural settings. The "peace structure" that had been in place in their previous worlds did not clearly apply in the urban, industrial environment.

In spite of its apparent atypicality, the history of Pasco, Washington, during this period is instructive. Prior to World War II, Pasco was a small agricultural transportation and marketing hub on the banks of the Columbia River in the east-central portion of Washington. After the U.S. government chose a site near the town for an atomic processing operation, Pasco was transformed. Tens of thousands of workers poured into the area in 1943 and 1944 to assemble the Hanford nuclear facility. Contractors demanded so much labor that DuPont resorted to recruiting African Americans from the south. Uneasy city officials in Pasco convinced DuPont to guarantee round-trip train fare so that blacks could easily depart after construction was completed (Burgess, 1949).

When construction stopped in 1944, some African Americans left, but they did not return to the South. Instead, most went to Portland, Seattle, San Francisco, or Los Angeles. Pasco's black population briefly dropped to perhaps a third of its wartime peak, but then renewed hydroelectric dam building on the Columbia River reinvigorated the town and bolstered the reemployment of many African Americans. Federal involvement thus left Pasco a changed town. Whereas in 1940 it had slightly less than 4,000 residents, only 27 of whom were black and some 57 who appeared as "other" in the census, by 1948 estimates placed the total population at about 10,000, including 2,000 to 2,500 African Americans. One researcher noted at the time: "One cannot drive through Pasco and its surrounding area, read a local newspaper, or talk with local citizens without realizing that a critical racial situation is present" (Burgess, 1949, p. 2).

White residents perceived the very presence of blacks in the town as a problem. They felt that African Americans were "intruding" on their social space. More than half believed that segregation would solve some of the problems. Indeed, that same group thought that there was no segregation in the city. Virtually every African American, and the several sociologists conducting field surveys at the time, agreed that the town was highly segregated. In spite of a long-standing state statute against discrimination on the basis of race, color, or creed in public accommodations and several court rulings that upheld the law, whites in Pasco had put into effect Jim Crow practices in public accommodations (restaurants, stores, theaters), housing, and transportation. Not only did some 80 percent of whites believe that African Americans received fair treatment in the town, but slightly more than a third saw no contradiction between democratic practices and "keeping Negroes in their place" (Burgess, 1949, pp. 3, 48, 71–80).

Because of Pasco's striking transformation and its centrality to the new "defense" needs of the emerging Cold War, racial tensions in the town drew the attention of scholars as well as of national African American organizations. In 1948, the NAACP organized a Tri-Cities Branch that encompassed Pasco, Kennewick, and Richland (even though most African Americans lived in east Pasco). In that same year, Thurgood Marshall protested to Washington state officials about mistreatment of blacks in Pasco, asking the state to address the problem before a potential race riot erupted (Taylor, 1977, p. 221; Wiley, 1949, p. 135). Simultaneously, the Seattle Urban League launched a series of investigations regarding General Electric's employment practices at the nearby Hanford plant.[33] Neither organization transformed race relations in the town; but their involvement demonstrates the ways in which African Americans in the West used national organizations to exert political pressure.[34]

Observers of race relations in Pasco made only the briefest, passing references to Native Americans, Asian Americans, or Mexican Americans in the town despite the fivefold increase in the numbers of these groups. The rapid appearance and high proportions of African Americans and newly arrived "whites" understandably upset the existing social hierarchy and refocused the debate along a black-white axis. Nonetheless, Pasco was an exaggeration rather than an exception, for much the same reordering of social relations took place in rural settings as well as in larger urban centers throughout the West.

In Butte County, California, during 1946, the forty nut and fruit orchardists in the Growers' Farm Labor Association (GFLA) faced a record almond crop, high yields and prices for their other produce, and a shortage of labor. A largely "Mexican" workforce had come to the county but had begun to move on before the nut harvests to other jobs, harvesting other crops at better pay. The GFLA looked 200 miles to the southwest, to the Emergency Farm Labor Program (EFLP) in the San Francisco-Oakland area, for help. EFLP officials, in turn, connected the growers with ten "part-time preachers" and labor contractors in the African American community of Richmond, California. Richmond had been a major site of wartime black employment, but defense layoffs in the postwar period and a reluctance of African Americans to leave western urban areas resulted in high unemployment. The GFLA and federal officials arranged for the recruitment of up to 300 of Richmond's African Americans to supplement the basic harvest labor force of about 1,300 workers, based in part on the EFLP estimates that the 1946 harvest in Butte county would require about 1,700 laborers (Johnson, 1993; Record, 1951, pp. 95–101, 129–131, 133).

For African Americans in the postwar West, agricultural field work was an option of "last resort," and the GFLA had trouble finding many Richmond residents willing to make the trip. The initial group of black recruits who showed up amounted to only 80, and not more than 125 were in the county at any one time in the 1946 season. Still, the prospect of African Americans among the harvest laborers caused a widespread panic among many growers outside the GFLA and especially with the townspeople of Chico, the largest urban center in the county. Whites in the area believed this small group of recruited workers housed at the Chico Fair Grounds by the GFLA to be the advance guard of a "tidal wave of color that was sweeping up from the Bay Area" in the wake of defense plant layoffs. White fears were numerous: Blacks might be "incompetent" laborers, they might be "thieves" ready to prey upon open rural whites, they might attack white women, or worse yet, they might stay. Most whites in Chico believed that "a lot of race trouble" would result from the presence of blacks in the town. It did. Unable to stop the labor migration, whites in Chico turned to displaying "White Trade Only" signs in the windows of their businesses. White property owners even drafted racially restrictive covenants into their deeds. Before the summer 1946 arrival of the "outside laborers," whites in Chico had largely overlooked African American residents in the town. Some longtime black residents complained that the migrants from Richmond upset the racial order, driving all African Americans, in the eyes of whites, down into the same category as "Mexicans, prisoners of war, and Hindus" who had been used by growers as harvest laborers. As observers in the national black press noted, white Chico residents were attempting to apply the same "caste lines and caste distinctions" to African Americans that had been applied to Chinese, Filipinos, and South Asians. The press account assured readers that Chico was not an isolated case and that these circumstances were repeated throughout California and the West (Record, 1951).

Chico's story illustrates the complexities of class and race relations, of urban and rural economies in conflict, and supports David Montejano's contention that a "provincial thesis"—that is, attention to the uneven capitalist development of a region—is just as useful in explaining race relations as

macro-level analyses such as world systems theory or notions of urbanization and industrialization (1987, pp. 316–318). Provincialism, if taken to
mean attention to different constructions of race, of different racializations,
proves quite useful as a framework for analysis. This concept enhances the
understanding that beyond cultural distinctions lay very different avenues to
power, to the political system. In the same vein, the editors of *The Crisis*, in
publishing the Chico story, meant their statements about western "caste
lines" to be taken more as a motivator for political action and as a warning
than for as a description of a fait accompli (Record, 1951).

In the larger western cities, from San Diego to Seattle, race relations were
complicated and contradictory. Nisei war service and citizenship and "ethnic" identity politics for other racialized groups stood alongside Zoot Suit
"riots," the Bracero Program, and internment. Yet as they had in Pasco and
Chico, whites in the West increasingly lamented the disordering of the social
hierarchy that they attributed to African American migrations. Some city officials explained that although "older" groups such as "the large Mexican
population" had "been absorbed, and we have no problem with them," the
new black migrants were "unassimilable." These officials called for a cessa-
tion of the in-migrations "until such time as these people can be properly absorbed into the community" (*Race Relations*, June 1946, p. 319).

As in Chico, whites could not stop the black migration. As a result, some
whites tried to restore segregation through the use of restrictive covenants
directed particularly at African Americans but generally against all racialized
peoples as well as Jews. Local courts upheld restrictive covenants. The battle
lines for the next two decades were drawn; not between whites and nonwhites, but between blacks and whites, for court actions depended upon extensive political organization directed toward city, county, state, and federal
institutions and upon the ability of the particular groups to have an impact.[35]
By default, African Americans were the only group available at the time.
Asian Americans, Mexican Americans, and Native Americans, though they
had achieved high levels of political organization, had not achieved the *national* sway, limited though it might have been, of organizations such as the
NAACP, the Urban League, or the network of black churches. Each of
those groups also had to contend with an "alienation" or "marginalization"
inapplicable to blacks.

The approaches that unions took provide an example of how local institutions were affected by national organizations. In the 1930s, Communist party
members and other leftists led the way in bringing white labor to the table
with racialized peoples. Because the latter had been so poorly treated in the labor markets and because so many unions excluded them in spirit or letter, they
"bargained collectively" through community labor contractors, company
unions, or fully segregated locals. After 1936, the competition that arose between the Congress of Industrial Organizations (CIO) and the American Fed-

eration of Labor (AFL), combined with the CIO's attention to race (condoned by left-leaning organizers and officials, and made imperative by the base of workers that CIO locals had to organize), forced AFL unions to reconsider their racial policies. By the end of World War II, both the CIO and the AFL had in place programs to account for race, though these were often resisted by many white union members. The unions took different approaches to the question of race: CIO unions tended to encourage integration, whereas the AFL chartered racially homogeneous locals (Friday, 1996b).

In the West, these new policies encouraged a dramatic shift in the relationships between racialized peoples and organized labor. It was not an easy transition. On the local level, many white unionists steadfastly resisted the switch. In the International Longshoremen's and Warehousemen's Union, generally recognized as a leader in interracial organizing on the West Coast and Hawaii, the Portland local resisted the entrance of blacks until 1961 (Nelson, 1988; Rosswurm, 1992; Taylor, 1977, pp. 210–211). Elsewhere in the West, the competition between the AFL and the CIO was connected with competition between factions in the communities of racialized peoples. Until about 1948, though, it looked as if multiracial unions might be possible. The full-blown emergence of the Cold War and anticommunist pogroms forced labor unions at the national level to take new directions. Loose, localized control of organizing gave way to more careful control at the upper echelons. This translated into the narrowing of "race" from its multiple local manifestations to a polarized vision of the "national" black-and-white construction. Non–African Americans, in this sense, were the last organized and the first ignored.

Between 1948 and 1954, left-led unions, which had already alienated a goodly portion of African Americans with their wartime "sacrifice" of civil rights to the "fight against fascism," continued to organize and represent many racialized peoples, but concentrated their defensive energies on the symbolic fight for unity between blacks and whites. At this time the unions, including a number of CIO affiliates and most AFL affiliates, conducted their own internal antileftist coups and purges. The CIO expelled those affiliates that refused to participate in the purge. By the time the CIO and the AFL merged in 1955, organized labor's attention to the "racial question" was severely limited, even in respect to African Americans.[36] The narrowing of attention to African Americans and then the diffusion of that limited focus reflected broader changes in western race relations as well as the manner in which national organizations redirected the discussion at the local level in the West.

Federal agencies charged with assuring economic equality dealt with the multiracial West even more poorly than organized labor. Hearings held by the Committee on Fair Employment Practice (CFEP) are illustrative. When the CFEP convened hearings, which were more public and influential than its investigations, its officials invariably privileged African American concerns in the shipyards, aerospace, and other government contract–dependent industries in Seattle, Portland, San Francisco, and Los Angeles. In the Southwest, CFEP-conducted investigations of labor practices affecting Mexican American miners received some attention, but the Committee held no formal hearings and took very limited action. Federal officials took an approach that limited Mexican American concerns to an individual level rather than defining them as group or racial concerns—a status reserved for the interests of African Americans and Native Americans. Competition for authority within the federal government, particularly between the State Department and CFEP, further watered down federal responses. Moreover, the location of the greatest political influence in the State Department largely nullified the efforts of CFEP officials in the Southwest. Only vague, voluntary compliance measures by mining companies resulted from CFEP activities in the Southwest (Daniels, 1991; *Race Relations*, 1943, December, p. 18, and 1944, Feb.-March, pp. 12–13; May, p. 18; Aug.-Sept., p. 1; and Dec., p. 18; Taylor, 1977).

At the same time, Asian Americans and Native Americans fared worse. Federal agencies charged with assisting them faced dismantlement. The War Relocation Authority (WRA), which ran an extensive propaganda program to smooth the reentry of Japanese Americans into postwar society, barely outlasted the war and had only begun to implement its programs before its demise (Leonard, 1992, pp. 226–276, 314–345; *Race Relations*, June 1946, p. 358).[37] The Bureau of Indian Affairs (BIA), just as problematic in its activities as the WRA, oversaw two key programs—urban relocation and termination—designed to end federal assistance and support for Native Americans. Supporters of relocation believed it an effective device for "modernizing" Indian peoples. They held the notion that if they placed Indians in urban centers and arranged for their initial housing in the city and employment in industry, then Indians could be assimilated into "modern" urban society—just as nineteenth-century officials believed that the imposition of land ownership, commercial agriculture, and domestic and industrial "arts" would result in assimilation. Supporters of urban relocation did not foresee cultural persistence, the emergence of new ethnic identities, and discrimination in labor markets (Weibel-Orlando, 1997).

The now infamous policy of the 1950s was an attempt at forced assimilation on a much grander scale than relocation: Through the dispersal of tribal holdings to individuals, the withdrawal of federal assistance programs, and the nullification of treaty status, the policy was aimed at transforming whole reservations and tribal groups rather than individuals. Between 1945 and 1968, the set of federal programs now informally known as "Termination" affected an estimated 109 tribes, rancherias, and pueblos; almost 12,000 people, in all. Although this amounted to only about 3 percent of federally recognized Indians, the implications of the policies were ominous. Quite early in the process, support among Native Americans for Termination quickly dissipated, and a great many of the policy's non-Indian supporters backed away as well. Although the policy had dire effects on those "terminated," it also had the unintended consequence of strengthening pan-Indian or supra-tribal identity and politics in addition to generating a greater sympathy and support from whites. By the early 1960s, the federal government had all but abandoned Termination, though the policy remained officially in effect until the end of the decade (Blackhawk, 1995; Fixico, 1986; *Race Relations*, Aug.-Sept. 1945, pp. 34–35, March 1947, p. 232, April 1947, p. 278, and March 1948, pp. 144–145; Wilkinson and Briggs, 1979).

In contrast, the federal and local governments took much more supportive positions, relatively speaking, for African Americans than for other racialized groups. African Americans' recognition of the power of their votes was a key factor. In the 1944 elections, black organizations began to realize that in northern and western cities, their votes could be decisive in the outcomes (*Race Relations*, Aug.-Sept., 1944, p. 1). Suddenly, where politicians previously had paid little attention to African Americans, they began to listen. At the community level in the West, African Americans demanded and received representation on Civic Unity Councils, which were designed to combat segregation in housing and in schools as well as to address other issues of health and welfare. While these committees might also have Japanese American, Chinese American, Mexican American, and Native American members, their influence was limited in comparison to that of African Americans, who brought significant blocs of voters to the bargaining table (*Race Relations*, Dec. 1944, p. 18, Feb.-March 1944, pp. 12–13, Oct. 1946, pp. 78, 83–85, and April 1947, p. 278).

Especially in California, African Americans became politically more visible as city, county, and state executives began to appoint blacks to higher positions—for example, on prison boards and housing authorities and in the office of the attorney general. Many city mayors formed special advisory commissions on race relations and civil rights, which were often staffed largely by African Americans. African Americans and their organizations, from the NAACP and the Urban League to community churches, clearly stood out above the crowd of racialized groups (*Race Relations*, May 1947, p. 18, Aug.-Sept. 1945, p. 3, and Jan. 1946, p. 166).

By using local events, such as the plight of Emmett Till and the Montgomery bus boycotts, and tying them to civil rights issues, African Americans in the West convinced many, black and white, that theirs was *the* national race relations issue (Sitkoff, 1993, pp. 37–60). With their growing influence on local and even national politics, blacks carefully guarded and cultivated their base of strength during the ensuing decades. One incident that occurred in Seattle between 1962 and 1963 is illustrative. During that period, Mayor Gordon S. Clinton set up a Human Rights Commission after African American community leaders there forced him into action. Clinton miscalculated, though, when he appointed only two blacks to the commission and named Japanese American Philip Hayasaka as executive secretary. The Reverend Mance Jackson, one of the two key organizers of the initial protest that had forced the mayor's hand, declared that members of the African American community "feel that in his recommendations the mayor has closed his channel of communications with the Negro community and that his action shows he is no longer willing to let the Negro take an active part in reaching solutions to inequality" (Taylor, 1977, p. 250). The incident antagonized Seattle's black leaders, whose protests suggest that African Americans expected representation and the leading positions on such commissions. Yet the incident also reveals that after nearly two decades of blacks' occupying a privileged if subordinate position in western racial politics, a more complicated political landscape had begun to emerge.

At first slowly, but with increasing regularity by the mid-1960s, Mexican Americans and Asian Americans operated out of local power bases to assert some degree of power and demand attention. But they did so out of coalition-building efforts rather than by sheer numbers. For Mexican Americans, the necessity of coalition building became clear as early as 1947, when Edward R. Royobal ran for a Los Angeles city council seat but lost. Between then and 1949, when Royobal won a seat, his supporters within the Mexican American community linked up with the Progressive Party, which had many Jewish members, and with organized labor to gain the post. Royobal's election signaled that in Los Angeles, as in much of the West, racialized groups standing by themselves had little chance of gaining political influence. Western cities and states were not split into competing European American ethnic political machines with which racialized people had to ally themselves. Whites in the West were more unified than in eastern and midwestern cities, forcing racialized groups to form coalitions. Yet because Asian Americans and Mexican Americans faced so many "roadblocks to political power," argues political scientist Raphael J. Sonenshein, "the eventual leadership of the progressive movement in Los Angeles flowed in the direction of the black community" (Sonenshein, 1993, p. 31). Other scholars also have remarked on this trend (Camarillo, 1984, p. 81; Leonard, 1992, pp. 304–308).

However, economic influence did not "flow" to western African Americans at the same rates as did political leadership. Postwar data on family incomes in the West reveal just how slow any movement was and demonstrate the reality that African Americans and all people of color remained in subordinate positions. In 1950, black families earned only 44 percent of the regional average income. Among peoples of color, only Native American families earned less (20.3 percent). Chinese Americans, Japanese Americans, Filipinos, and Mexican Americans fared somewhat better, with earning levels at 55.6 percent, 51.6 percent, 45.6 percent, and 44.9 percent of the median family income in the West, all remarkably lower than whites. By the 1960 census, all people of color in the West had made gains but still stood well below whites. The family incomes of African Americans, benefiting from political gains and greater representation in unions, had more than doubled in the decade since 1950. They had bettered their position vis-à-vis the regional average, earning almost ten points more than in 1950 (53.5 percent). By 1960, they had also moved up in rank among people of color, standing third behind Japanese Americans, whose average earnings had increased to 67.7 percent of the regional average, and Chinese Americans, whose family incomes had grown to 63.6 percent of the median income of families in the West. Below African Americans, Filipino family incomes had increased only slightly, to 47.3 percent of the West's average income, while Mexican Americans remained in virtually the same spot, earning only 44.2 percent of the median regional income. Native Americans had improved their economic lot, but still earned only 28.4 percent of the regional average. The data reveals that the African American economic position among people of color and in relationship to whites did improve, but at rates that disappointed African Americans.[38]

Perhaps due to these very gradual economic gains, there was significant disunity after World War II within the ranks of African American organizations such as the Los Angeles NAACP, disunity that was exacerbated by the anticommunism of the late 1940s and 1950s. African Americans living in the western states found themselves with the sustained (if qualified and limited) support of labor organizations, liberals and progressives, state, county, and city governments, and even of other racialized peoples as they took up a "war of position" to engage the racial state and to reformulate racial policies. From the 1940s into the 1960s, African Americans occupied a subordinated but privileged racial position. Their connections to national organizations, their abilities to swing the vote in elections, and the attention that they garnered from the federal government, combined with significant shifts in the understanding of racial inequality, democracy, and the general American polity, made western race relations look little different from those in the North. In western urban and even rural areas the discussion of black and white relations predominated and all disputes arising from other interracial relationships were interpreted as of lesser significance—as unconnected, local spats with aliens and immigrants that could be put on hold for future resolution.

A "War of Position"

Beginning in the 1960s, particularly within Native American, Mexican American, and Asian American communities in the West, pan–ethnic group identities began to emerge. These identities were not simply reactions to or emulations of African American strategies. They were linked to movements that emerged organically from the respective ethnic communities. The movements, understandably, often found themselves responding to similar political, economic, and social issues and using a common vocabulary to describe their circumstances. Returning war veterans, college students, and community activists in each racialized group lobbied for a voice in politics. In doing so, they undermined the short-lived racial order in the West, which had placed blacks above other racialized groups, and created a more democratic vision—sometimes through coalitions and other times through separatist, cultural nationalist, or feminist agendas (Chavez, 1994; Cornell, 1990, pp. 380–382; Espiritu, 1992; Garcia, 1994; Gutierrez, 1995, pp. 183–187; Wei, 1993).

For their part, African Americans found themselves still only slightly ahead of where their journey had begun, in spite of their "privileged" position. Some had managed to break out of inner cities, but most had not. Organized labor in particular industrial sectors belatedly brought blacks into full membership on the eve of the virtual collapse of those industries. Shipbuilding, automobile production, even airplane manufacture hit hard times in the West. African Americans continued to find themselves in vulnerable, volatile positions. As had long been the case, they were among the "last hired, first fired" as they continued to labor in highly competitive market sectors (Taylor, 1977, pp. 272–273).

To make matters worse, long-standing practices of privileging Asian Americans in school systems over African Americans, Mexican Americans, and Native Americans took a toll. The practice often took the form of very subtle—and at other times not so subtle—tracking of students on the basis of teachers' senses of differentness among racialized groups. A comparative study of postwar race relations in the intermountain Pacific Northwest revealed that white school teachers believed Japanese American students to be better, more responsive, less demanding of "special" attention, and even cleaner than African Americans. This resulted in greater praise for the former and more condemnation of the latter. Among African Americans, white teachers tended to favor the lighter-skinned black students, whom they described as "better-mannered," and these students often ranked near the top of their class. These influences, as much as any set of cultural values held by a particular "ethnic" group or an ethnic solidarity, gave Japanese Americans advantages. Very gradually, with the shift away from biological notions of race to notions of cultural difference, and the Cold War culture of individual opportunity, Japanese American business and academic "successes"—the "model minority thesis"—became a prime tool for the bludgeoning of African Americans, for blaming the victim (Skim, 1989; Kennedy, 1946).

Since the 1960s, racialized groups have been able to gain increased access to the political system by using the courts, the ballot box, the media, and their "purchasing power." This trend has no more engendered pluralism than did the era of the 1920s and 1930s. Instead, racialized groups have been pitted against each other in efforts to gain greater state attention. Racialized groups, though they have unprecedented access and influence in politics, still find themselves laboring under white hegemony. In many respects, the transition of attention to "reverse discrimination," the rise of the "angry white male," and the celebration of ethnicity in the context of postindustrial society are efforts to reassert white hegemony. Racial constructions based on biology, though still operative, no longer enjoy widespread public acceptance in the cultural and legal realms (Pascoe, 1996). Instead, more subtle forms of racism have emerged, as Eduardo Bonilla-Silva argues (see Chapter 4 of this volume). The postmodern tendency to deconstruct, encouraged by the apparent "fall of communism," has led us to focus on individual, cultural identity, and individual opportunity rather than on the structural, institutional, and collective aspects of racial formation. We might well need to develop more effective categories of understanding and better definitions of race and racism, as Michael Omi and Howard Winant argue in Chapters 1 and 2, in order to challenge the new racial state.

Conclusion

Race relations in the twentieth-century western United States have gone through a series of transformations. The first, lasting from the 1880s to about 1920, involved the establishment of a white hegemony throughout the region after a series of wars and political seizures. The capitalist transformation of the region made the task of negotiating social relations between indigenous peoples and the many newcomers to the region quite difficult, for it interwove class and race relations in contradictory ways. Nonetheless, an "accommodative agreement" emerged in which whites essentially controlled land and labor whereas racialized groups operated out of ethnic enclaves, worked in segmented labor markets, and negotiated paternalistic ties. "Wars of maneuver" emerged in the 1920s and 1930s as the various groups sought to use their relative positions of power, their "ethnic hegemonies," to secure privileged positions within white hegemony. In the 1940s and 1950s, African Americans capitalized on demographic and political shifts and on group differences to secure a privileged position among racialized groups, although all nonwhites remained subordinated. By the 1960s, African American privilege had declined. At first, this engendered a "war of position"; but more recently, the situation has degenerated into something increasingly akin to the earlier "wars of maneuver" because many whites believe that the political, economic, and social shifts threaten their hegemony—though most refuse to recognize that they operate within any hegemonic system.

An accurate understanding of these historical transformations in racial formation in the western United States undermines two very powerful and ultimately limiting historical narratives. One is the story of U.S. race relations as only black and white. By understanding racial formations before World War II as regional and acknowledging their transformations, we allow for the recognition that the *national* story of black and white is reflective of constructions of race that persisted during a quarter of a century and even then were highly problematic. The history of the multiracial West is more than the sum of individual stories of oppression and resistance. Western racial formations emerged through complex processes of suppression, contestation, negotiation, accommodation, maneuvering, and positioning among and within racialized groups and within a continuously changing "white" hegemony.

Recognizing the West as the site of national racial formations rather than as a separate, exceptional place conquered by white settlement helps to supplant narratives that no longer reflect our understandings of the past, present, or future. A West that reengages and transforms the "national" story is desperately needed. Changes in the immigration laws of the mid-1960s, combined with the gradual dispersal of Asian Americans and Mexican Americans throughout the country, make an understanding of the West's racial formations essential for interracial, interethnic relations today—relations that are much more complicated now than they were in the 1950s and early 1960s, when they were dominated by black and white. Race and racism must be confronted now: It is indeed "due time."

NOTES

1. Writing about race is difficult, particularly while avoiding essentialist categories. I have used *racialized* rather than *race;* but labeling people is always problematic. In this essay, I have used the terms *white* and *Anglo* interchangeably. I also use *African Americans* and *blacks*, and *Native Americans* and *Indians,* as synonyms. I have tried to use *Chinese American, Japanese American,* and *Mexican American* to encompass both the American-born and immigrant populations whenever possible. An exception to that pattern is the term *Filipino,* which I use partly because of the group's self-reference and its members' status as U.S. nationals. This chapter does not illustrate either how those categories came to be constructed or how they shifted over time.

2. Karen Isaken Leonard, *Making Ethnic Choices: California's Punjabi Mexican Americans* (Philadelphia: Temple University Press, 1992), provides important background on this little-known topic.

3. Like any definition of race, a definition of region is troublesome. *West* in this essay refers to the area from the western and southern stretches of Texas, north into the Canadian prairies, over to Alaska, and down to California. Most references are to the western United States, though at times I comment on Canada.

4. These are some of the more powerful recent works that tackle this myopia. Barbara M. Posadas, "The Hierarchy of Color and Psychological Adjustment in an Industrial Environment: Filipinos, the Pullman Company, and the Brotherhood of Sleeping Car Porters," *Labor History*, 23 (1982), pp. 349–373, is an early, rare exception in its approach—an approach that too few scholars have chosen to pursue.

5. In the works cited, Limerick discusses these images in an effort to undermine the common story. Her approach influenced my thinking on the subject.

6. Ray Allen Billington, *The American Frontier Thesis: Attack and Defense* (Washington, DC: American Historical Association, 1971) and Richard W. Etulain, ed., *Writing Western History: Essays on Major Western Historians* (Albuquerque: University of New Mexico Press, 1991) will introduce readers to the "old" western history. The "new" history of the West is most accessible in Patricia Nelson Limerick, *The Legacy of Conquest: The Unbroken Past of the American West* (New York: W. W. Norton, 1987) and Patricia Nelson Limerick, Clyde A. Milner II, and Charles E. Rankin, eds., *Trails: Toward a New Western History* (Lawrence: University Press of Kansas, 1991). A thick, but broad survey in the latter genre is Richard White, "*It's Your Misfortune and None of My Own": A New History of the American West* (Norman: University of Oklahoma Press, 1991). Clyde A. Milner, II, Carol A. O'Connor, and Martha Sandweiss, eds., *The Oxford History of the American West* (New York: Oxford University Press, 1994), is an attempt at developing a compromise between the two schools of thought.

7. William Cronon raised this point at the 1994 conference "Power and Place in the North American West," in Seattle, but suffered intense criticism for privileging a (white) national narrative that was neo-Turnerian over that of the nonnational experiences represented by Mexican Americans, Native Americans, Asian Americans, and many others who believed their experiences in the region not to be part of the U.S. national story.

8. In spite of an enormous and growing literature on separate racialized groups in the West, only a handful of authors have adopted multiracial perspectives. These works are among those that have most influenced my own.

9. Dana Y. Takagi in *The Retreat From Race: Asian-American Admissions and Racial Politics* (New Brunswick, N.J.: Rutgers University Press, 1992) and E. San Juan, Jr. in *Racial Formations/Critical Transformations: Articulations of Power in Ethnic and Racial Studies in the United States* (Atlantic Highlands, NJ: Humanities Press International, 1992) argue against any decline in the significance of race, whereas William Julius Wilson in *The Declining Significance of Race and Changing American Institutions* (Chicago: University of Chicago Press, 1978) argues the contrary. Lawrence H. Fuchs, *The American Kaleidoscope: Race, Ethnicity, and the Civic Culture* (Hanover, NH: Wesleyan University Press, 1990) wistfully seeks a pluralistic unity.

10. The scholarship on many of the points I make in this chapter is extensive. Because this is not a bibliographic review of the literature on the subject (or historiographical essay), I provide citations only for the works that have most influenced my thinking. The authors of those studies often had very different purposes in mind than that to which I am putting their works, and I hope I have faithfully represented their arguments. Those same works do offer good starting points for those interested in pursuing the bibliographic record in greater depth.

11. Przeworski provides a useful definition and critique.

12. I borrow this phrase from Richard Maxwell Brown, "Violence," in *Oxford History of the American West*, pp. 493–425. Brown speaks of a "Western Civil War of Incorporation," which was at an end by 1919.

13. Maps 34–38 and 56–60 provide a compelling visual illustration, particularly when rail lines are matched up with military wagon roads, mail routes, and rivers.

For a quick recent survey of railroads, see Keith L. Bryant, Jr., "Entering the Global Economy," in *Oxford History of the American West*, pp. 213–224.

14. See William G. Robbins, *Colony and Empire: The Capitalist Transformation of the American West* (Lawrence: University of Kansas Press, 1994), for the strongest statement on extractive enterprises and capitalism in the West.

15. Disease resulting from the influx of white settlers had the most devastating effects on Native American populations. I have not dealt with the subject in this chapter, in part because the greatest effects of disease were experienced long before the period on which this chapter is focused. See Albert L. Hurtado, *Indian Survival on the California Frontier* (New Haven: Yale University Press, 1988), for more on this subject.

16. The Dawes Act wrested reservation lands from Native American tribes, assigned some to individuals, and made the rest available to whites for purchase. In the 1880s, tribal lands amounted to about 155 million acres. By the end of the 1920s, only about 30 million acres remained in Native American hands, as much as 91 million acres having passed out of their control under the Dawes Act.

17. Control of financial institutions also had class implications, as the Populists attempting cooperative ventures and the residents of socialist utopian communities came to realize.

18. Sociologist Eduardo Bonilla-Silva has offered important insights in his conversations with me on how race is structured.

19. Charles J. McClain, *In Search of Equality: The Chinese Struggle Against Discrimination in Nineteenth-Century America* (Berkeley: University of California Press, 1994); Lucy E. Sayler, *Laws Harsh as Tigers: Chinese Immigrants and the Shaping of Modern Immigration Law* (Chapel Hill: University of North Carolina Press, 1995); and Sucheng Chan, ed., *Entry Denied*, provide rich details on how Chinese used the courts to resist racial law. Ian F. Haney Lopez, *White By Law: The Legal Construction of Race* (New York: New York University Press, 1996), looks at the issue more broadly and offers strong evidence to suggest the "value of whites to whiteness."

20. Sociologists define *ethnic enclave* in economic terms as the concentration of ethnically run small businesses in a "ghettoized area" (see Jiobu, "Ethnic Hegemony," p. 355). Historians often define the term more broadly to describe the clustering of racial or ethnic groups in an urban setting, usually with some small businesses included. In general, the phrase is a loose substitute for *ghetto*, a phenomenon that most historians would agree does not exist in any "true" form in the United States. For one example of the use of the term by a historian, see Deutsch, "Landscape of Enclaves," pp. 110–132.

21. Reservation lands could not be regulated by state laws, and no federal statute barred Asians or other aliens from owning or leasing land. Asian Americans quickly recognized and took advantage of this loophole.

22. Luckingham, for example, shows Chinese businesses spread throughout the city of Phoenix.

23. Note that *equilibrium* here does not signify equality, but something closer to sustained crisis.

24. It is ironic that Jiobu does not recognize the "natural" growth in the Nisei population as a replacement for "sustained immigration," which is part of the ethnic enclave definition. Hostilities were so high against Japanese Americans that it hardly

mattered that one group was of immigrant origin and the other American by birth. In this sense, his efforts to distinguish the ethnic hegemony thesis from the ethnic enclave theory is weakened. Nor does he recognize that social (cultural and legal) constructions of "otherness" or "differentness" may also sustain the notion held by whites that a group is "alien" or "immigrant."

25. I am indebted to Paul Wong, Rory Ong, Eduardo Bonilla-Silva, and Shelli Fowler for clarifying this point.

26. I realize that most social scientists will balk at the terms *virtual, substantial,* or even *local* as being far too vague. Without testing the model rigorously against empirical evidence, which for this historical era is highly problematic even if available, I would suggest as Jiobu does that control of roughly a quarter to a third of an economic enterprise or a labor market allows a given group to begin to assert significant power. That percentage may even decrease under special circumstances, such as the fad for Asian "schoolboy" household servants in pre–World War II Seattle, which displaced many African Americans.

27. Zamora provides a thorough discussion of Mexicans and organized labor prior to the 1920s.

28. Richard Griswold del Castillo, in "The International Dimensions of the Zoot Suit Riots" (a paper presented at the 1995 Western Historical Association Meeting, Denver, Colorado), points out that up to World War II, the Mexican government, press, and urban intelligentsia held mildly "anti-Pachucho" sentiments. During the war, those sentiments grew more negative, in part to justify inaction on Mexican American social problems and to aid in the Mexican government's courting of U.S. favor, which the government believed was "essential in order to continue with Mexico's economic progress."

29. For a brief overview of these policies, see Alvin M. Josephy, Jr., "Modern America and the Indian," in *Indians in American History,* ed. Frederick Hoxie (Arlington Heights, Ill.: Harlan Davidson, 1988), pp. 251–274.

30. For the impacts of internment on Japanese American women, see Valerie Matsumoto, "Japanese American Women During World War II," in *Unequal Sisters,* pp. 436–449.

31. See, for example, Park et al., *Tentative Findings of the Survey of Race Relations,* especially p. 24. Many of these works are discussed in Barry Goldberg and Colin Greer, "American Visions, Ethnic Dreams: Public Ethnicity and the Sociological Imagination," *Sage Race Relations Abstracts* 15, no. 1 (1990), pp. 5–60.

32. Johnson borrows the adjective *metropolitan-military* from Roger W. Lotchin, "The Metropolitan-Military Complex in Comparative Perspective: San Francisco, Los Angeles, and San Diego, 1919–1941," in *The Making of Urban America,* ed. Raymond A. Mohl (Wilmington, DE: SR Books, 1988), pp. 202–213.

33. The Seattle Urban League Records, Archives and Manuscripts Division, University of Washington Libraries, Seattle, Washington, contain several files detailing the disputes African Americans had with General Electric, one of the major contractors at Hanford.

34. For another example, see Melcher, "Blacks and Whites Together," pp. 195–216.

35. For one example, see Rebecca Moore, "Anyplace But Here: The Seattle Campaign for Open Housing, 1950–1969," master's thesis, Western Washington University, 1995.

36. For a good example of the problematic relations, see the debate encompassed by Ray Marshall, "Unions and the Negro Community," *Industrial and Labor Relations Review* 17 (1964), pp. 179–202; Herbert Hill, "Unions and the Negro Community," *ibid.*, pp. 619–621; and Ray Marshall, "The Racial Practices of the ILGWU: A Reply," *ibid.*, pp. 622–626.

37. The WRA, for example, fought against the application of restrictive covenants to Japanese Americans.

38. U.S. Bureau of the Census, *U.S. Census of Population: 1950*, vol. 4: *Special Reports*, part 3, chapter C, *Persons of Spanish Surname* (Washington, D.C.: Government Printing Office, 1953), pp. 23 and 27; U.S. Bureau of the Census, *U.S. Census of Population: 1950*, vol. 4: *Special Reports*, part 3, chapter B, *Nonwhite Population by Race* (Washington, D.C.: Government Printing Office, 1953), pp. 31, 36, 41, 46, 51, and 56; U.S. Bureau of the Census, *U.S. Census of Population: 1950*, vol. 2: *Characteristics of the Population*, part 1, *United States Summary* (Washington, D.C.: Government Printing Office, 1953), p. 137; U.S. Bureau of the Census, *U.S. Census of Population: 1960*, *Subject Reports*, *Nonwhite Populations by Race* (Washington, D.C.: Government Printing Office, 1963), pp. 102, 105, 110, 112, and 116; U.S. Bureau of the Census, *U.S. Census of Population: 1960*, *Subject Reports*, *Persons of Spanish Surname* (Washington, D.C.: Government Printing Office, 1963), p. 38. The data provided for Mexican Americans in the census are ambiguous and problematic at best. They apparently describe people with Spanish surnames and not those identifying themselves as "Mexican American." Moreover, the Bureau of the Census did not make the calculation for the West as a whole. The figures I use for 1950 come from a calculation based on figures for Arizona and California. I simply took 60 percent of the differential between the figures for the two states as the regional average. For 1960, the census bureau did give figures for the Southwest, by which it meant Texas, New Mexico, Arizona, Colorado, and California. While the figures provided by the Bureau of the Census are no doubt inaccurate, they can be used for some comparisons. It remains clear that Mexican Americans' economic position did not improve much, and always remained substantially lower than that of whites. (The figures cited in the text above are the regional median incomes, not white incomes, because the census bureau did not consistently report white incomes.)

Although the Census Bureau recorded family incomes in 1940, it did not calculate family incomes on the basis of race. The 1940 census does reveal a median national white family income of $1,325 and a national nonwhite family median income of $489—or 36.9 percent of that of whites. These data, when estimated for the West, suggest that whites earned only about $800 to $1,000, also lower than the national average. By 1950, the West ranked first in the nation in median family income, with $3,430—11.5 percent higher than the national mark of $3,073. The Northeast followed, with a median income of $3,365; north central states with $3,277; and the South with only $2,248. No data are available on the average income of people of color for 1940 (see U.S. Bureau of the Census, *Historical Statistics of the United States: Colonial Times to 1957* [Washington, D.C.: Government Printing Office, 1957], pp. 159, 167; *Census of the United States: 1940, Population*, vol. 3: *The Labor Force*, part 1, *United States Summary* [Washington, D.C.: Government Printing Office, 1943], pp. 12 and 119; and *U.S. Census of Population: 1950*, vol. 2: *Characteris-*

tics of the Population, part 1, *United States Summary* [Washington, D.C.: Government Printing Office, 1953], p. 137).

REFERENCES

Almaguer, T. (1994). *Racial Fault Lines: The Historical Origins of White Supremacy in California.* Berkeley: University of California Press.

Anderson, K. (1991). *Vancouver's Chinatown: Racial Discourse in Canada, 1895–1980.* Montreal: McGill-Queen's University Press.

Barrera, M. (1985). "The Historical Evolution of Chicano Ethnic Goals: A Bibliographic Essay." *Sage Race Relations Abstracts* 10, no. 1, pp. 5–14.

Beck, W. A., and Haase, Y. D. (1989). *Historical Atlas of the American West.* Norman: University of Oklahoma Press.

Beechert, E. D. (1985). *Working in Hawaii: A Labor History.* Honolulu: University of Hawaii Press.

Billington, R. A. (1971). *The American Frontier Thesis: Attack and Defense.* Washington, DC: American Historical Association.

Blackhawk, N. (1995). "I Can Carry On from Here: The Relocation of American Indians to Los Angeles." *Wicazo Sa Review*, 11, no. 2, pp. 16–30.

Boxberger, D. L. (1989). *To Fish in Common: The Ethnohistory of Lummi Indian Salmon Fishing.* Lincoln: University of Nebraska Press.

Broussard, A. S. (1993). *Black San Francisco: The Struggle for Racial Equality in the West, 1900–1954.* Lawrence: University of Kansas Press.

Brown, R. M. (1994). "Violence." In Milner, C. A. II, O'Connor, C. A., and Sandweiss, M., eds., *The Oxford History of the American West.* New York: Oxford University Press.

Bryant, K. L., Jr. (1994). "Entering the Global Economy." Pp. 213–24 in Milner, C. A. II, O'Connor, C. A., and Sandweiss, M., eds., *The Oxford History of the American West.* New York: Oxford University Press.

Burawoy, M. (1979). *Manufacturing Consent: Changes in the Labor Process Under Monopoly Capitalism.* Chicago: University of Chicago Press.

Burgess, M. E. (1949). "A Study of Selected Socio-cultural and Opinion Differentials Among Negroes and Whites in the Pasco, Washington, Community." Master's thesis. Department of Sociology, State College of Washington, Pullman.

Bustamante, A. R. (1995). "Mexican Mine Worker Communities in Arizona: Spatial and Social Impacts of Arizona's Copper Mining, 1920–1950." *Estudios Sociales* 5, no. 10, pp. 27–54.

Caramillo, A. (1984). *Chicanos in California: A History of Mexican Americans in California.* San Francisco: Boyd and Fraser.

Chan, S. (1986). *This Bittersweet Soil: The Chinese in California Agriculture, 1860–1910.* Berkeley: University of California Press.

Chan, S., ed. (1991). *Entry Denied: Exclusion and the Chinese Community in America, 1882–1943.* Philadelphia: Temple University Press.

Chan, S., Daniels, D. H., Garcia, M. T., and Wilson, T. P., eds. (1994). *Peoples of Color in the American West.* Lexington, MA: D.C. Heath.

Chavez, E. (1994). *Creating Aztlan: The Chicano Movement in Los Angeles, 1966–1978.* Doctoral dissertation. Department of History, University of California, Los Angeles.

Chinn, T. W., Lai, H. M., and Choy, P. P., eds. (1969). *A History of Chinese in California: A Syllabus.* San Francisco: Chinese Historical Society of America.

Chu, G. (1970). "Chinatowns in the Delta: The Chinese in the Sacramento–San Joaquin Delta, 1870–1960." *California Historical Society Quarterly* 49, pp. 21–37.

Conzen, K. N., Gerber, D. A., Morawska, E., and Pozzetta, G. E. "The Invention of Ethnicity: A Perspective from the U.S.A." *Journal of American Ethnic History* 12, no. 1.

Cornell, S. (1990). "Land, Labour, and Group Formation: Blacks and Indians in the United States." *Ethnic and Racial Studies* 13, pp. 380–382.

The Crisis. (1946). May. P. 138.

Daniels, C. (1991). *Chicano Workers and the Politics of Fairness: The FEPC in the Southwest, 1941–1945.* Austin: University of Texas Press.

Daniels, D. H. (1980). *Pioneer Urbanites: A Social and Cultural History of Black San Francisco.* Philadelphia: Temple University Press.

Deutsch, S. (1987). *No Separate Refuge: Culture, Class, and Gender on an Anglo-Hispanic Frontier in the American West, 1880–1940.* New York: Oxford University Press.

_____. (1992). "Landscape of Enclaves: Race Relations in the West, 1865–1990." In Cronon, W., Miles, G., and Gitlin, J., eds., *Under an Open Sky: Rethinking America's Western Past.* New York: W. W. Norton.

Deutsch, S., Sanchez, G. J., and Okihiro, G. Y. (1994). "Contemporary Peoples/Contested Places." In Milner, C. A. II, O'Connor, C. A., and Sandweiss, M., eds., *Oxford History of the American West.* New York: Oxford University Press.

Espiritu, Y. L. (1992). *Asian American Pan-ethnicity: Bridging Institutions and Identities.* Philadelphia: Temple University Press.

Etulain, R., ed. (1991). *Writing Western History: Essays on Major Western Historians.* Albuquerque: University of New Mexico Press.

Fixico, D. L. (1986). *Termination and Relocation: Federal Indian Policy, 1945–1960.* Albuquerque: University of New Mexico Press.

Fowler, L. (1987). *Shared Symbols, Contested Meanings: Gros Ventre Culture and History, 1778–1984.* Ithaca, NY: Cornell University Press.

Frank, D. (1994). *Purchasing Power: Consumer Organizing, Gender, and the Seattle Labor Movement, 1919–1929.* Cambridge, MA: Cambridge University Press.

Friday, C. (1993–1996). Interviews with Don ("Lelooska") Smith. Unpublished transcript.

_____. (1994). *Organizing Asian American Labor: The Pacific Coast Canned-Salmon Industry, 1870–1942.* Philadelphia: Temple University Press.

_____. (1996a). Interviews with Eddie Merchant. Unpublished transcript.

_____. (1996b). "The Marine Cooks and Stewards on the Narrowing Path: Race, Class, and Gender in Cold War America, 1948–1956." Paper presented in December 1996 at a conference of the Organization of American Historians, Chicago.

Fuchs, L. H. (1990). *The American Kaleidoscope: Race, Ethnicity and the Civic Culture.* Hanover, NH: Wesleyan University Press.

Gamboa, E. (1990). *Mexican Labor and World War II: Braceros in the Pacific Northwest, 1942–1947*. Austin: University of Texas Press.

Gibson, J. R. (1992). *Otter Skins, Boston Ships, and China Goods: The Maritime Fur Trade of the Northwest Coast, 1785–1841*. Montreal: McGill-Queens University Press.

Glenn, E. N. (1986). *Issei, Nisei, War Bride: Three Generations of Japanese American Women in Domestic Service*. Philadelphia: Temple University Press.

Goldberg, B., and Greer, C. (1990). "American Visions, Ethnic Dreams: Public Ethnicity and the Sociological Imagination." *Sage Race Relations Abstracts* 15, no. 1, pp. 5–60.

Goodwyn, L. (1978). *The Populist Moment: A Short History of the Agrarian Revolt in America*. New York: Oxford University Press.

Gutierrez, D. G. (1995). *Walls and Mirrors: Mexican Americans, Mexican Immigrants, and the Politics of Ethnicity*. Berkeley: University of California Press.

Harmon, A. (1995). *A Different Kind of Indian: Negotiating the Meanings of "Indian" and "Tribe" in the Puget Sound Region, 1820s–1970s*. Doctoral dissertation. Department of History, University of Washington, Seattle.

Hill, H. (1964). "Unions and the Negro Community." *Industrial and Labor Relations Review* 17, pp. 619–621.

Hoare, Q., and Smith, G. N., eds. (1971). *Selections from the Prison Notebook of Antonio Gramsci*. London: Lawrence and Wishart.

Hoxie, F. E. (1984). *A Final Promise: The Campaign to Assimilate the Indians, 1880–1920*. Lincoln: University of Nebraska Press.

Hurtado, A. L. (1998). *Indian Survival on the California Frontier*. New Haven: Yale University Press.

Ichioka, Y. (1988). *The Issei: The World of the First Generation Japanese Immigrants, 1885–1924*. New York: Free Press.

Iverson, P. (1994). *When Indians Became Cowboys: Native Peoples and Cattle Ranching in the American West*. Lincoln: University of Nebraska Press.

Jiobu, R. (1988). "Ethnic Hegemony and the Japanese of California." *American Sociological Review* 53, pp. 353–367.

Johnson, M. (1993). *The Second Gold Rush: Oakland and the East Bay in World War II*. Berkeley: University of California Press.

Johnson, S. L. (1993). *The Gold She Gathered: Difference, Domination, and California's Southern Mines, 1848–1853*. Doctoral dissertation. Department of History, Yale University, New Haven, CT.

Josephy, A. M., Jr. (1988). "Modern America and the Indian." Pp. 251–274 in Hoxie, F., ed., *Indians in American History*. Arlington Heights, IL: Harlan Davidson.

Kennedy, T. H. (1946). "Racial Survey of the Intermountain Northwest." *Research Studies of the State College of Washington* 14, no. 3, pp. 163–246.

Kim, H. (1994). *A Legal History of Asian Americans, 1790–1990*. Westport, CT: Greenwood Press.

Kitano, H.H.L. (1993). *Generations and Identity: The Japanese American*. Needham Heights, MA: Ginn Press.

Lemert, E. M., and Rosberg, J. (1946). "Crime and Punishment Among Minority Groups in Los Angeles County." *Research Studies of the State College of Washington* 14, no. 2, p. 136.

Leonard, K. A. (1992). *Years of Hope, Days of Fear: The Impact of World War II on Race Relations in Los Angeles*. Doctoral dissertation. Department of History, University of California, Davis.

Leonard, K. I. (1992). *Making Ethnic Choices: California's Punjabi Mexican Americans*. Philadelphia: Temple University Press.

di Leonardo, M. (1984). *The Varieties of Ethnic Experience: Kinship, Class, and Gender Among California's Italian-Americans*. Ithaca, NY: Cornell University Press.

LeWarne, P. (1975). *Utopias on Puget Sound, 1885–1915*. Seattle: University of Washington Press.

Lewis, D. R. (1990). "Reservation Leadership and the Progressive-Traditional Dichotomy: William Wash and the Northern Utes, 1865–1928." *Ethnohistory* 38, pp. 124–142.

Lewis, E. (1993). "Invoking Concepts, Problematizing Identities: The Life of Charles N. Hunter and the Implications for the Study of Gender and Labor." *Labor History* 34, pp. 292–308.

Light, I. (1974). "From Vice District to Tourist Attraction: The Moral Career of American Chinatowns, 1880–1940." *Pacific Historical Review* 43, pp. 367–394.

Limerick, P. N. (1987). *The Legacy of Conquest: The Unbroken Past of the American West*. New York: W. W. Norton.

_____. (1992a). "The Case of Premature Departure: The Trans-Mississippi West and American History Textbooks." *Journal of American History* 78, pp. 1380–1394.

_____. (1992b). "Disorientation and Reorientation: The American Landscape Discovered from the West." *Journal of American History* 79, pp. 1021–1049.

_____. (1995). "Common Cause? Asian American History and Western American History." In Okihiro, G. K., Alquizola, M., Rony, D. S., and Wong, K. S., eds., *Privileging Positions: The Sites of Asian American Studies*. Pullman, WA: Washington State University Press.

Limerick, P. N., Milner, C. A., II, and Rankin, C. E. (1991). *Trails: Toward a New Western History*. Lawrence: University of Kansas Press.

Lippin, L. M. (1994). "There Will Not Be a Mechanic Left: The Battle Against Unskilled Labor in the San Francisco Harness Trade, 1880–1890." *Labor History* 35, no. 2, pp. 217–236.

Lopez, I. F. (1996). *White By Law: The Legal Construction of Race*. New York: New York University Press.

Lotchin, R. W. (1988). "The Metropolitan-Military Complex in Comparative Perspective: San Francisco, Los Angeles, and San Diego, 1919–1941." Pp. 202–213 in Mohl, R. A., ed., *The Making of Urban America*. Wilmington, DE: SR Books.

Luckingham, B. (1988). *Minorities in Phoenix: A Profile of Mexican American, Chinese American, and African American Communities, 1860–1992*. Tucson: University of Arizona Press.

_____. (1994). *Phoenix: The History of a Southwestern Metropolis*. Tucson, AZ: University of Arizona Press.

Lukes, T. J., and Okihiro, G. (1985). *Japanese Legacy: Farming and Community Life in California's Santa Clara Valley*. Cupertino, CA: De Anza College, California Historical Center.

Lyman, S. (1974). "Conflict and the Web of Group Affiliation in San Francisco's Chinatown, 1850–1910." *Pacific Historical Review* 43, pp. 474–499.

Marchak, P. (1987). "Organization of Divided Fishers." In Guppy, N., McMullan, J., and Marchak, P., eds., *Uncommon Property: The Fishing and Fish Processing Industries in British Columbia*. Toronto: Methuen.

Marshall, R. (1964a). "Unions and the Negro Community." *Industrial and Labor Relations Review* 17, pp. 179–202.

_____. (1964b). "The Racial Practices of the ILGWU: A Reply." *Industrial and Labor Relations Review* 17, pp. 622–626.

Matsumoto, V. J. (1993). *Farming the Home Place: A Japanese American Community in California*. Ithaca, NY: Cornell University Press.

McClain, C. J. (1994). *In Search of Equality: The Chinese Struggle Against Discrimination in Nineteenth-Century America*. Berkeley: University of California Press.

McKinney, J., and Magnuson, W. G. (1943, Sept. 17). Warren G. Magnuson Papers, file 7, box 17, accession 3181–2. University of Washington Libraries, Archives and Manuscripts Division, Seattle.

Melcher, M. (1991). "Blacks and Whites Together: Interracial Leadership in the Phoenix Civil Rights Movement." *Journal of Arizona History* 32, pp. 195–197.

Miller, K. A. (1990). "Class, Culture, and Immigrant Group Identity in the United States." Pp. 96–129 in Yans-McLaughlin, V., ed., *Immigration Reconsidered: History, Sociology, and Politics*. New York: Oxford University Press.

Milner, C. A. II, O'Connor, C. A, and Sandweiss, M., eds. (1994). *The Oxford History of the American West*. New York: Oxford University Press.

Miyamoto, F. (1984 [1939]). *Social Solidarity Among the Japanese in Seattle*. Seattle: University of Washington Press.

Montejano, D. (1987). *Anglos and Mexicans in the Making of Texas, 1836–1986*. Austin: University of Texas Press.

Montoya, M. E. (1993). *Dispossessed People: Settler Resistance on the Maxwell Land Grant, 1860–1901*. Doctoral dissertation. Department of History, Yale University, New Haven, CT.

Moore, R. (1995). *Anyplace But Here: The Seattle Campaign for Open Housing, 1950–1969*. Master's thesis. Department of History, Western Washington University, Bellingham.

Mumford, E. H. (1989). "Washington's African American Communities." Pp. 79–81 in Solberg, S. E., and White, S., eds., *Peoples of Washington: Perspectives on Cultural Diversity*. Pullman: Washington State University Press.

Nelson, B. (1988). *Workers on the Waterfront: Seamen, Longshoremen, and Unionism in the 1930s*. Urbana: University of Illinois Press.

Nomura, M. (1987). "Within the Law: The Establishment of Filipino Leasing Rights on the Yakima Indian Reservation." *Amerasia Journal* 13, no. 1, pp. 99–117.

Okihiro, G. Y. (1994). *Margins and Mainstreams: Asians in American History and Culture*. Seattle: University of Washington Press.

Omi, M., and Winant, H. (1994). *Racial Formation in the United States from the 1960s to the 1990s*. New York: Routledge.

Park, R., et al. (1925). *Tentative Findings of the Survey of Race Relations: A Canadian-American Study of the Oriental on the Pacific Coast*. Stanford: Stanford University, Survey of Race Relations.

Pascoe, P. (1991). "Western Women at the Crossroads." Pp. 40–58 in Limerick, P., Milner, C. A. II, and Rankin, C. E., eds., *Trails: Toward a New Western History*.

Pascoe, P. (1996). "Miscegenation Laws, Court Cases, and Ideologies of 'Race' in Twentieth-Century America." *Journal of American History,* June.

Peck, G. (1993). "Padrones and Protest: 'Old' Radicals and 'New' Immigrants in Bingham, Utah, 1905–1912." *Western Historical Quarterly* 24, pp. 157–178.

Philpott, S. B. (1963). "Trade Unionism and Acculturation: A Comparative Study of Urban Indians and Immigrant Italians." Master's thesis. University of British Columbia, Vancouver.

Posadas, B. M. (1982). "The Hierarchy of Color and Psychological Adjustment in an Industrial Environment: Filipinos, the Pullman Company, and the Brotherhood of Sleeping Car Porters." *Labor History* 23, pp. 349–373.

Powers, W. K. (1988). The Indian Hobbyist Movement in North America. Pp. 557–561 in Washburn, W. E., ed., *Handbook of North American Indians: Vol. 4, History of Indian-White Relations.* Washington, DC: Smithsonian Institution.

Przeworski, A. (1980). "Material Bases of Consent: Economics and Politics in a Hegemonic System." *Political Power and Social Theory* 1, pp. 21–66.

Race Relations. 1943–1948. Various issues.

Record, C. W. (1951). "The Chico Story: A Black and White Harvest." *The Crisis* 58, no. 2, pp. 95–101, 129–131, 133.

Reuss, C. F. (1944). "Assimilation of Wartime Migrants into Community Life." *Research Studies of the State College of Washington* 12, no. 1, p. 25.

Robbins, W. G. (1994). *Colony and Empire: The Capitalist Transformation of the American West.* Lawrence: University of Kansas Press.

Roediger, D. R. (1994). *Towards the Abolition of Whiteness: Essays on Race, Politics, and Working Class History.* London: Verso.

Rosswurm, S., ed. (1992). *The CIO's Left-Led Unions.* New Brunswick, NJ: Rutgers University Press.

Sanchez, G. J. (1993). *Becoming Mexican American: Ethnicity, Culture, and Identity in Chicano Los Angeles, 1900–1945.* New York: Oxford University Press.

———. (1994). "'Go After the Women': Americanization and the Mexican Immigrant Woman, 1915–1929." Pp. 284–297 in DuBois, E. C., and Ruiz, V. L., eds., *Unequal Sisters: A Multicultural Reader in U.S. Women's History.* New York: Routledge.

San Juan, E., Jr. (1992). *Racial Formations/Critical Transformations: Articulations of Power in Ethnic and Racial Studies in the United States.* Atlantic Highlands, NJ: Humanities Press International.

Saxon, A. P. (1971). *The Indispensible Enemy: Labor and the Anti-Chinese Movement in California.* Berkeley: University of California Press.

Sayler, L. E. (1995). *Laws Harsh as Tigers: Chinese Immigrants and the Shaping of Modern Immigration Law.* Chapel Hill: University of North Carolina Press.

Scharff, V. (1995). "Woman Suffrage in Wyoming and the Ironies of Empire." Paper presented at the meeting of the American Historical Association's Pacific Coast Branch, Maui, Hawaii, January 8, 1995.

Scheuerman, R. D., and Trafzer, C. E., eds. (1986). *Renegade Tribe: The Palouse Indians and the Invasion of the Inland Pacific Northwest.* Pullman: Washington State University Press.

Schmid, C. (1945). "Pre-war and Wartime Migration to Seattle." *Research Studies of the State College of Washington* 13, no. 1 (March), pp. 14–15.

_____. (1946). "Wartime Trends in the Population of the State of Washington." *Research Studies of the State College of Washington* 14, no. 2 (June), pp. 128–132.

Schorr, D. L. (1946). "'Reconverting' Mexican Americans." *New Republic,* Sept. 30, pp. 412–413.

Schwantes, C. A. (1979). *Radical Heritage: Labor, Socialism, and Reform in Washington and British Columbia, 1885–1917.* Seattle: University of Washington Press.

Seattle Post-Intelligencer. (1963). July 20.

Sitkoff, H. (1993). *The Struggle for Black Equality: 1954–1992.* New York: Hill and Wang.

Smith, M. E. (1943). "A Comparison of Judgement of Prejudice Toward Certain Racio-National Groups Before and Since the Entry of the United States into World War II." *Journal of Social Psychology* 18, pp. 393–400.

Sone, M. (1979 [1953]). *Nisei Daughter.* Seattle: University of Washington Press.

Sonenshein, R. J. (1993). *Politics in Black and White: Race and Power in Los Angeles.* Princeton: Princeton University Press.

Spivak, R. G. (1943). "The New Anti-Alien Drive." *The New Republic,* November, pp. 740–741.

Takagi, D. Y. (1992). *The Retreat from Race: Asian-American Admissions and Racial Politics.* New Brunswick, NJ: Rutgers University Press.

Takaki, R. (1983). *Pau Hanna: Plantation Life and Labor.* Honolulu: University of Hawaii Press.

Tamura, L. (1993). *Hood River Issei: An Oral History of Japanese Immigrants to Oregon's Hood River Valley.* Urbana: University of Illinois Press.

Taylor, Q. (1977). *A History of Blacks in the Pacific Northwest, 1788–1970.* Doctoral dissertation. Department of History, University of Minnesota, Minneapolis.

_____. (1994). *The Forging of a Black Community: Seattle's Central District from 1870 Through the Civil Rights Era.* Seattle: University of Washington Press.

Tolbert, E. J. (1994). "The UNIA in Los Angeles, 1920s." Pp. 407–417 in Chan, S., Daniels, D. H., Garcia, M. T., and Wilson, T. P., eds., *Peoples of Color in the American West.* Lexington, MA: D. C. Heath.

Toll, W. (1996a). "The Transit of Families: The Japanese Migration to Portland." Unpublished article.

_____. (1996b). "Black Portland in 1920: The Origins of Working Class Stability." Unpublished article.

Tsai, S. H. (1986). *The Chinese Experience in America.* Bloomington: Indiana University Press.

U.S. Department of Commerce. (1975). *Historical Statistics of the United States. Part 1: Colonial Times to 1970.* Washington, DC: GPO.

U.S. House of Representatives. (1930). Exclusion of Immigration from the Philippine Islands. Hearings Before the Immigration and Naturalization Committee, 71st Congress, 2nd Session. Pp. 178–190.

U.S. House of Representatives. (Dec. 1937–Jan. 1938). Amending Merchant Marine Act, 1936. Hearings Before the Committee on Merchant Marine and Fisheries, 75th Congress, 2nd and 3rd Sessions. Pp. 61–68, 714.

U.S. Senate (July 1939, Feb.–April, 1940). Deportation of Aliens. Hearings Before a Subcommittee of the Committee of Immigration, 76th Congress, 2nd and 3rd Sessions.

Utley, R. M. (1982). *Indian Frontiers of the American West, 1846–1890.* Albuquerque: University of New Mexico Press.

Van Kirk, S. (1980). *Many Tender Ties: Women in Fur-Trade Society, 1670–1870.* Norman: University of Oklahoma Press.

Vargas, Z. (1993). *Proletarians of the North: A History of Mexican Industrial Workers in Detroit and the Midwest, 1917–1933.* Berkeley: University of California Press.

Warren, W. H. (1986–1987). "Maps: A Spatial Approach to Japanese American Communities in Los Angeles." *Amerasia Journal* 13, no. 2, pp. 137–151.

Washburn, W. E. (1975). *The Assault on Indian Tribalism: The General Allotment Law (Dawes Act) of 1887.* Philadelphia: Lippincott.

Weber, D. (1994). *Dark Sweat, White Gold: California Farm Workers, Cotton, and the New Deal.* Berkeley: University of California Press.

Wei, W. (1993). *The Asian American Movement.* Philadelphia: Temple University Press.

Weibel-Orlando, J. (1997). *Indian Country, LA: Maintaining Ethnic Community in a Complex Society.* Urbana: University of Illinois Press.

West, E. (1991). "A Longer, Grimmer, but More Interesting Story." In Limerick, P. N., Milner, C. A. II, and Rankin, C. E., eds., *Trails: Toward a New Western History.* Lawrence: University of Kansas Press.

White, R. (1986). "Race Relations in the American West." *American Quarterly* 38, pp. 397–416.

_____. (1987). *The Roots of Dependency: Subsistence, Environment, and Social Change Among the Choctaws, Pawnees, and Navajos.* Lincoln: University of Nebraska Press.

_____. (1991). *It's Your Misfortune and None of My Own: A New History of the American West.* Norman: University of Oklahoma Press.

_____. (1994). "Animals and Enterprise." Pp. 237–274 in Milner, C. A. II, O'Connor, C. A, and Sandweiss, M., eds., *The Oxford History of the American West.* New York: Oxford University Press.

Wiley, J. T. (1949). "Race Conflict as Exemplified in a Washington Community." Master's thesis. State College of Washington, Pullman.

Wilkinson, C. F., and Briggs, E. R. (1979). "The Evolution of Termination Policy." Pp. 91–95 in Getches, D. H., Rosenfelt, D. M., and Wilkinson, C. F., *Cases and Materials on Federal Indian Law.* St. Paul: West.

Wilson, W. J. (1978). *The Declining Significance of Race and Changing American Institutions.* Chicago: University of Chicago Press.

Wong, K. S. (1995). "Chinatown: Conflicting Images, Contested Terrain." *Melus* 20, pp. 3–16.

Worster, D. (1987). "New West, True West: Interpreting the Region's History." *Western Historical Quarterly* 18, pp. 141–156.

Wyatt, V. (1987). "Alaskan Indian Wage Earners in the 19th Century: Economic Choices and Ethnic Identity on Southeast Alaska's Frontier." *Pacific Northwest Quarterly* 78, nos. 1–2, pp. 43–50.

Zamora, E. (1993). *The World of the Mexican Worker in Texas.* College Station: Texas A & M University Press.

six

A Formal View of
the Theory of Racial Formation

RICHARD NAGASAWA

In 1987, with the publication of their book *Racial Formation in the United States*, Omi and Winant boldly opened a debate about the adequacy of current theories to explain race relations in the United States, asserting that these theories did not account for recent dynamic changes in the landscape of those relations. Critics of Omi and Winant (Gordon, 1989; Nagel, 1988; Hamilton, 1988; Driver, 1988; San Juan, Jr., 1992; and Webster, 1992) have taken them to task for suggesting that the three major paradigms in race theory—ethnicity, class, and nation—failed to fully explain race, while Omi and Winant themselves failed to offer a more effective theoretical statement of race.

The purpose of this chapter is to formally restate the most significant ideas formulated by Omi and Winant in order to expose the logical skeleton of their informal theory of race. My objective is to strive for clarity and precision, and in doing so, to uncover the theory's weaknesses—assuming they exist. Omi and Winant's ideas are complex, held together by a mixture of logic, rhetoric, and data. My strategy is to pare down the semantic layers in order to state the theory as simply as possible. I will attempt to meet the two criteria suggested by Cohen: (a) that the theory be explicit and relatively precise; and (b) that the theory clearly exhibit the structure of the argument. In Cohen's words, "the syntax of the theory should allow an examination of the logical skeleton of the theory apart from its content" (Cohen, 1989, p. 194).

The Utility of Formal Theory

There are no rules one can follow in formalizing a theory, and the logic by which a theory proceeds is not always obvious. So why attempt to formalize a theory? Formalization clears up problems of scope, conditions, and form. The goal of formalization is to expose the theory and strip it down so that it is as simple and clear as possible. The process of formalization consists of operations performed on the theory to see what it says (Skidmore, 1975). In the course of performing these operations, one must select from among various possibilities. No set of rules exists by which the desired outcome can be produced without distortions or omissions resulting from this process of selection.

In selecting the basic principles for the formalization of the theory of racial formation, I have necessarily relied on my own insights and understanding of the theory. Others might disagree with my decisions in selecting these basic sentences, or axioms. To enable my readers to understand why I have chosen particular principles, I have quoted specific passages from Omi and Winant pertaining to the principle in question.

The Defects of Race Theory

Omi and Winant first addressed the defects of current race theories and then introduced their own theory as a more valid explanation of race relations. Omi and Winant asserted that class-based theory and nation-based theory emerged in response to ethnicity-based theory, which they identified as the predominant race theory. Their critique of ethnicity-based theory centered on the claim that this type of theory applies only to white ethnic history and ignores the different historical experiences of ethnic minorities, and that it therefore distorts the true nature of race relations in the United States. Moreover, they maintain, ethnicity-based theory gave rise to the neoconservative policies that led to reversals of the civil rights gains of the 1960s and 1970s. Omi and Winant viewed class-based theory as reductionist because it subsumes the category of race into that of class and thereby diffuses the role of race in class identities. Hence, they have argued that class-based theory dismisses race as the force that drives conflict and racial divisions.

Finally, since nation-based theory is closely related conceptually to class-based theory, Omi and Winant noted that the former has the same defects as the latter. Referring to the world systems model, Omi and Winant suggested that the core nations continue to exploit former colonies and peripheral nations in much the same way that interest groups exploit blacks in the United States. Omi and Winant therefore rejected the theory of internal colonialism (for a description of the latter, see Chapter 12 in this volume), considering it yet another example of the limitations and inadequacies of nation-based theory for explaining race relations in the United States.

Critics' View of the Theory of Racial Formation

Having identified flaws in each of the three most prevalent paradigms, Omi and Winant presented a new theory that they argued was far more effective than the old models. Like most of social science theory, Omi and Winant's theory is not immune to criticism. For example, Gordon has asserted that Omi and Winant "overstate the negation of race and racism among ethnicity-based theoreticians" (1989, p. 133) and that they implicitly discard, by exclusion, critical efforts to modify the defects of ethnicity-based theses. In their critique of class-based theory and nation-based theory as reductionist, Omi and Winant selectively drew evidence for their conclusion from the available literature (Gordon, 1989).

Nagel went so far as to state that the "lack of rigor" of Omi and Winant's 1987 book rendered it "ultimately not very compelling or useful" (1988, p. 1026). Hamilton identified three "blatant flaws" in Omi and Winant's work. First, Hamilton noted that they had ignored a number of major analyses by political scientists in the 1970s. Second, he asserted that the twenty years that had passed since the events of the 1960s and 1970s did not provide enough historical perspective within which to develop a theory explaining those events. Lastly, Hamilton suggested that Omi and Winant had failed to discuss the concept of "institutional racism," which he claimed "serious scholarship on the period would not permit ignoring" (1988, pp. 158–159). Despite such criticism, Driver viewed Omi and Winant's theory as "elegant and plausible" and asserted that they had "magnificently accomplished what they were asked to do: to provide a statement on race for a series of books 'on critical social thought'" (1988, p. 283).

Some scholars have criticized Omi and Winant for erecting straw men that they could knock down easily to make way for their own race theory. Yet if the foundation of a theory is defective, then it will ultimately self-destruct; and in this light, critics have had little to say about the theory itself. Even though Nagel (1988) took issue with Omi and Winant's use of the concepts of "ethnicity" and "race" and their failure to define either, the theory outlined in the book escaped serious criticism. For example, the theory's ability to explain minority protest action and white racial reaction has hardly been touched upon, apart from Gordon's (1989) comment that it appeared to be only a variation of the "action-reaction-action dynamic interracial thesis" (pp. 134–135). In spite of that, Gordon praised the authors for taking on the "riskier" and more valuable task of prediction, as reflected in the theory's statement about the trajectory of racial politics, rather than the safer task of explaining past events. In particular, the theory asserts that race will continue to determine the course of political and social history and that the political right will try to control further large-scale mobilization by blacks in society (Driver, 1988).

Often the polemics of critics tend to get in the way of constructive analyses of a theory. The most important question critics can ask is: What can be done to identify and correct the theory's inadequacies? That is the question I have attempted to answer in this chapter.

Overview of the Theory of Racial Formation

The theory of racial formation outlined by Omi and Winant (1987) can be easily understood within the framework of the social construction paradigm. Omi and Winant argue that racial categories are based on racist ideologies and are not—as previously conceptualized—biological and "immutable." The focus of their own theory is on how we think and use the categories to structure our experiences and view the world. Omi and Winant's theory in fact challenges the basic premise of biological determinism as it applies to race. Hence, this view fits well within the social constructionist perspective.

Briefly, the theory asserts that all members of society are subjected to racial projects that provide the means by which race is identified. Once race is identified, it is routinized and standardized by the state, which Omi and Winant describe as a "racial state." Hence, racial projects form the basis for the racial formation process. According to Omi and Winant, we all learn some sketch of the rules of racial classification and of our racial identity. The meaning of race is framed in collective identity, in the social structure. So race becomes second nature to us in understanding, explaining, and acting in society. It is the "central axis" of social relations. Moreover, the meaning of race is constantly being transformed by political struggle between the collective actions of groups and the reactions of the racial state. The racial order thus is in "unstable equilibrium." It follows from this that racial categories are not "fixed and immutable" but are defined by meanings of race that shape individual and collective identities, which in turn frame collective action toward the state.

Race operates on two levels: the micro and the macro levels. Individuals (micro level) are mobilized in response to an unjust racial order (macro level). The social and political struggle between the collective and the state (trajectory) that follows results in a new meaning of race and in change in the racial order. The newly altered racial order, in turn, is likely to become the target of new challenges from ideological opponents in an ongoing dialectic.

The theory thus explains (a) how the racial order and the meaning of race and the political role it plays affect individuals and the state. It suggests that individuals mobilize and collectively challenge the unjust racial order. Since the state organizes and enforces the racial order in terms of programs and policies, the state is the focus of the demands in the political struggle between the collective and the state. The theory also explains (b) how the racial order is changed and maintained in an unstable equilibrium. The racial order changes when the state initiates either reforms or repressive measures in response to the demands by the racially based collective. The meaning and the role played by race thus are constantly transformed in an unstable equilibrium.

Basic Principles of
the Theory of Racial Formation

The first assumption on which Omi and Winant's theory of racial formation is based is the assumption that race is the core, the "central axis," of political and social relations in the United States. (*Racial formation* refers to "the process by which social, economic, and political forces determine the content and importance of racial categories, and by which they are in turn shaped by racial meanings" [Omi and Winant, 1987, p. 61].) The politics of race and the state are so intimately related in American society that Omi and Winant link the two conceptually as the "racial state." They write: "The state from its very inception has been concerned with the politics of race. For most of U.S. history, the state's main objective in its racial politics was repression and exclusion" (1994, p. 81). Because "the state is inherently racial" (1994, p. 82), it is often the site of racial conflicts. The state organizes and enforces the racial order in everyday life; thus, the state shapes and is shaped by the politics of race: "The racial state . . . has been historically constructed by racial movements; it consists of agencies and programs which are the institutional responses to racial movements of the past" (1994, p. 86). From Omi and Winant's observations on the nature and consequences of the racial state, I have deduced the following basic principles of their theory of racial formation.

The Principle of Disrupted Equilibrium

Omi and Winant view the racial order as an "unstable equilibrium" (1994, p. 84), meaning that racial conflict persists in society. Opposition groups continually seek to politicize racial identities and challenge the racial order and normal politics: "The state is the focus of collective demands both for egalitarian and democratic reforms and for the enforcement of existing privileges" (1994, p. 82). The ideological challenge results in conflict between the state and the racially based collective, disrupting the equilibrium. How does the challenge come into being? Omi and Winant claim that racial movements arise as the result of political or racial projects that:

> summarize and explain problems—economic inadequacy, absence of political rights, cultural repression, etc.—in racial terms. The result of this ideological challenge is a disparity, a conflict, between the pre-existing racial order, organized and enforced by the state, and an oppositional ideology whose subjects are the real and potential adherents of a racially defined movement. (1994, p. 86)

The principle of disrupted equilibrium thus may be stated as follows: *The state organizes and enforces the racial order. Therefore if the racial order is unjust, then racial projects will mobilize racially based collectives to demand changes in the unjust racial order.*

The Principle of Collective Action

The collective challenge to the preexistent racial order disrupts the unstable equilibrium, and an ideological struggle follows. The collective action creates a crisis for the state. The state thus will seek to stabilize the racial order and will initiate reforms in light of the demands by the collective to change the unjust racial order. Omi and Winant state:

> In racial terms the state's trajectory of reform is initiated when movements challenge the pre-existent racial order. Crisis ensues when this opposition upsets the pre-existing *unstable equilibrium*. The terms of challenge can vary enormously, depending on the movement involved. Opposition can be democratic or authoritarian, primarily based in "normal" politics or in disruption; opposition can even reject explicit political definition, as in the case of cultural movements. (1994, p. 87)

Hence, let us formulate the principle of collective action as follows: *The ideological struggle between the state and the collective will occur if and only if racial projects mobilize the collective to demand changes in the racial order.*

The Principle of Trajectory

The concept of "trajectory" links the two major actors in the drama of racial politics—the racial state and the racially based collective. Omi and Winant write: "By 'trajectory' we mean the pattern of conflict and accommodation which takes place over time between racially based movements and the policies and programs of the state" (1994, p. 78). The ideological struggle forces the state to adopt policies of absorption and insulation and initiate moderate reforms in light of the demands, which set the conditions for a change in the racial order: "Ultimately a series of reforms is enacted which partially meets oppositional demands. Reform policies are initiated and deemed politically effective in establishing a new 'unstable equilibrium.' These policies are then regularized in the form of agencies and programs" (1994, p. 87).

However, if the state confers more than the level tolerated by the political conservatives, a new political meaning of injustice will emerge and become linked to conservative ideology. In this instance, the state will adopt reactionary responses to the demands of the collective. In this context, Omi and Winant describe the situation that occurred in the 1970s:

> In attempting to eliminate racial discrimination, the state went too far. It legitimated group rights, established affirmative action programs which, according to the right, debilitated, rather than uplifted, its target population. In this scenario,

the victims of racial discrimination had dramatically shifted from racial minorities to whites, particularly white males. (1994, p. 117)

Hence, the white majority rearticulated the meaning of racial equality, which led to a new "unstable equilibrium": "Racial reaction repackaged the earlier themes—infusing them with new political meaning and linking them to other key elements of conservative ideology" (1994, p. 117). It follows from this that *if the state and the collective engage in an ideological struggle, then the state in response will either (a) adopt policies of absorption and insulation, and initiate reforms; or (b) adopt policies linked to conservative ideology, and initiate repressive responses.*

The Principle of Unstable Equilibrium

In either case, liberal reform or conservative reaction, the racial order will undergo change. Hence, the racial order is characterized as an "unstable equilibrium," which suggests the cyclical pattern of "passing through periods of rapid change and virtual stasis, through moments of massive mobilization and others of relative passivity" (1994, p. 86).

> The racial order is equilibrated by the state—encoded in law, organized through policymaking, and enforced by a repressive apparatus. But the equilibrium thus achieved is unstable, for the great variety of conflicting interests encapsulated in racial meanings and identities can be no more than pacified—at best—by the state. (1994, pp. 84–85)

It follows, then, that *if the state adopts either (a) or (b), then the racial order will change, disrupting the unstable equilibrium, and the altered racial order will in turn become the target of a new ideological challenge in an ongoing dialectic.*

In summary, the *principle of disrupted equilibrium* establishes the racial state as the source of injustice in the social order and the focus of the demands of the collective. Under the conditions of an unjust racial order, racial projects politicize racial identities and mobilize members of society to collectively challenge the preexisting racial order and normal politics. The *principle of collective action* suggests that the ideological challenge by the collective results in conflict between the state and the racially based collective. The *principle of trajectory* states that the political or ideological struggle results in changes in the racial order when the state initiates either moderate reforms or repressive responses. Finally, the *principle of unstable equilibrium* asserts that the changes will disrupt the unstable equilibrium and the racial order will once again be challenged by new ideological opponents in an ongoing dialectic. These four principles are the basis of the formal theory developed in the next section.

FIGURE 6.1   Model of the Theory of Collective Action (Unstable Equilibrium)

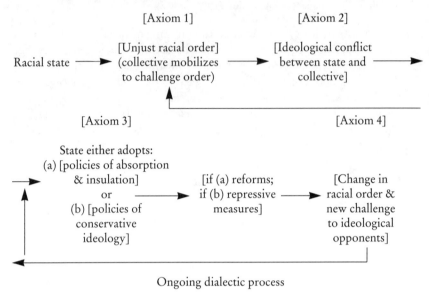

Ongoing dialectic process

Formal Theory: Definitions and Uses

In the social sciences, theories are likely to contain unstated premises and historical and philosophical digressions as well as formal hypotheses that shed light on the phenomena in question. Because social science theories are often written in ordinary language, which lacks the precision of formal language, it is often difficult to identify a theory's major propositions. Some theories are so vague and flexible that they defy logical and empirical evaluation.

A "good" theory is one that helps us (1) to organize our thinking, (2) to make sense of the data, and (3) to go beyond the data and suggest implications that are not evident from the data. The ideal model of a theory, if there is one, is the deductive system stated in some formal language. Braithwaite (1953) defines a deductive theory as "a deductive system in which observable consequences logically follow from . . . the fundamental hypotheses in the system" (p. 22). The value of a theory of this kind resides in the fact that (1) empirical findings can be subsumed under its fundamental hypotheses and that (2) the theory can be tested by testing a few critical hypotheses derived from its axioms.

A *formal deductive theory* is a theory that has been specified in relatively exact terms by means of a formal language. Theories that are stated strictly in symbolic or mathematical terms have an advantage over theories that are stated in natural language: The formal language greatly clarifies and simplifies the theory and thus produces information about the theory itself that otherwise might be overlooked.

The formal deductive theory contains terms that are formally defined, axioms that are explicitly stated, and theorems that are derived from the axioms. In the formal deductive theory, then, it is possible to decide mechanically whether a given statement follows from the axioms by means of formal rules. The formal deductive theory is able to handle a large amount of data with relatively few axioms and to go beyond the data to discover facts not yet observed. It is extremely useful if we wish (1) to subsume existing facts, and (2) to derive precise implications of matters of fact.

Formal systems consist of two parts: a calculus and an interpretation. The calculus is the formal language (or apparatus) of the theory by which the system's sentences are stated. In the formal deductive system, some of the sentences are specified as axioms. The system is completely specified so that the theorems of the system are stated in terms of the axioms and explicitly stated rules of inference. In addition to the calculus, formal theories have an interpretation. The symbols of the system are given an interpretation, a substance. In most instances, the meanings of the symbols are treated informally or intuitively.

The calculus of the formal system generally consists of four elements: vocabulary, formation rules, axioms, and rules of inference. The *vocabulary* of the formal system consists of terms used in writing the sentences or statements of the theory. The terms of the vocabulary denote variables, logical constants, and punctuations. *Formation rules* are rules that tell us how to construct the sentences, as does grammar in ordinary language. The *axioms* are a set of sentences that are assumed to be true, and from which other sentences of the theory (theorems) are derived by rules. And finally, the *rules of inference* provide the means to proceed step by step in deriving the theorems from the axioms.

Let us now restate Omi and Winant's theory of racial formation in more formal terms. Formal language systems are content free in much the same way that logic and mathematics are. In a strict sense, formal system are abstract calculi composed of symbols and formulas. The only concern is with the deduction of sentences, not with the truth or falsity of the sentences. For this purpose, I shall take the theory of racial formation and express it in terms of the calculus of *propositional logic*.[1] We begin by formalizing the four principles outlined above as axioms from which we will subsequently derive theorems by rules of logic.

A Formal Theory of Collective Action

This theory consists of four axioms. I shall first state the axioms in English, symbolize them in propositional logic, and then derive from them a number of theorems using the rules of logic.

Axioms:

Ax. 1: If the state organizes and enforces the racial order only if the racial order is unjust, then the racial projects will mobilize the collective to demand changes in the unjust racial order.

Ax. 2: An ideological struggle will follow between the state and the racially based collective if and only if the racial projects mobilize the collective to demand changes in the unjust racial order.

Ax. 3: If the state and collective engage in an ideological struggle, then the state will either (a) adopt the policies of absorption and insulation and initiate reforms or (b) adopt the policies linked to conservative ideology and initiate repressive responses.

Ax. 4: If the state adopts either (a) or (b), then the existing racial order will change and disrupt the unstable equilibrium and become the target of a new ideological challenge in an ongoing dialectic.

The axioms may be restated in symbolic terms to enhance our ability to determine the deductive relations between sentences. The symbols of the formal theory are listed in Table 6.1.

The theorems derived from the four axioms are listed in Table 6.1 and identified in Figure 6.2. Note that the diagram shows the links between the axioms and theorems. Let us examine two of the theorems from the theory that bear on the state's reactions to the ideological demands of the collective and see how they relate to events described by Omi and Winant. Consider T6 and T7:

T6: *If the racial order is unjust, only if the state and collective engage in an ideological struggle, then the state will adopt policies of absorption and insulation and initiate reforms.*

$$T6: (q \; s) \; v$$

T7: *If the racial order is unjust, only if the state and collective engage in an ideological struggle, then the state will adopt conservative policies and initiate repressive measures.*

$$T7: (q \; s) \; w$$

The two theorems suggest that if the racial order is unjust and if the state and collective engage in an ideological struggle, then the state will adopt reforms (T6) or the state will adopt conservative measures (T7). The former suggests that the state will attempt to neutralize or pacify the demands through moderate reform measures, as happened in the "first phase" of the civil rights reforms of the mid-1960s. According to Omi and Winant: "The resulting concessions were limited but real: policy shifts through executive order and legislation, judicial action against specific racist practices, establishment of new state programs and agencies with 'equal opportunity' mandates, and the hiring

TABLE 6.1   Theorems

Theorems						Premises
T1:	q		r			Ax. 1
T2:	r		s			Ax. 2
T3:	(p		q)	s		Ax. 1 & T2
T4:	q		s			T3
T5:	(p		q)	(v	or w)	T3 & Ax. 3
T6:	(q		s)	v		T4
T7:	(q		s)	w		T4
T8:	s		(y & z)			Ax. 3 & Ax. 4
T9:	w		(y & z)			Ax. 4
T10:	(v	or	w)	y		Ax. 4
T11:	v		y			T10
T12:	w		y			T10
T13:	v		(y & z)			Ax. 4
T14:	v		y			T13
T15:	v		z			T13
T16:	y		v			T13
T17:	y		z			T15 & T16
T18:	(y		z)	w		T17
T19:	s		v			Ax. 3
T20:	s		w			Ax. 3
T21:	s		r			Ax. 2
T22:	p		r			Ax. 1
T23:	(p		q)	r		T3 & T21
T24:	(q		r)	s		T1
T25:	(q	&	r)	s		T2

FIGURE 6.2   Structure of the Theory of Racial Formation

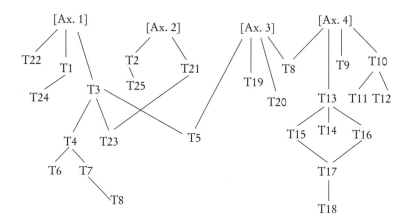

of many black activists by state institutions" (1994, p. 104). The latter (T7) suggests that the state will adopt conservative measures. From the mid-1960s to the early 1970s, changes took place in the racial order. The events that occurred in the 1970s are thus captured by T7. The policies of the "welfare state" were questioned by conservatives with popular support, and the state initiated measures to slow and reverse the changes that began in the 1960s. According to Omi and Winant: "Conservatives argued with increasing popular support, to stop 'throwing good money after bad.' In attempting to remedy problems of poverty and inequity, the state, they charged, only made them worse and instilled a parasitic dependency in its clients" (1994, p. 116).

Theorem 18 addresses the shift from the state's liberal reforms to the more conservative reaction. It states:

$$\text{T18: (y z) w}$$

If changes in the racial order disrupt the unstable equilibrium and if the new racial order is the target of ideological opponents, then the state will adopt conservative ideology and initiate repressive measures. In other words, if the state reforms go too far and disrupt the unstable equilibrium, the state will be challenged by conservatives to adopt new measures to slow or reverse the changes. This deduction explains the "backlash" of the 1980s. The model of the theory of collective action may be used to describe the process, as shown in Figure 6.3.

Omi and Winant describe the change in the climate of racial politics as follows:

> On the policy level, the Reagan administration took its cue from both the new right and neoconservatives, arguing that the important forms of racial discrimination had been eliminated. Thus most civil rights remedies and mechanisms for achieving racial equality were suddenly considered to discriminate *against whites* (1994, p. 134).

The examples above illustrate how the theorems of the formal theory subsume the facts of changes in racial politics and the reactions of the state, and thus, how the theorems capture historical changes in the politics of race. Let us now turn to an example of how the theory may be used deductively to explain the facts.

The Explanatory Usefulness of the Theory

In science, there are two modes of theoretical explanation: (a) statements (empirical regularities or generalizations) explained as deductive consequences of a theory, and (b) events explained as deductive consequences of a

FIGURE 6.3   State Reaction and Opposition Ideology

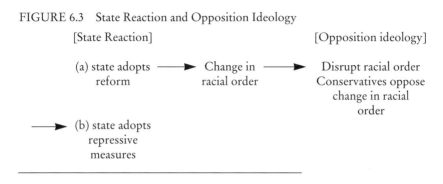

[State Reaction]   [Opposition ideology]

(a) state adopts ⟶ Change in ⟶ Disrupt racial order
    reform   racial order   Conservatives oppose
                                        change in racial
                                        order

⟶ (b) state adopts
      repressive
      measures

hypothesis. Popper states that to explain by means of theory is "to deduce a statement that describes it [the theory], using as premises of deduction one or more universal laws together with certain singular statements, the initial conditions" (1959, p. 59). In other words, theory explains in a hierarchical form; that is, it deductively explains hypotheses that in turn also explain facts or events by deduction.

The deductive process by which a hypothesis is used to explain a fact or to predict an event consists of the following elements (Salmon, 1967):

H: Hypothesis selected to explain fact
I: Initial conditions (auxiliary hypotheses)
O: Observational consequences

The first two elements are premises. The second premise specifies the antecedent conditions (or initial conditions) that are inherent both in the first premise—that is, the hypothesis—and in the fact to be explained. The third element, the conclusion, may be in the form of a prediction (if the event has not yet occurred) or an explanation (if the event has occurred).

Briefly, *theory* as used here consists of a set of statements (or fundamental propositions) from which other statements follow by logical principles. The statements of the theory can usually be divided into two parts: (a) the primary theory, which is composed of general statements or propositions, and (b) auxiliary hypotheses, which serve to link the general propositions of the primary theory to the regularity or fact in question.

To see how the statements of the theory of collective action can be used deductively to explain the facts, let us consider the case outlined below.

Fact: In the late 1980s, Asian Americans collectively mobilized to confront the leading U.S. universities, which they felt had adopted unjust informal quotas for admission of Asian American students.

Theorem 1, which follows from Axiom 1, may be used to explain the fact as regards quotas for the admission of Asian American students.

T1: Racial projects will mobilize the collective to demand changes in the racial order, if the racial order is unjust.

There is no obvious connection between the statement of the theory and the fact to be explained. To make this linkage, we use auxiliary hypotheses, the main purpose of which is to connect the general statement of the theory to the statement of the fact in order to explain the latter. Hence, the following auxiliary hypotheses are introduced in the deductive format.

Auxiliary hypotheses:
  (i) In the late 1980s, the leading U.S. universities had informal quotas for the admission of Asian American students. (Unjust racial order)
  (ii) The problem was viewed in racial terms as unjust and in violation of civil rights laws by Asian American academics, civil rights leaders, and students. (Racial project)

It follows that Asian Americans collectively mobilized and actively confronted university administrators to change the unjust quota system (fact). Hence, the hypothesis derived from Ax. 1 plus the auxiliary hypotheses (i) and (ii) allow us to deductively subsume the fact in question—that is, to explain the fact in the deductive sense.

The Empirical Adequacy of the Theory

Even though the theory may be fruitfully used to explain the facts in question, it must also be tested by new data. It stands or falls on whether or not such empirical tests confirm its plausibility. If the hypothesis is proved false, this result indicates either the falsity of the primary theory or the falsity of the auxiliary hypotheses used to link the primary theory to the fact(s) in question. The theory is disconfirmed only to the extent that one believes that the auxiliary hypotheses are confirmed.

The formal theory can be tested by testing only a few crucial statements to shed light on its plausibility. From the structure of the theory (Figure 6.2), it is clear that tests of Theorem 5 will indirectly affect Axiom 3 and Theorems 2 and 3 as well as Axioms 1 and 2, since they are linked to the derivation of Theorem 5. So if T15 is refuted by data, then the data throw into question three of the four axioms of the theory. A theory is created in order to be tested against the facts and proven false. To refute a theory is to advance science. In this context, Popper states: "Every refutation should be regarded as a great success; not merely as a success of the scientist who refuted the theory, but also of the scientist who created the refuted theory and who thus in the first instance suggested, if only indirectly, the refuting experiment" (1962, p. 243).

In the final analysis, the theory of racial formation, like any theory, must be evaluated in terms of its empirical adequacy. It is not the purpose of this chapter to examine the formal theory's empirical adequacy; I leave this task to others.

Summary and Conclusions

To introduce their own racial theory, Omi and Winant examined critically the three competing paradigms in race and ethnic studies—ethnicity-based theory, class-based theory, and nation-based theory—for the purpose of finding the paradigm in question deficient in terms of its ability to explain race relations in the United States. In analyzing Omi and Winant's theory, in turn, I found it a more natural competitor for models that describe social change or large-scale social movements than for the three models cited in Omi and Winant's critique. This observation might have been a result of my chosen focus; however, the formal theory clearly suggests that Omi and Winant's work offers another approach to the study of social movements, explaining the organized collective promotion of or resistance to change. Omi and Winant's work can justifiably be compared to Smelser's value-added theory (Smelser, 1962) or to the resource-mobilization perspective (Zald and Ash, 1964; Zald and McCarthy, 1987). In fact, Omi and Winant did consider these models briefly in their discussion of the modern civil rights struggle but found them deficient in explaining the "politicizing of black identity" that led to the emergence of the radical agenda of the 1960s (1994, p. 98).

I therefore concluded that the theory as formalized in this chapter should be viewed as a "special theory" (specific for race) of collective action and social change. Like Omi and Winant's analysis, on which it is based, the theory avoids the dilemma of circularity that the two other models sustain in the sense that it does not depend on the concepts of strain or reward as evidence for collective action. The great utility of the theory lies in its ability to describe and explain the origin, character, and change of social or political movements in the United States. Clearly, Omi and Winant's work can gainfully be considered alongside Smelser's and Zald and Ash's—the two most widely used and cited sources on social movement theory in the past thirty years.

CONCEPTS AND DEFINITIONS

Absorption: the process by which the state adopts demands in suitably moderate form (cooptation)

The source of these definitions is M. Omi and H. Winant, *Racial Formation in the United States,* 2nd ed. (New York: Routledge, 1994), pp. 3, 55–56, 78, 82, 88–91, 106, and 163.

Articulation: the process of defining political interests and identities

Insulation: the process by which the state confines demands to areas that are not crucial to its operation

Racial categories: political classifications that establish the boundaries of racial identity

Racial formation: the process by which racial categories are created, inhabited, transformed, and destroyed

Racial order: the "rules of the game" that define the scope of state activity vis-à-vis race; the rules by which racial politics is organized

Racial project: the effort to reorganize and redistribute resources along racial lines

Racial state: a state that is inherently racial; concerned with the politics of race

Rearticulation: the redefinition of political interests and identities by recombining familiar ideas and values

Trajectory: the pattern of conflict and accommodation that takes shape over time between racially based social movements and the policies and programs of the state

NOTES

1. For a more precise and expressive analysis, quantifier logic may be the method of choice. The decision to use quantifier or propositional logic depends on the objective in mind. I selected propositional logic—the simpler of the two—as the formal language, since the objective is simply to isolate the logical form of the sentences or arguments.

REFERENCES

Braithwaite, R. B. (1953). *Scientific Explanation*. New York: Cambridge University Press.

Cohen, B. P. (1989). *Developing Sociological Knowledge*. 2nd ed. Chicago: Nelson-Hall.

Driver, E. D. (1988). "Featured Essay." *Contemporary Sociology* 17, no. 3, pp. 280–286.

Gordon, L. (1989). "Racial Theorizing: Is Sociology Ready to Replace Polemic Causation Theory with a New Polemic Model?" *Sociological Perspectives* 32, no. 1, pp. 129–136.

Hamilton, C. V. (1988). "Book Review: 'Racial formation in the United States from the 1960s to the 1980s,' by Omi, M., and Winant, H." *Political Science Quarterly* 103, no. 1, pp. 158–159.

Nagel, J. (1988). "Book Review: 'Racial formation in the United States from the 1960s to the 1980s,' by Omi, M., and Winant, H." *American Journal of Sociology* 93, no. 4, pp. 1025–1027.

Omi, M., and Winant, H. (1987). *Racial Formation in the United States: From the 1960s to the 1980s*. New York: Routledge and Kegan Paul.

_____. (1994). *Racial Formation in the United States: From the 1960s to the 1980s*. 2nd ed. New York: Routledge.

Popper, K. (1959). *The Logic of Scientific Discovery*. New York: Harper and Row.

_____. (1962). *Conjectures and Refutations: The Growth of Scientific Knowledge*. New York: Basic Books.

Salmon, W. C. (1967). *The Foundations of Scientific Inference*. Pittsburgh, PA: University of Pittsburgh Press.

San Juan, E., Jr. (1992). *Racial Formation/Critical Transformations*. Atlantic Highlands, NJ: Humanities Press.

Skidmore, W. (1975). *Theoretical Thinking in Sociology*. New York: Cambridge University Press.

Smelser, N. (1962). *Theory of Collective Behavior*. New York: Free Press.

Webster, Y. O. (1992). *The Racialization of America*. New York: St. Martin's Press.

Zald, M. N., and Ash, R. (1964). "Social Movement Organization: Growth, Decay, and Change." *Social Forces* 44, pp. 327–341.

Zald, M. N., and McCarthy, J. D. (1987). "Social Movement Industries: Competition and Cooperation Among SMOs." In Zald, M. N., and McCarthy, J. D., eds., *Social Movements in an Organizational Society: Collected Essays*. New Brunswick, NJ: Transaction Books.

seven

Social Ecological Contexts of Prejudice Between Hispanics and Blacks

YOLANDA FLORES NIEMANN

> Prejudice: an aversive or hostile attitude toward a person who belongs to a group, simply because he belongs to that group, and is therefore presumed to have the objectionable qualities ascribed to the group.
>
> —G. W. Allport (1954, p. 7)

With few exceptions (e.g., Guthrie and Hutchinson, 1995; Bach, 1993; Portes and Stepick, 1993; Oliver and Johnson, 1984), the vast majority of research on race relations and prejudice in the United States has focused on attitudes between blacks and whites. *Race* is assumed to mean black people and white people, and *minority* is equated with *black* (Moore, 1981). This biracial assumption is enshrined in the U.S. census, where statistics are provided for the categories "white" and "nonwhite," with most people understanding *nonwhite* as meaning "black" (Moore, 1981).

Given the history of slavery and the civil strife of the 1960s, this focus on blacks and whites previously might have been justifiable. However, the color of America is rapidly changing, and reality is masked by the assumption that issues dealing with racial minorities are a question of black or white. According to 1990 census figures (United States, Bureau of the Census, 1990), the population growth of Hispanics and blacks, the largest minority groups in the United States, far exceeds that of whites. Whereas the white population is expected to grow by 13 percent, black and Hispanic population growth is projected at 24 percent and 45 percent, respectively. Since contact between these populations will inevitably increase, an examination of attitudes, perceptions, and situations that might affect relations between blacks and Hispanics is timely.

In this chapter, we will undertake precisely this sort of examination. In the first section, we will review the literature on black and Hispanic intergroup attitudes and prejudices, stereotypes, social distance, and conflict or hostility. In the second section, I have outlined the literature on the social ecological contexts of blacks and Hispanics, which might underlie negative perceptions and relations between these groups. These contexts include disparities in housing, education, employment, poverty, health, and political power. The third section contains a discussion of conclusions that might be reached from a review of this literature, especially regarding projections of future black–brown relations.

The literature currently available indicates that prejudice between blacks and Hispanics might well be a function of disparities between the two groups in domains of power, resources, and status. These disparities appear to precipitate socially shared prejudices between blacks and Hispanics as categories rather than between individual members of those groups (Brown, 1995). The evidence also indicates that prejudices are a function of ethnic group stereotypes and of the level and quality of contact between the groups.

Black–Brown Intergroup Attitudes and Prejudices

Although research that directly examines black–brown prejudices has been sparse, recent literature allows for some conclusions. For instance, Mindiola, Rodriguez, and Niemann (1996) interviewed 1200 randomly selected blacks and U.S.-born and foreign-born Hispanics (600 of each racial group) in Houston, Texas, regarding different aspects of the relationship between blacks and Hispanics. When asked for perceptions of conflict, 59.1 percent of foreign-born Hispanics agreed that there was much conflict between the groups, compared to 46 percent of U.S.-born Hispanic and 45.1 percent of black respondents. Additionally, 52.7 percent of foreign-born agreed that blacks are prejudiced against Hispanics, whereas only 32.1 percent of U.S.-born Hispanics and 21.6 percent of blacks agreed. When asked if they agreed that most Hispanics are prejudiced against blacks, 35.9 percent of blacks, 24.2 percent of U.S.-born Hispanics, and 35.4 percent of foreign-born Hispanics agreed. When asked if Hispanics and blacks fear one another, 42.7 percent of foreign-born and 26.2 percent of U.S.-born Hispanics agreed that Hispanics fear blacks. There was general agreement among all three groups that blacks do not fear Hispanics.

However, when describing the impact of immigrants in the Houston area, 53.6 percent of blacks said it was bad, whereas 63.0 percent of foreign-born and 56.1 percent of U.S.-born Hispanics said the impact was good. When asked whether government programs designed for minorities favor blacks or Hispanics, 57.9 percent of foreign-born and 49.6 percent of U.S.-born Hispanics agreed that programs favor blacks, whereas 75 percent of blacks disagreed that most government programs designed for minorities favor blacks.

Using an index of hostility created from a 1980 *Los Angeles Times* survey, Oliver and Johnson (1984) found Hispanics more antagonistic toward blacks than vice versa on almost every indicator. In contrast, black antagonism toward Hispanics was grounded in a single belief—that immigrants take away jobs. This finding is also consistent with Mindiola, Rodriguez, and Niemann's (1996) results regarding the perceived impact of immigrants in Houston. Oliver and Johnson (1984) found black respondents more likely to indicate that relations were getting worse between blacks and Hispanics.

In a recent focus group study that examined Hispanics' self-identifying markers, Niemann and Romero (1995) found that Mexicans and Mexican Americans in Houston report that one thing they have in common is conflict with blacks. These respondents, who were generally of low socioeconomic status, reported much firsthand discrimination by blacks. They stated that the many blacks employed at places that provide services for the poor (for example, the Women, Infant, and Children (WIC) program, food stamp program, Aid to Families with Dependent Children (AFDC), health clinics, and so on) treat Hispanic women badly. The feelings of the group were voiced by one respondent who said that blacks pretend they don't see the Hispanic women waiting for services; they "talk down" to them, treat them disrespectfully, and claim they don't understand them, even when they speak English.

In summary, Hispanics report more prejudice against blacks than vice versa, although they believe the opposite to be true. That is, Hispanics believe that blacks are more prejudiced toward them than vice versa. However, Mindiola, Rodriguez, and Niemann's (1996) data indicate a difference in perceptions between U.S.-born and foreign-born Hispanics on the issues of black–brown relations. These findings show the complexity of the relationships between these minority groups.

Social Distance Between Blacks and Hispanics

Mindiola, Rodriguez, and Niemann (1996) also examined social distance between blacks and Hispanics. Once again, findings indicated significant differences between U.S.-born and foreign-born Hispanics and blacks regarding intergroup contact. For instance, 71.5 percent of blacks and 63.2 percent of U.S.-born Hispanics indicated frequent interaction with Hispanics, compared to only 34 percent of foreign-born Hispanics; 45.8 percent of foreign-born and 15.1 percent of U.S.-born Hispanics said they never or almost never interact with blacks. In contrast, 10.1 percent of blacks said they never or almost never interact with Hispanics. The vast majority of respondents in this survey also indicated that given an opportunity, they would be willing to work alongside or in close contact with the other and to live in a neighborhood with the other. However, these data contradict those of Oliver and Johnson (1984), who found that Hispanics indicated less willingness to have blacks in their neighborhoods (22 percent) than vice versa (16 percent).

Mindiola, Rodriguez, and Niemann (1996) also found some contradictions regarding willingness for respondents' children to have intergroup contact. For instance, 41.8 percent foreign-born and 46.8 percent of U.S.-born Hispanics said they would approve of their children marrying a black person, whereas 59.4 percent of blacks said they would approve of their children marrying a Hispanic. Regarding dating, 45.8 percent of foreign-born and 54.0 percent of U.S.-born Hispanics said they would approve of their children dating blacks, whereas 61.6 percent of blacks said they would approve of their children dating Hispanics.

These latter data are consistent with those of Lambert and Taylor (1990), who found that Mexican Americans were more willing to accept whites than blacks as family members through marriage. In a survey of black, Anglo, and Hispanic college students, Lampe (1981) found that more Anglo females indicated they had dated blacks than did Hispanic females, which coincided with the finding that black males dated more Anglo females than they did Hispanics. Blacks indicated that Hispanic females who refused an invitation to date said the refusal was often explained by differences in language, religion, values, and family control (Lampe, 1981). Black males who acknowledged they invited Anglo females to go out more often said they did so because of more frequent contact and/or a greater feeling of cultural similarity (Lampe, 1981). A few also mentioned a greater fear of reprisals by Hispanic males, particularly if the date necessitated going into the barrio (Lampe, 1981).

Social distance was also measured by researchers in the Changing Relations Project (Bach, 1993), who used ethnographic research methods to analyze the relations between longtime residents and newcomers from different cultures in Chicago, Houston, Miami, Philadelphia, Monterey Park (California), and Garden City (Kansas). They found language was a source of conflict, and the most contested issue in relations among newcomers and established residents in all six sites. They report: "Language is more than a means of communication. It binds individuals together and separates groups. It conveys tremendous complexity of purpose and meaning, and contains both the instrument value of enabling communication and the symbolic values of personal and group identity" (Bach, 1993, p. 36). In these six research sites, language-based problems emerged through separate services that reduced interactions between monolingual Hispanics and their English-speaking counterparts, including blacks. This language barrier also pertained to church services. Bach (1993) quotes one Houston parishioner as saying that the most segregated hour of the week is 11:00 A.M. on Sunday.

Dyer, Vedlitz, and Worchel (1989) measured intergroup prejudice with social distance items that assessed level of acceptance or rejection of members
of the other groups in nine standard social distance settings: marriage, children in same school, work with at job, swimming together, have as boss,
have at home gathering, have as neighbor, children have as college room-
mate, and children have as teacher. Their research, with a respondent random Texas sample of 708 Anglos, 249 Blacks, and 256 Hispanics, identified
some possible mediators and moderators of social distance between blacks
and Hispanics. For instance, they found that younger Hispanics have an acceptance level of blacks significantly higher than that found among older
Hispanics, and Hispanics with higher education are significantly more positive toward blacks than are their less educated fellows. Higher educated
blacks are significantly more positive toward Hispanics than are less educated black citizens, and non-Baptist Protestant blacks are more positive toward Hispanics than are Catholic and Baptist blacks.

In somewhat inconsistent findings, Johnson and Oliver (1994) report that
on all measures of social distance, Hispanics are from two to three times more
likely to express xenophobic attitudes toward blacks than vice versa—attitudes that are not changed by controlling for sex, education, and social class.
Johnson and Oliver believe that these prejudicial attitudes are a function of the
Mexican tradition, which is not one of tolerance. They argue that Hispanics
bring with them prejudices toward blacks from their host countries. Spanish
and Mexican culture have historically denigrated dark skin, which translates
into desire on the part of some Mexican Americans to be white and into negative attitudes toward contact with blacks (Johnson and Oliver, 1994).

Overall, data indicate that the social distance maintained between blacks and
Hispanics is greater than that between each minority and the majority Anglo
groups (Dyer, Vedlitz, and Worchel, 1989). Dyer and colleagues concluded:

> Minorities maintain at least as much social distance from each other as Anglos
> maintain toward the two minority groups. . . . Minority group members hold
> values similar to those of the majority, accepting the majority while rejecting the
> other minority. Hence, we cannot rely on the experience of discrimination to
> reduce discrimination. Interestingly, rejection of an out-group minority by a
> minority group may be broader and less selective than rejection of the minority
> by the majority group. (1989, p. 614)

Stereotypes

One measure of prejudice that may predict group relations is an assessment
of intergroup stereotypes. Mindiola, Rodriguez, and Niemann (1996) asked
600 U.S.- and foreign-born Hispanics and 600 blacks, all randomly selected
from among Hispanic and black residents of Houston, to suggest three

words that in their opinion best described the other group, and to indicate how positive that word was when used about that group. With that methodology, the favorableness of the provided terms was determined by respondents and not by researchers. Findings indicated that of words used by U.S.-born Hispanics to describe blacks, 52 percent were favorable, 38 percent were negative, and 10 percent were neutral. Of words provided about blacks by foreign-born Hispanics, 43 percent were favorable, 47 percent were negative, and 10 percent were neutral. Of words used by blacks to describe Hispanics, 68 percent were favorable, 25 percent were negative, and 7 percent were neutral. Thus, blacks held more favorable perceptions of Hispanics than vice versa, with foreign-born Hispanics' perceptions being the most negative.

Lambert and Taylor (1990) also assessed intergroup attitudes in a study of working-class adults in a Michigan metropolitan area. They found that Hispanics perceived blacks as not hardworking, not trustworthy, not law abiding, and not unfairly treated. They perceived blacks as particularly violent and aggressive, powerful, and likely to stick together as a group. Hispanics described themselves positively and as very hardworking. There was no dimension in which blacks were perceived as similar to Hispanics. Oliver and Johnson (1984) found that Hispanics were twice as likely as blacks to agree that the other group was more violent than the average group. Twenty-one percent of Hispanics agreed that blacks were not as intelligent as other people.

In contrast, blacks described themselves as very American but very unfairly treated. They did not perceive that any other group was as unfairly treated as blacks. They saw themselves as aggressive and violent, but no more so than other groups (Lambert and Taylor, 1990). Lambert and Taylor found that blacks held favorable views of other ethnic groups: "Although tempered with particular shortcomings . . . , they do not feel the need to put other groups down in the process of keeping self-respect" (p. 145). However, Oliver and Johnson (1984) found that one-third of their black respondents thought that Hispanics did not try hard enough to speak English.

Sigelman, Shockey, and Sigelman (1993) reported on a 1989 survey that indicated that Hispanics expressed many of the same stereotyped perceptions of blacks that were widespread among Anglos. Regarding conflict, they stated that the "we-them" mentality was defined in terms of race and not victimization. Blacks might view Hispanics as whites rather than as fellow victims of discrimination. Nevertheless, these data indicated that blacks were neither more nor less likely than whites to engage in stereotyping of Hispanics.

To assess current ethnic/racial group stereotype content, Niemann, Jennings, Rozelle, Baxter, and Sullivan (1994) asked an ethnically diverse group of 259 urban college students to list the first words that came to mind when they thought about Mexican Americans and blacks. The resultant data showed blacks most frequently using the following descriptors of Mexican

American males: *antagonistic, hard workers, pleasant, caring, lower class, intelligent, alcohol users, short, dark hair, attractive, speak loudly, speak softly, criminal, family oriented,* and *humorous.* Terms chosen by blacks to describe Mexican American females were: *pleasant, attractive, caring, overweight, intelligent, baby makers, unmannerly, long hair, dark hair, bad tempered, passive, ambitionless, talkative, sociable,* and *sexy.*

Terms used of black males by Mexican American respondents were: *athletic, antagonistic, pleasant, speak loudly, muscular, criminal, tall, dark skin, unmannerly, sociable, good dancers, lower class, intelligent, achievement oriented,* and *egotistical.* Terms used by Mexican Americans to describe black females were: *speak loudly, athletic, egotistical, unmannerly, sociable, dark skin, antagonistic, fashion conscious, lower class, ambitionless, pleasant, intelligent, complainer, tall,* and *good dancers.* These data indicate that although each group listed some positive traits about the other, most traits were negative, and black traits described by Hispanics were more negative than vice versa. Furthermore, most of these traits were consistent with those enumerated by Anglo respondents (Niemann et al., 1994), indicating that these stereotypes may be socially consensual rather than group specific. These data are also consistent with the reported finding that blacks hold more favorable views of Hispanics than Hispanics hold of blacks.

Perceptions of Mutual Affinity and Conflict with Out-Groups

Intergroup relations also might be affected by feelings and perceptions of affinity and/or conflict with the same out-group. In the case of blacks and Hispanics, an affinity or perceived alliance of Hispanics with Anglos may particularly lead to mistrust between the two minority groups. In her discussion of conflict between blacks and Puerto Ricans, Ginorio (1987) states that blacks attribute Puerto Rican blacks' insistence of identification as Puerto Rican first and black second to a denial of "negritude." Ginorio (1987) explains that although in the United States race relations are seen in terms of black and white, in Latin America the concept of race is one of a continuum. Puerto Ricans therefore insist that they are Puerto Rican first, and a given color, second. However, the degree to which blacks interpret this identification as identification with whites contributes to conflict and mistrust between blacks and Hispanics.

Niemann and Romero (1995) found that Hispanics seemed to have a keen awareness of negative attitudes among Anglos and blacks toward Mexican immigrants. Their male focus group respondents reported anger and frustration at having been injured on the job and then discarded by their Anglo bosses. Respondents indicated that Hispanics believe that they are more easily "used" and mistreated by the system than are blacks, who have the safety net of U.S.

citizenship. These Hispanic respondents also reported their perception that neither Anglos nor blacks want Mexicans or Mexican Americans to call themselves "Americans." As one respondent said, "They always correct us and say, 'No, you're Mexican!'" They indicated frustration about their fear of complaining when their civil rights are violated, stating that teachers and other authority figures know that all they have to do is mention the INS (Immigration and Naturalization Service) for the complainant to go away. This response came forth also from Mexican American U.S. citizens. Although they do have citizenship, they resent the hassle associated with being asked to prove they are in the United States legally. Respondents believed that since Hispanic immigrants cannot claim the prerogative of nativism, they cannot complain about injustices in the way that blacks can, leading to resentment against blacks. This perceived social reality may also lead to the beliefs among Hispanics that blacks are better off in this society than are Hispanics, and that blacks have more affinity with whites than do Hispanics.

In an argument consistent with Niemann and Romero's (1995) findings, Johnson and Oliver (1994) argue that Mexican Americans have historically viewed blacks as black Anglo-Saxons due to their affinity for Anglo culture. On the other hand, blacks believe that Mexican Americans can fit into the mainstream more easily than blacks because they can "anglicize" themselves and assimilate (Johnson and Oliver, 1994).

Affinity is also perceived between blacks and Whites by Miami's Hispanics. Portes and Stepick (1993) report that blacks and whites in Miami have common outlooks in their belief that native-born groups, regardless of color, should resist the inroads of a foreign culture and complete the immigrants' assimilation (p. 195). In terms of the anti-Cuban affinity, Portes and Stepick (1993) report that one black informant claimed that native whites, although racist, were more acceptable than Cubans because at least they "are racist by tradition and they at least know that what they're doing is not quite right. . . . Cubans don't even think there is anything wrong with it. That is the way they've always related, period" (p. 197).

Other researchers have reported affinity between Hispanics and Asians, who traditionally have conflict with blacks (Cheng and Espiritu, 1989). Cheng and Espiritu's (1989) research on Korean businesses in black and Hispanic neighborhoods showed none of the hostility indicative of collective resentment between Koreans and Hispanics that was reported from 1972–1987 in city or community newspapers in Los Angeles. In contrast, both black and Korean newspapers and the *Los Angeles Times* published numerous articles on Korean-black conflicts. Cheng and Espiritu (1989) explain that Koreans and Mexicans share an immigrant ideology:

> Immigrants are often willing to work extra hard because they hold on to the possibility of rising within the system. . . . Many blacks appear to have largely

rejected this dream. As fellow immigrants vying for a place in the American system, Hispanic immigrants may regard Koreans as fair competitors in a capitalist economy rather than as unfairly advantaged enemies (p. 528).

On the other hand, Cheng and Espiritu (1989) found that "many blacks are angry because they perceive Koreans as foreigners who take advantage of the black communities" (p. 528). Here, then, is evidence of a mutual affinity between Hispanics and Koreans, whom blacks perceive as enemies. Such an affinity, in turn, could lead to conflict and mistrust between blacks and Hispanics.

A difference in levels of conflict with out-groups tends to precipitate or aggravate a lack of trust between blacks and Hispanics especially if the two groups are played against each other by Anglos. Acuña (1988) reported that in blue-collar workplaces such as steel manufacturing plants, management has indeed deliberately played black and Mexican workers against one another in order to gain the advantage. Such interactions at the very least would tend to perpetuate conflict and hostility between groups.

Perceptions of Racism

Differential interpretations of whether certain behaviors and attitudes are indicative of racism, and perceptions of different levels of racism targeted toward groups, might also lead to conflict between groups. Skerry (1993) states that Hispanics feel much less discriminated against than do blacks. His conclusion is based on a 1970 survey of Houston Hispanics and blacks and on a 1984 survey of Californians that indicates that whereas 42 percent of blacks in California felt blacks "get fewer opportunities than they deserve," only 23 percent of Hispanics described their situation in such terms. In the same survey, 21 percent of blacks in California felt "most Americans are not prejudiced" against them, and 36 percent of Hispanics felt that way. In the same survey, 61 percent of blacks claimed to have "personally experienced discrimination," compared to 35 percent of Hispanics.

In his discussion of a 1989 poll by the *Los Angeles Times* in Southern California, Skerry (1993) reports that 49 percent of blacks claimed to have personally experienced discrimination, but only 29 percent of Hispanics made the same claim. This poll also indicated that over 60 percent of blacks disagreed with the assertion "These days you hear too much about the rights of minorities and not enough about the rights of the majority," whereas only 49 percent of Hispanics disagreed. To the question "Do you think the government is paying too much attention to blacks and other minority groups, or paying about the right amount of attention to them, or do you think the government is paying too little attention to blacks and other minority groups," 74 percent of blacks—compared with 45 percent of Hispanics—said "too little."

In the same review, Skerry (1993) cites a 1982 survey that asked Californians whether they agreed with the statement "Government should not make a special effort to improve the position of blacks and minorities because they should help themselves." Only 18 percent of blacks agreed, whereas 33 percent of Hispanics and 50 percent of whites agreed. On the statement "To make up for past discrimination women and members of minority groups should be given special treatment in getting jobs and places in college," agreement was quite varied—67 percent of blacks, 45 percent of Hispanics, and 19 percent of whites agreed. On the statement "Business should be required to hire a certain number of minority workers and women even if this means some whites and men would not be hired," 62 percent of blacks, 43 percent of Hispanics, and 25 percent of whites agreed.

In a 1988 poll reported by Skerry (1993), 56 percent of California blacks favored being granted "special preferences" in hiring and promotional practices, compared to only 36 percent of Hispanics; and 55 percent of blacks favored special preferences for college admission, compared to 37 percent of Hispanics. Interestingly, a 1988 Los Angeles poll of delegates to the Democratic National Convention revealed fewer differences between blacks and Hispanics regarding their support for affirmative action, indicating that Mexican American leaders are more supportive of affirmative action, especially quotas, than their rank and file (Skerry, 1993). Skerry concludes that "even in San Antonio, where memories of Texas-style discrimination are still fresh, Mexican Americans are less preoccupied with gaining restitution for past wrong than with taking advantage of present and future opportunities" (p. 297). He states that the concept "fair" is less emotionally charged for Mexicans than for blacks.

In a study that examined perceptions of racism, Niemann and Jones (1995) asked respondents to indicate whether agreement or disagreement with items on a symbolic racism scale was indicative of racism. Results indicated that regarding racism, blacks and Hispanics may have opposing interpretations of whether behaviors and beliefs are racist. For instance, 40 percent of blacks said the statement "Our society is shaped by the national media" would be perceived as racist by them because the media portray blacks as criminals and habitual welfare recipients. On the other hand, 100 percent of Mexican American respondents said that the statement would not be perceived as racist because they believe the media do not influence society in that manner. Regarding a statement about interracial marriage, 60 percent of blacks said that love matters more than color, whereas only 7 percent of Mexican Americans provided that response (to the statement "It is a bad idea for blacks and whites to marry one another").

Stack and Warren (1992) also found different experiences of racism between groups. They discuss a *Miami Herald* poll of racial and ethnic attitudes in which 34 percent of blacks reported that they or someone they knew had faced discrimination in seeking a job or promotion, in contrast to 14 percent of Anglos and 13 percent of Hispanics. Additionally, 32 percent of blacks blamed Hispanics for discrimination, whereas 40 percent blamed Anglos. "Dade County's massive Hispanic immigration has at once created severe competition for entry-level jobs; an enclave economy largely closed to blacks; and continuing resentment over federal, state, and local aid to political refugees that is not available to native blacks" (p. 173).

A Summary of Black–Brown Perceptions

The foregoing review leads to several conclusions: First, Hispanics report that they view blacks as more prejudiced toward them than vice versa. Relatedly, Hispanics maintain more social distance from blacks than vice versa, although other factors also might be mediating this social distance. Second, Hispanics report more negative stereotypes of blacks than do blacks of Hispanics. Third, blacks perceive more racism than do Hispanics, and are in greater favor of programs favoring minorities. These conclusions likely are a function of direct and indirect experiences of blacks and Hispanics with each other and within society generally.

People's social reality is largely a function of the social ecological contexts in which they live (Niemann and Secord, 1995). Disparities in contexts that lead one group to have a lower quality of life than another may lead to conflict between the compared two groups and may thus underlie intergroup prejudice. This conceptualization is summarized by Oliver and Johnson (1984), who argue that the urban context in which blacks and Hispanics find themselves is ripe for the development of mutual distrust and hostility. In the case of blacks and Hispanics, the comparative state of employment, education, power, housing, and health may be a source of conflict. Following is a discussion of these specific contexts as they relate to blacks and Hispanics.

The Effects of Social Ecological Context

Housing

In 1981, Massey argued that with passing time and socioeconomic advance, residential segregation of Hispanics would decline from what it was in 1970. He wrote, "There is no reason to believe that the pace and process of residential desegregation will be any different for these groups than for the many other immigrant groups who have successfully adapted to life in the United States" (p. 320). Yet segregation continues in 1998. Since residential segregation determines where people shop, work, and become educated, it increases social distance, with deleterious effects on intergroup relationships (Bach, 1993).

Massey and Denton (1988) investigated trends in suburbanization for blacks, Asians, and Hispanics, and effects of suburbanization on segregation from 1970–1980 in 59 U.S. metropolitan areas. They found that blacks are much more segregated than Hispanics or Asians, and that Hispanics are much less segregated within central cities than are blacks. The researchers state, "In spite of recent increases in suburbanization, Blacks, compared with other minority groups, remain highly concentrated in central cities, and, within these areas, they experience very high levels of residential dissimilarity and spatial isolation from non-Hispanic whites" (p. 621). Furthermore, black segregation shows considerable persistence from city to suburb. Massey and Denton (1988) conclude that Hispanics have far greater access to suburbs than do blacks. Furthermore, in metropolitan areas where they are heavily represented, Hispanics are considerably more integrated than are blacks. This conclusion is consistent with other research. Matre and Mindiola (1981) investigated the residential segregation of Anglos, Mexican Americans, and blacks in southwestern metropolitan areas. Using an index of dissimilarity, they found that blacks are the most segregated group, and Hispanics, the least.

Moore (1981) states that ghettoization (groups locked into poverty areas of cities with poor institutional services and poor housing) does not seem to be a valid concept for Mexican Americans, though it is widely considered valid for blacks. She states that the reason for the relative lack of ghettoization of Mexican Americans is twofold: First, many southwestern cities were founded by Mexicans, and prevailing residential patterns reflect many decades during which new Anglos competed with original Mexicans for space. Second, since many of these cities grew by annexation, these areas included traditional Mexican settlements. "These patterns contribute to a lower level and a more variable pattern of residential segregation" (Moore, p. 281). Although differences in ghettoization can be explained in terms that do not reflect preferential treatment of one group over another by the dominant Anglo majority, most lay persons are unaware of the factors that precipitate particular housing patterns. Thus, differential segregation could breed resentment and underlie prejudice. Consistent with Moore (1981), Skerry (1993) states that Mexican Americans have found considerable shelter in their homogeneous enclaves, in contrast to blacks, who were deprived of their own distinctive institutions. He states, "The barrio has never borne as heavy a stigma for Mexicans as the ghetto has for blacks" (p. 298).

Furthermore, Johnson and Oliver (1994) state that blacks are concerned that the movement of immigrants into their residential neighborhoods represents a displacement that is motivated by racism and economic gain. For example, they cite the pattern in Los Angeles of blockbusting. That is, once a Hispanic family moves into an apartment building, the tenement rapidly becomes all Hispanic. Landlords perceive Hispanics to be better tenants, and landlords charge Hispanics more, due to the doubling up of families in dwellings.

Cuciti and James (1990) report evidence suggesting that poor Hispanics are more isolated in high poverty neighborhoods than are poor blacks. They state that "patterns of Hispanic segregation have long resulted in a much greater separation of Hispanics by economic class than has been the case for blacks" (p. 56). Overall, their data imply extreme isolation of poor Hispanics. As a result of this isolation, blacks may not be aware of Hispanic poverty, and may thereby believe that poverty is restricted to blacks. Such a belief could exacerbate feelings of competition and conflict between the groups.

Education

Another context of differential experience for blacks and Hispanics is in the domain of education. Cuciti and James (1990) found that Hispanics do less well than blacks on education-related measures. In 26 southwestern cities, dropout rates between the groups were significantly different—32 percent for Hispanics and 15 percent for blacks. In the largest cities, the Hispanic dropout rate was 33 percent, compared to 20 percent for blacks. Other data are consistent with Cuciti and James (1990). For instance, Moy (1995) reports that in 1984, about twice as many blacks (841,336) were in public higher education institutions as were Hispanics (452,514). He reports that in 1988, there were 881,000 blacks and 587,000 Hispanics enrolled in educational institutions of all types.

Regarding returns from education, Thomas, Herring, and Horton (1995) report that nationwide, Latino men have higher mean personal earnings than blacks across educational levels, except for college graduates. As shown in Table 7.1, the findings were less consistent for women.

Another education-related issue that could lead to intergroup conflict between blacks and Hispanics is education values. Ginorio (1987) found that whereas blacks emphasize integration, Hispanics emphasize bilingual education as a means of obtaining quality education for their children. Such differences in participation in and expectations from the educational system may contribute to Hispanics' perceptions that government programs help blacks more than Hispanics, and may underlie conflict and resentment.

Employment

The extent and quality of a person's employment has far-reaching effects on the quality of their housing, health, education, and many other aspects of life. Significant, group-based differences in job opportunity, therefore, could lead to intergroup conflict. In their discussion of interethnic conflict, John-

TABLE 7.1   Annual Mean Earnings Compared for Blacks and Hispanics, 1990 (By Gender and Education)

	Males		*Females*	
	Black	*Hispanic*	*Black*	*Hispanic*
Some high school	8,043	10,767	3,398	3,996
High school grad	11,096	15,094	7,688	6,713
Some college	14,300	16,432	11,079	10,206
College grad	32,058	31,940	19,383	18,406

Source: M. E. Thomas, C. Herring, and H. D. Horton, "Racial and Gender Differences in Returns from Education," in G. E. Thomas, ed., *Race and Ethnicity in America* (Washington, D.C.: Taylor and Francis, 1995).

son and Oliver (1994) state that the basic bone of contention, especially between blacks and members of immigrant minority groups, is the issue of jobs. They cite a 1983 Urban Institute survey assessing attitudes toward immigration, in which blacks strongly agreed (66 percent) with the contention that undocumented Mexicans living in the United States take jobs away from American citizens.

In their examination of the relative effects of race/ethnicity on levels of employment, Horton and Thomas (1995) found that in nearly every case, blacks had the lowest level of employment, Hispanics had slighter higher levels, and Asians and whites alternated in first place. They emphasized that in 1990, blacks were the only group that was more likely to be unemployed than employed. Horton and Thomas found these results consistent with studies documenting that blacks have experienced and continue to experience the greatest level of discrimination in American society. Moreover, they argue that as the size of the middle-class segments of Asian and Hispanic populations increase, blacks are expected to experience greater disadvantage in the job market. Horton and Thomas conclude, "This study provides some evidence that racial and ethnic conflict is likely to be exacerbated in the 21st century" (p. 236).

There may also be significant group differences in the level of employment and in gains from employment. Cuciti and James (1990) report that Hispanic poor have a much greater attachment to the work force than do poor blacks, as evidenced by the fact that the "working poor" constitute a larger percentage of Hispanic poverty than of black poverty. For instance, their data indicated that in 1979, 59 percent of poor Hispanic households had earnings, and one-third of poor Hispanic households worked at least 40 hours per week; whereas among poor blacks, 49 percent had earnings and 23 percent worked regularly.

Outright competition for jobs may also lead to intergroup conflict. For instance, Oliver and Johnson (1984) found that 66 percent of black respondents agreed that undocumented Mexicans living in the United States take jobs away from American citizens, whereas only 39 percent of Hispanics responded similarly. In the survey conducted by Mindiola, Rodriguez, and Niemann (1996), 53 percent of black respondents agreed that immigrants take away jobs from blacks, compared to 25 percent of U.S.-born and 13 percent of foreign-born Hispanics.

A reflection of this perceived and real discrimination is the black policemen's discrimination suit in Miami. The suit cites that the number of blacks on the force has remained unchanged from 1975 to 1980, despite an increase in the city's black population, whereas the number of Hispanic police on the force has increased (Stack and Warren, 1992). In addition to lack of police representation for blacks, black representation in Miami workplaces has decreased in conjunction with increased Cuban immigration for clerical workers, machine operators, service workers, and household workers (Stack and Warren, 1992). Blacks' perception that immigrants take away jobs is thus, at least in part, founded on their experiential and ecological reality.

Poverty

Another contextual domain related to employment that could lead to conflict is poverty. Cuciti and James (1990) report that the poverty rate for Hispanics was 27.3 percent in 1986, 5.7 percent higher than the 21.6 percent 1978 rate, whereas the Black poverty rate remained relatively stable at 31.1 percent over the same period. However, the economic status of Hispanics depends on country of origin (Cuciti and James, 1990). The highest poverty is found among Puerto Ricans, and the lowest among Cubans, whereas Mexican Americans fall in between. In places like Miami, then, where Cuban Americans are the predominant Hispanic group, black residents may have a distorted view of national poverty rates for Hispanics, thinking them lower than they actually are. Such a view may be compounded by the reality that 10 percent of residents of underclass tracts (areas with poverty rates above 40 percent) are Hispanic, whereas the majority of the underclass tract residents are black (Cuciti and James, 1990). Additionally, Hispanics are less dependent on public assistance than are blacks; 41 percent of all poor black families received public assistance income in 1979, compared to 29 percent of Hispanic families (Cuciti and James, 1990). High poverty rates may increase conflict between blacks and Hispanics as the two groups compete for scarce resources available to the poor (Ginorio, 1987).

In their discussion of group relations and job competition in Miami, where Cuban Americans have become a powerful group, Stack and Warren (1992) state that "even more disastrous from the black viewpoint was the apparent ease with which the Hispanics rooted themselves financially in the economy of the city" (p. 195). Further exacerbating the conflict is the perception that Hispanics can get government loans but blacks cannot. Stack and Warren (1992) state, "Particularly galling to Blacks was the fact that much of the capital that Hispanics needed for their business success was provided by the U.S. government" (p. 196). Cuban Americans also qualified for special government contracts as a minority group, in addition to receiving more loans from the U.S. Small Business Administration. Blacks received only one-seventh of what Hispanics got from the SBA, although their population strength was one-half that of Hispanics (Stack and Warren, 1992).

Portes and Stepick (1993) reported that by 1989 the average family income of Hispanics in Miami had nearly reached parity with the non–Hispanic white population, but blacks were still far behind, and this gap had become a source of tension. Portes and Stepick also asserted that the Cuban presence was doubly offensive to blacks because it was successful and foreign. They stated that Cubans always disclaimed intentional racism and claimed that discrimination was a function of their preoccupation with their own success, leaving them no time for attention to complaints from blacks. Although Cubans said they provided economic resources to blacks—for example, loans—blacks insisted that investment in black areas was aimed only at exploitation, especially since Cuban shops did not employ blacks.

Health

Another contextual domain that could lead to intergroup conflict is the area of health, where there is a poverty-related discrepancy between blacks and Hispanics at several levels. For example, blacks have an infant mortality rate of 18.2 percent, compared to 8.5 percent for Hispanics (Eberstein, 1995). Additionally, the neonatal mortality rate is 12 percent for blacks, 5.5 percent for Hispanics; and the post–neonatal mortality rate for blacks is 6.2 percent, and 3.0 percent for Hispanics (Eberstein, 1995). Such discrepancies are especially important because they involve the highly emotional issue of the survival of babies. Blacks might attribute this difference in infant mortality to differential discrimination favoring Hispanics over blacks.

Politics

Perhaps the contextual domain that has the most far-reaching effects is that of political power. A group's political power can affect job opportunities, health, poverty, education, and perhaps to a lesser extent, housing. Dunn and Stepick (1992) report that Miami's black community appears to have missed out on political changes and growth. Using the phrase "Miami syndrome" to denote the futility of blacks' attempts to alter or amend a political system that is fundamentally unresponsive to their needs, Stack and Warren (1992) confirm that blacks find themselves pitted against Hispanics in what amounts to a zero-sum relationship, with the cultural power of Hispanics transforming Dade County politics. "The result of increased Hispanic political power is the further erosion of black political strength" (p. 167).

Dunn and Stepick conclude that blacks are the most frustrated residents of Miami since Cubans have gained political control over much of the local government. However, in a study published almost a decade earlier, Oliver and Johnson (1984) reported that blacks had more political power and held more elected offices than Hispanics in Los Angeles. Oliver and Johnson discussed a 1980 *Los Angeles Times* survey that had asked Los Angeles respondents about ethnic groups' power. In that survey, blacks were the least likely group to express the view that Mexican Americans had too much political or economic power, which contrasted significantly with Mexican Americans' views that blacks had too much power. Echoing these research findings from Miami and Los Angeles, Mindiola, Rodriguez, and Niemann (1996) found that Houston Hispanics perceive blacks as having more power than Hispanics.

Discussion

In undertaking the preceding review of the literature, I expected that the process would reveal a direct relationship between disparity in contextual domains affecting quality of life and prejudice between blacks and Hispanics. Based on this review, however, it seems that in most social-contextual domains, with the exception of comparatively low levels of education and political power for Hispanics, blacks are worse off than Hispanics. This conclusion is consistent with work that indicates that the analytical framework of an underclass does not apply to Hispanics as it does to blacks (Cuciti and James, 1990). At the same time, however, Hispanics report more prejudice toward and social distance from blacks than vice versa.

However, the one context in which blacks seemed to be better off than Hispanics was political power; and as stated earlier, this domain may have more far-reaching implications than any other. Just as researchers have focused on black–white issues, the perception among Hispanics seems to be that politicians also have focused on blacks and whites, in effect allocating more relative power to blacks while generally ignoring the concerns and rights of Hispanics. Related to this issue is the fact that many U.S. Hispanics are relatively recent immigrants with no citizenship rights. Even when Hispanics are citizens, stereotypes facilitate perception and treatment of them as outsiders and/or foreigners, which leads to discrimination, especially in today's anti-immigrant climate. Hispanics may thus perceive that they are relatively powerless and have more discrimination issues to deal with compared to blacks.

On the other hand, blacks may perceive that Hispanics have power and do not experience discrimination because discrimination against Hispanics has not been legal, as it has been against blacks. Blacks may not be aware of the de facto discrimination against Hispanics. They may not be aware, for instance, that drugstores in Texas towns were closed to Mexicans until the late 1940s; restaurants and movie houses did not open to Mexicans until the early 1950s; hotels were exclusively reserved for Anglo patrons until about 1958; barber and beauty shops were segregated until 1969; and in the early 1970s, the bowling alleys, cemeteries, and swimming pools still remained segregated (Montejano, 1987). There was no real change until blacks in the south mobilized to present a challenge to Jim Crow. Thus, Mexican Americans benefited from civil rights legislation prompted by blacks' demands of the 1960s (Montejano, 1987). Because they benefited from blacks' demands, however, Hispanics' fight for civil rights has not been in the foreground of American society as was blacks' fight for civil rights. Therefore, blacks' social reality may be that they, and not Hispanics, have been the targets of discrimination, whereas the reality of Hispanics may be that due to the political attention conferred on blacks, discrimination is no longer the problem for blacks that it is for Hispanics.

Recommendations for Future Research, Teaching, and Social Action

With few exceptions, researchers have not differentiated between attitudes of U.S.-born and foreign-born Hispanic respondents. Given that the issue of power has emerged as critical to relations between these two groups, it seems highly likely that other research on intergroup prejudice may find differences in attitudes between Hispanics with and without U.S. citizenship. Further research on intergroup relations should attempt to isolate the role of citizenship in prejudice.

The available literature also does not indicate what role, if any, knowledge of another group's political and economic oppression has on relations between minority groups. It may be possible to alleviate negative attitudes by furthering the awareness of discrimination toward groups other than one's own. For instance, in some research that has emerged from university classes on racial and ethnic experiences, data indicate that increased awareness of the plight and experience of another group may increase feelings of empathy, leading to a reduction of prejudice (Niemann, 1996).

In addition, more research is needed on the role of contact between blacks and Hispanics in intergroup relations, since most work on the effects of contact has thus far focused on blacks and whites. Foreign-born Hispanics have significantly less contact with blacks than do U.S.-born Hispanics, which likely plays a role in the more negative stereotypes that the foreign-born have of blacks (Mindiola, Rodriguez, and Niemann, 1996). Present levels of contact also affect future contact, or social distance. Our review of the literature indicates that due to the segregation and in some cases the isolation of poor Hispanics, these groups may not be aware of the experience of the other, which could certainly affect feelings of empathy. Contact between persons of *equal status* has been shown to reduce negative stereotypes and intergroup hostility (Brown, 1995). It is possible, therefore, that increased contact between blacks and Hispanics may bring awareness of their mutual plight as members of oppressed groups, increasing perceptions of affinity between the groups, and thus, reducing prejudice. Without this awareness, however, it is also possible that increased contact will lead to increased intergroup tension and prejudice. Therefore, it is imperative that researchers pursue various avenues related to contact that might lead to reduction of prejudice.

In the final analysis, increased hostility and conflict between blacks and Hispanics is likely if the disparity evident in present social ecological contexts remains unchanged. Given the growing population rates of these two groups, action must be taken to enhance the quality of life of both and to close the gap between them.

REFERENCES

Acuña, R. (1988). *Occupied America: A History of Chicanos.* New York: Harper and Row.

Allport, G. W. (1954). *The Nature of Prejudice.* Reading, MA: Addison-Wesley.

Bach, R. (1993). *Changing Relations Project: Newcomers and Established Residents in U.S. Communities.* New York: Ford Foundation.

Brown, R. (1995). *Prejudice: Its Social Psychology.* Oxford, UK: Blackwell.

Cheng, L., and Espiritu, Y. (1989). "Korean Business in Black and Hispanic Neighborhoods: A Study of Intergroup Relations." *Sociological Perspectives* 32, no. 4, pp. 521–534.

Cuciti, P., and James, F. (1990). "A Comparison of Black and Hispanic Poverty in Larger Cities of the Southwest." *Hispanic Journal of Behavioral Sciences* 12, no. 1, pp. 50–75.

Dowden, S., and Robinson, J. P. (1993). "Age and Cohort Differences in American Racial Attitudes: The Generational Replacement Hypothesis Revisited." In Sniderman, P. M., Tetlock, P. E., and Carmines, E. G., eds., *Prejudice, Politics, and the American Dilemma.* Stanford: Stanford University Press.

Dunn, M., and Stepick, A. (1992). "Blacks in Miami." In Grenier, G. J., and Stepick, A., eds., *Miami Now! Immigration, Ethnicity, and Social Change.* Gainesville: University Press of Florida.

Dyer, J., Vedlitz, A., and Worchel, S. (1989). "Social Distance Among Racial and Ethnic Groups in Texas: Some Demographic Correlates." *Social Science Quarterly* 70, no. 3, pp. 607–616.

Eberstein, I. W. (1995). "Social Background, Risk, and Racial/Ethnic Differentials in Infant Mortality." In Thomas, G. E., ed., *Race and Ethnicity in America.* Washington, DC: Taylor and Francis.

Ginorio, A. B. (1987). "Puerto Rican Ethnicity and Conflict." In Boucher, J., Landis, D., and Clark, K. A., eds., *Ethnic Conflict, International Perspectives*. Newbury Park, CA: Sage.

Guthrie, P., and Hutchinson, J. (1995). "The Impact of Perceptions on Interpersonal Interactions in an African American/Asian American Housing Project." *Journal of Black Studies* 25, no. 3, pp. 377–395.

Horton, H. D., and Thomas, M. E. (1995). "The Impact of Population and Structural Change on Racial Inequality in the United States: An Examination of Employment Toward the 21st Century." In Thomas, G. E., ed., *Race and Ethnicity in America*. Washington, DC: Taylor and Francis.

Johnson, J. H., and Oliver, M. L. (1994). "Interethnic Minority Conflict in Urban America: The Effects of Economic and Social Dislocations." In Pincus, F. L., and Ehrlich, H. J., eds., *Race and Ethnic Conflict*. Boulder: Westview Press.

Lambert, W. E., and Taylor, D. M. (1990). *Coping with Cultural and Racial Diversity in Urban America*. New York: Praeger.

Lampe, P. E. (1981). "Towards Amalgamation: Interethnic Dating Among Blacks, Mexican Americans and Anglos." *Ethnic Groups* 3, pp. 97–109.

Massey, D. S. (1981). "Hispanic Residential Segregation: A Comparison of Mexicans, Cubans, and Puerto Ricans." *Sociology and Social Research* 65, no. 3, pp. 311–322.

Massey, D. S., and Denton, N. A. (1988). "Suburbanization and Segregation in U.S. Metropolitan Areas." *American Journal of Sociology* 94, no. 3, pp. 592–626.

Matre, M., and Mindiola, T. (1981). "Residential Segregation in Southwestern Metropolitan Areas: 1970." *Sociological Focus* 14, no. 1, pp. 15–31.

Mindiola, T., Rodriguez, M., and Niemann, Y. F. (1996). *Intergroup Relations Between Hispanics and Blacks in Harris County*. Houston, TX: University of Houston, Center for Mexican American Studies.

Montejano, D. (1987). *Anglos and Mexicans in the Making of Texas, 1836–1986*. Austin: University of Texas Press.

Moore, J. W. (1981). "Minorities in the American Class System." *Daedalus* 110, no. 2, pp. 275–299.

Moy, M. W. (1995). "Asian American Education: Better or Worse in the 21st Century?: A Look At One State." In Thomas, G. E., ed., *Race and Ethnicity in America*. Washington, DC: Taylor and Francis.

Niemann, Y. F. (n.d.). "A Model for Teaching Cultural Differences Through Subjective Construal." Unpublished paper.

Niemann, Y. F., Jennings, L., Rozelle, R. M., Baxter, J. C., and Sullivan, E. (1994). "Use of Free Response and Cluster Analysis to Determine Stereotypes of Eight Groups." *Personality and Social Psychology Bulletin* 20, no. 4, pp. 379–390.

Niemann, Y. F., and Jones, M. (1995). "A Psychometric Evaluation of Racism Scales." Paper presented at the annual meeting of the American Psychological Association, New York, August 14, 1995.

Niemann, Y. F., and Romero, A. (1995). "Social Realities of Mexican Residents of the Southwestern United States: Patterns of Conflict and Identity." Paper presented at a conference of the National Association of Chicano Studies, Spokane, Washington, March 15, 1995.

Niemann, Y. F., and Secord, P. (1995). "The Social Ecology of Stereotyping." *Journal for the Theory of Social Behavior* 25, no. 1, pp. 1–14.

Oliver, M. L., and Johnson, J. H. (1984). "Inter-Ethnic Conflict in an Urban Ghetto: The Case of Blacks and Hispanics in Los Angeles." *Research in Social Movements, Conflict and Change* 6, pp. 57–94.

Porter, B., and Dunn, M. (1984). *The Miami Riot of 1980.* Lexington, MA: D. C. Heath.

Portes, A., and Stepick, A. (1993). *City on the Edge: The Transformation of Miami.* Berkeley: University of California Press.

Sigelman, L., Shockey, J. W., and Sigelman, C. K. (1993). "Ethnic Stereotyping: A Black-White Comparison." In Sniderman, P. M., Tetlock, P. E., and Carmines, E. G., eds., *Prejudice, Politics, and the American Dilemma.* Stanford: Stanford University Press.

Simpson, G. E., and Yinger, J. M. (1985). *Racial and Cultural Minorities: An Analysis of Prejudice and Discrimination.* Fifth Edition. New York: Plenum Press.

Sitton, S. N. (1992). "Los quinientos anos de dominacion y colonialismo y los pueblos etnicos de Mexico." *Estudios Sociologicos* 10, no. 3, pp. 651–675.

Skerry, P. (1993). *Mexican Americans: The Ambivalent Minority.* Cambridge, MA: Harvard University Press.

Stack, J. F., and Warren, C. L. (1992). "The Reform Tradition and Ethnic Politics: Metropolitan Miami Confronts the 1990s." In Grenier, G. J., and Stepick, A., eds., *Miami Now! Immigration, Ethnicity, and Social Change.* Gainesville: University Press of Florida.

Thomas, M. E., Herring, C., and Horton, H. D. (1995). "Racial and Gender Differences in Returns from Education." In Thomas, G. E., ed., *Race and Ethnicity in America.* Washington, DC: Taylor and Francis.

United States. Bureau of the Census. (1990). *The Population of the United States.* Washington, DC: U.S. Government Printing Office.

eight

Racial Formation and Chicana/o Identity: Lessons from the *Rasquache*

MARC PIZARRO

As the dawn of the twenty-first century hangs just over the horizon, Latinas/os may be the most significant population in the United States. Latinas/os may, in fact, shape and even determine the social, economic, and political future of the United States. Throughout the southwest Latinas/os already make up the majority of many major metropolitan areas as well as the majority of the school population, and early in the next century they will be the largest minority group in the country. The Chicana/o population, constituting more than two-thirds of the total Latinas/o population, is a particularly important subgroup both because of its size and its subjugation: the educational outcomes of Chicana/o youth are the lowest of any major racial/ethnic group in the United States, and they have improved little in the past twenty-five years—and in some areas have actually worsened (Reddy, 1995). Correspondingly, Chicana/os have made little progress in the job market, particularly with regard to measures such as relative incomes and unemployment (Reddy, 1995). Clearly, with official high school dropout rates of Chicana/os hovering at 35 percent and other estimates ranging from 50 to 75 percent, understanding the struggles of Chicanas/os will be essential for the United States as we enter the new millennium (Reddy, 1995; Valencia, 1991).

One of the most crucial issues facing the Chicana/o community at this time is a persistent inability to apply critical analyses of the social context in which Chicana/o find themselves to making productive change for large numbers within the community. As the numbers suggest, this is an urgent issue because of the large portion of the Chicana/o population that needs access to empowering experiences for the benefit of the Chicana/o community and the larger society. The first generation and newly emerging second generation of Chicana/o scholars[1] have had to fill the huge void that existed in social, political, and economic research given the previous invisibility of the Chicana/o in these areas. For this reason, a large portion of their work has been descriptive or preliminary analyses. Only very recently have scholars been able to turn attention to Chicana/o development and outcomes with an eye toward developing interventions that might be widely applicable.

This project makes such an effort. It analyzes Chicana/o identity formation[2] to understand the major influences on Chicana/o identity. Focusing exclusively on the identity formation process, this chapter reveals the significance of identity to the larger Chicana/o experience and to efforts at empowerment.[3] The underlying logic here is that these identities are not only multifaceted but that the different components of identity (familial, ethnic, academic, occupational, and so on) are interwoven, and thus, individuals' outcomes are in some way linked to the sense of social self that emerges in their formative processes. If we can understand the development of identity in Chicana/o youth, we may expose insights into how these formations can be shaped to enhance outcomes. I have therefore chosen to begin this chapter by deconstructing Chicana/o identity and placing it in the larger social context (using the racial formation model), and then proceeding with a consideration of one individual's life experiences as a prospective model for change.

Despite increasing acknowledgment of the significance of ethnic identity in the lives and outcomes of Chicanas/os, little research has yet been undertaken into Chicana/o identity formation. Most research that analyzes Chicana/o identity actually deals with specific, quantified facets of Chicana/o ethnic identity (such as ethnic affiliations, preferences, or values) and considers the relationships between these variables and outcomes, adaptation strategies, and the like. The following authors and their referenced works represent these current trends in the research: Bernal and Knight, 1993; Bernal and Martinelli, 1993; Hurtado, 1994; Hurtado, Gonzalez, and Vega, 1994; Knight, Cota, and Bernal, 1993.

In short, while Chicana/o identity is at the core of understanding the Chicana/o experience and the potential means of reshaping and redirecting Chicanas/os toward identities that are empowering, little consideration has been given to deconstructing identity. A few works, however, have suggested the potential importance of developing this understanding. Both Bernal, Saenz, and Knight (1991) and Mehan, Hubbard, and Villanueva (1994) challenge the notion that strong ethnic identities are inherently linked to academic failure. They suggest that in certain instances and through specific intervention programs, strong ethnic identities are in fact linked to (and may be a primary motivation for) academic success. These works do not look into the identity formation processes by which this occurs, but they do provide a strong rationale for the current project.

Chicana/o Students' Racialized Identity Formations

The core of this analysis is grounded in a research project conducted with Chicana/o youth that explored their identity formations, the influences behind these formations, and the connection between both and the educational outcomes of the students. The project began with the development of a general framework of Chicana/o identity that attempted to incorporate all the different potential arenas of Chicana/o students' identity formations (identified in the literature and in research with the participants). It was determined that family identity is important but that it is a precursor to social identity and that school identity is also important (with regard to outcomes) but that this is heavily influenced by familial and social identities in general. Thus, the construct of Chicana/o identity included the potentially significant realms of: class, community, gender, race/ethnicity, sexuality, and religion/spirituality (along with family and school).[4] Additionally, participants included other realms of identity formation when relevant.

In sum, the construct of Chicana/o identity, as operationalized in this chapter, encompasses those social realms in which Chicanas/os have the potential for significant interactions that contribute to their sense of social self. I have used a different means of operationalizing identity than those employed in quantitative analyses, which define the terms that determine the nature of an individual's ethnic identity. Instead, the students were asked about the social issues that were important to them, so as to discover the role of different arenas of identity within their overall social identities. Even more importantly, they were asked to explain who they were in their own minds and which identities were most pertinent in their lives.

The rationale underlying this approach was the need for researchers to understand how individuals define their own identities and why, so as to avoid defining students' identities through measures that are unable to grasp the value, meaning, and influences behind these individuals' responses.[5] In the project, Chicana/o students at a major university, a community college, and a high school in metropolitan Los Angeles completed surveys and participated in interviews. In their answers to open-ended and closed-ended questions, the students revealed their self-constructed identities and the forces at work in their development.[6]

Clear patterns emerged from the qualitative analysis that are crucial to our understanding of contemporary Chicana/o identity. First of all, race is by far the most dominant facet of these students' identities. That is, when they are asked about the issues that have been most important in their development, race/ethnicity comes up more often than any other issue. Nine of the thirteen students interviewed brought up race as a central part of their development and who they are. A few students provided examples of this as they responded to a question asking which of a number of issues was most important to who they are:

> [Race is] really the basis of who I am. Like, I mean class will always change. You can get poor. . . . You can always change everything, to a certain degree, but your ethnicity is who you really are. It's not something that's instilled in you. . . . You're basically born into it.
>
> I have to say race, ethnicity, and culture. And the reason why my race is very important to me [is because it's] my roots, where I come from. . . . With culture, it all stems from heritage for me. Things that my ancestors went through. . . . I believe that my culture is being targeted in [an] immigrant-bashing type of way.
>
> . . . [Race . . .] It's always been very important. . . . See, I grew up in [the barrio]. And we went to . . . elementary school [there], me and my brother. And then, when it was time to go to junior high, at that time, in the late seventies, it's gangs and so it's crazy. So my brother and I, we went out to school in the [white area]. They had better schools and stuff. So we got bused. We always had pride in being Mexicanos, but I think it was more emphasized when we went out there, where me and my brother were [two] of the few Mexicanos who were in the honors classes, who played sports, and were good at it. It was kind of like we were representing Mexicans. So it became a little more important. . . . We always took pride in it.

Although the students interpreted race/ethnicity in different ways, it was clearly the dominant theme in their discussions, usually with regard to the sociopolitical position of Chicanas/os (and based in the larger context of racial discrimination). As the first student explained, race/ethnicity is something that Chicanas/os can neither avoid nor change.

Five of the thirteen students interviewed felt their socioeconomic status was a key part of their development and who they were (four of them felt it was central); but three of these students viewed class as part of their ethnic or racial experience. One student provided a good example as she discussed experiences and issues that dealt with class (after introducing race issues earlier) but also integrated race issues into this discussion.

> [Class] was the big problem for me as I was growing up, class. Because I've always been discriminated [against]. We grew up in a upper-middle-class environment and we were the only minorities, my sister and I, growing up with most of the student population [in] elementary school being Anglo. . . . And growing up I always felt like an outcast. They would say like racial remarks like "wetback" and [another Chicana's] name was Rosa so they used to call her "Rosarita Beans." Things like that, so class was a big problem for me because even when I went to my girlfriends' house, they lived in these big houses up in the hills, where[as] we lived in a little small little underdeveloped, impoverished house where my mom kind of always made us feel embarrassed for living there. She never liked us bringing friends over. . . . So class in that sense, that was a big problem for me growing up.

Another student provided a more detailed example of how Chicanas/os link race and class:

> I mean race, race was important. Races fighting against other races and being put down. . . . And the different levels of society. You've got your upper class, middle class, and lower class. Most of the lower class is two races, Mexican and black. Middle class, you've got your Orientals, some whites, some Mexicans, and stuff. . . . And your upper class: all the white-collar society. All your executives [are] mostly Anglo.

MP: When did it become an issue for you?

> When I started working, I was working in a bank, and I'd see the separation. I'd see supervisors, the majority of supervisors were all white, you know they were the decision makers. They handled your money, they handled your paycheck. . . . It was hard for someone of a different race to climb that ladder. You saw more white people getting promoted, more white people getting the job spots and all that. That's when I started seeing that this ain't right.

As these examples show, when students brought up other realms of potential identity formation that were involved in their development, these often were embedded within the construct of race (if not confused with it) in their discussions. Class, for example, was most often either consciously or subconsciously deemed a part of, or defined by, being Chicana/o (as seen in the two excerpts above). With regard to their total identities, race/ethnicity was the most important realm in which students defined themselves.

Later, when asked whether the different realms of identity were linked (in their lives), students explained how race encompassed many of the different realms of identity formation. One student provided a good example of how the different facets of identity were linked when asked if the issues he had been discussing were connected or distinct.

> I'd say distinct in their definition but connected in their function. . . . I can give you a definition of each one of these issues, like what it means to me, separately. But, if I discuss gender, sexuality is going to come up, class is going to come up, spirituality and religion is going to come up, community is going to come up, race and ethnicity is going to come up. I can't talk about one without the other, they're all connected in the way they operate, in the way they affect me.

In fact, seven students felt that all of the different realms of identity formation were related and mentioned this within their discussion of specific issues. More specifically, race was seen by many as encompassing class, religion, family, community, and gender. Similarly, when students were asked about the importance and impact of specific aspects of their racial/ethnic experience, they also lumped these issues into their larger racial experience so that issues like language background, country of origin, and skin color were not central to identity formation beyond the fact that they were used by non-Chicanas/os as criteria for determining their racial status and therefore were related to racial discrimination.

Two students did a good job of explaining what they and their peers meant when they linked the different realms of identity. As one student said, the family incorporates a number of different areas of students' identity development. She referred specifically to religion, sexuality, gender, and class within the cultural aspects of family life and identity formation. Another student was more specific as he explained that there are different categories within the linkages of these different identity themes. He linked gender, race, and sexuality as related identity themes in their connections to discrimination, while linking community, class, religion, and race (again) as a more general area of identity development.

> They're all connected. . . . I think I would view community, class, race, and religious spirituality more in one sense. Gender, sexuality, and then race would be more in terms of discrimination that's going on out there. . . . I would say gender, sexuality, and race in terms of discrimination; others . . . community, class, race, and spirituality are more separate.

This student cut to the heart of the distinctions within students' identity development, suggesting that students' racial/ethnic experiences can be perceived in two different ways: as political, in response to discrimination (racial identity); and (although he did not emphasize the other aspect) as cultural (ethnic identity).[7] The political facet of this identity is linked to discrimination, and therefore, to gender as well as sexuality (depending on the individual), while the cultural aspects are linked to family, community/class, and religion.

Still, there is no black-and-white categorization of these different areas, as specific experiences shape individuals in different ways. Class, for example, is typically incorporated within students' interpretations of their experiences as Chicanas/os, but it is linked more to the cultural aspects of these experiences rather than as a political, discrimination-based area. This is simply because most students do not have a class consciousness. One student, however, clearly interpreted class as a political issue, and his configuration of identity linkages was quite different from that of the others. Similarly, gender can be seen both as cultural and as political, depending on the individual. In fact, only a few students felt gender and gender discrimination were crucial issues that they *had* to deal with, while most saw gender and differential treatment of males and females as embedded in local, familial histories and not addressable. This is not to suggest that gender is never a crucial arena of identity formation for Chicanas/os. Rather, gender becomes central in Chicanas' identities when power is asserted across gender lines in ways that parallel or exceed the exertion of racial power. It is critical to acknowledge that the unique gender dynamics within the Chicana/o community (e.g., the often-discussed role of machismo) are not central to how most students define themselves because of the fact that other facets of identity formation are dominant and overriding (at least, at this stage in their lives).

The most important finding overall was simply that there are two distinct realms of identity formation within the Chicana/o student population, a political arena and a cultural arena. Not all students have both; but the distinction clearly exists. Furthermore, as students describe themselves and their identities, they reveal that (as they see it) their ethnic-cultural identity is the part of their experience as Chicanas/os that is local and embedded in the lives of all Chicanas/os. In many ways it is an assumed facet of identity, because most believe that Chicana/o experiences and characteristics are internal, intrinsic, and universal. The racial-political identity thus predominates in Chicana/o perceptions of self. Their sense of self evolves from experiences with, and observations of, discrimination in their communities and schools. It is reinforced by the life experiences of their families and their oral histories describing legacies of racial confrontation (examples will be provided later).

The evolution of Chicana/o racial-political identities in the late twentieth century shows the racial formation process at work in vivid detail. Chicana/o students in Los Angeles grow up being defined not as an ethnic group, not in terms of their cultural capital or with respect to their socioeconomic status, but as a racialized group. This is how they are most obviously constructed in their daily lives, despite the formation of school and familial identities.

In addition to their more general explanations of the significance of race in their identities (covered in the previous section), several of the students talked specifically about the racial confrontations that had critically shaped their identity formation. One student discussed the significance of race on two separate occasions during our interview:

> And we had a substitute one day [in sixth grade] and everybody, the whole class was messing around, it was [a] ruckus. And the teacher came up to me and she said, "If you don't like it, you can go back where you came from." And then she told that to my friend, and we were the only two Mexicans in the class, and I think there was one black guy. . . . And so that was the theme of the day, every time everybody else messed up, it was "Shut up, shut up!" but when we messed up it was "Go back to Mexico!" And so we already knew by sixth grade, I guess we were already socialized, like, not to make a big deal out of it. . . . And in junior high, like, it was more evident. You know, like, if you [a Chicana/o] ditched, they had to call the cops. But if, like, a white kid ditched, they would

just send X teacher to go get him. So, like, that was different. I was constantly, like, suspended, expelled.

Another student's school experiences (as she worried over getting into college) reflect a somewhat less direct, racialized incident—the connotations of which, however, are clear:

I was still worried about whether or not I was going to [get into the university]. I mean, I graduated with, like, a three-nine [3.9 GPA]. But I was still really worried. . . . Probably because I had a counselor who I despised in high school. I told her I wanted to go to [the university] and she saw my grades and she said, "You know I don't think you're going to get into [the university]," and she said, "But you might, because you are a minority, so you might get in." And, I thought, I know it plays a big part, but it still really upset me that she said that. . . . I had good grades and she was just like, "I don't know if you'll get in, but you might because you're Mexican."

Some students also described how important the messages conveyed by family members were to their dealing with these issues and even to their identity formation itself. For example, one student provided the following explanation when she was asked where her pride (which she mentioned earlier) came from:

My uncle, because he was like another father. He was the kind that'd listen to you, and you could say whatever you wanted to him, and he would help you out, just tell you, "You're Mexican and you have to be proud of it, 'cause that's who you are." My grandpa too, he sat me and my nina down to talk about where we come from so that later on it won't be a question to us.

Other students described powerful racial confrontations outside of the school that were critical to their evolving views of themselves:

But a lot of the cops, they treat me bad. . . . Me and my friend, we were in my car and they stopped us. I turned off the car and he told me to turn down the radio, and I turned it down, and for no reason he took out a gun and put it on my head. And both of 'em [the police] were white. And my friend had a beanie with the Mexican eagle on the front. He took off his beanie, he threw it on the floor and stepped on it. And he [the police officer] pulled me out of the car and then he put my hands on my back, he took out that little black [rubber stick]. . . . And he smacked me in the head with it and he told me that we were in [a white neighborhood], and . . . what were we doing over there, that we belong in [the barrio]. That over here that it's pure white people . . . and that us wetbacks should go back over there. . . . But there's nothing I could do about it. It's just hate, that's why. . . . My dad too, they treat him bad. Because they arrested my dad because supposedly he was hitting my mom, but it was just a neighbor calling because they were arguing. And they were two white cops too, and they tied my dad from the hands and feet and they dragged him all the way to the cop car.

The backlash against liberal politics and policies like affirmative action has transformed the sociopolitical discourse by revisioning the melting pot, appropriating "color-blind" imagery, and criticizing ethnic groups that avoid the meltdown. However, the reality of the Chicana/o experience reveals that the lives of these individuals, from a very early age, are defined and categorized for them as a function of the color of their skin. The experiences of these students and their impact on students' identity formations are a powerful illustration of Omi and Winant's (1994) racial formation model.

The severity of this situation becomes more dramatic as we look back on the history of the Chicana/o experience. Tomás Almaguer (1994) provides an in-depth look at the experiences of the first Chicanas/os (as well as other racial groups in California after its annexation by the United States). In his work, Almaguer exposes the significance of race and the racialization of the Chicana/o population as the key organizing principle around which the hierarchical relations of inequality in California were structured. Almaguer critiques other theoretical approaches to understanding the stratification of early Californian society as incomplete and inaccurate in that they ignore the complexity of the ideological forces at work during this period and overlook the way in which race became a central issue in interpreting one's location in society and one's power over others, regardless of class. He asserts that "racialization fundamentally shaped the class- and gender-specific experiences of both the white and nonwhite populations" (p. 209).

The point of this reference is not to summarize Almaguer's work but rather to show that the same means of hierarchical stratification are being invoked in the subjugation of Chicanas/os as we move into yet another century. The Chicana/o students of modern-day Los Angeles suggest that the primary changes that have occurred are related to the advancement of the ideological weaponry employed to maintain the hierarchy. In place of the blatantly racist ideologies that argued the inherent or embedded inferiority of certain races, today the hierarchy is reinforced through a racialization process that intersects with class and gender injustices to deny Chicanas/os the opportunity to demonstrate their equality. This is achieved by limiting Chicana/o access to the resources needed to succeed in contemporary society. Underlying the current popular discourse on race is the belief that past reforms have led us to a point where effort is all that is needed for people of color to succeed (as evidenced in the anti–affirmative action, color-blind ideology currently advocated). Omi and Winant (1994) and Apple (1993) provide a detailed analysis of this process in the contemporary sociopolitical climate of the United States.

The voices of Chicanas/os as young as 15 years give evidence that "equality of opportunity" is, in many ways, popular fiction. As the students suggest, racializing forces and their impact on their identity formation in and out of school are a crucial part of the massive failure facing the Chicana/o community. Students are forced to deal with their placement at the low end of the school hierarchy as a function of their race, and few have opportunities to understand the multitude of forces at work in this process. They respond by lashing out, which often results in their own failure and denied access to opportunities for advancement.

Resistance, *Rasquachismo,* and Hope

The ideological assault being leveled against Chicanas/os is meeting with resistance. As we look to better understand Chicana/o identity and move toward empowering interventions, the students reveal powerful possibilities. The final interviews I conducted with the college students exposed the significant impact of their and their families' experiences with racial confrontation: These students integrally tied the concept of change to their identity. These students saw themselves as Chicanas/os with strong ties to their culture and community and with a clear understanding of the subjugated role of Chicanas/os in the larger society (as a result of the racism they have witnessed and faced). Within this identity, they included their visions of themselves involved in efforts geared toward the empowerment of the Chicana/o community. The importance of effecting change in the power of Chicanas/os is central to who they are, and it shines a light of hopefulness on the lives of other Chicanas/os whom they might help.

The hopefulness embedded in these students' self-images, however, must be balanced by an equal measure of realism. Successive generations of Chicana/o students have entered the university with politicized, strong Chicana/o identities that incorporated the goal of seeking change but that were abandoned later, during losing battles against the institutional forces that demand conformity and limit the spaces in which transformation can be sought. One student I interviewed provided a vivid example of the ease with which this occurs, despite one's earlier commitment to change:

> When I was in high school, I came up [to the university] and there was some guy from 23rd Street in [the barrio]. He was going to school, he was going to be a lawyer. He was talking me into going, you know like all the old *veteranos*[8] do, like, "You got to go to school. I'm doing this to help out my community, my homeys and stuff like that." And, I was like "Oh wow, that dude's cool." And then three years later, I found out that he became like some rich lawyer in . . . [an upwardly mobile neighborhood], driving a Mercedes.

While the individual described here and others like him may be making contributions to the Chicana/o community, the reality being lived by the majority of Chicanas/os (as described earlier) implies the limits of these contributions. This history suggests the need to redefine and reconstitute success among the Chicana/o populations and to avoid placing Chicana/o empowerment in the institutionally sanctioned and subsequently gutted entities of acceptable Chicana/o "resistance."

Rasquachismo is such a redefinition. While there are a number of varied interpretations of *rasquachismo,* it generally refers to an approach to life that reconceives "lower-class cultures" as powerful by invigorating specific cultural icons with reinterpreted significance. As a larger construct, it encompasses the reconstruction of the underdog into a subject (rather than object) who employs her/his agency to transform and empower the downtrodden. Tomas Ybarra-Frausto explains this concept, first in his tri-part "non-linear, exploratory, and unsolemn" description, and then in two more specific definitions:

> Very generally, *rasquachismo* is an underdog perspective—a view of *los de abajo*—an attitude rooted in resourcefulness and adaptability yet mindful of stance and style.
>
> *Rasquachismo* presupposes the worldview of the have-not, but it is also a quality exemplified in objects and places (a *rasquache* car or restaurant) and in social comportment (a person who is or acts *rasquache*).
>
> Although Mexican vernacular traditions form its base, *rasquachismo* has evolved as a bicultural sensibility among Mexican Americans. On both sides of the border it retains its underclass perspective. (1991, p. 156) . . .
>
> As a way of being in the world, *rasquachismo* assumes a vantage point from the bottom up. It proclaims itself from the margins and borders of the culture. Often it is the disenfranchised subgroups within the Chicano community who best exemplify a *rasquache* sensibility. . . .
>
> *Rasquachismo* feigns complicity with dominant discourses while skillfully decentering and transforming them. (1991, p. 160)

Perez takes these definitions and makes applications to Chicanas/os in the educational system as she explains, "To be Chicana/o on one's own terms within the educational system is to be *rasquache* with respect to it" (p. 277). These ideas and images became vividly real through conversations I had with a Chicana/o university student that might help us better understand Chicana/o identity, racial formation, *rasquachismo,* and the possibility for transformation and Chicana/o educational empowerment.

Perhaps the most successful Chicana/o student I worked with was Ernesto. At the time of our last interview, Ernesto was less than a month from graduating from a major California university and would start a graduate program at that same university with a fellowship the following fall. Our discussions were filled with colorful stories of a number of aspects of his life, from encounters with the police, gangs, and racist teachers, to his travels in Mexico, his family history, and his intellectual emergence.

The story of Ernesto's identity formation begins much like those of many other Chicana/o students with whom I worked. Growing up in an emerging barrio in the Los Angeles area, he attended schools with a large number of white students and white teachers. This interracial context played a big role in his identity formation. When we talked about his social sense of self, both through a checklist and in open-ended questions, race was at the center of his identity. As he discussed the influences on this identity, he returned to his school experiences immediately.

Racism and race issues are embedded in each of the stories he recounted from his elementary and secondary school experiences. One of the earliest experiences where, for him, race became a distinguishing characteristic was through English as a Second Language (ESL) classes. While ESL class participation is technically based on linguistic background, through his experiences it became a stigmatizing, race issue.

> So, I remember I went through ESL . . . 'til fifth grade. And I would always get all these awards, you know, they would take me to these big banquets. And it wasn't a big deal to me. Because I was like, "Man, I've been knowing English for, like, a long time." So every year they would give me this award and I would be like "Okay, you know." So every year I would go to ESL and I'd be like "All right [already], I think I'm pretty good at English . . . because it was a stigma, you know. It's like, "Okay, it's time for you people to go to the ESL class," and so that kinda affected me, but it wasn't as bad for me as for others 'cause my friends spoke English whereas other people in the ESL didn't even have any friends who spoke English. So that was kind of heavy.

Ernesto's experiences in ESL were, in his mind, racial, because it was Chicanas/os who were in ESL, whereas large numbers of the other students were not Chicana/o (and specifically white). As Ernesto explains, his racial awareness really became clear toward the end of elementary school. Perhaps the most memorable experience he had in elementary school was with a substitute teacher. He remembers that when the teacher had problems with other students, she told them to "Shut up!" But when she had problems with the two Chicana/o students, she told them, "Go back to Mexico!" Ernesto, however, was born in the United States, so his understanding of this incident was that he was being racially categorized.

His experiences with race and racism became frequent as he entered junior high school. He recalls getting jumped by skinheads at the school because he intentionally invaded their space in the yard. Ernesto also explained that the school staff exacted punishment differentially, often suspending only the Chicana/o students for truancy although white students also failed to attend classes. Continuing, Ernesto mentioned a number of racial incidents with both teachers and students when he began talking about high school. As with most instances of racism, observers (readers) can interpret many of these examples in different ways, suggesting that other means of differentiation might have been employed; but in Ernesto's world, the means of differentiation were clear. For example, Ernesto described an interaction he had with a teacher that clearly pushed him over the edge:

> I remember this, one time, there was this teacher who taught architecture. . . . And everybody's [saying], "Oh, he's the bomb, you got to take it. He's the man." And I didn't realize it, but it was like white and Chinese kids that would say that. So I took him, and he was an asshole to me. And he was the one that got me expelled from school, because he told me, "I'll never ever listen to you or call on you if you raise your hand." I was, like, looking for attention, and he walked by my desk and he wouldn't call on me. I had my hand raised. So I stood up on my desk with my hand raised, and he still wouldn't answer me; so when he came back around, I jumped off and I head-butted him. And so I got kicked out of school, and my dad made a big thing of it, and then the principal started talking shit to my dad and I cussed out the principal and I said, "Don't talk to my dad like that." Because he was being real paternalistic to my dad. And so, that's when I was like, "Man, fuck white people. I mean these people are just assholes."

This incident had strong racial connotations for Ernesto simply because his teacher treated him very differently than he treated the white and Asian students who liked his class so much, and because of the way his father was treated (elsewhere he refers to the power and respect white parents commanded in his schools). Ernesto recalls other instances of racial confrontations that he had with other teachers as well as a coach. During these high school years he also became more aware of the underlying racism that was present in his earlier school experiences with white students.

> When I went to high school, like, that's where everybody goes, the *raza*,[9] the black, brown, everybody. So then I started seeing my Chicano friends and started hanging out with them, and that was probably one of the first times I really thought about race because I noticed the difference. Because when I hung out with white dudes, like X white boy was "big nose," you know, you joke around. This white boy was "big butt" . . . and I was always "beaner." Like that was the joke. . . . It was, like, good-hearted, so I thought, but then I thought about it and thought, "No, that's bullshit, that's fucking racist." And so then I just told all my white friends "Shine you" and started hanging with the Mexicans again. And they always said, "Oh, look, he changed, he became a gang member," you know, that's what the white dudes would say. And, like, to me, I was kind of, like, reacting against the way they treated me.

In a subsequent discussion, Ernesto provided further detail:

> E: So I was always clear on race. I knew when I hang around with the whites, this is the treatment I'm gonna get. When I hang around

with the *raza,* this is treatment I'll get. And the blacks, I knew a
lotta blacks but I didn't really hang out with 'em that much.

MP: So, how did that affect you in terms of, like, how you dealt with
this situation?

E: I have to admit that I always thought that I wasn't as smart as white
kids, like that was just natural. Not that it was, like, naturally biological or anything, but I just couldn't compete with them if I
wanted to, for some reason or another. So then I was, kinda like,
you know, "Well, then, fuck school."

MP: Because of the way that you saw the divisions, I mean, the way
people were?

E: I don't know, I couldn't place it, but it was, like, in class they ask a
question and, like, a white kid answers it. You just see that all the
time. . . . I'm sure that it was [because of] the way you were
treated and stuff, but you just grow up always having this feeling.
I remember a good example. I remember in eighth-grade U.S. history, we were covering the war with Mexico, and, like, I had this
total feeling, I couldn't tell you what we talked about that day. I
couldn't show you the book. I couldn't say that's the story we
read. But I had this horrible feeling that I was supposed to stand
up and apologize, like, that's how the history was covered. I had
this feeling, like it's time for [me] to stand up and say, "Sorry for
making you take our land and having this war with us, wasting
your time with us." But that's how, like, I felt. So, like, I always
had this feeling that—maybe it was before that or maybe it started
then—that this education wasn't for me, it wasn't about me,
maybe I was included in it in, like, certain incidents, but it wasn't
for me, and that's why they got it and I didn't.

And then I remember this other history class the next semester,
the teacher Miss Johnson, she was, like, really cool, and everybody could play around except me. And I was the only Mexican
in the class. And there was this guy named Abdul who was from
Africa, but he was, like, really assimilated. . . . And there was this
white kid named Jim Hernandez. I know their names because I
went to [community college] with them too, and they're like
clowns, just total clowns. And Jim's dad is a Inca but his mom is
white and he looks real white. His mom's Jewish, so he's got curly
hair and stuff. And like they could fuck around all you could, but
she just couldn't take it when I would, it was weird. 'Cause we
would always have to do this thing, like, you had to ask a question
every time somebody gave a presentation, which was every day.
And when you said it, you had to act like you were a journalist, so
you had to name a magazine. So I remember, like, [they] would

say, "Hi, I am Abdul from *Guns and Ammo*," and the whole class would chuckle, and the teacher would chuckle. And I would say, "I am Ernesto, I'm from *Lowrider*," right, and then [she would say] "Ah, come on, *Lowrider* magazine." And so it was like I couldn't fuck around like they could. And so, I've always had this feeling like school wasn't for me.

In these stories, Ernesto shows the underlying racial script that mediated his interactions with students and teachers. These included confrontations that were not blatantly racist but whose racial overtones were clear to him. During his high school years, Ernesto also dealt with race and racial confrontations outside of the school. He recounted experiences working in fast food restaurants and being relegated to duties that whites did not have. He described being assaulted by police and the role this played in his perception of police and police brutality. This incident was, in some ways, a turning point for him. On the one hand it crystallized his racial understanding of his world; but at the same time, it exposed him to community groups who assisted him and others who were beat up by the police.

A short time later, Ernesto went to a local community college (on his father's promise to get him a car if he did). As his connection in the community became stronger and he was exposed to readings and ideas that helped him to better contextualize his racial experiences, he slowly became more interested in education. He still organized his world along the racial lines that had been so pivotal at the different stages in his life, as he hung out with other Chicanas/os and participated in Chicana/o organizations. It was a drive-by shooting that really turned him around, however. As he saw friends shot and killed one night, he decided to focus on making change and acquiring an education as part of that process. Ernesto centered his studies on those courses and issues that helped him deal with the reality of his experience, and this is what pulled him further into education. Soon he transferred to a four-year university, where he became a sociology major (with an emphasis on Latin America).

Throughout his experience, there were obviously other issues that came into play besides race. As mentioned in the early part of this chapter, however, most of these issues he understood as they meshed with race and racism. When he discussed the importance of class during one interview, he explained:

And a lot of it has to do with race, too, 'cause I remember we were building a skateboard ramp, at this Chinito's house, this Japanese dude's house, but he lived, like, where all the rich white people lived. And we were trying to figure out a way to explain to his dad how we got the wood, 'cause we were stealing all the wood from construction sites. So, I remember this guy was, like, "I got an idea, we'll just tell him that Ernesto's dad is a construction worker, and he gave us all the wood." So I was, like, "Yeah, that's a great idea!" And then I thought about it, I was, like, wait a second, that's a trip, like right away they would believe my dad was a construction worker but they never thought to say, "Well, let's pick whose dad's gonna be the construction worker."

Ernesto recalls other experiences that were based on class (related to school lunch programs and buying gifts), but these stories too, in the end, are about race. Making a theoretical point (that emerged from his experiential analysis), Ernesto explained:

> You know, it's, like, harder to interpret class oppression. But it's easy to see the racial oppression . . . since *all* Chicanos are majority, like, poor, or, like, low income, like, you see the race thing. I mean, now I'm startin' to see, like, the class thing more often. But I still think that in this country, like, um, I don't say this too often, but I think the Chicanos have more to deal with along racial lines than class lines right now.

So different potential arenas of identity formation have come into play throughout Ernesto's life; but race, as constructed through myriad confrontations, is the lens through which issues like class, community, and religion are filtered and understood. This brief look into Ernesto's life has allowed us to see the contemporary manifestations of the racial formation process and its damaging impact on Chicanas/os in schools, as well as the means by which Ernesto formed a racial-political identity that allowed him to avoid being crushed by his schools. Much of this identity formation process occurred in Ernesto's response to the contexts in which he found himself. At the same time, however, his Chicana/o racial-political identity encompasses his own creative re-visioning of himself and his community, which in essence is a *rasquache* identity.

In many ways, Ernesto has turned traditional constructions on their end and helped us understand the ways in which identity, through a racial formation process, can be reconstituted to move Chicanas/os toward empowerment. In our conversations, Ernesto provided a number of examples of this redefinition. In one such case, he was discussing his feelings about grades:

> Like, I've had classes where I get, like, a C-minus and I'm, like, "Man, I got a 86 on the midterm. What's up with this dude, he gave me a C-minus." And I say I ain't even going to sweat it because if I start getting caught up in grades then I'm going to be like these dudes who are always, like, real individualistic. Last week [of class they ask], "How are you going to grade the final?" And it's like those people aren't here to learn. They're here to get a 4.0 and go to law school or just graduate. So I never complain about my grades.

In essence, Ernesto is redefining the popular conception of the university student's objective from the position of the underdog. Rather than trying to compete and to show he is as smart as his peers (as "smart" is popularly constructed), he focuses on acquiring knowledge that is applicable to his interests—he seeks knowledge rather than acclaim. Although one might criticize him for being naive or for potentially damaging his future chances, Ernesto believes that his future "success" in trying to achieve social change will be shaped by knowledge rather than grades. This redefining is a crucial facet of *rasquachismo*, and it is something that he has continuously done at different stages in his life. Looking back at high school, he provides another example:

> We appropriate the cheapest pizza, or the cheapest meal was *our* spot. And even though, like, the white kids didn't go there because they had money to go to these other places, we hid that, like, that was us. We went to go eat at the truck. We went to the truck. You know, and it's like white kids never go eat at the truck. They wouldn't eat that crap. But it was like we made our stuff cool. We made Dickies that cost fifteen bucks cool.[10]

Ernesto and his friends created a social space that was their own and through which they could access power. They made their socioeconomic limitations the symbols of their strength. On an individual basis, he has done this in other areas of his life to help him feel comfortable with who he is and move toward his own goals. A good example is how he has dealt with skin color.

> I'm, like, one of the dark ones, so, like, it's always a discussion. 'Cause I have an uncle who has four kids and two of 'em are really light and two of 'em are, like, really, really dark. So it's always brought up, it's always a discussion, and now I just say, "I'm proud to be browner than white." It sounds fucked up to people who aren't dark, but I guess I'm just turning it around like I don't have a problem with it.

Ernesto has reclaimed the location of the Chicana/o in society, abandoning popular notions of success and power and replacing them with self-empowering interpretations. While these can be seen simply as survival strategies, they become much more as Ernesto applies them to making change. This can be seen as he speaks specifically about the *rasquache* orientation as he first responds to the question of who he is and later explains the influences behind his identity:

> But, above all, . . . I like to think of myself as, like, somebody who cares, you know, somebody who wants to pull over and help people on the freeway but knows that in America you can't do that . . . and someone who takes the underdog cause, thinks about society, and likes to be critical of society, and enjoys a good fight, not a fist fight in the street, but I would prefer a open discussion in society. I would *love* to live in Mexico City and be, like, involved in all the

shit that's going on there. But I'm not in Mexico City, I'm here,
I'm a Chicano, I grew up here. I would say there's a lot to be done,
and I'm really concerned with it. That's where I would see myself.

MP: You're somebody who takes on the role of the underdog.
. . . Where do you think that came from for you?

E: Probably it's from growing up. Talking to my grandfather and my
dad a lot. Talking about all the things they gone through. 'Cause
ever since I was small, I remember this one dude socked my
brother and, like, I remember just thinking, like, "I'm gonna kick
his ass." You know, and he was a friend of mine, but I remember I
fought him for three days in a row, and he was beatin' my ass
every time. But I [said] I'm gonna fight this dude every day until I
win. . . . But I've always felt that you shouldn't let wrong things
slide. There's some points in your life where you're sort of embar-
rassed for not doing it or not sticking up. But I've always, like,
you know, world series, if it ain't my team, I'm votin' for the, the
sorrier team. I've always been like that, 'cause my grandfather
used to always tell me all these stories [about his difficult experiences as a Mexican in the United States], and I would always think
that was fucked up, you know. I always kind of had this feeling
inside like "I wouldn't do that to anybody." Or "I wouldn't leave
anybody hanging," you know.

Growing up with vivid examples of the difficulty of being the underdog,
Ernesto (perhaps both consciously and subconsciously) decided to fight for
the underdog. His views parallel those of the Zapatistas in Mexico whom he
visited and made reference to several times. He explained his feelings by this
example:

In Mexico they say *Todos somos Marcos.*[11] You know, and they ask Marcos, you
know, "Who are you?" And he said, "I'm a gay in San Francisco, black in South
Africa, I'm a Palestinian in Israel, I'm a *mojado*[12] in East L.A. . . . I would say,
like, I'm just one person in this fucked-up world and no different from anybody else that's fucked. I'm not in the ruling class. I'm in the dominated class.

Ernesto went on to explain his connection to the oppressed everywhere,
creating linkages based on this underdog perspective. In short, he has responded to racism by looking at the world through *rasquache* eyes that allow him not only to gain a sense of pride but to redefine the Chicana/o existence and empower his community with cultural symbols that are valued
and beneficial. This *rasquache* mentality emerges from the history of Chi-
canas/os, as revealed by his comment, "I think everybody should remember
who they are, and what got 'em where they go."

As we moved beyond defining and understanding the *rasquache* mentality (as introduced by Ybarra-Frausto, 1991) and began to look toward employing *rasquachismo* as an agent of change (as suggested by Perez, 1993), Ernesto revealed that this *rasquache* mentality was firmly grounded in the pursuit of change (in two separate instances):

> And that's one of the things my boss told me. Because she helped me a lot with my confidence. She went to [the university], she was a counselor, and she says, "Look, when people talk about issues, they talk about them from conceptual knowledge." She said, "You have practical knowledge of 'em and that's why people will listen to you." Because I've spoken to, like, students and stuff, and I don't say things have to change. I say, "This is what happened to me and this is what we need to do," you know, "Just do something, I don't care what you do."
>
> I remember when we had this interesting conversation when I was in Chiapas with all these, like, activists that stayed at this hotel. And they were saying all this theoretical stuff. And it was interesting. And I just said, "Hey you know what, I figure, like, I have to die one day and I hope that before I die I have time to reflect on my life, and I just hope that I'm proud of what I did in my life."

At the same time as he creates a Chicana/o identity grounded in his contributions to changing and improving things for Chicanas/os, Ernesto is still struggling with exactly what he wants to do. He is enrolled in a Ph.D. program and sees himself moving toward a point where he can apply his education and theoretical analyses to activist work. He debates about becoming a full-time activist, a researcher in communities, or an applied theoretician. He also considers pursuing his activist interests outside of the United States (in Latin America). He is caught in the dilemma that confronts many Chicanas/os at this turning point—seeking change but unsure of where or how to engage in that process. At the same time, however, Ernesto has created a space for himself in the university that is his own; a space that allows him not only to retain his racial identity but to inject it with *rasquache* icons and reconstitute it so that it simultaneously moves him toward endowing others with a *rasquache* mentality that allows self-empowerment and the pursuit of changes that will empower Chicana/o communities. He has begun a process of empowerment and change that can be passed on to Chicanas/os as a group by Chicana/o communities.

Conclusion

Through an in-depth qualitative investigation that engaged Chicana/o students in discussions about their self-conceptions, we have begun to understand contemporary Chicana/o identity formation in ways that have not previously been tapped. While the construct of Chicana/o identity includes a multitude of manifestations and continually evolves in fluid, amorphous ways, the overriding role of race in the experiences of Los Angeles Chicanas/os from a very early age results in the predominance of racial-political Chicana/o identities. Despite the fact that other facets of their experiences are important in students' identity formations and that they classify themselves as members of other social entities, the racial formation process results in many of these other facets of Chicana/o identity being subsumed under the construct of their racial-political or their ethnic-cultural identity.

The objective of this investigation was to obtain an understanding of Chicana/o identity formation with the hope that it might reveal insights into how identity is linked or can be linked to Chicana/o empowerment, given the overwhelming "failure" faced by members of the community in the schools, for example. By focusing on the intricacies of one particular student's life, we have not only better understood the process of Chicana/o identity formation but gleaned possible connections to empowerment.

One of the most successful of the students who participated in the study revealed how he has struggled with racial oppression and reconstructed his image of himself and the Chicana/o experience to endow it with a cultural capital that he in turn taps into as he not only achieves success but also positions himself to empower other Chicanas/os.

As we turn our eyes to the horizon and gradually walk into the twenty-first century, Chicana/o students, and one in particular, have important lessons to help us begin this journey. It is clear that race is crucial to how Chicanas/os understand and organize their world. One of the fundamental means by which this comes about is their experiences with and observations of racism and discrimination. As the statistics on educational failure along with individual students' stories suggest, many Chicanas/os are unable to deal with these issues in empowering ways and instead strike out against the mouths and hands of racism (as Ernesto himself did in high school).

Ernesto's story, however, shows us the possibility for transformation. Ernesto has boldly met the challenge posed by Perez as she proposed invoking *rasquachismo* in Chicana/o educational struggles: "We must creatively continue to exploit unexpected sources in the construction of identities and politics that challenge the norms of thinking and practices within the educational system" (Perez, 1993, p. 277). By acknowledging the role of race in Chicanas'/os' lives and deciphering the complexities of the racial formation process, Chicanas/os can contextualize their experiences. Through this process they, in turn, can look within the community for symbols of power and strength and turn the popular conceptions of "success" on end. By acknowledging *rasquache* roots and nurturing them, Chicanas/os—the inheritors of many southwestern metropolitan and rural areas in the twenty-first-century United States—can embark on paths toward empowerment that, although they are diverse, lead to the development of their communities and the larger society that depends on them.

The precise means by which this can be done has yet to be worked out; but it can become reality as researchers, community leaders, individual schools or teachers, and most importantly, parents look to help Chicana/o youth understand the processes of racial formation and racism that exist around them, the strength in the cultural capital and Chicana/o icons that have been popularly devalued, and their ability to engage in transformative processes that are personally stimulating and rejuvenating.

The twenty-first-century experiences of the Chicana/o will no doubt be shaped by race. The challenge is to reconstruct racial formation processes and to develop Chicana/o[13] identities that are grounded in *rasquachismo.* This effort can best be generated by Chicana/o communities rather than by immovable institutions, and it can lead us along multiple paths toward empowerment and social change.

NOTES

1. The first generation of Chicana/o scholars includes those who were trained and began their scholarly careers in the 1960s and early 1970s, and the second generation is the cohort that emerged in the later 1980s and early 1990s. There was a very small number of Chicana/o scholars that can be classified as an earlier generation, whose work was very important to the development of research in these areas as well as the training of future scholars. Being so small, however, this group hardly constitutes a cohort of scholars. See Muñoz (1989) for an extended discussion.

2. *Chicana/o* refers to females and males of Mexican descent who are living, and have been socialized, in the United States. (Other descriptors can be used for this population; but this label is grounded in the larger argument of this chapter, as is discussed in the chapter's conclusions.) In this chapter, *Chicana/o identity* refers to the social identity that Chicanas/os establish for themselves. This social identity is simply how given individuals define themselves in their own social world, specifically with regard to the social groups in which the individuals place themselves and with which they interact. Thus, Chicana/o identity theoretically includes the identity of all Chicanas/os, including those who define themselves as upper middle class or as homosexuals, for example, but who do not consciously ethnically identify. It also includes Chicanas/os who define themselves as Catholic, Mexicano, and working class simultaneously, as another example. This investigation then considers the self-perceptions of all types and categories of Chicanas/os, to understand the full complexity of these identity formations, with the goal of addressing the needs of large numbers.

3. It is beyond the scope of this chapter to directly analyze all of the connections between Chicana/o identity, its influences, and educational outcomes, although several linkages are obvious.

4. Employment is another potentially crucial realm of identity formation; but since the sample in this research consists of students, employment was not a primary

focus. Still, students were able to bring up the role of their jobs and employment in their identity formations when relevant.

5. The analysis that follows is grounded in social justice research methodology. The fundamental principle of this research approach is that both the objective and the method of research should be grounded in social justice. One means toward this end is to allow "participants" to become authorities as co-researchers. Although this project was conducted while the model was still being developed, this chapter was written with these principles in mind. See Pizarro, 1998, for an extended discussion of these issues.

6. Students volunteered to participate in the study through classes in their respective schools. As mentioned, students' identities were understood through their responses to the social issues they deemed important (such as racism, sexism, and community issues) as well as who they said they were in their social worlds. These issues were covered repeatedly in each of the research tools through multiple closed- and open-ended questions. Students spent thirty to forty-five minutes completing surveys, and those interviewed spent one to one and one-half hours discussing these issues, while some also participated in a second interview of similar length. The interviewees were also challenged with regard to the strength of their beliefs through discussions of opposing views. Each individual student's responses were then analyzed to determine the nature of their identities and the influences on them. Afterward, each student's experiences were incorporated into an all-encompassing model. The analyses in this paper are based on data collected through surveys with over 150 Chicana/o students (fairly equally divided among high school freshmen, high school seniors, community college students, and university students), as well as interviews with 13 students (also equally divided among the different cohorts, with an additional graduate student participant at the university).

7. Other identity researchers have noted these potential distinctions in both theoretical discussions and in analyses of quantitative data. See L. Gutiérrez, "Critical Consciousness and Chicano Identity: An Exploratory Analysis," in *Estudios Chicanos and the Politics of Community: Selected Proceedings of the National Association of Chicano Studies* (Ann Arbor, MI: McNaughton and Gunn Lithographers, 1989) pp.35–53; J. Rodriguez and P. Gurin, "The Relationship of Intergroup Contact to Social Identity and Political Consciousness," *Hispanic Journal of Behavioral Sciences* 12, pp. 235–255.

8. *Veteranos* refers to older gang members, who are considered the ultimate authorities by young Chicana/o gang members and wanna-bes.

9. *Raza* is a loosely used ethnic identifier that includes Chicanas/os and all Latinas/os depending on the context.

10. The "truck" refers to food trucks that are often present in areas where Chicanas/os work and live. They are similar to food trucks that cater to construction sites and other working-class job sites, but their menus reflect their Chicana/o clientele. "Dickies" are work pants that were integrated into the *cholo* attire in the 1970s. Gang members and wanna-bes often wear them oversized, with deep creases.

11. Marcos is one of the leaders of the Zapatista revolt in Chiapas, Mexico, in which a unified indigenous front is renewing revolutionary leader Emiliano Zapata's cry for land redistribution. *Todos somos Marcos* is a slogan used among the people, which means, "We are all Marcos."

12. *Mojado* (wet) is a Spanish word used to describe an illegal alien. It is usually translated as "wetback."

13. *Chicana/o* has been used throughout this work because it symbolizes the racial-political identities that the participants exposed as central to their experience. When Ernesto was asked what ethnic label he used, he mentioned several but focused on *Chicano*. He went on to explain, "For me, 'Chicano' is like an affirmation of a political awareness. . . . Saying you're Chicano . . . is like an awareness of what it means to identify with your people and [to be] culturally and politically conscious of your situation in life."

REFERENCES

Almaguer, T. (1994). *Racial Fault Lines: The Historical Origins of White Supremacy in California*. Berkeley: University of California Press.

Apple, M. (1993). "Constructing the Other: Rightist Reconstructions of Common Sense." Pp. 24–39 in McCarthy, C., and Critchlow, W., eds., *Race, Identity, and Representation in Education*. New York: Routledge.

Bernal M., and Knight, G., eds. (1993). *Ethnic Identity: Formation and Transmission Among Hispanics and Other Minorities*. Albany: State University of New York Press.

Bernal, M., and Martinelli, P., eds. (1993). *Mexican American Identity*. Encino, CA: Floricanto Press.

Bernal, M., Saenz, D., and Knight, G. (1991). "Ethnic Identity and Adaptation of Mexican American Youths in School Settings." *Hispanic Journal of Behavioral Sciences* 13, pp. 135–154.

Gutiérrez, L. (1989). "Critical Consciousness and Chicano Identity: An Exploratory Analysis." In *Estudios Chicanos and the Politics of Community: Selected Proceeding of the National Association of Chicano Studies*. Ann Arbor, MI: McNaughton and Gunn Lithographers.

Hurtado, A., Gonzalez, R., and Vega, L. (1994). "Social Identification and the Academic Achievement of Chicano Students." Pp. 57–74 in Hurtado, A., and Garcia, E., eds., *The Educational Achievement of Latinos: Barriers and Successes*. Santa Cruz, CA: Regents of the University of California.

Hurtado, S. (1994). "Latino Consciousness and Academic Success." Pp. 17–56 in Hurtado, A., and Garcia, E., eds., *The Educational Achievement of Latinos: Barriers and Successes*. Santa Cruz, CA: Regents of the University of California.

Knight, G., Cota, M., and Bernal, M. (1993). "The Socialization of Cooperative, Competitive, and Individualistic Preferences Among Mexican American Children: The Mediating Role of Ethnic Identity." *Hispanic Journal of Behavioral Sciences* 15, pp. 291–309.

Mehan, H., Hubbard, L., and Villanueva, I. (1994). "Forming Academic Identities: Accommodation Without Assimilation Among Involuntary Minorities." *Anthropology and Education Quarterly* 25, pp. 91–117.

Muñoz, C. (1989). *Youth, Identity, Power: The Chicano Movement*. New York: Verso Press.

Omi, M., and Winant, H. (1994). *Racial Formation in the United States: From the 1960s to the 1990s*. 2nd ed. New York: Routledge.

Perez, L. (1993). "Opposition and the Education of Chicana/os." Pp. 268–279 in Mc-Carthy, C., and Critchlow, W., eds., *Race, Identity, and Representation in Education*. New York: Routledge.

Pizarro, M. (1997). "Power, Borders, and Identity Formation: Understanding the World of Chicana/o Students." *Perspectives in Mexican American Studies* 6.

_____. (1998) "'Chicana/o Power!': Epistemology and Methodology for Social Justice and Empowerment in Chicana/o Communities." *Qualitative Studies in Education* 11.

Reddy, M. (1995). *Statistical Record of Hispanic Americans.* 2nd ed. Detroit, MI: Gale Research.

Rodriguez, J., and Gurin, P. (1990). "The Relationship of Intergroup Contact to Social Identity and Political Consciousness." *Hispanic Journal of Behavioral Sciences* 12, pp. 235–255.

Valencia, R. (1991). The Plight of Chicano Students: An Overview of Schooling Conditions and Outcomes. Pp. 3–26 in Valencia, R., ed., *Chicano School Failure and Success: Research and Policy Agendas for the 1990s.* London: Falmer Press.

Ybarra-Frausto, T. (1991). Rasquachismo: A Chicano Sensibility. Pp. 155–162 in del Castillo, R. G., McKenna, T., and Yarbro-Bejarano, Y., eds., *Chicano Art: Resistance and Affirmation, 1965–1985.* Los Angeles: Wight Art Gallery.

nine

Agribusiness Strategies to Divide the Workforce by Class, Ethnicity, and Legal Status

FRED KRISSMAN

The social networks that immigrant and ethnic communities depend upon for economic survival have long been used by U.S. industries to obtain new employees. An example is agribusiness in California and Washington state. Growers in California have tapped networks based in Mexico for decades to obtain their workers. Their preference for binational networks transformed rural California, undermined conditions for the farm workforce, and provided an excuse for a resurgence of white nativism. In contrast, growers in Washington state depended primarily upon networks of workers based in the southwestern states, bringing milder impacts on the Pacific Northwest. However, I contend that agribusiness in Washington state has recently adopted the California model. In this chapter I describe how binational networks are manipulated by agribusiness in each state, outline the negative consequences, and suggest an alternative model.

Introduction

The now entrenched international migration flows from thousands of rural Mexican communities are documented to have been created and sustained by labor recruiters representing industries in the United States.[1] Nevertheless, virtually all of the solutions adopted by the U.S. government focus on the supply side of the immigration equation, due to the widespread belief that Mexico, Mexicans, and immigrants in general are to blame for myriad socioeconomic problems in the United States. The continued demand by U.S. firms for new immigrants is still conveniently ignored, even as new governmental initiatives make these workers ever more desirable to U.S. employers. I contend that the influx of new immigrants continues unabated because U.S. employers can more easily divide immigrants by class, ethnicity, and legal status, leaving them vulnerable to exploitation in the workplace.

To document the demand side of the immigration issue I have examined the agribusiness sector, which has recruited tens of millions of immigrants during the past century. U.S. agribusiness still employs about 3 million farm workers annually, an ever increasing majority of whom are so-called illegal aliens (that is, undocumented workers) from Mexico. Furthermore, the demand for immigrant workers has expanded exponentially as their use has spread to a growing number of nonfarm industries such as meat packing, manufacturing, construction, and janitorial, domestic, and tourist-related services.

In conducting research in the primary farming regions in California and Washington—the San Joaquin and Yakima valleys—I was literally comparing apples and oranges, with grapes thrown in for good measure. Each of these three labor-intensive crop industries generates more than $1 billion annually; is dominated by relatively few large growers and/or major corporations; is subject to increasing vertical integration; and is promoted and protected in a variety of ways by the government. A great deal of research documents all of these characteristics of U.S. agribusiness.[2] What has remained largely unexamined is how these major agribusiness industries maintain access to an ample supply of immigrant workers regardless of public opinion and public policy.

In this chapter I illustrate four points about farm labor markets in the United States. First, the successful recruitment of unlimited numbers of new immigrants has permitted agribusiness to keep its workforce divided from one generation to the next. Second, historical-structural specificities account for the variations found among farm labor markets, including the influence events in one rural region may have on another. Third, international social networks are crucial to the recruitment of new immigrant workers. And fourth, the negative consequences of the current system can only be remedied by significantly increasing the penalties levied on the ultimate benefactors of a constant influx of new immigrants—the corporations that continue to recruit new immigrant workers.

These four points are documented in four sections: (1) the macro context, within which international labor recruitment occurs, examining the roles played by agribusiness, the government, labor intermediaries, and farm workers and their labor unions; (2) the micro context, within which labor recruitment occurs, describing the operation of migrant social networks; (3) three case studies, illustrating how labor recruiters manipulate social networks to maintain an ample labor supply; and (4) a review of the divisions suffered by the nation's farm workers, and of alternative public policies that would limit the ability of agribusiness to exploit workforce cleavages. New policies would improve working conditions for the current farm labor force, benefiting impoverished families as well as the destitute rural communities in which these families reside on both sides of the U.S.-Mexican border, while eliminating the many consequences, often unintended, of current U.S. immigration, labor, and bilateral policies.

Labor Recruitment By Agribusiness in the San Joaquin and Yakima Valleys

Can labor-intensive crop industries in California and Washington be compared? California is the number one agricultural producer in the United States: Farming is California's single largest economic sector, with $22 billion in annual crop revenues produced by more than 700,000 workers. Crop industries within California's three top agricultural counties—all in the San Joaquin valley[3]—generate more than $7 billion in revenues annually with the labor of about 250,000 workers (Agricultural Commissioner [AC], 1990–1995; Employment Development Department [EDD], 1990). Agricultural jobs constitute an average of more than 20 percent of total employment across the three counties, while the inhabitants of scores of "farm worker enclaves" are dependent upon the region's farm labor market for more than half of their total employment opportunities. Indeed, the high demand for low-cost farm labor during the past three decades has transformed at least fifty-nine rural Californian communities, the majority in the San Joaquin valley, into enclaves populated primarily by families of Mexican origin (Palerm, 1991, pp. 124–127).

Agriculture is one of most important economic sectors in Washington state, and the top goods-producing sector in eastern Washington, generating about $7 billion annually with a workforce of more than 135,000 (WSES [Washington State Employment Service], 1994a, p. 12; *Yakima Herald-Republic*, Aug. 21, 1991). The Yakima valley is the state's top farm district, producing over $1 billion in crops per year with the labor of more than 50,000 workers, making agriculture the dominant regional economic and employment sector (Larson and Bullamore, 1995). Agricultural jobs constitute more than 25 percent of total employment in Yakima county and more than 50 percent of job opportunities in five farm worker enclaves that have been transformed into majority Mexican-origin towns during the past decade.

The San Joaquin valley has been the most important crop producing region in the world since at least the 1950s, and the Yakima valley has been among the top ten agricultural regions in the nation since the 1930s (Krissman, 1996, chapter 2; *Yakima Herald-Republic*, April 11, 1965). However, the successful development of the principal crop industries in these valleys was not assured upon agrarian settlement in the 1850s. Two types of "outside" assistance have been required to transform the San Joaquin and Yakima valleys into highly productive farm regions.

First, both valleys required massive government-funded projects to provide rural infrastructure: rail lines, all-weather roads, electrical power, and irrigation. Each of these projects was accomplished in stages, and—in the case of the irrigation projects—over the vigorous protests of U.S. farmers to the east, who saw government largesse in the Pacific region as providing unfair benefits to their competitors (Krissman, 1996, chapter 2; *Yakima Herald-Republic*, April 11, 1965, p. 12F). Furthermore, both regions' growers benefit from the ongoing research conducted at taxpayer-subsidized land-grant universities, to the tune of tens of millions of dollars annually.

The second type of outside assistance required by the agricultural sector in each region was ample and low-cost labor. For more than a century labor-intensive agricultural production in the Pacific region has required the importation of vast armies of seasonal labor. Native Americans and indentured workers from Asia were early sources of farm labor (Monroy, 1990; Cheng and Bonacich, 1984). However, during most of the present century, Mexicans have predominated in both Washington and California. Lawrence Cardoso (1980) and Erasmo Gamboa (1990) have documented the active recruitment of Mexicans and Mexican Americans by agribusiness in the western United States since before 1910. Growers accelerated their recruitment activities right up to the 1930s depression, when they acquiesced in the nationwide campaign to repatriate to Mexico as many farm workers as could be coerced (Hoffman, 1974). Nevertheless, Mexicans, Filipinos, and Native Americans provided the bulk of the harvest workforce in the Pacific Northwest during the depression (Gamboa, 1990, p. 13), whereas in California, a core labor force of Mexicans was supplemented by so-called "Okies," who had been displaced from the south-central United States (Gregory, 1989).

Much of the southwestern United States—until the 1840s, part of Mexico—had been initially settled and partly developed by Mexican nationals (Acuña, 1981, part I). At least 100,000 Mexicans were thus incorporated into the U.S. economy when the northern Mexican provinces were annexed. *El norte* remained a haven during times of famine, civil war, and revolution, all of which plagued Mexico between the 1880s and 1920s, during which time at least another 100,000 Mexicans crossed the northern frontier. The northward flow of political and economic refugees was promoted by U.S. economic penetration into Mexico, as well as labor recruitment by U.S. industries (Cardoso, 1980). Early agribusiness industries such as Californian citrus and Texan cotton encouraged Mexican workers to settle in scores of rural settlements near orchards and fields, where they were segregated and confined by law and custom to manual labor.[4]

Most Anglo agricultural investors did not recruit, train, and supervise Mexican workers themselves. Spanish-speaking supervisors were required to take charge of the labor force. As Mexicans came to dominate regional farm labor markets in the southwest, some advanced into supervisory positions, taking on the task of labor recruitment as either formal or informal interme-diaries.[5] Informal intermediaries provided labor services to their agricultural employers as part of their official duties. Formal intermediaries, known as farm labor contractors (FLCs), contracted their labor services to a number of growers. FLCs became an integral cog in the social relations of produc-tion in the western United States; many of the earliest farm worker protests focused on friction with FLCs, not with the growers that hired the contrac-tors and set the basic conditions of employment (see Fisher, 1953; Williamson, 1947). Although worker abuse was common, FLCs were gener-ally successful at containing class conflict as a result of the dependence of farm workers for basic services such as job placement, transportation, hous-ing, and short-term loans. Furthermore, the intermediaries were typically tied to the labor force by national, ethnic, and kinship ties, and sometimes sided with workers against growers attempting to keep wages low.

A significant portion of the Mexican workforce in the southwestern United States settled near the industries that they served. In contrast, most Mexican farm workers came to the northwest only as one part of a migration circuit with a series of geographically and seasonally distinct jobs since the peak labor demands were too brief to sustain a locally based farm labor force. FLCs based in California and Texas provided a mobile workforce for growers in the northwest; Texan contractors alone brought 60,000 migrant workers north annually (Gamboa, 1990, p. 14).

In addition to the seasonal needs of employers and a high dependence upon FLCs, Mexican migrants were also constrained by federal policies that differ-entiated Anglo farm workers from non-Europeans. For example, New Deal legislation specifically excluded "non-white"[6] farm laborers from education and housing programs, segmenting workers such as Mexicans at the bottom of farm labor markets (Gamboa, 1990, p. xiii; Krissman, 1997a, p. 14).

Although an ethnically mixed workforce combined in 1933 to stage the largest and longest strike up to that time in California (Chacon, 1984), a longtime strategy of growers involved the recruitment of different ethnic groups to undermine strikes. Growers used Japanese to confront Anglo workers, Filipinos to defeat Japanese, and Anglos to replace Mexican strikers time and again; the governmental apparatus played a principal role in helping scab labor to cross picket lines (see Williamson, 1947). Large agribusiness in-terests also financed a vigilante group, Associated Farmers, which has been compared with the American Ku Klux Klan and the German Nazi party due to its methods (Pichardo, 1995). Only the onset of World War II opened new avenues of employment for nonwhite farm workers. Both expanding war-time industries and the armed services were willing to accept farm workers, including Mexicans.

Due to alternative employment opportunities, growers were under pressure
to improve wages and conditions for their workers at a time when farm production was expanding rapidly (Galarza, 1964, pp. 41–45). Rather than compete to retain their current workforce, agribusiness convinced the federal government to sponsor a contract labor system to flood the farm labor markets
with new immigrant workers. The so-called bracero program displaced private FLC firms, since the government and growers combined to recruit and
supervise immigrant workers, with the taxpayers paying much of the bill.

At the program's peak, hundreds of thousands of braceros were brought
to the United States annually to compete in the farm labor market with Mexicans, Mexican Americans, and others already working in agriculture. Even
in its first few years, the influx of new workers led to a deterioration in labor
conditions, and Mexican braceros responded to violations of their contracts
with protests, including full-scale strikes (Gamboa, 1990, chapter 4; Acuña,
1981, p. 146). Repression and deportations by the government, combined
with the terror tactics of the Associated Farmers, helped keep wages at De-
pression-era levels through the harvest of 1946. The program was so effective at oversupplying farm labor markets that growers applied pressure to
extend the program beyond its "wartime emergency" mandate.

Whereas the bracero program persisted in the southwestern United States
until 1965, it was short-circuited in the northwest. When World War II
ended, negotiations between the U.S. and Mexican governments led to
slightly better guarantees for braceros. Furthermore, the federal government
shifted some costs from the taxpayers to the growers. For example, transportation was now assessed to the growers, with round-trip expenses to
Washington state estimated at $162.95 per bracero (Gamboa, 1990, p. 122).
Growers in the northwestern states began to abandon the program even
though the shortage of low-cost labor was greater than ever due to the displacement of the migrant workforce by braceros during the war (Gamboa,
1990, pp. 126, 127). Therefore, agribusiness in the northwest began recruitment activities in the southwestern United States again. During the next
three decades the apple industry became heavily dependent upon Mexican-
origin residents of south Texas (*Tejanos*).

The government played a key role in supporting a two-track migratory system in the western United States between 1947 and 1965. While the bracero
program continued in the southwestern United States, governmental institutions helped agribusiness in the northwest recruit Tejanos by implementing
the so-called Interstate Job Clearance system (Kissam et al., 1993, p. 230;
Gamboa, 1990). This system encouraged people in the southern Rio Grande
valley to migrate by dropping them from the relief rolls as soon as growers
claimed there was work available.[7] Tens of thousands of Tejanos were forced
of economic necessity to migrate to the northwest to work, at the same time as
hundreds of thousands of Mexican braceros were being imported into the

southwest to work at even lower wages. These complementary migrant networks kept total farm labor costs throughout the western United States very low—about half the wage paid unskilled manufacturing workers during the same period (Galarza, 1964, chapter 15; Gamboa, 1990, p. 127).

The depressive effects of the bracero program on wages and working conditions led to increased protests from unions and community activists. Cesar Chavez, who organized primarily among urban-based Mexican Americans during the 1950s, staged a series of protests against the bracero program in Oxnard, California, in 1961 (Taylor, 1975, pp. 94–96). Chavez's activists succeeded in revealing the regional citrus growers' preference for bracero workers despite chronic underemployment among local residents. The protests led to major revisions in bracero policy, which helped seal the fate of the long-lived contract program. Within a year, Chavez left his job with the Community Service Organization to begin a campaign to organize farm workers in the San Joaquin (Chavez, 1992).

When the bracero program was finally terminated at the end of 1964, the government documented hundreds of thousands of former braceros to keep the southwestern United States oversupplied, weakening the emergent farm labor movement in California for a time (Fineberg, 1971). A number of unions and worker advocacy groups made forays into regional farm labor markets in this period, appealing to different portions of a diverse farm worker population (Krissman, 1997b, p. 15). The United Farm Workers (UFW) union, led by Cesar Chavez, was based among Mexican and Mexican American residents settled in the San Joaquin. This support was grounded in years of canvassing the small rural settlements, handing out flyers, soliciting members in house meetings (*juntas caseras*), and providing a variety of community services (Taylor, 1975, p. 113). Chavez emphasized religious faith, nonviolent activism, and a civil rights message—an approach unique within the organized labor movement. Although Chavez's approach broadened the UFW's message beyond the usual worker constituencies, a high level of sacrifice was required of UFW union members, and this alienated many farm workers.

Growers exacerbated every cleavage within the heterogeneous labor markets to divide the workforce. The legalized former braceros, along with new, undocumented workers, migrant families, supervisory personnel, and disaffected non-Latino farm workers such as some Anglo "fruit tramps" and dissident Filipinos, all were used to counter the organizing efforts of the UFW. These factions were used by growers during strikes as "scab labor," and the UFW did whatever it could to get them out of the fields.[8] Former braceros and the undocumented feared the UFW for its use of the Immigration and Naturalization Service (the INS) to enforce immigration laws.[9] Migrant families opposed Chavez's active support for increased regulation of child labor. Supervisors, including many of Mexican origin, were divided between their ethnic and economic loyalties; based on their class interests, many were more closely allied with growers than with workers. And some Anglo and Filipino workers were put off by the ubiquitous use of the Spanish language and of Mexican symbols such as images of the Virgin of Guadalupe and the Mexican flag at meetings and rallies. However, most farm workers in California were understandably united in wanting to improve conditions that had remained substandard for a generation (Majka and Majka, 1982; Jenkins, 1985, chapter 6). When the UFW began to win contracts, the growers turned to a rival union to impede the farm workers' movement.

Growers formed an alliance with the International Brotherhood of Teamsters (the IBT). The IBT was already infamous for its raids on other unions to gain new contracts and members (Krissman, 1997b, pp. 7–11). For example, the Teamsters first entered the agricultural sector in the 1940s, when the cannery industry turned to the IBT in order to stymie the militant, multiethnic labor union United Cannery, Agricultural, Packing, and Allied Workers of America/Food, Tobacco, and Agriculture (known as the FTA). Indeed, the IBT's destruction of the FTA, as chronicled by Vicki L. Ruiz in *Cannery Women, Cannery Lives* (1987), reads like a primer for the Teamsters' subsequent campaign against the UFW. In 1961 the Teamsters had obtained a contract with lettuce grower Bud Antle in his attempt to evade a strike called by the Agricultural Workers Organizing Committee. The IBT sealed its deal with Antle by providing him a loan of $1 million out of the membership's pension fund (Taylor, 1975, p. 100).

The IBT argued that theirs was a "real" union, rather than a "civil rights organization" like the UFW. Indeed, the UFW did frame its movement in terms of race rather than those of class.[10] However, the Teamsters had also abandoned a class approach to labor organizing as early as the 1930s. Furthermore, the IBT revealed itself as discriminatory in the treatment of Mexican union members (*Los Angeles Times*, April 28, 1973), as well as unwilling to fight for the whole panoply of improvements sought by the UFW. The mere threat of UFW organizing activities drove countless growers, including the bulk of the table grape, citrus, and vegetable industries, into the arms of the Teamsters. Nevertheless, the IBT was forced by the strategies of the upstart UFW to back out of most of its "sweetheart" contracts, and finally, in 1977, to cede the fields to the UFW (*Los Angeles Times*, May 11, 1977).

By the late 1970s the UFW represented at least 110,000 farm workers (about 10 percent of the state's farm labor force). The union's impacts extended far beyond its membership, forcing the average farm wage up about 20 percent, adding benefits previously unheard of in any U.S. farm labor market, introducing a state law recognizing farm worker rights, and providing a new icon to the Chicano power movement (Wells, 1996, p. 94; Acuña, 1981, chapter 9). However, agribusiness continued to seek an alternative to the UFW. Increasingly, growers resorted to another old ally in their strategy to divide the labor force—formal labor intermediaries.

The FLC system had been all but eliminated from California during the bracero program. Government agencies and grower associations had combined to provide most of the services (recruitment, transportation, housing, food, training, and supervision) once rendered by intermediaries. By the end of the bracero era, private FLC firms controlled less than 10 percent of the state's total farm labor force. However, in the 1970s, California growers turned increasingly to FLCs to displace employees who were attempting to organize. Most FLCs are Mexican- or Mexican American–owned, while virtually the entire supervisory hierarchy is made up of Mexicans. FLCs tapped a seemingly inexhaustible supply of new immigrant workers, and the UFW found its race-based approach blunted in a fight against Mexican firms. The number of farm workers in California employed by FLCs doubled in the 1970s, then doubled again by the mid-1980s (Commission on Agricultural Workers [CAW], 1993; Rosenberg et al., 1992). By the early 1980s, the UFW's membership plummeted to less than 10,000 as new, undocumented immigrants under the control of FLCs replaced unionized workers.

Undocumented immigration surged under the stimulus of FLC recruitment, introducing new flows of international migrants, such as indigenous Mexicans from southern Mexico (Kearney, 1986; Mines and Anzaldua, 1982). These workers are distinct from earlier flows of *mestizo*[11] Mexican farm workers, not merely in physical characteristics and historical circumstances, but even in language. These Mexicans speak indigenous languages as their native tongue, and a substantial portion have not learned much Spanish due to a lack of public schools in their isolated villages. At first a seemingly insignificant stream, international migration from indigenous regions rapidly swelled to become one of the largest sources of new farm workers in the United States. In California alone, indigenous workers now constitute at least 10 percent of the labor market (Zabin et al., 1993).

While social ferment heightened in California, the pattern of Tejano migration to Washington continued unabated for fifteen years after the bracero program ended. The influx of former braceros and new, undocumented Mexican workers into the southwestern United States kept wages static near the Mexican border. However, the success of the UFW's campaign for government enforcement of child labor laws in the 1980s discouraged Tejano families from migrating (Kissam et al., 1993; Carkner and Jaksich, 1993). Therefore, Yakima producers also increased their recruitment activities in California at the same time that the protracted conflict between management, labor, and the unions encouraged many farm workers to seek work elsewhere. The relatively low level of immigration enforcement in the northwest lured many undocumented Mexicans north; indeed, the Washington state contingent of the INS cooperated with growers to document workers.[12]

The new migrants to Washington established direct ties with growers or applied for jobs in agribusiness personnel offices, just as their predecessors had in the southwest, in the aftermath of the bracero program. Their quick placement was facilitated by the rapid expansion of agricultural production, which increased by more than 25 percent between the 1980s and the 1990s (Carkner and Jaksich, 1993). These farm workers who settled in Washington served as magnets for relatives and friends both in California and Mexico, especially when the "pioneers" moved into supervisory positions that allowed them to dispense jobs to others. The result was the waning of the FLC system in the northwest even as FLC firms reemerged in California.

In the mid-1980s the government exacerbated the post-bracero trends toward both the increased settlement of formerly migrant workers and oversupplied farm labor markets. Responding to politicians' complaints about the ongoing influx of undocumented migrants in the southwestern United States, Congress implemented the Immigration Reform and Control Act (or IRCA) in 1986. Its principal goal was to reverse seemingly unremitting undocumented immigration from Mexico (Bean et al., 1989). Therefore, employer sanctions on the use of undocumented labor and increased enforcement of immigration laws were its central provisions.

Agribusiness interests throughout the Pacific region claimed that labor shortages were likely to result from the implementation of IRCA. The governors of Oregon and Washington states both made highly publicized forays into the fields for "photo ops" showing them pitching in to harvest threatened crops, and California's U.S. Senator Pete Wilson lobbied for a new bracero-style program. Under the intense political pressures, the U.S. Border Patrol suddenly ordered the border opened to all undocumented workers who claimed to be returning to farm jobs previously held in the western United States. Farm labor markets were flooded, setting the stage for widespread fraud in obtaining the documents needed to qualify for legalization under IRCA.

The Washington apple industry added considerably to the general hysteria, unleashing an unprecedented advertising campaign in California to encourage workers to venture north. The resulting influx led to an industry-made disaster, with thousands of workers unable to obtain sufficient work to pay their living expenses, let alone finance a return trip south. Growers disavowed responsibility, saying that they could not be expected to pay seasonal workers until there was work to be done. After weeks of ad hoc local efforts to respond to the hungry and homeless migrants, the governor finally used emergency funds to ship the hundreds remaining back to California at the taxpayers' expense. The Washington Apple Commission and its advertising agency eventually settled a class-action lawsuit filed by the state's Legal Aid agency on behalf of destitute farm workers, paying out $617,000 (*Yakima Herald-Republic*, May 20, 1992).

Despite initial agribusiness fears, IRCA did not lead to farm labor shortages (Carkner and Jaksich, 1993; *Yakima Herald-Republic*, Aug. 21, 1991;

Los Angeles Times, Jan. 15, 1988, Nov. 19, 1991, and Nov. 26, 1991). Aside from the sudden opening of the border to undocumented workers in 1986, several amnesty provisions had been added to IRCA to appease the U.S. agribusiness lobby, which was seeking a new "guest worker" program. These provisions led to the legalization of more than 2.5 million undocumented immigrants and new farm workers. Whereas IRCA's employer sanctions have since been roundly deemed a failure due to a lack of rigorous enforcement, its amnesty provisions may have been too successful.

The documentation of millions of Mexicans increased resettlement of many former migrants in the United States and attracted new waves of undocumented immigrants, many of whom are family members of those legalized under IRCA's provisions (see *Yakima Herald-Republic*, May 3, 1987; *Los Angeles Times*, Nov. 26, 1991). In both the San Joaquin and Yakima valleys the settled Hispanic population increased by about 80 percent between 1980 and 1990, leading to a regional demographic transformation (Krissman, 1996, chapter 4; Yakima Chamber of Commerce, 1994, p. 26, 28). The continued growth of labor-intensive agricultural production during the same period further spurred Mexican immigration and settlement. However, the profitable expansion of labor-intensive crop industries has not resulted in higher earnings for the labor force.

Conditions for the farm labor force and the economies of the rural towns that house them deteriorated in the 1980s and 1990s. In California the rate of use of FLCs suddenly quadrupled in 1987, as growers sought to shield themselves from employer sanctions (Commission on Agricultural Workers, 1993). It is widely known that FLCs pay the lowest wages under the worst working conditions. In the San Joaquin valley, the three main farm counties contain four areas that have been designated "enterprise zones" due to their elevated rates of unemployment (Dowell et al., 1994, p. 10), as well as seven of the ten poorest incorporated towns in the state, with average per capita incomes of about $5,500 (*Los Angeles Times*, July 6, 1992). These seven towns are all farm worker enclaves,[13] with Latino-majority populations of Mexican origin and heavily dependent upon work in the agricultural sector.

Meanwhile, in the Yakima valley, farm workers report decreased earnings in the aftermath of IRCA due to an increasing oversupply of labor. Yakima county has been declared a distressed area eligible for Rural Enterprise Community funds, with an unemployment rate averaging 14 percent. The same enclavement pattern so pronounced in rural California has developed in Yakima in recent years.[14] Farm worker earnings average under $6,000 annually, with 58 percent earning too little to qualify for supplemental unemployment insurance (WSES, 1994a, appendix IV; WSES, 1994b, p. 13; WSES, 1994c, p. 8; *Economist*, July 18, 1992).

These dramatic demographic and socioeconomic changes that occurred within a single generation have led to greatly increased interethnic tensions in both regions. In California the return of a nativist movement has substantial support across ethnic lines. For example, Proposition 187, a particularly harsh anti-immigrant measure, was supported by about a third of Latinos, half of African Americans, and two-thirds of Anglos (Krissman, 1997a, p. 22). Joint raids of the local police and the INS on Latino-majority communities in the San Joaquin valley, after a long hiatus, recurred in the early 1990s as some longtime mestizo residents from Mexico joined with the Anglo minority to support the deportation of new, undocumented workers, many of whom are ethnically distinct indigenous immigrants from southern Mexico (*Visalia Delta-Times*, Nov. 13, 1992; Krissman, 1996, pp. 185–187).

Journalists and researchers have commented on the rise in local nativist sentiments in Yakima (*Economist*, July 18, 1992; *New Yorker*, March 25, 1996; Buzzard, 1992, p. 145). Perhaps the single best evidence of the immigration backlash in this northwestern region was inadvertently unleashed as a result of an attempt by the region's newspaper to increase interethnic understanding. An eight-day series (*Yakima Herald-Republic*, Feb. 26 through March 5, 1995) focusing on the Mexican state of Michoacan, the homeland of most members of the local Mexican community, led to a barrage of voice- and editorial-mail, 115 of which were printed verbatim in a series of editorial-page columns. More than 80 percent were negative, questioning the paper's positive portrayal of Mexico, Mexicans, and farm workers.[15] Of course, strong public sentiment has officials sitting up to take notice. While some local politicians have attempted to straddle the fence (*Yakima Herald-Republic*, Nov. 10, 1994), the region's congressman is solidly behind federal efforts to curb legal immigrants' rights and blockade the border and supports a Republican plan to implement a new, bracero-style, guest worker program.[16] The same congressman called for the regional contingent of the INS to delay enforcement of immigration laws until after the harvest season is concluded in order to avoid inconvenience to farm employers (*National Public Radio*, June 26, 1997).

While agribusiness, FLCs, and the federal government were all attempting in various ways to ease the effects of IRCA, the new law inspired 500 Washington state farm workers to meet in Yakima in 1986. They hoped that impending implementation of the law might improve conditions for the current farm labor force by providing them documents and eliminating the incessant recruitment of new workers in Mexico by grower representatives. The group founded the independent United Farm Workers of Washington state. Regional analysts downplayed the prospects for this organization, doubting that Washington farm labor could be organized in the foreseeable future due to internal dissension and the lack of a state farm labor law requiring growers to recognize employee representatives (Kissam et al., 1993, p. 285). Indeed, ninety members left the union in 1993 when it affiliated with the California-based UFW (*Yakima Herald-Republic*, Sept. 1, 1994). However, periodic industry downturns, static wages, and poor working conditions, as well as legislation to exclude farm workers from coverage under a state health-care reform act, helped labor organizers make their case for union representation during the past decade (Buzzard, 1992, pp. 143–144; *People's Weekly World*, May 22, 1993).

In 1994 Cesar Chavez died in Arizona while fighting a lawsuit filed more than a decade earlier by lettuce grower Bruce Church. After a meeting of the union's leadership, Cesar's son-in-law Arturo Rodriguez ascended to the presidency without a membership election. Some criticized the selection of a member of the family, arguing that inherited leadership is inappropriate in the modern labor movement (Wells, 1996, p. 96). Most pundits agreed that the death of Chavez and the awkward passing of the mantle to his little-known son-in-law signaled the death knell of the UFW as a labor union. However, critics were proved wrong.

A number of factors helped resuscitate the UFW. Rodriguez tacitly admitted that the UFW had made strategic errors in recent years, especially in its failure to continue organizing farm workers (*San Francisco Chronicle*, May 5, 1994). Rodriguez has promoted a more aggressive strategy, increasing the organizing portion of the UFW's budget of $4.6 million to 41 percent, and signing eleven contracts in the first year of his tenure. UFW membership increased 25 percent between 1994 and 1997, making it the fastest-growing union in the labor federation.[17]

The election of John Sweeney in 1995 to the presidency of the American Federation of Labor–Congress of Industrial Organizations (AFL-CIO) was also helpful. The former head of an immigrant-dominated union, Sweeney pledged to target minority workers for organization, and backed up his promise with a plan to spend a total of $100 million on union organizing in 1996 and 1997 (*Nation*, March 24, 1997). As head of the Latino-dominated and highly symbolic UFW, Arturo Rodriguez was placed on the powerful executive council that coordinates the federation's actions.

Compared to the limited and largely cynical coverage typically accorded unions, the media have shown remarkable goodwill toward the "new" UFW. There have been myriad feature articles and reports touting an imminent return of the union to its former greatness (for one example, see *Time*, Nov. 25, 1996). Partly in response to the overwhelmingly positive coverage, progressives generally, and the Chicano/Mexican American community specifically, continue to assemble in record numbers at marches organized by the UFW, even in out-of-the-way locales. Rallies of 10,000 in Watsonville, California and of 2,000 in Mattewa, Washingon in summer 1997 stimulated even more media coverage and community pride than usual (see *Yakima Herald-Republic*, Aug. 11, 1997).

However, another, less-publicized factor might help explain the resurgence in numbers of farm workers under UFW contract. The Rodriguez-led

UFW is considerably more pragmatic in its negotiations with employers than was the union in decades gone by. In 1995 it signed a contract with Bruce Church after a long-standing law suit was settled out of court. Unfortunately, the reported terms of the new contract indicate that it provided very modest gains. A revised contract with agribusiness giant Sun World (after the company declared bankruptcy due to speculation in leveraged buy-outs and exotic crops) *reduces* wages and other benefits, at least in the first years of the contract, penalizing workers for the mistakes of management (*Rural Migration News*, April 1996, p. 4; Krissman, 1996, p. 112). Such compromise agreements were not a feature of the Chavez years, when growers bitterly complained about the union's lack of flexibility.

Meanwhile, in the Pacific Northwest, the Yakima UFW culminated a seven-year organizing campaign, effectively using a boycott strategy, to sign the state's first farm worker contract with Yakima valley winery Chateau Saint Michelle in fall 1995. Buoyed by this unexpected victory, on February 22, 1996 the UFW announced its intention to work with its old nemesis— the Teamsters—to organize Washington state's billion-dollar apple industry[18] (*Rural Migration News*, April 1996, p. 4). However, a short time later Arturo Rodriguez decided to launch a major campaign to organize California's $600 million strawberry industry, with the AFL-CIO contributing $100,000 per month (*San Francisco Chronicle*, Nov. 24, 1996). The strawberry campaign was the single largest labor action under way in the United States in 1997 (*Nation*, April 14, 1997).

The UFW's Washington project was clearly relegated to a secondary status, with only four organizers working among a harvest labor force of 40,000. The strawberry effort made little concrete progress despite a crew of forty organizers working among 20,000 workers. Press releases have stressed that the UFW is in Watsonville for the long haul. One UFW organizer said, "One worker at a time. [If there are no elections next year,] ... maybe the year after that, or the year after that" (*San Francisco Chronicle*, Nov. 24, 1996). The bulk of the Yakima staff—including the UFW regional director and the apple industry researcher—have been working in Watsonville since December 1996.

Although the strawberry effort is regarded as a good opportunity to gain experience in running a major, industry-wide campaign, apple harvesters have grown restive since the announcement of the campaign in Washington. The skeleton crew at the UFW's regional office was kept busy in 1997 responding to workers who staged five impromptu walkouts and strikes (see, for example, *Yakima Herald-Republic*, Aug. 19 and Sept. 4, 1997). The UFW has been successful in negotiating short-term wage hikes in three cases, although other issues, including the need for collective bargaining, have not been considered by growers. The spontaneous outbursts of orchard workers show that there is plenty of discontent; but without enough resources for careful organizing, the UFW is hamstrung. While the UFW primarily responds to sudden firestorms, the Teamsters have proceeded with the task of organizing workers for a sustained campaign in which increased wages is only one of many issues at stake.

The Teamsters have a longtime presence in the Yakima valley, having signed scores of contracts in the region's food processing facilities in the 1940s.[19] However, many Washington companies have revoked union contracts in decertification drives in recent decades. Regional Teamsters locals still have contracts with a number of major regional food processors, including Del Monte, Simplot, McCain Foods, and Tree Top, Inc. Tree Top is the Pacific Northwest's 2,500-member cooperative apple juice processor, generating about $225 million in 1994 with more than 1,000 workers (*Washington CEO*, May 1995; *Yakima Herald-Republic*, April 12 and Oct. 24, 1992). It was while conducting field work at some of these plants that I discovered the previously unreported presence of FLCs in Yakima's apple industry.

The Teamster locals have permitted the introduction of so-called "temp agency workers" into their closed shops. These temporary employment agencies are registered farm labor contractor firms. One FLC alone provides more than 700 trainees annually to Teamster-covered plants. Under federal labor regulations governing unskilled "trainees," these FLCs can require new hires to work for the first week without pay.[20] These workers also suffer double supervision, by agency as well as company overseers. As a result of these conditions, temp workers have turnover rates three times higher than among direct employees at the same facilities. Therefore, about half the temporary workers do not complete a thirty-day probationary period,[21] depriving the locals of union members. However, the locals have not made an issue about the use of such workers.

Why have the Teamster locals failed to represent these workers? One explanation may be the sociocultural rift between the leadership and these workers. The hierarchy in the locals, and in the now defunct western conference, has long been dominated by white men, most of whom come out of trucking operations, while the processing facilities are now staffed primarily by Spanish-speaking immigrant women. Furthermore, some of these officials may no longer identify themselves as members of the working class.[22] For example, the secretary-treasurer of one of the locals that would like to represent packing house workers again told me that he used to be an apple orchard owner himself. Finally, it may be that officials within the locals or at the old conference level made a deal of some sort with the processing facilities, of the type that the old Teamsters were infamous for.

Under these conditions the early successes of the Teamsters "United for Change" campaign came as a surprise. Packing house suspensions and firings of activist workers have been countered systematically by a series of proworker rulings at the National Labor Relations Board, while compromise rulings have been pursued to the appeals level. Thus far the companies have been forced to rehire most of the workers. The Teamsters also repeatedly have challenged the grower-biased role of the quasigovernmental Washington Apple Commission, picketed and leafleted apple industry promotions and meetings, produced two bilingual newsletters, and even participated in Christmas season *posada* protests in front of local INS offices[23] (and then sent out Christmas cards to supporters depicting this classic example of street theater).

The success of the apple campaign is attributed to international labor organizers, not local Teamster officials. In order to understand the difference between the international and local officials, one must be aware of recent changes in the union movement.[24] Just as the AFL-CIO underwent a major metamorphosis after the recent election of insurgent candidate John Sweeney, the International Brotherhood of Teamsters (the IBT) has undergone a veritable revolution since the election of reformer Ron Carey in 1991. Indeed, the votes that Carey controlled in the federation's single largest union made the later election of Sweeney possible. However, many Teamsters locals remain bastions of old-time corruption, resistant to democratic unionism.

Although the international union is careful to keep the locals informed via periodic meetings, the locals have not contributed to United for Change activities in a meaningful way. There is a potential quagmire in the making under these circumstances. If the international is fortunate enough to obtain packing house contracts, what fate would these workers suffer at the hands of disinterested locals? The IBT is wrestling with this issue across the nation, as it joins other AFL-CIO affiliates in aggressively organizing new, labor-intensive industries with large numbers of women, minority, and immigrant workers (see *Nation*, March 24, 1997).

Creative solutions will be required to protect the interests of a new, diverse membership, while avoiding a complete rupture between the international and the traditional union base. One proposal is to organize the new membership into industry-wide "locals" that span entire regions, while permitting the white-dominated, traditional locals to maintain their current structures. Of course, a great deal of resistance can be expected from the locals to losing the revenues that the new membership would generate to new, region-wide locals.

Aside from these emerging problems, the facts on the ground indicate that even the IBT-led organizing campaign is proceeding much more slowly than might have been expected from the early press releases. In spite of strong declarations of financial support, the IBT only has about a dozen full-time organizers working on the apple campaign. Since the focus of organizing is geographically dispersed between two packing houses (one in the city of Yakima and one in Wenatchee, about two hours away), their forces are stretched quite thin. If the IBT had additional organizers, the campaign could grow rapidly to take advantage of preexisting contacts with workers in a dozen other facilities. Since the apple crop is packed by 125 houses, the IBT fears that the targets of individual strikes will merely result in growers' shifting of their product from the affected houses to those conducting business as usual.

The principal strategy of packing house managers appears to focus on dividing the workforce, particularly by ethnicity and legal status. Anglos represent at least 10 percent of the packing house workforce. Supervisors, often relatives of the Anglo packing house owners, are reported to frequently taunt workers of Mexican origin, saying that non-English speakers are lucky to have any job at all in the United States. Furthermore, activists report that supervisors often threaten to invite agents of the INS to pay a visit, which is not taken lightly by a workforce estimated to be at least 50 percent undocumented. The main Yakima packing house currently targeted for organization, Washington Fruit and Produce Company, recently tried to implement a review of workers' documents, including those of workers that have been employed at the plant for as many as twenty years. The IBT has assisted the workers in protesting this practice, which is regarded as illegal harassment.

In dividing the labor force, the packing house owners have received assistance from the federal government. Raids, arrests, and deportations by immigration officials in Washington have more than doubled in the past two years, while the budget for the state's regional INS has more than tripled. As labor activism increased in fall 1996, the INS conducted at least three raids at packing sheds in Selah (where Tree Top is headquartered and maintains its largest plant). Another INS raid occurred in nearby Sunnyside, at Independent Food Processors—a wholly owned and privately held subsidiary of Washington Fruit and Produce (*Yakima Herald-Republic*, Dec. 18, 1996). Independent Food alone employs about 300 workers, generating about $60 million annually (*Washington CEO*, May 1995). Thus far, no fines have been levied against the owners for employing undocumented workers; only farm workers have suffered for violating the immigration laws by working in the United States. Considering the intrusion of the federal government, a great deal of additional effort will be required to organize a major portion of the state's 10,000 packing house workers.

Summary

Above I have profiled the macro context within which agribusiness, the government, farm labor contractors, farm workers, and labor unions have shaped two of the most important farm labor markets in the United States during the past century. The incessant recruitment of Mexican workers by agribusiness firms has led to the development of dense socioeconomic linkages between rural areas of Mexico and the United States. Formal and informal ethnic intermediaries have been used to keep the labor markets oversupplied, except when the federal government has intervened directly to provide an ample supply of new immigrant workers to farm employers.

Over time many hundreds of thousands of the more than 10 million Mexican farm workers brought to the western United States have been encouraged to resettle with their families in rural towns near where they have obtained jobs with agribusiness firms. However, the substandard conditions maintained in U.S. farm labor markets are insufficient for a domestic workforce to support their families, leading to increased labor activism. Agribusiness has responded to efforts to reform farm labor markets by dividing the labor force by class, ethnicity, and legal status in order to keep wages and working conditions substandard.

The federal government has generally been an active collaborator in recruiting, settling, and constraining the farm labor force. However, political factors have led to contradictions in its pro-grower policies, especially in regard to immigration policy.[25] Activists and unions have tried, with mixed results, to exploit this fault line between agribusiness and government. Meanwhile, unions that purport to represent these workers have often aided and abetted employer strategies due to a lack of effective countermeasures, their own institutional interests, and/or methods of organizing that fail to include a class-based analysis of conditions in farm labor markets. Long-term divisions within the labor force have resulted in a rise in nativism, a resurgence of labor intermediaries, and a decline in union representation. Although unions have belatedly begun to reconsider their traditional approach, the substandard conditions prevailing within the nation's farm labor markets do not yet reflect their increased activities.

II. In the second and third sections of this chapter, I shift to a micro organizational description of how the nation's farm labor markets are kept oversupplied. By documenting the incessant recruitment of new workers from Mexico, we can reframe the immigration debate as a phenomenon driven by the demand for low-cost labor in the United States and can refocus attention on the fault line between agribusiness and the federal government.

The remainder of the chapter describes the stimuli that encourage impoverished peasants in Mexico to make the decision to cross a highly militarized international border and arrive in specific towns in the United States to work at prearranged jobs, thousands of miles from their remote villages. The three case studies in the third section illustrate the techniques by which agribusiness firms continue to recruit new immigrants in spite of the sociocultural barriers between employers and employees, and in defiance of public policies concerning labor and immigration. First, the elaboration of social networks is discussed in the second section, since the development of these

TABLE 9.1   Bases of Informal Social Networks

Blood kinship—*Familia*
Fictive Kinship—*(Compadrazgo) Compadres*
Common locality, ethnicity, or nationality—*(Paisanaje) Paisanos*

networks among migrants is what provides agribusiness labor recruiters an entree into rural Mexican communities where would-be immigrants live.

What are social networks? Networks develop from the ubiquitous informal interactions that arise between new migrants and established immigrants. As Lane Hirabayashi (1993) notes in a study of rural to urban migration within Mexico, newly arrived migrants seek out settled residents with whom they can claim a commonly shared heritage based upon mutually agreeable criteria (see Table 9.1), including kinship by blood or marriage; fictive kinship (*compadrazgo*[26]); or other ties, such as a common locality of origin or an even broader shared identity such as ethnicity or nationality (*paisanaje*[27]). Based upon such ties, immigrants may provide new migrants with vital assistance such as the provision of food, lodging, loans, and employment opportunities. Such networks have been widely noted on every continent, and they occur both among migrants who have few material resources at their disposal and among ethnic entrepreneurs who make use of their social networks to invest resources in enterprises, from small-scale family stores to multimillion-dollar industrial projects.[28]

How are informal networks institutionalized within firms? Larissa Lomnitz (1982) explains how firms can manipulate informal social networks based upon her study of diverse organizations in Mexico. Formal enterprises that use patronage to fill jobs typically institutionalize social networks to obtain their workers. Under a patronage system the employer (or *patron*) can demand unswerving loyalty from subordinates in exchange for jobs. Control over the workforce is highly personalistic and involves two types of patron-client relationships. *Vertical* relations among the levels within the firms' hierarchies signify asymmetrical power linkages and reflect class differences. *Horizontal* relations also develop within and between firms—typically among families of the same class at the higher levels in the hierarchies. Lomnitz found in her study of networks in Mexico that employment positions are filled by patronage in all economic sectors, from day laborers at construction sites to the upper levels of academia and the government.

In the United States, both agribusiness enterprises and farm labor contractor firms (FLCs) use patronage to obtain and supervise their seasonal workforce.[29] Management personnel and their assistants at every level of the organizational hierarchy (see Table 9.2) use both vertical and horizontal relations to ensure an adequate supply of compliant workers.

TABLE 9.2   Hierarchy of U.S. Farm Labor Markets

	1. Agribusiness and/or FLC Owners or Managers—*Patrones*	
	2. Field Supervisors—*Supervisores*	
	3. Crew Foremen—*Mayordomos*	
	4. Crew Assistants—*Ayudantes*	
Transporters:	Tally Counters:	Machine Operators:
Raiteros	*Checadores*	*Maquinistas*
	5. Crew Field Workers—*Campesinos*	

As the following case studies demonstrate, all five levels are comprised of individuals who can serve as recruitment agents (Rosenberg et al., 1992).

The Case Studies

The three cases below provide a representative and interesting comparison of the various ways in which new farm workers are currently recruited from Mexico. Each case is derived from a different crop industry, recruiting its workforce in a different labor-sending region with a different migratory pattern and history of interactions with labor markets in the United States. Each recruitment agent varies by ethnicity, immigration history, placement in the organizational hierarchy of each firm, and level of kin, compadre, and paisano support. Nonetheless, all three have their origins as labor brokers in the strike-breaking strategies of agribusiness; have seen a marked deterioration in the conditions for their workers; admit that they have high levels of employee turnover; and engage in constant replenishment activities in the labor-sending and -receiving regions. Each was documented under a different government program, yet all are in labor markets that provide upward mobility only to farm workers who participate in recruitment activities for agribusiness firms.

The activities engaged in by intermediaries, including those described here, can only be understood within the macro context of the conditions prevailing within the agricultural sector, discussed earlier in this chapter.[30] Agribusiness interests and the federal government have structured farm labor markets in the United States in such a way that they are made up almost entirely of new immigrant workers who have few avenues to achieve upward mobility. Farm labor uses up the average worker within about ten years as a result of the onerous piece-rates and hard labor most crop tasks involve. Indeed, U.S. farm workers have an average life expectancy of less than 60 years—lower than the average for those who remain in underdeveloped Mexico. In an economic sector where most jobs are seasonal and lacking the protection and security of union contracts, one of the very few opportunities for lengthening a farm labor career is to become a recruitment agent. Agents garner more waged income, endure less physical hardship, earn nonwage income through the provision of services to their clients, and rise in social status from the rank of worker to that of labor manager.

Recruitment agents play critical roles in the development of their social networks, even as they rise socioeconomically above their working brethren. Successful agents become important members of their social networks by virtue of their access to coveted resources. Furthermore, as Martha Menchaca (1995) illustrates for a citrus belt community in southern California, intermediaries may be at the forefront of causes that benefit their farm worker clients, such as improved housing, political representation, and even desegregation of neighborhoods and schools. However, in each case, the labor boss and family also benefit from these struggles.

There have been important instances when labor intermediaries in California supported or even led labor actions by their workers against agricultural employers. Chinese farm workers engaged in effective strikes in the 1890s despite their contractor bosses (Chan, 1986). The ethnic solidarity of Japanese contractors with their workers at the turn of the century was renowned (Lloyd, 1953). Mexican crew leaders organized in the San Joaquin valley cotton strike of 1933 (Weber, 1995, chapters 2 and 3). Filipino contractors led the first table grape strike, which forged the United Farm Workers union in 1966 (Scharlin and Villanueva, 1992). And some crew leaders played leading roles in the vegetable strikes in the Salinas valley in the mid-1970s (Wells, 1996). Furthermore, the Farm Labor Organizing Committee also gained crucial support in its fight to organize vegetable pickers from some recruitment agents in the midwest in the late 1970s (Barger and Reza, 1994, p. 100).

Therefore, it is clear that some recruitment agents may respond to the needs of their workers at the cost of good relations with their employers. Further research may reveal how these divergent cases led to contractor alliances with their workers. Undoubtedly, specific historical-structural circumstances, as well as micro level distinctions among movements, leaders, and workers, may cut across class differences. However, the available literature on the agricultural sector and my own fieldwork demonstrate that growers, contractors, unions, and farm workers all recognize that the use of FLCs are a major obstacle to the organization of farm workers.[31] For example, when the workers in the Menchaca study went on strike for job security, improved wages, and a union contract, the intermediary that had fought for their civil rights in the community recruited scab labor for the growers and even served as a spokesman for the Anglos in order to disguise the racial component of the conflict (Menchaca, 1995, p. 136).

Indeed, this contractor readily agrees that the dominance of FLCs in California today makes organizing farm workers all but impossible.[32] Whereas the historical record demonstrates that only the credible threat of union activity improves farm wages and working conditions (Wells, 1996, pp. 86, 94), the thriving intermediary trade usually guarantees the static or deteriorating labor market conditions found in the agricultural sector today. Therefore, the widespread use of FLCs imposes a constraint on the freedom of labor to increase its value through collective bargaining. FLCs are also a principal cause of the perpetuation and deepening of rural poverty throughout the rural United States.[33] The following cases each illustrate a variety of the conditions under which FLC agents serve the interests of agribusiness, even as they provide vital assistance to new farm workers for a price.

Whose Interests Do FLC Agents Serve?

Umberto, a 46-year-old mestizo man, came with his family from Huanusco, Zacatecas[34] in north-central Mexico in the mid-1960s. In 1968, at age 16, he joined his parents and older siblings in the fields in the San Joaquin valley, harvesting a variety of crops (including table grapes). The family became members of the United Farm Workers union (UFW) when their principal employer, a corporate subsidiary with 700 acres of vineyards, signed a collective bargaining agreement in 1970. The new contract raised wages by more than 30 percent and provided unprecedented benefits.

Umberto became a company crew foreman in 1975, and a field supervisor in 1976. Although the company refused to renew the union contract in 1973, the UFW persisted in attempting to renegotiate an agreement. Therefore, the corporate manager of the vineyard approached Umberto with a proposition—to start an FLC to provide the company with its harvest labor.[35] As Umberto recalls, it was an offer he could not refuse. The manager helped Umberto obtain a loan to cover initial business expenses and arranged for an accountant to provide payroll and other business services.

Along with the assistance of the corporation, Umberto had his large family as an asset. The family's collective work experience enabled Umberto to fill the supervisory positions for four crews. Each crew was headed by a sibling or an in-law, and was supported in other key positions by their spouses, parents, or other close relatives. The FLC's new workers were initially recruited from among the corporation's preexisting labor force. All benefits not mandated by the government were eliminated, permitting the corporation to obtain total labor savings of more than 10 percent.[36]

The elimination of the union threat was followed by a slow but marked decline in wages.[37] Umberto told me that increased FLC competition for contracts had forced wages down. While he claimed that working conditions in his firm were better than those prevailing among his competitors, Umberto admitted that the firm suffered turnover rates of more than 60 percent annually. He replenished his workforce by ongoing recruitment activities among the paisanos from his native town in Zacatecas. Umberto's entire management hierarchy is from Huanusco, permitting easy and ubiquitous access to the community's social network. His efforts are facilitated by the fact that Zacatecan migration to the San Joaquin has become well entrenched.

With the growth of Umberto's firm, and the periodic fissioning off of management,[38] FLCs controlled by immigrants from Huanusco soon provided at least 5,000 seasonal jobs in the valley. In fact, more paisanos are resettled in the San Joaquin than continue to reside in Huanusco, which is now experiencing negative population growth.[39]

Although the large immigrant population in the San Joaquin attracts many first-time migrants from Huanusco, I documented efforts by Umberto's FLC agents to increase their influence in the labor-sending community itself during my Mexico-based fieldwork. Umberto has been able to strengthen his position in the community largely by building horizontal ties within his large kindred and by engaging in hometown philanthropy of benefit to the community as a whole.

For example, Umberto is a founding member of a social club that was established in the San Joaquin. The social club engages in a number of small projects in Huanusco, including providing a $20 monthly stipend to about a dozen destitute individuals. Umberto is also among the expatriate elite whose names are emblazoned on plaques commemorating donors to the community's revitalization fund. Although Umberto has not returned to Huanusco in more than a decade, his parents sponsor both a public Christmas party (a *posada*) and a portion of the sacred rite of the dressing of the infant Jesus there; both are "honors" bestowed by the priest in return for a high level of financial support to the parish.

While Umberto focuses upon horizontal relations and philanthropy, his large family, mainly FLC management agents, is working to strengthen vertical relations. Many serve as godparents (*compadres*), providing financial sponsorship for the material expenses that families incur in baptisms, *quinciañeras*, and marriages. Furthermore, a general store owned by Umberto's in-laws permits would-be migrants to apply for FLC jobs as well as obtain cash loans needed to make the journey north for the summer grape harvest. The store's loans, provided at an interest rate of 30 percent *monthly*, ensure that migration is within the reach of virtually any able-bodied adult in Huanusco, while serving as a principal recruiting tool for Umberto's FLC.

During the 1990 summer harvest I canvassed two of Umberto's work crews in the vineyards. In each crew I found a "family," with each foreman a *paterfamilias*, while the foremen, in turn, were closely related to Umberto. *Paisanos* from Zacatecas filled every position on both crews (each had forty-odd members). When I questioned the dominance of the Zacatecans, Umberto replied that "his people" trained *paisano* newcomers at no cost to him, caused no trouble, and had a special talent for harvesting table grapes. Each vine row had a core picker/packer team (*equipo*), almost all of whom were young people between the ages of about 18 and 30. Most of the teams were composed of close kin—a husband and wife, siblings, or first cousins (*primo hermanos*). In addition, in many rows elderly and preteen relatives augmented the labor of the core team.

Verbal indicators of both vertical and horizontal relations within the FLC were habitually displayed among the different levels of the hierarchy (see Table 9.2). When Umberto came by to check on harvest progress, he was generally greeted as *don* (sir) or *patron* by crew workers, whereas crew foremen hailed Umberto more familiarly as *hermano* (brother), *tio* (uncle), *compadre*, or *paisano*. In a similar fashion, foremen were referred to by familial terms, or as *compadres*, by their crew workers. Within each level of the hierarchy, generally comprised of close kin related directly through blood or marriage relations, horizontal relations were more pronounced. Evidence of horizontal relations included the provision of low- or no-interest loans, mutual aid, and cooperative exchanges of labor and other resources throughout the year.

Upward Mobility on the Farm Job Ladder

Refugio, a 45-year-old indigenous Mixtec man, is a longtime harvester in the San Joaquin valley's citrus industry and an FLC agent who has moved up the farm job ladder (from field harvester, to transporter and machine operator, to foreman; see Table 9.2).

Raised in a remote hamlet near Tecomaxtlahuaca (known by its diminutive, Teco) in the southern Mexican state of Oaxaca, Refugio worked from age 7 to provide for himself (as well as to help support his single mother and her two other children). He began earning his living by shepherding goats for a childless village couple; but at age 12 he joined the hundreds of thousands migrating from the Mixteca,[40] leaving Teco to labor first in a Mexico City tortilla-producing plant for four years before seeking work in the American-controlled agribusiness sector, first on a north Mexico tomato plantation,[41] and then in California.

In 1981, at age 29, Refugio settled in the San Joaquin valley with his common-law wife, two of her brothers, and a family of *paisanos*. They found employment through another *paisano* on a citrus harvest crew. The firm, one division of a national conglomerate, controls about fifteen thousand acres of navel oranges in the region. However, the firm divested itself of both its field labor and trucking operations as a result of labor organizing activities in 1983.[42] The company encouraged key supervisory personnel within these two divisions to become independent entrepreneurs, providing harvest labor and transport services under contract to the firm.

Refugio was recruited into a new harvesting FLC through his foreman. The FLC offered the same piece-rate but annulled all previously negotiated (non–government mandated) benefits. The piece-rate has remained static in the intervening eleven years,[43] thereby declining by more than 20 percent vis-à-vis the ongoing rise in the cost of living.

Worker complaints about the loss of hard-won benefits were met with selective discharge. These punitive firings, along with the high employee turnover rate that is common to FLCs, has led to a recurrent need to replenish the crews. Refugio has obliged his foreman by recruiting *paisanos* from Teco. By assisting the foreman, Refugio benefited in three ways: First, he enhanced his status within the Oaxacan expatriate community; second, he was awarded a *raitero* franchise (transporting 7 to 10 workers to and from the fields in his van each day, at $3 per person—increasing his daily earnings by an average of 60 percent); and, third, he was eventually promoted to the less arduous field task of forklift operator. The foreman further secured Refugio's role as a recruiter upon this last promotion by requiring that henceforth they would cooperate equally in maintaining the crew's size.

Refugio has reinforced preexisting ties within Teco, improving access to his native social network. He has provided a "safe house" to scores of migrant *paisanos* passing through in search of seasonal work along the far-flung Pacific coast migrant circuit.[44] Furthermore, he has remained a member in good standing in his home community. In 1987 Refugio received U.S. residency documents, legalizing his status as a U.S. worker, and began making periodic return visits to Oaxaca.

In Teco he purchased a house lot, officially married his wife, and distributed gifts brought from California. Refugio also greatly expanded his compadrazgo relations, participating in many of the celebrations that visiting migrants indulge in during visits home. With his new van, well-fed and -dressed family, and fat billfold, Refugio serves as yet another local example of the benefits of international migration, relative to the endemic poverty of the Mixteca. Refugio also passes on information about living and working conditions in California to villagers who may be considering a trip to the United States, as well as loans to migrants who cannot afford to finance their own migration.

On trips back up to the U.S. border, Refugio often ferries new migrants in his van. He has developed contacts with labor smugglers (*coyotes*) who help the undocumented Oaxacans across the border and reunite them with Refugio in San Diego. In addition, he has aided many others by making periodic trips south from his California home to the border in response to collect phone calls from new migrants who needed a ride north.

The new migrants are required to stay with Refugio in his California household until their transportation, housing, and meal expenses have been paid off through payroll deductions at 20–30 percent interest per month. Between 1988 and 1992, the size of Refugio's household during the winter/spring harvest season has averaged about twenty-two adults and five children, lodged in various rooms within the main house, as well as in several improvised shelters erected on the house lot.

In 1991 Refugio was elevated to foreman status by his *patron*, who began his own FLC. He often asserts that he is working harder and longer as a foreman than he ever has before. Refugio stresses the difficult responsibility a foreman has to satisfy the grower and the FLC owner on the one hand, and the crew members on the other. He says that the crew members exert considerable influence on him to provide reasonable wages and decent working conditions. After all, Refugio notes, these are his *paisanos*, even family, not mere strangers.

Perhaps in part due to this tension, Refugio is often critical of the FLC owner, remarking that the *patron* brings in "easy money." When I asked Refugio what he meant, he retorted with a litany of the material possessions that the FLC owner has accumulated, including a restaurant (and two catering trucks that sell the restaurant's food to farm workers in the orchards), several houses, and ostentatiously equipped four-wheel-drive vehicles that the owner and other family members use to supervise the six harvest crews. However, Refugio also displays new wealth as a result of becoming an FLC agent—in 1990 he purchased a ramshackle four-bedroom home on a one-acre parcel, where the constant flow of *paisanos* passing through can be more easily accommodated. He also has purchased a large enclosed van that permits him to carry fifteen crew members to the field each day (at the fee of $3 per head).

Ethnic Solidarity or Exploitation?

"Lorenzo," a 44-year-old mestizo Mexican immigrant, is an orchard manager who oversees two crews for an intermediate-sized apple grower in the Yakima valley, Washington state. Reared in the rural municipality of Pajacuaran, Michoacan[45] in central Mexico, he first migrated to the United States at age 17 in 1970. He went to Salinas, California, where he joined his father in harvesting lettuce and other vegetables for ten months annually.

In 1975 the agribusiness firm was organized by the UFW, raising wages more than 40 percent and instituting benefits including a seniority system that helped guarantee jobs for older farm workers such as Lorenzo's father in spite of their lower productivity. However, in 1980 the firm decertified the union and abandoned the seniority system. The following year Lorenzo's father retired to Pajacuaran and Lorenzo's household migrated north to the Yakima valley.

Lorenzo's youngest brother worked for an apple grower in Washington. The grower had free housing in the orchards for his workers. Although the housing consisted of one-room cabins, it was an improvement: Lorenzo had been spending more than half his earnings in Salinas on rent alone. Furthermore, the grower had contacts at the Immigration and Naturalization Service who advised his workers on how to regularize their status. Finally, the workplace had no management-labor conflict. With these benefits, Lorenzo says that he attracted five other disgruntled Salinas workers to move north as well.

The grower is a farm equipment retailer who has purchased about 250 acres of apple orchards bit by bit, primarily from clients who either retired or went bankrupt. Lorenzo claims that the owner's interest in the orchards is limited to obtaining tax breaks that reduce his total liabilities. Lorenzo says that he rose to the position of field supervisor in four years, becoming "both a general and private." The owner provided Lorenzo with a larger cottage, a company truck, and a simple mandate: Keep production costs low.

Lorenzo's promotion occurred at a time when the U.S. government was awarding residency papers to millions of undocumented immigrants and new farm workers in 1986. The *patron*, fearful that implementation of the new immigration laws might lead to labor shortages, financed Lorenzo's return visit home to recruit new workers in Michoacan. Lorenzo helped at least thirty *paisanos* qualify for the program by providing them with papers certifying that they had worked at least ninety days picking apples, although he admitted to me that few had ever been as far north as Yakima, while some had never been to the United States at all. Several *paisanos* that I interviewed in Pajacuaran claimed that Lorenzo actually sold the certification papers for up to $500 each. If this was true, Lorenzo and/or his *patron* may have earned ten thousand dollars or more.

The paisanos came to Yakima in 1987 as instructed, only to find the apple harvest delayed due to unseasonal weather. Without adequate funds to support themselves, they needed loans to purchase necessities. Lorenzo says that the grower refused to advance wages due to uncertainty about the harvest. Stung by their reception, the *paisanos* began agitating for compensation for their long wait. The *patron* became edgy about the situation, making Lorenzo worried about retaining his own post. Lorenzo decided not to hire eighteen of the *paisanos* even when the harvest finally did begin. Although he claims that many owed him money for cash advances, Lorenzo says that he could not rely upon these workers.

Therefore, Lorenzo had one of his machine operators, an indigenous worker from the Purepeche plateau of central Michoacan, solicit workers from his hometown. The indigenous workers were willing to bunk up six to a cabin until Lorenzo's mestizo *paisanos* moved on in search of work elsewhere. Lorenzo still employs ten workers from Pajacuaran, but seven are close kin. Instead, Lorenzo now delegates responsibility for obtaining tractable workers to his foremen, insulating himself from direct pressures by either the *patron* or the workforce.

Lorenzo admits that the current situation for his apple workers is poor. Wages have been stagnant for more than a decade, the cabins have deteriorated due to age and high occupancy, work crews have been expanded, and total hours of work have declined.[46] He says that even he is not paid very well—his annual salary of $18,000 breaks down to about $7 an hour. Although his family lives in an orchard cottage and he has a ranch pick-up truck at his disposal, Lorenzo says that his own standard of living has declined since he moved to Washington. His wife doesn't like the rural isolation of their home, far from neighbors, stores, and other conveniences. However, the isolation of the orchards has economic advantages. Workers must rely on Lorenzo or a foreman to ferry them to town to cash their checks and pick up basic supplies. The convenience store owner, who charges each worker 5 percent to cash a check, gives Lorenzo a six-pack of beer for each check cashed by a crew worker. Lorenzo puts the beer on ice and sells it to crew workers in the orchards for a dollar a pop.

Summary

Let us briefly analyze the three cases presented above. First, the case studies support the explanatory power of two theoretical frameworks: the historical-structural approach and the articulation of modes of production.[47] The narratives reveal the dynamic roles played by the government, agribusiness, farm workers and their unions, and intermediaries. The studies also document the strong and ever expanding linkages between rural Mexico and farm labor markets in the United States. The intermediary in each case recruits most of his workers from a different labor-sending state in Mexico, revealing the ability to increase the heterogeneity of a labor force almost exclusively from a nation often thought of as homogeneous. Although all of these workers are Mexican citizens, they vary by region of origin and by ethnicity, and include native speakers of three distinct languages. This variability serves agribusiness interests that are seeking to divide the work force.

Intermediaries are able to stimulate ongoing out-migration across broader regions of rural Mexico due to the ever present and increasing under- and unemployment endemic to communities largely engaged in subsistence agricultural production. This vast labor reserve is an unorganized and low-cost workforce indebted—literally—to the recruitment agents who provide workers the opportunity to earn U.S. wages. Furthermore, the reproduction of the U.S. farm labor force is accomplished in rural Mexico—more than 90 percent of contemporary farm workers in California and Washington state were born and raised in Mexico, not in the United States.

Although the historical-structural approach and articulation theory provide the macrocontext, the case studies underscore the role of microorganizational processes—that is, the institutionalization of social networks—in recruitment and supervision practices. Recruitment agents expend a great deal of effort to build up and "bank" what Lane Hirabayashi (1993) calls "cultural capital." These efforts are fully documented using an ethnographic approach.

In case study #1, the mestizo owner of a moderate-sized FLC firm is generally above the face-to-face provisioning of "services for indenture." Instead, Umberto cultivates horizontal relations among the upper tiers of agents in his firm, while engaging in philanthropy in both California and Mexico to maintain his status as a *paisano* within the community. In turn, a score of his management agents elaborate vertical relations with members of the workforce that facilitate the continued recruitment of new migrant workers for the FLC.

The vertical relations between recruitment agents and new workers are underscored in the second and third case studies. Refugio is a new foreman from the Mixteca, Oaxaca, a region in southern Mexico inhabited primarily by indigenous peoples. He must engage in constant recruitment to fill his work crew in the face of high turnover rates. Periodic trips home, labor smuggling activities, and the provision of loans and services are all necessary to secure sufficient low-cost labor. Since most Mixtec adults must periodically migrate from their villages in order to earn sufficient wages to support their families, this region serves as a large reserve of surplus workers available to agribusiness recruiters. However, because the pay is so poor and the working and living conditions so harsh in the FLC for which Refugio is a foreman, new migrants must be constantly recruited to replace those that abandon the FLC after paying their debts. Although sociocultural ties diffuse overt labor conflict, "cultural capital" is rapidly expended under such substandard conditions.

Lorenzo is a mestizo immigrant from western Michoacan, Mexico who is now an informal intermediary in the Pacific Northwest. Although he works directly for his Anglo *patron* as orchard manager, Lorenzo is responsible for recruiting and supervising the apple harvest crews. He can offer grower-provided housing but cannot charge rent. He also does not control the writing up and paying out of payroll checks, limiting his ability to tap workers' wages directly. Nevertheless, Lorenzo has found ways to pad his salary by providing services required by a vulnerable workforce. Furthermore, he has passed on most recruitment responsibilities to his foremen, labor agents who can tap their own social networks in the indigenous Purepeche plateau region of central Michoacan, insulating Lorenzo from direct ties to, or complete responsibility for, the workforce. Lorenzo finds these indigenous workers more accommodating than his own mestizo paisanos, while the orchard owner can be deflected from criticizing Lorenzo for any actions these workers might undertake, instead blaming the foremen who recruited them.

In sum, the efforts of agribusiness to thwart government policy aimed at reducing undocumented immigration and the attempts of farm workers to organize in order to bargain collectively for improvements in working conditions, combined with the entrepreneurial ambitions of some farm workers, have led to the resurrection and rapid growth of formal FLCs in California. Growers in Washington have managed thus far to stave off farm labor reforms through the use of informal intermediaries. However, a system of patronage based on the incessant recruitment of new immigrants is entrenched in the social relations of production in both regions.

Conclusions

The recruitment of new workers undergirds agribusiness strategies to divide the farm labor force. Divisions by class can be observed in the ubiquitous manipulation of horizontal and vertical relations between Mexicans with differential access to key resources, including cash and contacts. Both FLCs and supervisory personnel have the ability to tap resources desperately sought by would-be immigrants. Class contradictions extend beyond the intermediary system, however; the union historically preferred by growers, the Teamsters, has also been internally divided along class lines, with much of the union leadership split from its membership.

The continuous recruitment of new immigrant workers promotes ever more divisions based upon ethnicity within the workforce. Although more than 90 percent of the farm labor force was born and raised in Mexico, these workers have become clearly divided along ethnic lines (between the traditional sources of mestizo workers from north-central Mexico and the new major source of indigenous workers from southern Mexico). These workers are divided by a historical legacy that includes racism in Mexico, which has been exacerbated during the entire postconquest period, as well as by physical characteristics and distinct languages.

Finally, differences in legal status have long divided the labor force, as one immigrant flow follows another, and as the government and agribusiness employers differentially bequeath rights and/or impediments upon each historical flow. The variations are distinct—U.S. citizens, legal immigrant residents, legal international migrants, short-term foreign contract workers, and undocumented workers—differentiating the labor force both on and off the job, within the United States and at the international border. These distinctions were created and structured by the government, but employers have habitually lobbied for their perpetuation and have refused to defer to government unless its policy coincides with the agricultural sector's interests. Complicating the problem for the farm labor force, unions have typically played into this agribusiness strategy to divide the workforce by targeting only a portion of the labor force as a constituency and even collaborating with government in the enforcement of these distinctions. The "new" union movement is still attempting to recover from these mistakes: The UFW is still regarded warily by many undocumented workers, and the Teamsters are still seen as racist by many non–U.S. citizens. This is a crippling legacy for farm worker unions because an ever larger majority of farm workers are undocumented and more than 90 percent are not U.S. citizens.

While exploitation by intermediaries is pervasive across U.S. farm labor markets, it is exacerbated within formal FLCs, since contractor operations handle the workers' payrolls and are less prone to government regulation than the more highly visible agribusiness firms. And, as described above, FLCs can manipulate sociocultural mores directly to diffuse class conflict. Therefore, as bad as conditions currently are for Washington state's farm labor force, they may deteriorate further if the state's apple industry shifts to the Californian model.

My current research in Yakima suggests that the key factors leading to the resurrection of the FLC system in California—government and union intervention to reform the farm labor market—are now increasingly present in the Pacific Northwest's apple industry. Both the government and labor unions have recently stepped up regulatory and reform activities in Washington state, much as they did in California in the 1970s. Furthermore, a number of processing facilities have begun to use large numbers of workers recruited through temporary employment agencies, and an increase there in vertical integration means that an ever greater proportion of field and postharvest workers are controlled by the same employers. To avoid the costly mistakes and wretched outcomes of California's experience, alternative policies must be implemented in Washington.

Public policy must accomplish the following five tasks. First, conditions for the current workforce must be improved in order to stabilize regional farm labor markets. Second, the government must actively support the right of farm workers to organize and collectively bargain with their wealthy and powerful employers. Third, government agencies must target the "demand side" of the immigration equation by funding adequate regulatory activities and by penalizing the ultimate employers (and benefactors) of undocumented workers—the agribusiness firms that attempt to evade a variety of laws by using informal supervisory personnel or formal FLCs. Fourth, if immigrant workers are deemed necessary for agribusiness industries, all of these needed workers must be guaranteed the same human and labor rights enjoyed by all other workers in the United States. Fifth, given the current trend of global economic integration, policy on immigration must address the deteriorating conditions in rural Mexican labor-sending communities. Each of these recommendations must be implemented in order to counter the patronage system that has institutionalized social networks linking rural Mexico to the United States.

NOTES

1. See Barrera (1979), Acuña (1981), Gamboa (1990), Galarza (1964), Massey et al. (1987), and Krissman (1997a).

2. For a discussion of the early development of "industrial" agriculture, see Gold-schmidt (1978 [1947]). See Krissman (1996, chapters 2 and 3) for a description of corporate agribusiness in California's table grape and citrus industries. And see Schotzko, R. T. (1994), *Good Fruit Grower* (August 1996 and January 1997), and *New York Times* (Oct. 28, 1996) concerning recent trends toward concentration and vertical integration in Washington state's tree fruit industries.

3. Fresno, Kern, and Tulare counties are all located in the southern portion of the San Joaquin valley.

4. For California's citrus industry, see Gonzalez (1994) and Menchaca (1995, chapters 2 and 3); for Texan cotton, see Taylor (1934) and Leeper Buss (1993).

5. This labor model had already been established in California, beginning with the Chinese intermediaries who provided immigrant gangs for the construction of the railroad and development of farms by the 1870s (Chan, 1986). The Japanese influx during the 1890s followed this model, but the Japanese intermediaries pressured growers for improvements in wage rates and working conditions (Cheng and Bonacich, 1984; Fisher, 1953). It was partly in reaction to the activism of the Japanese that growers shifted to the use of Mexican workers. The government played important roles in the recruitment, importation, regulation, and segmentation of these workers (Krissman, 1997a).

6. Although the U.S. census includes Mexicans among the white population, the federal and state governments long categorized most Mexicans as Indians in order to deny them many basic rights, including citizenship, education, and property ownership (Menchaca, 1993).

7. Furthermore, the State conspired to keep Tejanos in U.S. farm labor markets, developing strategies to force Mexican-origin children out of the school system by age twelve (Taylor, 1934, pp. 194–197).

8. For examples, see Fineberg (1971) on the strike-breaking former braceros; Taylor (1975, pp. 29 and 30) on the dissident migrant families; and Scharlin and Villanueva (1992) on divisions between the Mexican majority and Filipino minority concerning the UFW.

9. For distinct instances of the use of the INS by the UFW, see Taylor (1975, pp. 218, 287, 288); Garcia (1994, pp. 249 and 250); Mooney and Majka (1995, pp. 180 and 181); and Wells (1996, pp. 89 and 90).

10. Cesar Chavez (1992) consistently raised the issue of grower racism, without ever discussing the class bases for the strife between growers and farm workers.

11. *Mestizaje* has racial, ethnic, linguistic, and cultural connotations, all favoring the dominant national image in Mexico; mestizo traits are generally defined negatively, as in opposition to a cluster of indigenous traits that are best exemplified by the diverse pre-Columbian native traditions; see Nagengast and Kearney (1990, pp. 61–92) and Wolf (1959, chapter 11). Of course, 500 years of colonial and neocolonial oppression have made any attempt to distinguish between indigenous traditions and European-imposed patterns of behavior problematic.

12. Eight farm workers I interviewed in Yakima mentioned unsolicited visits by friendly INS officials to their homes resulting in the provision of documents during the late 1970s. Many others mentioned that their initial migration and/or settlement in Washington was due to the low profile of the INS in Washington (interviews conducted between September 1995 and January 1996).

13. These are the Latino-majority towns of Farmersville, Huron, McFarland, Mendota, Orange Cove, Parlier, and San Joaquin (U.S. Census, 1990). Only two of the ten poorest cities in California are in urban areas, in spite of a public policy focus on inner-city ghettos and barrios.

14. The Latino-majority towns of Grandview, Sunnyside, Toppenish, Granger, and Wapato (U.S. Census, 1990).

15. Four representative examples (*Yakima Herald-Republic*, March 5, 1995) include: "I am not at all happy with the Mexico [newspaper] project. . . . I have enough of Mexicans in the everyday world." "I picked up my . . . paper today and thought I was in Mexico. . . . I have never found one Mexican in the war when we imported them people up here to work for us and do you find them here now [sic]. I do not approve of this one bit." "I think we see enough of the Mexican culture all around and what it's doing to our country today without opening the [paper] and reading about it too. That's really too disgusting." "I'm sick of the [paper] shoving this Mexican s– down our throats."

16. Congressional aide Todd (Oct. 2, 1995); "Doc" Hastings on *National Public Radio* (Sept. 20, 1996) promised a guest worker program if the 1996 immigration reform legislation hampered access to migrant labor. I have argued elsewhere that efforts to create new, improved, bracero-style programs will only exacerbate most of the negative consequences noted above for the nation's farm labor markets by increasing labor market heterogeneity (Krissman, 1997a, p. 22).

17. See *Los Angeles Times* (April 24, 1993 and July 18, 1994), *Labor Management Decisions* (1994), California Institute of Rural Studies (1994), and *Time* (Nov. 25, 1996).

18. See Krissman (1997b) for a comparative historical analysis of both unions and the effects of their presence in the farm labor markets of California and Washington.

19. Based on interviews with the Yakima Teamsters local secretary-treasurer.

20. Interview with one of the temp agency's managers.

21. Interview with a processing facility personnel manager.

22. Ronald Taylor (1975, pp. 182 and 183; emphasis in original) describes the traditional union leaders: "[T]he [union] leaders . . . —with their posh offices, six-figure salaries, and fat expense accounts . . . —are from *organized* labor, where the emphasis is on structure and formalized conduct. They meet management on an equal footing; they play golf at the same clubs, dine at the same expensive restaurants, send their children to the same schools. Management and labor are 'friendly adversaries' . . . who understand the use of power and politics."

23. See, for example, *Seattle Times* (Jan. 8 and Feb. 5, 1997), *Wenatchee World* (Sept. 12, Nov. 7, and Dec. 12, 1996), *Yakima Herald-Republic* (Jan. 7, 1997), *Apple Warehouse News* (Wenatchee, Washington), *am Apples* (Yakima, Washington), and "Who's Crunching Whom (in the apple industry)" Teamster leaflets. *Posadas* are important religious processions among rural Mexicans that reenact the travails of Joseph and Mary in Bethlehem, as strangers looking for a place to stay before Mary gave birth.

24. See Krissman (1997b) for an in-depth discussion of the international Teamsters reform movement, as well as the perpetuation of corruption at the level of the union locals.

25. See Majka and Majka (1982) for a discussion of how policy contradictions can arise within and between agencies of the government.

26. See Hirabayashi (1993, chapter 2) for a thorough description of *paisanaje* (he calls it *paisanazgo*). See Massey et al. (1987, pp. 142–145), who use *paisanaje* with the same intent in a study of international migration. Indeed, Mexicans share with Italians a referential tie to their *paisanos*, leading even the Mexican government to usurp its strong sentiments for a showcase migrant protection program called "Paisano" (Krissman, 1996, pp. 273 and 274).

27. See, for example, Bonacich (1973) concerning small-scale family enterprises, and the *Los Angeles Times* (April 6, 1994) for the case of expatriate investments in mainland Chinese factories.

28. Wells (1996, pp. 199, 200, and 206–210) differentiates the use of patronage based upon the ethnicity of the employer. I argue that patronage persists even in agribusiness firms owned by Anglos or Japanese Americans, although its existence may not be obvious at the level of the owner. Rather, non-*paisano* owners of firms depend upon patronage among their supervisory personnel in order to gain access to social networks for recruitment; see Wells (1996, pp. 201 and 202) concerning patronage within a large Anglo-owned firm.

29. Ethnic enterprises arise due to the larger structural conditions prevailing in those sectors in which they are found (Guarnizo, 1992).

30. See, for example, Fisher (1953), Lloyd et al. (1988), and Krissman (1995).

31. Interview with Ralph A. Lopez (March 18, 1997).

32. Others have gone further, condemning FLC firms on a variety of grounds. For example, Cesar Chavez stated in testimony before the U.S. Senate select subcommittee on agriculture: "One must first understand that a farm labor contractor does not contract work in the full sense of the word. . . . He buys and sells human beings. His profit is based on the sweat and toil of the workers. . . . All the farm labor contractor does is promise hourly workers at the lowest rate he can find men to work at. . . . What is happening in Delano on this strike, the farm labor contractor becomes the professional strikebreaker" (from Taylor, 1975, p. 164; the editing is Taylor's).

33. Zacatecas is one of four Mexican states that have sent many tens of thousands of wage laborers to the United States since before 1900; see Cardoso (1980). In the 1990s, an estimated half million Zacatecans resided in California; see INEGI (1991) and *La Paloma* (Jan. 3, 1992). Currently, remittances from the United States provide about 80 percent of total revenues in southern Zacatecas, the most impoverished portion of the state; see INEGI (1991), CNC (1987) and Mines (1981). As a whole, formal remittances to Zacatecas (more than U.S.$104 million annually) top the total federal (Mexican) investment of U.S.$84 million in the state; Lozano Ascencio (1993, p. 67). Formal remittances include telegraph and bank transfers only; informal remittances include cash sent in the mail, with friends, or carried by the migrant upon return to Mexico.

34. The correlation between the activities of the UFW and the decision to subcontract the bulk of labor-intensive jobs out to FLCs was made by both the vineyard manager and Umberto himself.

35. Data obtained in interviews with the corporate manager and FLC owner in 1992.

36. Wages had risen by about 20 percent as a result of the union contract; Jenkins (1985) and Majka and Majka (1982). In the decade since the union was decertified, wages remained fixed for six years (dropping in relative terms due to inflation) and

then dropped absolutely during the past several years from the $5.25 per hour union benchmark of 1978 to as little as $4.85 by 1990 (Krissman, 1996, p. 90).

37. Within five years, several of his siblings started their own FLCs, replicating employment opportunities more than fivefold. The tendency for FLCs to fission—foremen and other FLC agents commonly strike out on their own—is well documented; Rosenberg et al. (1992, pp. 20–23) and Fisher (1953, p. 47). Fissioning is a fundamental feature of patronage relationships; Alvarez and Collier (1994, pp. 606–627) and Lomnitz (1982, pp. 51–74).

38. Huanusco lost 11 percent of its population between 1980 and 1990 (Krissman, 1996, p. 262)—a rarity in rural Mexico, where the birthrates have remained stubbornly high.

39. The Mixteca, mainly within western Oaxaca, is considered one of the most impoverished regions in Mexico. More than 80 percent of total regional revenues are generated by the remittances of out-migrants; Fernandez Ortiz (1989). A large proportion of its inhabitants have either emigrated or have been migrating seasonally since at least the 1800s; Kearney (1986). Although Oaxacans only began to migrate to the United States in significant numbers in the 1970s, Oaxaca is now among Mexico's top ten labor-sending states, generating at least $55 million in formal remittances in 1990; Cornelius (1993) and Lozano Ascencio (1993).

40. There is a strong relationship between tens of thousands of the new post-IRCA undocumented immigrants and the burgeoning north Mexico tomato industry (Krissman, 1994).

41. A causal relationship between the company's divestment of these labor-intensive operations and increased labor organizing efforts was drawn in interviews with several representatives of the firm's management. The relationship is reflected in the regional history of labor organizing and the use of FLCs to break strikes during the 1982–1983 citrus harvest season (*Valley Voice*, April 1983).

42. The average piece rate paid per 1,000-pound bin is $9; each bin holds about fifteen seventy-pound pick bags; the average worker can fill three to four bins per day in the average orchard, for an average gross pay of $27–36, hovering near the minimum wage baseline (Krissman, 1996).

43. There are alternative Mixtec migratory circuits to the U.S. west and east coasts (Krissman, 1994).

44. Michoacan is one of ten Mexican states that have sent many tens of thousands of wage laborers to the United States since 1940 (Arbingast et al., 1975, p. 32). In the 1990s it was believed to be the number one labor-sending state in Mexico, with 2 million residing for at least part of each year in the United States (*El Financiero*, Oct. 19, 1994, p. 36). The state government estimates that half a million Michoacanos who reside in the United States return during the Christmas season each year (*El Sol de Morelia*, Dec. 7, 1995, p. 6A). As a whole, formal remittances to Michoacan (almost U.S.$310 million annually) are higher than those to any other Mexican state, and are almost equal to the total federal (Mexican) investment of U.S.$361 million in the state (Lozano Ascencio, 1993, p. 67).

45. The average piece rate paid per 1,000-pound bin varies by variety. However, the vast majority of acreage is planted to red and gold delicious apples, which pay between about $9 and $11 respectively. The average worker can fill three to four bins

per day in the average orchard, for an average gross pay of $30–44—slightly above the minimum wage baseline at $6 per hour (Kissam et al., 1993, p. 251).

46. See, for example, Meillassoux (1981), Wolpe (1980), and Palerm (1976).

47. No Note Text.

REFERENCES

Acuña, R. (1981). *Occupied America: A History of Chicanos.* New York: Harper and Row.

Agricultural Commissioner [Fresno, Kern, and Tulare Counties] (AC). (1990–1995). *Agricultural Crop and Livestock Report: Sacramento and the Counties.*

Alvarez, R. R., and Collier, G. A. (1994). "The Long Haul in Mexican Trucking: Traversing the Borderlands of the North and the South." *American Ethnologist* 21, no. 3 (August).

Arbingast, S. A., et al. (1975). *Atlas of Mexico.* Austin: University of Texas Press.

Barger, W. K., and Reza, E. M. (1994). *The Farm Labor Movement in the Midwest: Social Change and Adaptation Among Migrant Farm Workers.* Austin: University of Texas Press.

Barrera, M. (1979). *Race and Class in the U.S. Southwest.* Notre Dame: University of Notre Dame Press.

Bean, F. D., Vernez, G., and Keely, C. B. (1989). *Opening and Closing the Doors: Evaluating Immigration Reform and Control.* Santa Monica, CA: RAND.

Bonacich, E. (1973). "A Theory of Middlemen Minorities." *American Sociological Review* 38, pp. 583–594.

Buzzard, S. (1992). "Case Study 3: The Apple Industry in Yakima County, Washington." In Heppel, M. L., and Amendola, S. L., eds., *Immigration Reform and Perishable Crop Agriculture.* New York: University Press of America.

California Institute of Rural Studies (CIRS) newsletter. (Fall 1994). "Elections Signal Revived UFW." P. 2.

_____. (Winter 1995). "UFW Scores Another Election Victory." 5.

Campesinos de Americas Unidos (CNC). (1987). *Reunion Nacional para el Analisis de la Migracion Campesina.* Zacatecas City, Zacatecas: CNC.

Cardoso, L. A. (1980). *Mexican Emigration to the U.S., 1897–1931.* Tucson: University of Arizona Press.

Carkner, R. W., and Jaksich, J. (1993). *IRCA and Washington Agriculture: Dependence on Migrant and Seasonal Farm Workers.* Presented at the Conference on Immigration Reform and U.S. Agriculture, Washington, D.C., March 29–30.

Chacon, R. (1984). "Labor Unrest and Industrialized Agriculture in California: The Case of the 1933 San Joaquin Valley Cotton Strike." *Social Science Quarterly* 65, no. 2 (June), pp. 337–353.

Chan, S. (1986). *This Bittersweet Soil: The Chinese in California's Agriculture, 1860–1910.* Berkeley: University of California Press.

Chavez, C. (1992). Notes from his course "Farm Labor Movements in the U.S.." Chicano Studies 191HH, University of California, Santa Barbara, Spring.

Cheng, L., and Bonacich, E. (1984). *Asian Workers in the U.S. Before World War II.* Berkeley: University of California Press.

Commission on Agricultural Workers (CAW). (1993). "Employment Trends in the U.S. and Seven Key Agricultural States." In *Case Studies and Research Reports, Appendix 1.* Washington, DC: Commission on Agricultural Workers.

Cornelius, W. A. (1993). "Mexican Immigrants in California Today." In Light, I., and Bhachu, P., eds., *Immigration and Entrepreneurship.* New Brunswick, NJ: Transaction Publishers.

Dowell, D. E., Beyeler, M., and Wong, C-C. S. (1994). *Evaluation of California's Enterprise Zone and Employment and Economic Incentive Programs.* Berkeley: University of California, California Policy Seminar.

Economist. (1992). "Hispanic Bad Apples?: Yakima, Washington." July 18, p. 29.

Edid, M. (1994). *Farm Labor Organizing: Trends and Prospects.* Ithaca, NY: Cornell University, Industrial and Labor Relations Press.

El Financiero. (1994). "Michoacan, Principal Expulsor de Migrantes." October 19, p. 36.

El Sol de Morelia. (December 7, 1995). p. 3.

Employment Development Department (EDD). (1990). *Agricultural Employment Pattern Study: San Joaquin Valley Region.* No. 5-A. Sacramento, CA: EDD.

Fernandez Ortiz, L. M., ed. (1989). *Los Factores que Condicionan el Desarrolla Rural en la Mixteca Oaxaquena.* Mexico City: Universidad Autonoma Metropolitana.

Fineberg, R. A. (1971). *Green Card Workers in Farm Labor Disputes: A Study of Post-Bracero Workers in the San Joaquin Valley.* Ph.D. thesis. History Department, Claremont Graduate School, Pomona, CA.

Fisher, L. H. (1953). *The Harvest Labor Market in California.* Cambridge: Harvard University Press.

Galarza, E. (1964). *Merchants of Labor.* Santa Barbara, CA: McNally and Loftin.

Gamboa, E. (1990). *Mexican Labor in the Pacific Northwest.* Austin: University of Texas Press.

Garcia, M. T. (1994). *Memories of Chicano History: The Life and Narrative of Bert Corona.* Berkeley: University of California Press.

Goldschmidt, W. (1978) [1947]. *As You Sow: Three Studies in the Social Consequences of Agribusiness.* Montclair, CA: Allanheld, Osmun.

Gonzalez, G. (1994). *Labor and Community: Mexican Citrus Worker Villages in a Southern California County.* Urbana: University of Illinois Press.

Good Fruit Grower. (1996). "Top 100 [Tree Fruit] Growers." August, pp. 5–13.

_____. (1997). "Special Focus: Apple Research." January, pp. 7–15.

Gregory, J. N. (1989). *American Exodus: The Dust Bowl Migration and Okie Culture in California.* New York: Oxford University Press.

Griffith, D., and Kissam, E. (1995). *Working Poor: Farm Workers in the United States.* Philadelphia: Temple University Press.

Guarnizo, L. (1992). *One Country in Two: Dominican-Owned Firms in New York and in the Dominican Republic.* Ph.D. thesis. Baltimore, MD: Johns Hopkins University.

Hirabayashi, L. (1993). *Cultural Capital: Mountain Zapotec Migrant Associations in Mexico City.* Tucson: University of Arizona Press.

Hoffman, A. (1974). *Unwanted Mexican Americans in the Great Depression: Repatriation Pressures, 1929–1939.* Tucson: University of Arizona Press.

Instituto Nacional de Estadistica, Geografia e Informatica (INEGI). (1991). *La Situacion Actual de la Migracion Zacatecana.* Zacatecas City, Zacatecas: INEGI.

Jenkins, J. C. (1985). *The Politics of Insurgency: The Farm Worker Movement of the 1960s.* New York: Columbia University Press.

Kearney, M. (1986). "Integration of the Mixteca and the Western U.S.-Mexico Region via Migratory Wage Labor." In Rosenthal-Urey, I., ed., *Regional Impacts of U.S.-Mexican Relations.* La Jolla, CA: University of California at San Diego, Center for U.S.-Mexican Studies.

Kissam, E., Garcia, A., and Runsten, D. (1993). "The Apple and Asparagus Industries in Washington." In *Case Studies and Research Reports, Appendix 1.* Washington, DC: Commission on Agricultural Workers.

Krissman, F. (1994). "The Transnationalization of the North American FVH Agricultural Sector: Mechanization or 'Mexicanization'?" Paper presented at a meeting of the Latin American Studies Association in Atlanta, in September 1994.

_____. (1995). "Farm Labor Contractors: The Processors of New Immigrant Labor from Mexico for Californian Agribusiness." *Agriculture and Human Values* 12, no. 4 (Fall), pp. 18–46.

_____. (1996). *Californian Agribusiness and Mexican Farm Workers (1942–1992): A Bi-National Agricultural System of Production/Reproduction.* Ph.D. thesis. Department of Anthropology, University of California, Santa Barbara.

_____. (1997a). "California's Agricultural Labor Market: Historical Variations in the Use of Unfree Labor, ca. 1769–1994." In Brass, T., and van der Linden, M., *Free and Unfree Labour.* Berne: Peter Lang.

_____. (1997b). "Comparing Apples and Oranges: The Teamsters and United Farm Workers in the San Joaquin and Yakima Valleys, 1966–1996." Working papers series. Seattle: University of Washington, Center for Labor Studies.

Labor Management Decisions (LMD). (1994). "Changing of the Guard: 'New' UFW Makes Gains."

La Paloma [Mexico City]. (January 3, 1992). "Los Angeles Zacatecanos Aid Their Homeland."

Larson, A., and Bullamore, B. (1995). *Assessment of Farm Worker Housing in Yakima County, Washington.* Yakima, WA: Housing Foundation.

Leeper Buss, F. (1993). *Forged Under the Sun/Forjada Bajo El Sol.* Ann Arbor: University of Michigan Press.

Lloyd, J., Martin, P., and Mamer, J. (1988). *The Ventura Citrus Labor Market.* Giannini Information Series, No. 88–1. Berkeley: University of California, Agriculture and Natural Resources Division.

Lomnitz, L. (1982). "Horizontal and Vertical Relations and the Social Structure of Urban Mexico." *Latin American Research Review* 17, no. 2.

Los Angeles Times. (April 28, 1973). "Role of Farm Workers in Teamsters Stalled: Union Official Denies Racism Is Reason for Two-Year Wait." B1.

_____. (May 11, 1977). "Teamsters to Withdraw, Leave Field to Chavez." A1.

_____. (January 15, 1988). "Some Firms Dodge Law on Immigration, Study Finds." A3.

_____. (Nov. 19, 1991). "Arrests Rise for Illegal Immigrants: The 1.1 million figure is the highest in four years . . . fading influence of employer sanctions." A3.

_____. (Nov. 26, 1991). "The Illegal Worker Problem: Do Hiring Sanctions Work?" A5.

_____. (July 6, 1992). "California Cities: Rich and Poor." A3.

_____. (April 24, 1993). "Cesar Chavez, Founder of UFW, Dies at 66." A1.

_____. (April 6, 1994)."Networking Pays Off for the Chinese: Emigrants Are Fueling Their Homeland's Growth." A1.

_____. (July 18, 1994). "[UFW] Union's Focus on Fields Starts to Bear Fruit." A3.

Lozano Ascencio, F. (1993). *Bringing It Back Home: Remittances to Mexico from Migrant Workers in the U.S.*. La Jolla, CA: Center for U.S.-Mexican Studies.

Majka, T., and Majka, L. C. (1982). *Farm Workers, Agribusiness, and the State.* Berkeley: University of California Press.

Massey, D., Alarcon, R., Durand, J., and Gonzalez, H. (1987). *Return to Aztlan: The Social Process of International Migration from Western Mexico.* Berkeley: University of California Press.

Menchaca, M. (1993). "Chicano Indianism: A Historical Account of Racial Repression in the U.S." *American Ethnologist* 20, pp. 583–603.

_____. (1995). *The Mexican Outsiders: A Community History of Marginality.* Austin: University of Texas Press.

Meillassoux, C. (1981). *Maidens, Meal, and Money.* Cambridge: Cambridge University Press.

Mines, R. (1981). *Developing a Community Tradition of Migration to the U.S.* La Jolla, CA: Center for U.S.-Mexican Studies.

Mines, R., and Anzaldua, R. (1982). *New Migrants vs. Old Migrants: Alternative Labor Market Structures in the California Citrus Industry.* Monograph no. 9. La Jolla, CA: Center for U.S.-Mexican Studies.

Monroy, D. (1990). *Thrown Among Strangers: The Making of Mexican Culture in Frontier California.* Berkeley: University of California Press.

Mooney, P. H., and Majka, T. J. (1995). *Farmers' and Farm Workers' Movements: Social Protest in American Agriculture.* New York: Maxwell Macmillan International.

Nagengast, C., and Kearney, M. (1990). "Mixtec Ethnicity: Social Identity, Political Consciousness, and Political Activism." *Latin American Research Review* XXV, no. 2.

Nation. (March 24, 1997). "Labor Deals a New Hand." Pp. 11–16.

Nation. (April 14, 1997). "The UFW Picks Strawberries: . . . the largest, most intense organizing drive in America." Pp. 18–23.

New York Times. (Oct. 28, 1996). "Huge Orchards Increase Apple Crops: Corporate Farms Threaten Family Farms." A16.

New Yorker. (March 25, 1996). "The New Americans: Mexican farm workers once believed in the American dream. Why are their children living the American nightmare?" Pp. 52–60.

Palerm, A. (1976). *Modos de Produccion.* Mexico City: Ediciones Gernika.

Palerm, J. V. (1991). *Farm Labor Needs and Farm Workers in California, 1970–1989.* Sacramento, CA: Employment Development Department.

People's Weekly World. (May 22, 1993). "Washington State Does It Again: Farm Workers Left Out in the Cold." P. 7.

Pichardo, N. A. (1995). "The Power Elite and Elite-driven Countermovements: The Associated Farmers of California During the 1930s." *Sociological Forum* 10.

Rosenberg, H., Vaupel, S., and Villarejo, D. (1992). *Farm Labor Contractors in California.* Sacramento, CA: Employment Development Department.

Ruiz, V. L. (1987). *Cannery Women, Cannery Lives: Mexican Women, Unionization, and the California Food Processing Industry, 1930–1950.* Albuquerque: University of New Mexico Press.

Rural Migration News. (April 1996). "Farm Workers: UFW settles with Bruce Church, Inc." P. 4.

Sacramento Bee. (May 1, 1996). "State Digging Away at $100 Billion Underground Economy."

San Francisco Chronicle. (May 5, 1994). "Union Seeks Ways to Replant Its Productivity." A1.

_____. (Nov. 24, 1996). "Strawberry Fields Forever United?" B1.

Scharlin, C., and Villanueva, L. V. (1992). *Philip Vera Cruz: A Personal History of Filipino Immigrants and the Farm Workers Movement.* Los Angeles: University of California, Los Angeles Labor Center.

Schotzko, R. T. (1994). "Changing Times in the Tree Fruit Industry." Unpublished manuscript.

Seattle Times. (Jan. 8, 1997). "Ruling: Grower Unfairly Fired Unionizers." D1.

_____. (Feb. 5, 1997). "NLRB Charges Stemilt with More Labor Violations."

Taylor, P. (1934). *An American-Mexican Frontier: Nueces County Texas.* Chapel Hill: University of North Carolina Press.

Taylor, R. B. (1975). *Chavez and the Farm Workers.* Boston: Beacon Press.

Time. (March 29, 1993). "The Temping of America." Pp. 40–47.

_____. (Nov. 25, 1996). "Picking a New Fight: UFW Has Turned to Organizing Strawberry Fields." Pp. 64, 65.

Valle, I. (1994). *Fields of Toil: A Migrant Family's Journey.* Pullman: Washington State University Press.

Valley Voice. (April 1983). "United Farm Workers Activity in the Citrus Industry."

Visalia Delta-Times. (Nov. 13, 1992). "Farmersville Protests: Most Speakers Defend Police in Tense Farmersville Meeting." 1A.

Washington CEO. (May 1995). "The Private 150: Our Annual Look at the State's Top Private Companies." Pp. 31–40.

Wells, M. J. (1996). *Strawberry Fields: Politics, Class, and Work in California Agriculture.* Ithaca, NY: Cornell University Press.

Wenatchee World. (Sept. 12, 1996). "Fruit Workers Take Complaints to Growers." P. 10.

_____. (Nov. 7, 1996). "Farm Workers Sit in on Apple Meeting." P. 14.

_____. (Dec. 12, 1996). "Apple Packers Demonstrate At Hort[iculture] Trade Show."

Williamson, P. G. (1947). *Labor in the California Citrus Industry.* Master's thesis. Department of History, University of California, Berkeley.

Wolf, E. (1959). *Sons of Shaking Earth.* Chicago: University of Chicago Press.

Wolpe, H., ed. (1980). *The Articulation of Modes of Production.* London: Routledge and Kegan Paul.

WSES (Washington State Employment Service). (1992). *Yakima County Profile.* Olympia: WSES.

_____. (1994a). *Agricultural Employment in Washington State 1994.* Olympia: WSES.

_____. (1994b). *Annual Demographic Information.* Olympia: WSES.

_____. (1994c). *Washington State Labor Market and Economic Report.* Olympia: WSES.

_____. (1994d). *Annual Demographic Information.* Olympia: WSES.

Yakima Chamber of Commerce. (1994). *Economic Development Profile.* Yakima: Chamber of Commerce.

Yakima Herald-Republic. (April 11, 1965). "A Century of Irrigation: Special Report." Section F.

_____. (May 3, 1987).

_____. (Aug. 21, 1991). "A Lot More Workers Than Jobs: Farm Workers . . . Average . . . $5,845 a Year in State." A1.

_____. (April 12, 1992). "The Price Isn't Right." A1.

_____. (May 20, 1992). "Farm Workers to Receive Settlement: Apple Commission Pays in Suit Over Worker Ads." A1.

_____. (Oct. 24, 1992). "Check's in the Mail: Tree Top Returns $30 Million to Growers." A1.

_____. (Sept. 1, 1994). "Then There Were Two: New Farm Worker Union Forms." A1.

_____. (Nov. 10, 1994).

_____. (Feb. 26 through March 5, 1995). "Vecinos—Neighbors: [a special series on Michoacan, Mexico and Mexican farm workers in Yakima]."

_____. (June 3, 1995). "Vineyard Workers Vote to Unionize." A1.

_____. (Dec. 18, 1996). "Activists, Immigrants Picket INS Office Over Raid?"

_____. (Jan. 7, 1997). "NLRB Slaps Stemilt Over Labor Practices." A3.

_____. (Aug. 19, 1997). "Uncertain Future: Walkout May Be Costly for Protesting Harrah Farm Workers.) C1.

_____. (Sept. 4, 1997). "Rain Doesn't Cool Fruit Strike's Fury." C1.

_____. (Sept. 11, 1997). "Farm Workers Protest Pay By Marching Near Mattawa." A3.

Zabin, C., Kearney, M., Garcia, A., Runsten, D., and Nagengast, C. (1993). *Mixtec Migrants in California Agriculture: A New Cycle of Poverty.* Davis: University of California at Davis, California Institute for Rural Studies.

ten

The Thinking Heart:
American Indian Discourse and
the Politics of Recognition

KATHRYN SHANLEY

> Cartesianism tells us that we are schizoid creatures, one-half of which is little more than a mechanical rig for getting us about in the world. When we unquestioningly accept this diagnosis of our nature, we give up living in our bodies and enter a cultural insanitarium. . . . Through a recognition and contemplation of the "deep structures" of our bodily selves, we have the possibilities of rediscovering and reaffirming wholeness, self-healing, emotions, tactile-kinesthetic experience—all those dimensions of our bodily selves which we deposited at the doorstep when we entered.
>
> **—Maxine Sheets-Johnstone,**
> ***Giving the Body Its Due***

> . . . and I wonder where all the Skins disappeared to, and after a while I leave, searching the streets, searching storefronts, until I walk into a pawn shop, find a single heart beating under glass, and I know who it used to belong to, I know all of them.
>
> **—Sherman Alexie, "Pawn Shop,"**
> ***The Business of Fancydancing***

In the history of indigenous Americans' relations with Europeans, European discourses have gradually overwhelmed indigenous American discourses as the power relations have shifted to favor Europeans. The Western belief in the separation of mind from body, inherited from Descartes, has fostered another belief—that indigenous American peoples should, and will in time, disappear from the continent. The latter belief served to justify the colonization process, but it continues to the present day. Although several decades ago the so-called sexual revolution and the civil rights movement, and their attendant intellectual components, were supposed to have shaken the Cartesian binaries of mind/body and civilized/primitive loose from their Christian underpinnings, little has actually changed for Native Americans on the discursive level of popular ideology. Whether running in a vein of hatred or of love, the American discourse on primitivism stubbornly persists.[1]

Evolutionary narratives that code Native Americans for destruction by disease (today in terms of degradation through despairing poverty) or by cultural domination also persist in a range of spheres from Indiana Jones movies to Supreme Court decisions. Yet the need to reinvent "the primitive" also persists, and often within the same narratives, for, "[I]n this ideologically constructed world of ongoing progressive change, putatively static savage societies become a stable reference point for defining (the felicitous progress of) civilized identity" (Rosaldo, 1989, p. 70). Once "the primitive" comes to be seen as the "stable reference point" in the dominant discourse, then actual indigenous voices can no longer be heard. In the words of Norman Fairclough, "If a discourse type so dominates an institution that dominated types are more or less entirely suppressed or contained, then it will cease to be seen as arbitrary (in the sense of being one among several possible ways of 'seeing' things) and will come to be seen as *natural*, and legitimate because it is simply *the* way of conducting oneself" (1989, p. 91).

The irony of viewing American Indian discourses as *less natural* than those of European Americans is complex. In large part how Native discourses are dominated into disappearance in the first place is through being seen as *more natural* than discourses of West European traditions, and therefore as *too natural*.[2] Nevertheless, applying Fairclough's characterization of "natural" discourse to the American discourse of primitivism is not to say that Native resistance to domination has always and everywhere been absent or ineffective[3] or that accommodations have not occurred. Rather, it is to acknowledge that the first step in exploring features of American Indian peoples' discourse is to identify the silencing that has occurred and continues—specifically, the ideological mechanism of the silencing that must be examined.

In the nineteenth century, primitivism, as "a rhetorical tool of colonialisation," placed Native expression within the body rather than within the mind, as an unmediated "poetry of the heart" supposedly arising from "raw" emotion (Carr, 1996, pp. 66–67). Human speech has been considered in a similar vein as arising from primal emotions. On the Christian side of the paradigm, for "primitive" (hu)man to "advance," he must experience a religious conversion with a subsequent "mortification of the flesh." On the secular side of the paradigm, the Noble Savage is at his best when kept pristine, apart from the corruptions of "civilization." Until recently, perhaps up until the publication of Jerome Rothenberg's *Technicians of the Sacred*, so-called primitive "poetry of the heart" was actually thought to be at its best when spoken, or at least mediated, by non-Native people (Rothenberg, 1985 [1969]).[4] The rising number of American Indian writers since the 1960s has called attention to the need for more adequate ways of identifying the features of American Indian discourse, in addition to the need for a greater understanding of how the American discourse of primitivism functions.

This project involves both an excavation and an amplification of a central aspect of indigenous American thought and culture: the trope of the thinking heart in indigenous body-centered discourse, which has been overwhelmed, distorted, and silenced by Cartesian ideology. The discourse I employ in discussing this topic is a blend fashioned roughly out of academic and American Indian ways of "seeing." And while I want to be clear that I am not positing a superior position for indigenous epistemological and ontological values, I am asserting that such values are more functional in particular circumstances, places, and times. To borrow a question from Hayden White, "Could we ever narrativize without moralizing?" (1987, p. 25). Admittedly idealistic, my discourse does pivot on moral concerns. It is my hope that those concerns cross cultures, as all "quests for truth" generally do, but mostly I hope to promote a functional, perhaps liberating understanding of less assimilable cultural differences that some indigenous thinkers bring to the round tables of the world. In order to elucidate those indigenous values (at least on the level of cultural particularity that I engage) in a manner that does not reinvent the "primitive" of days gone by, I proceed with the assumption that "there is no single cognitive map that can guide one through the entire range of the human condition" (Littleton, 1985 [1926], p. xxxv). Yet some sort of generalizations are necessary, if points are to be made about the nature of ubiquitous misperceptions resulting from "caveman" primitives of popular imagination.[5] My focus in this chapter is on literary expressions of the postcolonial experience of indigenous peoples, as the thinking heart takes the shape of a constituting metaphor for community identification and community building.

Universals or Simulations of Universals

In *Manifest Manners*, Gerald Vizenor, Anishinabe writer and educator, speaks of how "Indians . . . must be the simulations of the 'absolute fakes' in the ruins of representation, or the victims in literary annihilation"(1994, p. 9). While it may not be immediately obvious, Vizenor is talking about a lose-lose situation for Indians, and the only way out of the "hyperreal" coding of Indians as "primitives" is through humor and dynamic orality—the restoration of "the real," the living. (In Vizenor's work, orality can be written as well, but that's another matter.) As David Murray so persuasively argues in his book *Forked Tongues*, about writing and representation in North American Indian texts, the early process of cross-cultural communication between indigenous and immigrant American peoples was frequently a lose-lose situation for Natives in that "while the bulk of the adaptation and translation was from the Indian side," Indians were being represented as possessing an inferior language (and, by extension, inferior culture, or no culture at all). Since indigenous cultures appeared to be tied closely to nature, Native peoples were thought to be more distant from "true" culture than were Europeans.

Given the long and obdurate tendency in American thought to misrepresent indigenous languages, literatures, and philosophies, it is important to reconceptualize the body-centered discourse of North American indigenous peoples in light of Native points of view,[6] showing how the location of thought within "the heart" reflects a less dualistic, more phenomenologically based ontology.[7] Such a discourse situates the "self" both more fully within its biological home (the whole of its thought base) and more fully within a nexus of relations to other living selves or beings. (I am trying here to avoid the binary of animate/inanimate, because indigenous epistemologies also reflect differences in what is regarded as a "self" and as living.) Rather than set up a dualism or opposition of my own, I hope to coax the dominant (academic and scientific) discourse(s) to loosen up. There is, after all, no absolute separation within or between human beings; rather, we are, as Linda Alcoff writes, "constitutively linked in various complex ways to that about which we are seeking to know" (1996, p. 13). Therefore, *relatedness* is a more key term in the discourse I'm dealing with than is *relativity,* for in the former term connectedness and ethics are emphasized, and in the latter, difference and distance. To speak of tribalism or indigenousness is, on the one hand, to speak of "aboriginal" human cultures, the original inhabitants; at the same time, it is imperative to avoid a return to the Noble Savage stereotype. Along with that, it is important to avoid suggesting that we are all as people equally close to indigenousness or tribalism, that getting there is a matter of making an imaginative leap. Opening some new space in the contemporary imagination for thinking about these old issues is vital but nonetheless difficult; it is like recovering truth from a cliche—to some it's so obvious as to be transparent, while to others it's attached to overly abundant sentiment.

As I mentioned above, Gerald Vizenor attempts to thwart and disconcert what have by now become usual expectations about the nature and truth of American Indian life, past and present. He terms the exoticizing and denigrating gestures "manifest manners" (1994), and looks to tribal peoples' oral traditions for continuing cultural dynamism. What he often uses to counter "manifest manners" are "comic holotropes" or "cultural stripteases,"[8] stopping short at the layer of breechcloth—all done as a sort of depiction of gesture language or mime. He also pulls frequently from postmodern writings to argue:

> The natural world is a venture of sound and shadows, and the outcome of the oral tradition is not the silence of discoveries, dominance, and written narratives. The natural development of the oral tradition is not a written language. The notion in the literature of dominance, that the oral advances to the written, is a colonial reduction of natural sound, heard stories, and the tease of shadows in tribal remembrance. (Vizenor, 1994, p. 72)

Vizenor's alternative view is particularly interesting from the standpoint of the spectacle/spectator—the striptease—as it relates to an embodied-sound-based value. The legacy of colonialism includes a domination of bodies as well as a predominance of sight-preference—the sign, the word (writing), and the image (commerce). As Maxine Sheets-Johnstone notes in the introduction to her book, *Giving the Body Its Due*, "Not only are stress, hypervisualism, popular body noise, a wholly material view of bodies, and the like, *cultural diseases*, Cartesianism itself is a cultural disease" (p. 13). Sheets-Johnstone's phrase "popular body noise" corresponds with Vizenor's phrase "natural sound," and both suggest the full range of environmental sounds surrounding experience.

Ethnographer Michael Jackson, in his book *Paths Toward a Clearing*, asserts that the "visualist bias [in American mainstream culture] has the effect of distancing the subject from the object, of seeing them as discontinuous entities" (1989, p. 5).[9] Jackson draws from John Dewey, the philosopher of American pragmatism, to add strength to his own argument in favor of what he terms *radical empiricism* in ethnography. Jackson defines radical empiricism as a method that "seeks to grasp the ways in which ideas and words are wedded to the world in which we live, how they are grounded in the mundane events and experiences of everyday life (Jackson, 1989, pp. 5–6). Dewey relates the supposed biology of vision to a "spectator theory of knowledge": "The theory of knowing is modeled after what was supposed to take place in the act of vision. The object refracts light to the eye and is seen; it makes a difference to the eye and to the person having an optical apparatus, but none to the thing seen. The real object is the object so fixed in its regal aloofness" (Jackson, 1989, p. 5).

The "object's" double-bind, in Dewey's description—being at once a "thing" who experiences nothing in being seen and an "object so fixed" that it possesses aloof sovereignty—fittingly compares to "the Indian" in American culture, perceived as pristinely noble, yet having no effective part in the process of his/her objectivization. No single theory or idea can reverse this situation; effective change must occur on many fronts.

The designation *the thinking heart* fittingly signals a major epistemological difference between European American and indigenous American discourses; yet to designate the difference as European Americans being more "mind-centered" and Indians more "body-centered" courts the risk of portraying Indians as possessing the sort of "stereotyped inarticulateness" evident in a range of non-Indian depictions, from scholarly writing to popular media since the sixteenth century (Murray, 1991, p. 7).[10] That is why it's important to begin again, to take another look at American Indian life, from the peoples' points of view insofar as is possible . Language provides a first glimpse into the way indigenous peoples order their worlds.

Gesture, Speech, and Memory

Among Plains Indians, where the use of sign language predominated, "the gestural lingua franca represented the words 'to think' or 'thought' by pointing to the heart before bringing the hand forward 'to gesture thought coming from the heart'" (Miller, 1980). According to another researcher who focuses on Plains signing, the anatomical heart is gesturally referred to in sign language to mean the physical organ, to mean "good" ("heart level"), "know . . . think" ("heart-drawn-front"), "remember" (memory, "heart know"), [and] annoy ("heart flutter") (Kroeber, 1978, p. 189). Carl Jung noted, when he visited the southwestern United States in the 1930s, that Pueblo people think with their hearts (Jung, 1981, p. 249). Other, similar reports suggest the phenomenon to be as far flung as from the East Coast of the United States (among the Delaware) to the South American Andes (among the Qollahuaya). Qollahuaya people not only regard thought and emotions as coming out from the heart of a person but they also see the person as analogous in structure and function to a mountain. The Qollahuaya have three distinct cultural communities inhabiting different elevations, different parts of the "body" of the mountain (Bastien, 1985). Closer to home, Jay Miller notes:

> In the [Pacific] Northwest, the widely used trade pidgin called Chinook jargon expressed the word for thinking as literally "to use the heart" (Gill 1933, p. 34). More specifically within this area, the word for "heart" in the Salishan language of the Moses-Columbia is based on the root for "think" (Kinkade, 1975). Also in the Pacific drainage, the Kalapuya had many expressions relating the heart to thought and emotions. For example, the phrase "Heart is not good" meant "I am angry" and "How is your heart" meant "What do you think?" (Jacobs 1945, pp. 95, 137) Similar idiomatic usage equating the heart, thought, and emotions is reported for other areas, such as the Great Lakes (Kinietz 1965, p. 200).

And finally, in my own Nakota tradition, thinking takes place in the heart's eye, *cante ista*. Seeing and feeling combine in "eye" as the initial interpreters of reality, and "heart" adds the final mediation. *Cante ista* is what some researchers term a "conduit metaphor." Brenda Farrell, in her study of Plains Indian sign talk and embodied action, entitled *Do You See What I Mean?*, writes:

> English speakers conceive of thoughts and ideas as 'things' and use numerous metaphors of getting, giving, putting, packing, and inserting ideas as objects of exchange in communication. In contrast, where PST [Plains Sign Talk] uses a visual metaphor in the variant of the verb TO LOOK (from the heart), it is one that emphasizes an active searching, a process of thinking rather than a product (p. 258).

The lack of separation of thought and feeling in Assiniboine epistemology is also reflected in the sign for "doubt": "two actions of the hand over the heart," and is "glossed in Nakota as *wacititipa*, not 'two hearts' but 'two minds,' performed over the heart" (p. 239).

In political terms, particularly relating to negotiation or collaboration, to think with and speak from your heart means many things: to speak honestly (not with a "forked tongue"), to keep your interconnectedness "in mind," and to engage in the communication process with sincerity of purpose (as if with blood kin). In the 1830s, Grizzly Bear of the Menominee commented astutely on the difference between Native and non-Native negotiations.

> We see your Council House—it is large and beautiful. But the Council House of the Red Man is yet larger. The earth is the floor—the clear sky is the roof-a blazing fire is the chair of the Chief orator, and the green grass is the seats of our Chiefs. You speak by papers, and record your words in books, but we speak from our hearts, and memory records our words in the hearts of the people. (Hazard, 1831, p. 23)

Just as Grizzly Bear sees "the Red Man's" Council House as larger and better than the White Man's, he also sees speaking from the heart and carrying the memory of what was agreed upon in the heart as preferable to relying on what gets recorded on paper and in books. His view, which is fairly representative of the views of many other Indian leaders, illustrates well the basic opposition that is reflected in the "thinking heart" trope.

"The Very Best Kind" of Bacon: Basic Understanding

Complementary and competing discourses are usually at work in cross-cultural negotiations, and that fact need not mean that deception is also involved; but in relations between the United States and the Plains tribes, in particular, the negotiators were often duplicitous from the start.[11] What follows is a story of the late-nineteenth-century negotiations between the United States government and the Sioux Nation, in which competing discourses are staged, literally and figuratively, by Lakota people in a manner intended to make clear that Lakotas understand the significance of cultural differences relative to discourse and power.

On one early fall day in 1875, a small group of Washington bureaucrats, referred to in history books as the Sioux Commission, gathered at a spot on the northern plains midway between the Red Cloud and Spotted Tail Indian Agencies in hopes of persuading Lakota leaders to sell their sacred Paha Sapa, or Black Hills.[12] Since gold had been discovered there the previous year, over twenty-five thousand miners had streamed into what was supposed to be land exclusively reserved for the use of the tribes that had negotiated the Laramie Treaty of 1868 (Welch, 1994).[13] After much humbling and fumbling on the part of negotiators for both sides during previous meetings in Washington, D.C., no accord had been reached regarding the sale of the Black Hills. The government was anxious to be done with the matter (and probably with Lakotas as well) and to move on with the business of the day, which included continuing to rebuild the country after the Civil War. The federal negotiators also hoped to satisfy Congress that they had dealt honorably and peaceably with Lakota people. On the Lakota side of the negotiations were Spotted Tail and Red Cloud. Having been to the nation's capital, they had seen how mightily the Whites outnumbered and outpowered them; from their experience in their familiar hunting grounds, they knew well how the numbers of wild game were dwindling. Moreover, they had begun to witness the movement of all sorts of outsiders—most ominous among them, missionaries—through and into Indian Country.

Both sides in the official encounter seemed to want to negotiate some sort of agreement, though the Indian people involved roughly broke down into three groups with differing ideas about the best route to take: reservation Indians led by Spotted Tail and Red Cloud, "who wanted to sell the Hills for a fair price"; a middle group led by Young Man Afraid, who worried that giving up the Hills would relegate them permanently to the reservation and cut them off from their hunting territory; and the "free" Indians, led by Sitting Bull and Crazy Horse, who "simply wanted the whites out of their lives and territory for good" (Welch, 1994, p. 86). Divisions existed also among the non-Indians, but the delegation from Washington represented those who preferred to obtain the Black Hills from the Plains Indian peoples by peaceful means.

As the commissioners waited for the leaders of all the Lakota bands to arrive, the numbers of Indians around them swelled to fifteen thousand. All of a sudden, their fear was heightened to near panic by the visage of two hundred warriors sweeping "down from the hills to the council site" and galloping around the gathered visitors as fast as their horses could carry them. According to James Welch, author of *Killing Custer*, "No sooner had these soldiers formed themselves in a line facing the commissioners than another group, then another and another, repeated the performance" (Welch, 1994, p. 85). A spectacle to behold, an estimated seven thousand mounted warriors formed into menacing tiers of men before the envoys. "Suddenly the lines parted," writes Welch, "and Little Big Man, a member of Crazy Horse's camp, rode up to the commissioners, stark naked except for a flowing war-bonnet. He had a rifle in one hand and shells in the other. He said he had come to kill the white men" (p. 86).

Due to the efforts of Young Man Afraid and the Indian policemen under his charge, the situation was defused, but it nonetheless delayed the parlay, giving the Indian "rank and file" an opportunity to decide against the sale of the Black Hills. Several days later, when the talks resumed, Spotted Tail insisted, "The amount must be so large that the interest will support us." Red Cloud, too, showed business savvy when he argued: "I want seven generations ahead to be fed. . . . These hills out here to the northwest we look upon as the head chief of the land. My intention was that my children should depend on these hills for the future." He also asked for wagons, cattle, horses, guns and ammunition for hunting, Texas steers, "the very best kind" of bacon, and all other manner of food, even salt and pepper. He asked for breeding stock—pigs, cattle, sheep, and chickens—for every family; in addition, he insisted on equipment to farm and a sawmill. That he thought his demands more than fair is evident in his declaration: "I am an Indian, but you try to make a white man out of me. I want some white men's houses at this agency to be built for the Indians. I have been into white people's houses, and I have seen nice black bedsteads and chairs, and I want that kind of furniture given to my people"(Welch, 1994, p. 87).

It goes without saying that the government was rarely willing to pay Indians the true value of land or resources they hoped to acquire from them; but in terms of gold alone, non-Indians had already taken an estimated $1.5 billion out of the Black Hills before 1875, the time of the Sioux Commission. Doing so was clearly in violation of the Ft. Laramie Treaty of 1868. The government, however, had even larger concerns than the wealth that the gold represented: The economy had begun to change from rural to urban, agricultural to industrial, and railroads were needed "to bring the whole country under one economic roof," to move immigrants west and resources east (Welch, 1994, p. 90).

Although the Lakota people were divided into three camps, as I mentioned above, all nonetheless recognized each other as Lakota, and each group in its own way sought to do what they thought best for their people. Little Big Man's display of confrontational warrior power, witnessed by the Sioux Commission, was one expression of resistance through a form of traditional Lakota discourse—an intensely individualized will absolutely subordinated to a larger, communal will. In other words, Little Big Man, through fulfillment of his own visionary power, expressed courageously the collective will. In order to understand the full import of Little Big Man's body-centered discourse, it is important to know what his nakedness signifies, how the horse he was riding figured into the display of courage, and the nature and source of his power. Although we do not have Little Big Man's words explaining his actions, George Kills in Sight (Brule Sioux), also

Lakota, tells a story passed down to him through his grandfather about Crazy Horse, a story that enables us better to understand the beliefs and customs surrounding Little Big Man's dramatic confrontation of the Sioux Commission:

> Crazy Horse was not a chief, but he was a medicine man. He was a real peace-loving man. The way my grandfather described him. . . . He was quite a medicine man. He could fix war bonnets where the man who wears the war bonnet gets into battle and never gets hit or wounded. [At the Battle of Little Big Horn] he sang his song and took sweet grass and tied it on his horse. He took loose dirt from around a gopher hole and sprinkled it on the horse from his nose to his tail. . . . He went up right in front of Custer's dismounted cavalry, and they started fifing. He rode from one end to the other singing his medicine song. They think any minute his horse [will] be shot down, but he rode on through. He showed the black bullet marks on his skin. . . . The bullets never went through (Lash and Hoover, 1995 [1971], p. 54).

The resemblance of the scene described above to Kevin Costner's opening performance as a Union officer before the Confederated troops in *Dances With Wolves* is not the first such appropriation of Indian heroism by Hollywood, but the full cultural import of the Crazy Horse scene apparently does not translate well across cultures. Assuming that Little Big Man's act corresponded culturally to Crazy Horse's death-defying feat, we can see cultural beliefs well beyond the reach of a soldier such as Kevin Costner's character.

In the Lakota language, feathered headdresses are called *wapaha-hetonpi* ("homed" or "many homed peak") or *iyuslobeto* ("with one tail") (Beuchel, 1970, p. 711). Both terms suggest virility, the courting or warring dance of a colorfully plumed creature. In Lakota traditions, there is nothing shameful about "borrowing" power from nonhuman relatives or from other elements of the natural world. Plains Indian feathered headdresses were apparently the object of scorn among Europeans, however, for as Richard C. Trexler remarks, "Having just completed their conquest of the allegedly 'effeminate' Moors, Iberian warriors now an ocean away [in America] faced feathered warriors and, fearing them, called them women" (1995, p. xi).[14] At the moment when the Plains warrior sings his death song, he is at his most powerful; because he is ready to face death, he is ready to live fully and make his life meaningful in the most altruistic way—for the people.

For Lakotas, the horse was regarded as a religious symbol, possessing "attributes of supernatural potency, analogous to 'medicine'" (Grosmith, 1981, p. 10). The dust from around a gopher's hole enables a person (and his horse) to disappear from sight, as gophers so frequently do, as well as to dodge bullets; the sweetgrass smoke purifies and imbues them with sacred power. Body-paint signifies dream images and therefore carries with it the holistic power of dream—the fullness of time in space. Welch described Crazy

Horse: "[He] painted his body with white spots, hailstones, and one cheek
with a red jagged line, a lightning bolt. He tied a pebble behind an ear and a
red hawk on his head. He sprinkled a handful of dust on both himself and
his horse before battle for protection from bullets and arrows" (Welch, 1994,
p. 118). In other words, Little Big Man was hardly naked; instead, he was
cloaked in power against his enemies.

Little Big Man's answer to the Sioux Commission's question plainly re-
sounded: No. That he chose to demonstrate "no" in a manner wholly unlike
that of European Americans suggests that the right to be Indian was at stake.
The words of Hole-in-the-Day, eminent Ojibway leader of the early nineteenth century, poignantly illustrate what many Indians from different tribes
understood of "the white man's" discourse relative to "the Indian":

> The [Creator], although he made the Indian and the white man of a different
> color, gave each a dialect by which they could understand each other. The Mas-
> ter of Life gave us a faculty of using our tongues, and we should use words
> enough to make ourselves understood. Take the white man, with all his wisdom,
> and he is not infallible to faults. Your words strike us in this way. They are very
> short. "I want to buy your land" (Miller, 1995, p. 201).[15]

Hole-in-the-Day suggests that the fallibility of white men is that they use
language poorly, but he leaves it to us to figure out the nature of the white
man's "faults." Can it be that European Americans talk too much and in the
process say many things that they do not mean, when what they truly want
is material, not spiritual? To Lakota people, as well as Ojibway, the two—the
material and the spiritual—are connected. Lakota means "ally" or "friend,"
and relations with others are always conducted within a kinship network.
Moreover, the Great White Father in Washington, whom the Sioux Commission represented, did not bring gifts for their Lakota "relatives," as
would be the customary way of visiting kin. Clearly, this was a sign that the
non-Indians preferred their own "dialect," their own terms of negotiation.

The words of Spotted Tail and Red Cloud leave no doubt that the two
men understood and effectively spoke in the discourse of the government
representatives. "Being and remaining Indian" did not mean they were unwilling to accommodate new technologies and customs—clearly they could
see the inevitability of adjusting to the non-Indian presence and influence
among them. They were led to believe that they could negotiate the terms of
their accommodation and that their way of seeing would be respected. But as
history would come to show, in this the Lakota were misled. In the words of
Colin G. Calloway, editor of a collection of Indian voices entitled *Our
Hearts Fell to the Ground: Plains Indians' Views of How the West Was Lost*:

> For Indian people, what was said at [Council] meetings was far more important
> than the written documents white participants produced. . . . Whites and Indi-

ans alike understood the council as a diplomatic forum, but they differed in their understanding of the concept of the treaty. For Indians, the council was an end in itself, . . . a meeting of hearts and minds. For white Americans, the council and its associated rituals were only a prelude to the real thing: A written agreement to which the requisite number of leaders 'touched the pen' while the scribe placed an X after their names. Indian leaders who touched the pen believed they were validating what they had said in council, but, under white American law, their names on the treaty committed them only to those statements contained in the final document. (1996, p. 22)

Red Cloud's words, "I am Indian, but you try to make a white man out of me," returned to haunt the government in 1980, when the Supreme Court finally ruled in favor of the Lakota. Because the agreement eventually signed by Lakota leaders did not include three-fourths of the adult male Sioux signatures and because the rations provided them were "*quid pro quo* for depriving them of their chosen way of life and was not intended to compensate them for the taking of the Black Hills," Lakotas were entitled to compensation plus interest (*United States v. Sioux Nation of Indians, et al.* 1980, p. 423). To date the Lakota have refused the money in lieu of court appeals to have the Black Hills—"the head chief of [their] land"—returned to them. "He" would no doubt behave more responsibly as their relative than did the Great White Father.

Political Recognition and Indigenous Peoples' Rights

The Supreme Court's decision in *United States v. the Sioux Nation of Indians* reflects the peculiar ambivalence that is American Indian law. Within it, the Lakota would seem to be regarded as sovereign, as a nation unto themselves, and yet under the ruling, the language of guardianship predominates. In the latter years of the twentieth century, hardly a week goes by that issues of Indian sovereignty versus either federal or state jurisdiction do not come up, relative most often to gaming. Some states want the right to tax Indians, while elsewhere citizens' groups and politicians seek to limit the amount of money that tribes *as foreign governments* can contribute to American political campaigns. Sorting out how American Indians figure into American mainstream culture is no easy matter, particularly for the courts at every level. The cultural and historical differences between Indians and other U.S. citizens fall subject to the discourse of primitivism when Indian status is in dispute, or get erased all together. Therefore, political recognition of Indianness hinges on non-Indians' understanding what is essentially at stake for Indians in their self-determination of their Indianness and self-governance of their communities. Debates around multiculturalism, moreover, often hinder more than help Indian causes because they so often miss the uniqueness of American Indians' status within the United States. The single most important difference between Indians and other American ethnic groups today, as in Crazy Horse's and Red Cloud's day, is the nature of their collective tribal identities. How does that difference fit with the obligations of liberal democracies to recognize the individual and collective identities of their citizens?

To begin with, where and how do tribal peoples enter the larger debate around multiculturalism? The discussion that follows centers on the discussion recorded in *Multiculturalism and "The Politics of Recognition"*, published in 1992. The text centers on Charles Taylor's essay "The Politics of Recognition" and offers responses to that essay by Steven C. Rockefeller, Michael Walzer, and Susan Wolf, with an introduction by Amy Gutmann. The text was reissued in 1994 as *Multiculturalism*, and expanded to include responses by K. Anthony Appiah and Jürgen Habermas.

Taylor took as his thesis in "The Politics of Recognition" that "identity is partly shaped by recognition or its absence, often by the *mis*recognition of others, and so a person or group of people can suffer real damage, real distortion, if the people or society around them mirror back to them a confining or demeaning or contemptible picture of themselves" (1994 [1992], p. 25). What Taylor proceeded to say suggests that the "post-" in *postcolonial* may indeed be premature for some people, since internalized subjugation lingers long after physical freedom has been won. Many would, in fact, argue that American Indians continue to be colonized in their "fourth-world," nation-within-a-nation status. Taylor continues: "Nonrecognition or misrecognition can inflict harm, can be a form of oppression, imprisoning someone in a false, distorted, and reduced mode of being."[16] The potentially powerful impact such negative mirroring can have on an individual's or group's quality of life necessitates an ethical principle: that cultural traits (or, in the case of individuals, personal traits) be recognized by the dominant group. To recognize means both to acknowledge and, in some way, to assure survival by not oppressing that life or the expression of that life experience. Although the extent to which the guarantee of cultural survival is, according to Taylor, subject to debate, the basic right to be what one is (individually or collectively) should, Taylor asserts, be granted as a matter of human dignity.

Aside from the now-versus-forever element in the controversial topic of recognition, Taylor's point is simple enough. It is important, however, to emphasize that his acknowledgment of the deleterious effect of negative images is nothing new. It comes decades after Franz Fanon described the same phenomenon in *Black Skin, White Masks* (Markmann, 1967)[17] and Vine Deloria, Jr., identified it in *Custer Died for Your Sins* (1969).[18] In fact, almost a century ago, in *The Souls of Black Folk*, W.E.B. DuBois referred to people similarly afflicted as possessing a "double consciousness" (1907, p. 3).[19] Seeing themselves one way and also seeing themselves as nonblack people see them. Understandably, such bifurcated vision often leads to a pained sense of imprisonment. William Apess, a Pequot Indian turned Christian minister, published *The Experiences of Five Christian Indians: Or, The Indians' Looking Glass for the White Man* in 1833, a text that attempts to correct the negative reflections held by non-Indian Christians about their Indian brethren (McQuade et al., 1994, pp. 746–749).[20] Apess states, "If black or red skins, or any other skin of color is disgraceful to God, it appears that [God] has disgraced himself a great deal—for he has made fifteen colored people to one white, and placed them upon the earth" (p. 746). Taylor's thesis, in other words, has been a given among scholars and thinkers from subjugated American ethnic minority groups for literally centuries.[21] What is new about Taylor's argument is that he traces these dominant projections to the development of certain philosophical assumptions through Western intellectual traditions, leading us to our contemporary dilemmas, and that he implicitly locates a central paradox within liberal democracies.

His argument is based, first, on a recognition of the fact of multiculturalism in "first-world" democracies, and, second, on a politics of recognition that highlights the inadequacy of Western paradigms for simultaneously accommodating a basic "right to be" and the right to a guaranteed cultural continuance or difference in perpetuity. The fact that acknowledgments or "recognitions" such as Taylor makes have been so long in coming suggests that some sort of privilege has been at stake for Western intellectuals until quite recently.[22] Clearly, a necessary means of puzzling out the challenges that multicultural societies face would be through the perspectives of formerly and currently subjugated people, who identified the problem long before it struck the academic establishment.[23] And while the dialogical form the conversation takes in *Multiculturalism* does model the recognition being valorized, I would argue that the model of equal exchange as presented in the text in effect eclipses perspectives from radically different worldviews, once again reflecting the extent to which those worldviews have suffered delegitimization.[24] Tribal discourses need more exposure in the media. Robert A. Williams, Jr., a legal scholar of Lumbee[25] descent, notes in *The American Indian in Western Legal Thought*, "A more elaborate, refined theory of the relation between law and power manifested as a will to empire awaits articulation on the foundations of a knowledge of colonizing discourse that has barely begun to emerge out of a non-Western history of decolonization" (1990, p. 8).

Taylor takes *recognition* to mean "equal recognition" in our contemporary global political climate, and traces its development in Western philosophical thought through at least two prior shifts. First, with "the move from honor to dignity has come a politics of universalism, emphasizing the equal dignity of all citizens, and the content of this politics has been the equalization of rights and entitlements" (Taylor, 1994 [1992], p. 37). Second, along with "the development of the modern notion of identity [has arisen] a politics of difference" (p. 38), also universalistic but somewhat in conflict with the universalism of a politics of equal dignity. Habermas extends the paradoxical predicament—to be (universal) or not to be (universal)—with this question:

> Does not the recognition of cultural forms of life and traditions that have been marginalized, whether in the context of a majority culture or in a Eurocentric global society, require guarantees of status and survival—in other words, some kind of collective rights that shatter the outmoded self-understanding of the democratic constitutional state, which is tailored to individual rights and in that sense is "liberal"? (Taylor, 1994, p. 108).

I would phrase the question somewhat differently: Is it possible that a "politics of difference" arises because the universalistic concept of human dignity requires a paradigmatic shift?

When K. Anthony Appiah enters the discussion, he extends the idea of the politics of recognition by acknowledging and fleshing out Taylor's parallel concept of an "ethics of authenticity." Appiah explains, "Other things being equal, people have a right to be acknowledged publicly as what they already really are" (Taylor, 1994, p. 149). Although what Appiah means by "other things being equal" cannot exactly be discerned from the context, he does add another layer to the term "recognition" by his emphasis on both "ethics" and "authenticity." A discussion of three terms—identity, authenticity, and survival—form the crux of his effort to come to grips with the problematics of defining recognition. For Appiah, individual identity is determined (yet never fully determined) by myriad social forces. He writes:

> Of course, neither the picture in which there is just an authentic nugget of selfhood, the core that is distinctively me, waiting to be dug out, nor the notion that I can simply make up any self I choose, should tempt us. We make up selves from a tool kit of options made available by our culture and society. We do make choices, but we do not determine the options among which we choose. *This raises the question of how much we should acknowledge authenticity in our political morality, and that depends on whether an account of it can be developed that is neither essentialist nor monological.* (Taylor, 1994, p. 155 [emphasis added])

Appiah's point is crucial to our discussion of the politics involved in the body-centered discourses of indigenous peoples, because it is often so difficult for Eurocentric peoples to recognize, in a deeper sense than is implied in the term *acknowledge,* the difference in being an indigenous person. The European American cultural bias against indigenousness, in other words, is so extreme that Native worldviews are not recognized unless they are cloaked in eroticism, exoticism, or degeneracy. As Appiah argues, "It is because someone is already authentically Jewish or gay that we deny them something in requiring them to hide this fact, to pass for something that they are not" (Taylor, 1994, p. 149). In liberal democracies an ethic of human dignity dictates that "what is to be avoided at all costs is the existence of 'first class' and 'second class' citizens" (Taylor, 1994, p. 37).

An account of authenticity, "neither essentialist nor monological," calls for consensus with and through diversity, it would seem, and therefore is doomed to failure as long as such representations are locked in binary terms. Moreover, the historically strategic moment of emergence of an individual or group into recognition may require a sort of staged essentialism for the point of difference to be adequately emphasized. Appiah put his finger on the elusive subtleties of the individual/collective blend when he says that "one reasonable ground for suspicion of much contemporary multicultural talk is that it presupposes conceptions of collective identity that are remarkably unsubtle in their understandings of the process by which identities, both individual and collective, develop" (Taylor, 1994, p. 156).

When Appiah steps onto the page for a moment to reveal something of his positionality as a black gay male, a fault line in Taylor's positionality becomes clear. Appiah writes: "In a rather unphilosophical nutshell, my suspicion is that Taylor is happier with the collective identities that actually inhabit our globe than I am, and that may be one of the reasons why I am less disposed to make the concessions to them that he does. These differences in sympathy show up in the area of group survival, to which I now turn." It is very clever of Appiah to characterize the difference between his and Taylor's thoughts on "collective identities" as Taylor's being "happier with the collective identities" that present themselves for recognition. I surmise that what Appiah means, at least in part, is that Taylor's "happiness" stems from a privilege conferred by social position and cultural perspective that he, Appiah, does not share. That difference may mean also that Appiah identifies with those peoples who are struggling to survive, literally and culturally, in a way that Taylor does not. The argument once again boils down to who has what at stake and the extent to which self-awareness informs any particular position.

The politics part of recognition thus enters the discussion fully and precisely when non-Western intellectuals and other like-minded thinkers begin to strip the mask from the face of the "will to empire." The process begins by our defining and negotiating the nature and extent of the recognition that we seek to encourage—in some cases, that we demand—while simultaneously identifying those unique aspects of being that an individual or group has a "right" to express and maintain, regardless of whether or not those personal or cultural traits serve the larger society. Recognition in liberal (or postliberal) democracies means that the voice of the formerly unrecognized will be heard first—and thus, will be authentically and freely expressed, and genuinely heard. Negotiation of difference can begin after that, followed by the implications for action or policy. As Taylor also asserts, "There must be something between the inauthentic and homogenizing demand for recognition of equal worth, on the one hand, and the self-immurement within ethnocentric standards on the other" (1994, p. 72).

For American Indians the idea of "a politics of recognition" has a distinctly different cultural and political history than it does for other ethnic minorities in the United States. Indians hold a peculiar position in global politics as well as a unique place within philosophical debates about the politics of identity. Given the radical difference in indigenous and Western worldviews, American Indians have consistently fought to be seen, first, as human beings who deserve to live; second, as cultural beings capable of morality, justice, and agency; third, as distinct and worthy political entities (sovereign nations, in the language of state politics); and last, as (post)colonial collectives striving to revitalize, reconstruct, and heal their traumatized individuals and communities. In order to see how American Indians fit in the "politics of recognition" that Taylor critiques, the aforementioned aspects of recognition require some gloss.

During the sixteenth century, when exploration and conquest of the so-called New World became a consuming passion in Europe, the resultant debates centered around whether or not American Indians were capable of salvation and proper citizenship in the new territories that Spaniards sought to dominate and build for Crown and Church. As Robert A. Williams, Jr., notes, regarding the experiments humanists were allowed to carry out to determine Indian capabilities, such "inquisitions . . . normally ended inconclusively, with each side trading anecdotes and assertions in a political contest of wills over who would possess that part of the Indian deemed most important. The priests sought the Indians' souls; the slavers required only their bodies. A debate proved a poor forum for adjudicating such incompatible possessory rights" (Taylor, 1994, p. 95). Thus, the "right" to be regarded as human was held in tandem with the right to escape enslavement and/or extermination.

NOTES

1. White, H. V., *The Content of the Form: Narrative Discourse and Historical Representation* (Baltimore and London: Johns Hopkins University Press, 1987), p. 105, defines discourse "with all the connotations of circularity, of movement back and forth that the Indo-European root of this term (*kers*) and its Latinate form (*dis*, "in different directions," + *currere*, "to run") suggest."

2. For the purposes of this essay, I prefer to outline more fully in the context of my argument what "natural" as well as "indigenous" or "American Indian" can mean.

3. For discussions of American Indian activism, see Paul Chaat Smith and Robert Warrior, *Like a Hurricane: The Indian Movement from Alcatraz to Wounded Knee*

(New York: New Press, 1996), and M. Annette Jaime, ed., *The State of Native America: Genocide, Colonialism, and Resistance* (Boston: South End Press, 1992).

4. I am thinking here of Walt Whitman as well as the British romantics. Carr traces the changing views toward "the primitive" through eighteenth- and nineteenth-century poetry in ways that add a texture to the discussion of American primitive discourse that time does not allow here. Also, see M. H. Abrams, *The Mirror and the Lamp: Romantic Theory and the Critical Tradition* (Cambridge: Oxford University Press, 1953; reprint 1971). Jerome Rothenberg, *Technicians of the Sacred: A Range of Poetries from Africa, America, Asia, Europe, and Oceania* (New York: Anchor Books, 1969; Berkeley: University of California Press, 1985). Also see Larry Evers, "Cycles of Appreciation," in *Studies in American Indian Literature: Critical Essays and Course Designs,* edited by Paula Gunn Allen (New York: Modern Language Association, 1983) pp. 23–31.

5. Sam Gill argues for replacing the term "primitive" with "nonliterate" (see "into the forest dimly: an introduction," in *Beyond "The Primitive": The Religions of Nonliterate Peoples* [Englewood Cliffs, N.J.: Prentice-Hall, 1982], pp. 1–9). Although he readily admits the limits of his new term for indigenous peoples, he prefers "nonliterate" because "it makes clear the category in which the relation is drawn" (p. 6). In introducing his edited volume of global indigenous peoples' "poetry," *Technicians of the Sacred,* Jerome Rothenberg argues that "primitive means complex."

6. Inasmuch as I am able to reconstruct and garner Native American points of view from historical source materials as well as living people.

7. I recognize that "body," "mind," and "heart" function as much as metaphors as they do as signifiers of actual body parts, functions, or sites.

8. Since Vizenor recycles his ideas, characters, and terms, many contextual definitions of terms are available in his various texts.

9. The passage quoted by Jackson appears in *The Quest for Certainty: A Study of the Relation of Knowledge and Action* (New York: Pedigree Books, 1980), on p. 23.

10. The phrase comes from David Murray, *Forked Tongues: Speech, Writing and Representation in North American Indian Texts* (Bloomington: Indiana University Press, 1991, p. 7), which makes a persuasive argument regarding the translation process, asserting that "a characteristic white approach . . . is to emphasize translation as an issue only when whites choose, or are forced, to do it, and to ignore it otherwise."

11. Calloway quotes an American commissioner regarding the negotiations to buy the Black Hills: "While the Indians received us as friends, and listened with kind attention to our propositions, we were painfully impressed with their lack of confidence in the pledges of the Government. At times they told their story of wrong with such impassioned earnestness that our cheeks crimsoned with shame. In their speeches, the recital of the wrongs which their people had suffered at the hands of the whites, the arraignment of the Government for gross acts of injustice and fraud, and the description of treaties made only to be broken, the doubts and distrusts of present professions of friendship and goodwill, were portrayed in colors so vivid and language so terse, that admiration and surprise would have kept us silent had not shame and humiliation done so" (p. 23).

12. Lakota people believe their tribe came from the Black Hills, when a Lakota man was instructed to follow a buffalo out of the hills onto the prairie.

13. My main source for events depicted here is James Welch's *Killing Custer: The Battle of the Little Bighorn and the Fate of the Plains Indians* (New York: W. W. Norton, 1994), written with Paul Stekler, pp. 74–94. Also see Stanley Vestal, *New Sources of Indian History, 1850–1891: A Miscellany* (Norman: University of Oklahoma Press, 1934) for primary source documents of the period, Indian and non-Indian; and Robert M. Utley, "Grant's Peace Policy, 1869–1876," in *The Indian Frontier of the American West, 1846–1890* (Albuquerque: University of New Mexico Press, 1984), pp. 129–155, for a sense of the government policy of the period.

14. Also see Laura F. Klein and Lillian A. Ackerman, eds., *Women and Power in Native North America* (Norman: University of Oklahoma Press, 1995).

15. National Archives, ratified treaty no. 287, RG 75, T–494, roll 5, p. 314; as quoted in Lee Miller, ed., *From the Heart: Voices of the American Indian* (New York: Vintage Books, 1995), p. 201.

16. Despite the gesture toward collective identities, Taylor actually followed a model of individualist identity.

17. Taylor mentions the contribution of Fanon to the discussion at hand but misses an excellent opportunity to deepen his own argument with the real-life consequences of the legacy of colonial expression.

18. Another of Deloria's books from that period insists on turning the mirror around: *We Talk, You Listen: New Tribes, New Turf* (New York: Macmillan, 1970). Over a decade later, Fred Big Jim played on Deloria's title for his text on Indian education, *We Talk, You Yawn.*

19. DuBois writes: "[T]he Negro is a sort of seventh son, born with a veil, and gifted with second-sight in this American world—a world which yields him no true self-consciousness, but only lets him see himself through the revelation of the other world. It is a peculiar sensation, this double consciousness, this sense of always looking at one's self through the eyes of others, of measuring one's soul by the tape of a world that looks on in amused contempt and pity." For some reason, Taylor stays away from discussing in any depth issues that relate to nonwhite ethnic minorities—American Indians, African and African American blacks, and so on—in favor of discussing the Quebecois.

20. Long before DuBois or Apess, Samson Occum (a Mohegan Indian who became a Methodist minister) spoke of Indians as despised by Christians, in his *A Sermon Preached at the Execution of Moses Paul* (Bennington: William Watson, 1772).

21. My purpose here is something other than tracing the fact of misrecognition of Native people in Western thought. I recommend Robert Berkhofer, Jr.'s *The White Man's Indian* as an introductory text. In this book, Berkhofer connects particular imagery of Indians to particular historical and political occurrences and traces a pattern of misrecognition over time.

22. I am making Taylor stand synecdochically for a particular whole, although I fully am aware that his position is his own.

23. Taylor all but ignores non-Western thinkers as he traces the trajectory of thought through Western philosophers such as Rousseau, Hegel, Kant, and the like.

24. The implication is that a level playing field exists, when in fact, survival may be at stake for some, whereas for others the discussion is at the level of rhetoric.

25. The Lumbee tribe resides in North Carolina.

REFERENCES

Abrams, M. H. (1971 [1953]). *The Mirror and the Lamp: Romantic Theory and the Critical Tradition.* Cambridge: Oxford University Press.

Acherran, L. A., eds. (1995). *Women and Power in Native North America.* Norman: University of Oklahoma Press.

Alcoff, L. (1996). *Real Knowing: New Versions of the Coherence Theory.* Ithaca, NY: Cornell University Press.

Bastien, J. W. (1985). Qollahuaya—Andean Body Concepts: A Topographical-Hydraulic Model of Physiology. *American Anthropologist* 87, pp. 595–611.

Berkhofer, R., Jr. (1978). *The White Man's Indian.* New York: Vintage Books.

Beuchel, E., Rev. (1970). *A Dictionary of the Teton Dakota Sioux Language.* Vermillion: University of South Dakota.

Calloway, C. G. (1996). *Our Hearts Fell to the Ground: Plains Indians Views of How the West Was Lost.* Boston: Bedford Books of St. Martin's Press.

Carr, H. (1996). *Inventing the American Primitive: Politics, Gender and the Representation of Native American Literary Traditions.* New York: New York University Press.

Cash, J. H., and Hoover, H. T. (1995 [1971]). *To Be An Indian: An Oral History.* St. Paul: Minnesota Historical Society.

DeLoria, V., Jr. (1969). *Custer Died for Your Sins: An Indian Manifesto.* New York: Macmillan.

_____. (1970). *We Talk, You Listen: New Tribes, New Turf.* New York: Macmillan.

DuBois, W.E.B. (1907). *The Souls of Black Folk: Essays and Sketches.* Chicago: A. C. McClurg.

Evers, L. (1983). "Cycles of Appreciation." Pp. 23–31 in Allen, P.G., ed., *Studies in American Indian Literature: Critical Essays and Course Designs.* New York: Modern Language Association.

Fairclough, N. (1989). *Language and Power.* London and New York: Longman.

Gill, S. (1982). "Into the Forest Dimly: An Introduction." In *Beyond "The Primitive": The Religions of Nonliterate Peoples.* Englewood Cliffs, NJ: Prentice-Hall.

Grosmith, E. S. (1981). *Lakota of the Rosebud: A Contemporary Ethnography.* Chicago: Holt, Rinehart, and Winston.

Jackson, M. (1989). *Paths Toward a Clearing: Radical Empiricism and Ethnographic Inquiry.* Bloomington: Indiana University Press.

Jaime, M. A., ed. (1992). *The State of Native America: Genocide, Colonialism, and Resistance.* Boston: South End Press.

Jury, C. J. (1961). *Memories, Dreams, Reflections.* New York: Vintage Books.

Klein, L. F., and Ackerman, L. A., eds. (1995). *Women and Power in Native North America.* Norman: University of Oklahoma Press.

Kroeber, A. L. (1978). "Sign Language Inquiry." In Umiker-Sebeoh, D. J., and Sebeok, T. A., eds. *Aboriginal Sign Languages of the Americas and Australia,* vol. 2. New York and London: Plenum Press.

Littleton, L. S. (1985 [1926]). "Lucien Levy-Bruhl and the Concept of Cognitive Relativity." In Levy-Bruhl, L., *How Natives Think.* Princeton: Princeton University Press.

Markmann, C. L., trans. (1967). *Black Skin, White Masks.* New York: Grove Press.

Miller, J. (1980). "The Matter of the (Thoughtful) Heart: Centrality, Focality, or Overlap." *Journal of Anthropological Research* 36, p. 339.

Miller, L. (1995). *From the Heart: Voices of the American Indian.* New York: Vintage Books.

Murray, D. (1991). *Forked Tongues: Speech, Writing and Representation in North American Indian Texts.* Bloomington: Indiana University Press.

Occum, S. (1772). *A Sermon Preached at the Execution of Moses Paul.* Bennington, VT: William Watson.

Rosaldo, R. (1989). *Culture and Truth: The Remaking of Social Analysis.* Boston: Beacon Press.

Rothenberg, J. (1985 [1969]) *Technicians of the Sacred: A Range of Poetries from Africa, America, Asia, Europe, and Oceania.* Berkeley: University of California Press.

Sheets-Johnstone, M. (1992). *Giving the Body Its Due.* Albany, NY: State University of New York Press.

Smith, P. C., and Warrior, R. (1995). *Like a Hurricane: The Indian Movement from Alcatraz to Wounded Knee.* New York: New Press.

Taylor, C. (1994). *Multiculturalism and "The Politics of Recognition."* Princeton: Princeton University Press.

Trexler, R. C. (1995). *Sex and Conquest: Gendered Violence, Political Order, and the European Conquest of the Americas.* Ithaca, NY: Cornell University Press.

United States v. Sioux Nation of Indians . . . et al. No. 79–639 (1980, June 30), p. 423.

Utley, R. M. (1984). "Grant's Peace Policy, 1869–1876." Pp. 120–155 in *The Indian Frontier of the American West, 1846–1890.* Albuquerque: University of New Mexico Press.

Vestal, S. (1936). *New Sources of Indian History, 1851–1891: A Miscellany.* Norman: University of Oklahoma Press.

Vizenor, G. (1994). *Manifest Manners: Past Indian Warriors of Survivance.* Hanover, CT: Wesleyan University Press.

Welch, J. (1994). *Willing Custer: The Battle of the Little Bighorn and the Fate of the Plains Indians.* New York: W. W. Norton.

White, H. (1987). *The Context of the Form: Narrative Discourse and Historical Representation.* Baltimore: Johns Hopkins University Press.

Williams, R. A. (1990). *The American Indian in Western Legal Thought: The Discourses of Conquest.* New York: Oxford University Press.

eleven

Virtual Defense:
Cyberspace Counterattack
Against White Supremacy

COLIN A. BECKLES

Race War in Cyberspace

That the Internet is and will continue to be a legitimate source of social power is accepted across a wide variety of circles. From the hallowed halls of the White House to the plethora of Internet books, Utopian descriptions of the Internet as "color-blind" and as a "virtual community" abound as the Internet continues to be championed across a variety of media.

By the same token, a few "critical" assessments of Internet communications are beginning to surface as well. The majority have focused on the dissemination of pornographic material. Others have centered on the polarization between the "information elite" and those without access to the Internet. This divide conspicuously follows along racial lines. Research conducted in 1995 by the RAND Corporation bears witness to this fact:

> An information elite still exists, made up of those with access to and knowledge about computers, e-mail . . . and computer networks. Specifically, computer access and use is positively related to higher levels of education and income. Also, race is independently related to computer and network access—whites being significantly more likely to have access to both than blacks and Hispanics. Apparently, if current trends continue without intervention, access to electronic information and communications technologies (and associated benefits) will be skewed in favor of traditionally advantaged groups. (RAND, 1995, p. xiv)

Compounding this problem of racial polarization of the Internet is that within this privileged group there exists a historically violent, white racist sector. A routine "surf" across the Internet or a glance at various newspapers will reveal that white racist groups such as the KKK and Skinheads have seized the electronic network as their latest propaganda tool. The goal seems clear: a twenty-first century, state-of-the-art, "cyber race war" complete with calls for verbal and physical aggression and violence against African Americans, Latinos, Asian Americans, and Native Americans.[1] On the road to accomplishing their "virtual" and "real-life" quest—"reestablishment" of their supreme position within the global racial order—these groups have taken mastery of the Internet as a primary strategy. Racist and violent information is archived and disseminated from dazzling white-supremacist home-pages and FTP sites. Discussion groups are monitored for potential recruits as well as for e-mail attacks and sabotage. White supremacy rallies and militant training camps are organized via e-mail, and new Internet links are continually being established with other racist individuals and organizations across the United States, Canada, Europe, and South America. See for yourself, if you haven't already: Skinhead U.S.A. (http://web2. airmail.net/bootboy/main.htm.); Portuguese Skinhead Page (http://www. geocities.com/capitolHill/1773/); Knights of the Ku Klux Klan (http:// www.geocities.com/capitolHill/1773/); Carolinian Lords of the Caucasus— CLOC (http://www.io.com/~wlp/aryan-page/cloc/); Stormfront (http:// 204.282.176.4/stormfront/); and Resistance Records (http://www.resistance. com). The following excerpts from Milton Kleim's "On Tactics and Strategy for Usenet" exemplify the militaristic role slated for the Internet:

> USENET offers enormous opportunity for the Aryan Resistance to disseminate our message to the unaware and the ignorant. . . . NOW is the time to grasp the WEAPON which is the Net, and wield it skillfully and wisely while you may still do so freely. . . . Furthermore, when a newbie posts a message sympathetic to us, CONTACT THEM IMMEDIATELY! Welcome them to the group, and offer them information about our activities. . . . I built my personal mailing list of over 80 activists largely through this means. As the Net grows, more and more people sympathetic to our Cause will journey onto it, and we need to greet them. . . . Don't use unnecessary "overkill"—if a "grenade" will do the job, DON'T use a "nuclear weapon." Watch for material that would be of use to us, such as news of enemy mailing lists or FTP and WWW sites. Relay such information to your comrades.(Kleim, 1995)

While Kleim and others have argued against white supremacists' advocating explicit violence in public forums such as the Internet, Kleim's militaristic language suggests otherwise. Moreover, his Internet writings are linked to white supremacist pages such as the Canadian page CNG (http:// www.io.com/~wlp/aryan-page/cloc/). CNG and other white supremacist factions' public advocacy of violence against minorities and/or "immigrants" is clear: "We are a white nationalist organization. . . . Our soldiers are here to KILL."

But anyone who picks up a newspaper, watches the news on television, or listens to the radio has undoubtedly heard about the genesis of "hate-net," at least to some extent. Although the phenomenon has been discussed in some detail in the media, the manner in which activist groups have utilized the Internet in order to "defend" and "empower" minority groups on the Internet and in "real life" has not been fully investigated and exposed. Thus the question remains, how is the Internet being utilized to combat white supremacy? In this chapter I offer an initial response to this question.

Defeating White Supremacy: Internet Strategies

A variety of tactics have been used by antiracists on the Net to directly halt racist attacks on minorities. While many strategies exist, we restrict our review to the following: the dissemination of antiracist education information, the monitoring and censoring of white supremacists, the organization of antiracist protests in the real world, and the formation of networks.

Cyber-Arsenals: Knowledge as Power for the Cyber-Warrior

Much of the ideology spouted by white supremacists on the Internet focuses on the "dehumanization" of other races and the "superhumanization" of whites. Indeed, various white supremacy themes suggest that the white race is the only positive contributor to world civilizations, that whites are chosen people of God, and that the white race is under siege by people of color via means ranging from affirmative action policies to miscegenation and immigration. Given the above, minority group activists have come to understand how the Internet is being used as an assault on their communities as well as how it can be used for empowerment. Racial minorities have sought to rehumanize themselves in this medium. Apparently functioning on the assumption that "knowledge is power," people of color have been using the Internet to educate themselves and others about their "true" histories by compiling their own information databases on line. With this virtual knowledge/power base as a resource, Internet users will be able to defend themselves and their communities by countering the racist information and representations disseminated by white supremacists. We therefore witness that worldwide, people of color and other racial minority activists are establishing and/or controlling their own "cyber- arsenals": home pages, FTP sites, and bulletin boards wherein people of color archive information about their history and culture:

Hook up to World Wide Web "Yellow Pages" like *Yahoo* or the *Universal Black Pages* and you'll find hundreds of home pages exploring the history and culture of the African diaspora. The Library of Congress African-American Mosaic, Birmingham Civil Rights Institute, Vibe (magazine) Online, AfriNET,

MelaNet, Griot Online, the Nation of Islam and NetNoir Online are just a few of the home pages where people of all races go to chat about black culture. African-Americans also often go to non–race-specific parts of the Web to get information about mainstream society and culture (Battle, 1996).

But African Americans are not unique in pursuing this activity. Indeed, cyber-arsenals also exist for people of Chicano/Latino descent (CLNet [http://latino.sscnet.ucla.edu]), Asian descent (Asian Community Online Network [http://www.igc.apc.org/acon/]), and indigenous descent (NativeWeb [http://web.maxwell.syr.edu/nativeweb]). Moreover, complementing these race-specific sites are the growing number of multicultural antiracist sites such as the Anti-Racism Resource Homepage (http://darwing.uoregon.edu/~dennisw/race.html). These sites tend to overlap with the educational empowerment goals of the race-specific sites, providing educational, cultural, business, legal, social, and health information for various racial groups.

Empowered with historical and demographic information obtained from the various cyber-arsenals, the antiracist cyber-warrior is now ready to challenge the white supremacist at the "front lines." A common strategy employed is what I term "virtual-verbal combat." This occurs via e-mail (electronic mail) directly to the white supremacist's e-mail address or by going through mailing lists or discussion groups frequented by white supremacists: alt.politics.whitepower or alt.politics.white nationalism. In addition to the attacking strategy, the information obtained via cyber-arsenal can be used for defensive purposes: to protect his/her discussion groups (e.g., soc.culture.-mexican.american, soc.culture.native.american, and so on) from the occasional "invasion" by white supremacist guerrillas. These frontline battles with white supremacists often become very aggressive. Indeed, some unmoderated interactions in newsgroups and chat rooms have been likened to saloon brawls in the "wild West."

Cyber-Hate Trackers: Virtual Reconnaissance

Guiding the antiracist cyber-warrior are a growing number of virtual reconnaissance agents, or "cyber-hate trackers." Their mission is to locate and monitor the growing number of home pages, mailing lists, bulletin boards, and FTP sites controlled by white supremacists. Thus we see the establishment of home pages such as "The Hate Page of the Week" (http://owlnet.rice.edu/~efx/hpotw.html/), "Nazism Exposed" (http://www.cs.uit.no/~paalde/ NazismExp), "Hate Groups in Cyber Space" (http://fas.sfu.ca/O/comm/c-mass/ issue2/), and "Net Hate" (http://vir.com/shalom/hatred1.html/). Pages often linked to white supremacist groups are also monitored, leading to the establishment of pages such as the "Militia Watchdog" (http://www.greyware.com/authors/

pitman). The founder of the "Hate Page of the Week" explained how he was moved to take action by his encounter with "cyber-hate":

"Racism and anti-Semitism remain great threats to our democracy. We cannot allow ourselves to ignore the hatred and intolerance," said Frank Xavier Placencia, a political science student at Rice University, who set up his own Net home page, *The Hate Page of the Week*. The home page is designed to draw public attention to the growth of hate groups in cyberspace, he said. "There were pages out there that so shocked and angered me that I wanted the whole world to see" (Sheppard, 1995).

In addition to information on the virtual whereabouts of white supremacists, information is also gathered on specifics of the racists' attacks as well, exposing the assailants. Virtual Varrio is a home page that does just this, specifically focusing on racist attacks against Latinos. Virtual Varrio has highlighted the Internet attacks on immigrants disseminated by "BajaRat"— a notorious Internet advocate of racist violence:

This scumbag maintains an anti-immigrant web site called alternatively the "Wetback Clearing-out House" and "http://www.hooked.net/users/junior1/mojado/madness." Quotes include: "Mojado Madness! The Infestation of the United States"; "Criminal Mojados Infesting U.S."; "Wetbacks Sucking Medi-Cal Coffers Dry!"; "this onslaught of third world parasites"; and "It's time to round up these animals and give them the boot." "BajaRat" makes very frequent anonymous racist postings to soc.culture.mexican.american and other newsgroups. A sampling: "Maybe the [Border Patrol] ought to just shoot these cockroaches on sight. . . . Building a piranha-stuffed moat from Imperial Beach to Brownsville with triple electric fences on either side would be better, though. . . . I say do whatever is necessary to stop the vermin." To a Chicana, "That pretty much affirms that you could well be in possession of a typical TJ gang-banger mentality, you hare-brained dingbat cunt. . . . Now FOAD, you incompetent bitch."

In addition to this individual white supremacist, members of the white supremacist group Carolinian Lords of the Caucasus (CLOC) have been notorious for attacking unsuspecting "Net civilians."

As can be expected from the above, whether it be during virtual discursive combat or just from stumbling across a white supremacist home page, casualties run high. Fortunately, counteracting the exposure given to racism by the Internet are the growing numbers of cyber-spaces wherein information can be collected about the incidents of racist violence occurring on the Net. Sites such as CyberWatch have been created that include a request to complete a survey of racism as it occurs on the Internet. Moreover, they provide a hotline to document particular racist incidents:

Welcome to the Simon Wiesenthal Center's CyberWatch Hotline.

Please use the form below to report any incidents of anti-Semitism, racism, or other forms of bigotry that you have experienced.
Description of incident:
Your name:
E-mail address:
Address:
City: State:
Zip/Postal: Country:
May we contact you via e-mail about this incident?
All reports are kept strictly confidential.
webmaster@wiesenthal.com

Using information gathered in this way, databases on Internet racism can be developed and used against the offenders.

In summation, the strategies described here have involved the development of weapons, surveillance, and dealing with casualties of the cyber race war. However, these strategies are focused on dealing with the individual white supremacist cyber-soldier. Other strategies focus on the destruction of cyber arsenals, supply routes, command centers, and/or "commanders" of the white supremacists. We turn now to these strategies.

Cyber-Site Censors

A variety of "censorship" methods have been advocated and/or employed to halt the spread of white supremacist discourse over the Internet. One common strategy is to terminate the operations of a white supremacist web site altogether. Activists identify sites from which white supremacist information is being disseminated and overload it with e-mail messages. This e-mail bombardment effectively causes a shutdown in site operations, as the site administrators are unable to handle the large volume of messages. The outflow of racist messages is stopped temporarily, or sometimes permanently (Clough, 1996).

Another more direct form of censorship, which is also more controversial, is to target servers that provide racists with Internet access—that is, Internet providers. The goal is to force providers not to host sites that disseminate white supremacist messages. Private groups, such as the Simon Wiesenthal Center in Los Angeles, in particular, have asked that providers adopt a code of ethics for Internet users:

> The Simon Wiesenthal Center of Los Angeles has asked Internet access providers to adopt a "code of ethics" that would prevent extremists from publishing their ideas on line. Internet providers that adopt the code would refuse service to individuals or groups that "promote violence and mayhem, denigrate and threaten minorities and women and promote homophobia." (Bray, 1996)

In addition to advocating that providers adopt such "self-regulation" strategies, various groups have asked the government to serve as an outside regulator. Government bodies have been asked to intervene and censor cyber-hate by taking legal action. European governments and commissions in particular are utilizing their powers to establish rules and regulations banning Internet communication that "incites" racial hatred and violence. Commissions have been established, such as the Consultative Commission on Racism and Xenophobia (CRAX), whose reported task is to "investigate and, using legal means, stamp out the current wave of racism on the Internet" . . . and to "take all needed measures to prevent the Internet from becoming a vehicle for the incitement of racist hatred." Internet providers have since been brought up on legal charges for hosting white supremacists. Because of such legal pressure, one of Germany's biggest providers, Webcom, cut off access to Ernst Zundel, a German neo-Nazi based in Canada. U.S.-based Internet providers such as Compuserve and America Online also have been targeted by German prosecutors:[2]

> America Online, Inc. said Friday that it is part of a broadening probe by German prosecutors into hate material on the Internet, joining CompuServe, Inc. and a European online service. The company said it may face charges in Germany for permitting German citizens to access neo-Nazi and anti-Semitic material on the global computer network. (*Los Angeles Times*, February 3, 1996)

The Antiracist Cyber-Structure: A Virtual Web of Resistance

In the cyber-war against white supremacy, many antiracist cyber-warriors have realized the value of increasing the scope of their Internet utilization by developing on-line networks. Thus, we witness the genesis of entities such as the Anti–Asian Violence Network [AAVN] (http://vc.apnet.org/~ebihara/aavn/html), which states its purpose as "to apply the Internet to further understand the issues of racial and ethnic violence, and to search for solutions." These race-specific networks have developed alongside multiracial networks. Once they are linked, the information they disseminate reaches local, national, and international points of contact. This information dissemination occurs in a variety of ways. First, Internet users from around the world can link up with their network pages by typing in the specific site address. Second, organizations such as the Anti-Racist Action group (http://www.infinet.com/~leep.ara.html) have established multiple sites in Canada and the United States, enabling them to function as an internal international network, relaying information from one ARA site to another. Third, groups such as the Anti-Racist Center in Holland have links from their sites to other antiracist sites cross-nationally. Fourth, in addition to providing information links in the network, providers can give or rent space specifically to those who want to create antiracist home pages and thereby increase the cyber-structural base. Similarly, providers such as the Institute for Global

Communications (IGC) rent low-cost space to organizations supporting "social justice" concerns such as fighting environmental racism.

As new links continue to be created to other Internet sites involved in the struggle against white supremacy, what becomes manifest is the existence of a multidimensional, growing, antiracist "cyber-structure" that spans the United States, Canada, and Europe, and reaches far beyond. The following excerpts from the General Anti-Racism Resource page (http://darwing.uoregon.edu/~dennisw/race.html) provide a clue to the extent of this antiracist cyber-structure.

Antiracist Organizations

1. The Black, Hispanic, and Anti-Racist Socialists' Home Page, administered by the Democratic Socialists of America, featuring Cornel West.
2. AFRANet, the Anti-Fascist and Anti-Racist Network, is a publisher of information, news, and forthcoming events that relate to the struggle against racism and fascism.
3. The National Rainbow Coalition is a multiracial, multi-issue national organization, founded by Reverend Jesse L. Jackson. Our mission is to move our nation and the world toward social, racial, and economic justice.

Pages with Antiracist Information

1. C.A.R.E., Computer Users Against Racist Expressions, fight against racism on the net. You can download their logo to add to your own page, showing that you oppose net racism.
2. Cyberwatch at the Wiesenthal Center is dedicated to tracking hate groups and hate speech on the Web and elsewhere. They will send you information on fighting racism in your community.
3. The Militia Watchdog by Mark Pitcavage.
4. The Nazism Exposed Home Page, devoted to fighting the Nazi Menace.
5. "Fighting Racism: A Key Struggle" tells how fighting racism is central to fighting capitalism.
6. *The Osgoode Web Press's Report on Systemic Racism,* a long and detailed in-depth study, published on the WWW by Osgoode Hall Law School.

Antiracist International Links

1. EFFECT, home page for environmental and developmental issues, against racism and violence, in Swedish. An English version is in the works.

2. The Anti-British National Party Page, administered by the Youth Against Racism in Europe (YRE).
3. The International Federation of Liberal and Radical Youth has some information on their fight against racism, xenophobia, anti-Semitism, and intolerance.

Cyber-Organizing: From Virtual to "Real-Life" Battlefields

Finally, in the battle against white supremacy, it must be stated that the scope of this network reaches beyond the virtual world. Indeed, the Internet has been utilized specifically to organize and recruit for "real-life" action against specific white supremacist groups and individuals. Cyber-warriors document and monitor on-line and real world occurrences of white racism. Antiracist home pages and e-mail lists are then used to inform other activists about the planned racist activity. Counterdemonstrations and rallies are planned, and net surfers are recruited to participate in the counterdemonstrations at upcoming racist rallies. The group Anti-Racist Action (ARA) in particular seems to favor this tactic. ARA members monitor white supremacist home pages and mailing lists in order to find out where the next white supremacist rally, march, or conference is to be held. This information is then posted on the ARA home pages in the United States, Canada, and Europe. All who can participate in the antiracist counterdemonstrations are encouraged to do so. The results of the "real-life" battle with groups such as the Klan, including pictures, are then posted on-line:

A faction of the Ku Klux Klan from Michigan, led by David Newman, obtained a permit to have a rally January 6th at the State House in Columbus, Ohio, "to protest against the Martin Luther King holiday." The ARA-Net and a coalition of other groups organized a counterdemonstration. As they have at two other previous Columbus rallies, the police had a massive presence, including a fenced-in pen to keep hundreds of protesters away from the dozen or so Klan members. The Klan was effectively shouted down for an hour, and the few who actually came to hear them were chased out. One took a beating, for which a man was later charged with felonious assault. Another protester was arrested for allegedly "assaulting a police horse" as the police cavalry attempted to disperse a large group that had gathered to confront the exiting KKK party. About 100 ARA-Net members from around the country held a meeting after the rally to discuss tactics and organizational structure. There was a tense debate over issues such as whether or not to enter "the cage" set up by the police and what method should be used to establish representation on an ARA-Net steering committee. The group discussion was cut short, but many members continued meeting at various social gatherings. All in all, it was a successful action against the Klan and a valuable exchange of ideas and positions in what will surely be an ongoing dialogue between ARA-Net members. For further info, or to get on the ARA News mailing list, write: ARA, PO BOX 82097, Columbus, Ohio 43202, or e-mail the address at the bottom of this page (http://www.infinet.com/ ~leep/rally.html). (1996)

Similarly, other cyber-warriors have developed Internet pages to keep other forms of systemic, institutionalized violence against people of color from occurring in the real world. Thus, we see the development of the "Free Mumia Abu-Jammal" (http://www.xs4all.nl/ ~tank/spg-l/mummia002.htm) home page and mailing lists used to raise funds, circulate petitions for electronic signature, and initiate e-mail letter-writing campaigns for the following: to end racist police brutality, to abolish the death penalty, and to release political prisoners.

These same strategies have been used to create real-world documents to solidify the fight against white supremacy. For example, AFRANet's home page (http://www.gn.apc.org/afranet/arc/arc.html/) provides space to examine their Anti-Racist Charter. This charter was conceived during England's 1995 National Assembly Against Racism. At that time, participants decided that in order to turn the tide against racism spreading across Europe, what was needed was "an Anti-Racist Charter to lay the foundations for the broad unity of the anti-racist struggle into the next millennium." Utilizing the Internet, antiracist activists worldwide can take their struggle into the "real world" by directly signing the charter on-line:

> I/we would like to call for an Anti-Racist Charter for the new millennium and would like to become a founder signatory to the Charter.
> I enclose £163 . . . to sponsor the Charter and become a founder signatory.
> Name/organization:
> Address:
> Tel.:
> As a founder signatory of the Charter you will receive information about the activities to further the objectives of the Charter. . . .
> Please make cheques payable to National Assembly Against Racism. Put an end to anti-immigration legislation; and an end to affirmative action repeal.

Forming antiracist coalitions on-line for real-world events is not an easy process. The further extension of the antiracist cyber network requires that participants understand that not all linked sites must be sponsored by groups whose primary purpose is fighting white supremacy or the antiracist struggle in general. Many antiracists are linked to "progressive" sites such as the ACLU home page; the U.S.-based Black, Hispanic, and Anti-Racist Socialist Page (http://ccmemac4.bsd.uchicago.edu/ DSArace/RaceComm), which is connected to the Democratic Socialists of America; and the England-based AFRANet (http://www.gn.apc.org/afranet/) which is associated with various groups, including the Campaign Against Racism and Fascism. Undoubtedly, the political histories of these real-world groups may influence the strategies adopted to combat racism on the Internet as well as the virtual and real-world networking that occurs.

However, it seems that because some cyber sites are dedicated to one specific issue, such as racist violence in the police force, the Internet can serve not only as a place to build networks between apparently "strange bedfellows" but also as a space to advertise the successes of these all too often difficult virtual and real-life attempts at coalition building. The excerpt below is from a mailing list operated by "NattyReb"(nattyreb@popd.1x.webcom.com) of the "African Frontline Network"(http://www.webcom.com.nattyreb), demonstrating the extent and the dimensionality of Internet networking in the fight against racism in general and white supremacy in particular:

You are invited to attend the:
MARCH AGAINST POLICE BRUTALITY
For Community Control of the Police and
Justice for Johnny Gammage
Featuring Mrs. Gammage and City Councillor Sala Udin
***
Saturday, June 29
11:00 A.M.
Meet at Freedom Corner in the Hill District
(Corner of Centre & Crawford, above the Civic Arena)
March to City Hall Downtown
Pittsburgh, PA

   DIRECTIONS: From Oakland, Squirrel Hill or Shadyside, take any 61 or 71 bus to Crawford & Fifth. From there you can walk up the hill to Centre or take the 84 up. By car, drive down Fifth Ave. to Crawford, take a right and drive up the hill to Centre.
   ENDORSED BY OVER 30 GROUPS: The Campus Coalition for Peace and Justice, NAACP, Million Man March Local Organizing Committee, ACLU, Coalition of African-Americans for Justice, Alliance for Progressive Action, Rainbow Coalition of Western PA, Merton Center, Campaign for a New Tomorrow, State Rep. Bill Robinson, Metropolitan Coalition of African-American Clergy, National Coalition on Police Accountability, Western PA Committee to Free Mumia Abu-Jammal, United Electrical Workers, Pittsburgh Labor Action Network on the Americas, International Socialist Organization, Buffalo Concerned Citizens Against Police Abuse, Citizens Coalition for Justice, Young Socialists, Libertarian Party of Pittsburgh, Malcolm X Holiday Commission, Nation of Islam, Unitarian Universalists for a Just Economic Community, Socialist Workers Party, the Silver Lake Association, Urban League, Coalition to Counter Hate Groups, Black Women's Political Crusade,

Unity Pittsburgh, Center for Campus Organizing of Cambridge, Mass., Solidarity National Organization, Citizens Against a Police State.

For more info: Call (412) 363–4410, e-mail pshell@cmu.edu or

see the web page http://www.cs.cmu.edu/~pshell/gammage/flyer.html.

Summary Comments

Following is a list of the methods that activists have used to fight white supremacy on the Internet:

1. Establishing information archives and disseminating information that represents the history of racial minorities in a nonracist fashion. The information is then used to challenge the assertions of white supremacists.
2. Monitoring and documenting the activities and incidence of white supremacism
3. Using e-mail and legal strategies to censor the activities of white supremacists on the Internet
4. Increasing the network of anti–white supremacist activism by establishing linkages and/or facilitating the creation of new sites and mailing lists. Thus, a local, national, and international cyber-structure against white supremacy is actively being spun across the Internet.
5. Planning, recruiting, and advertising "virtual" and "real-life" antiracist conferences, events, and rallies via the Internet.[3]

At this point, a comment about the effectiveness of the above strategies seems appropriate. First, although the monitoring of e-mail and home pages of white supremacists is a necessary and useful task, it seems at best a limited effort. This is due primarily to the vastness of the Internet, currently estimated at more than 7 million hosts and 35 million users worldwide.

Second, although using the Net to monitor public demonstrations of white supremacy is also necessary, it seems that the more surreptitious activities may be missed. In other words, in the cyber-war a distinction must be made between forces monitoring "aboveground" operations and forces devoted to monitoring "underground" maneuvers. Many of the white supremacists are utilizing the Internet for recruitment as well as propaganda. Having become aware of surveillance by antiracist and government forces, their "underground wing" could well be using the Internet under the cloak of secrecy or anonymity. This can be done with the use of "countersurveillance" devices such as PGP—an encoding device—or "remailers"—another type of anonymity device. Thus, white supremacists can send e-mail messages to one another—to strategize, organize, and execute their activities—with little fear of detection by the common antiracist activist. Moreover, racist events planned publicly on-line might in fact be mere decoys, diverting antiracists' attention and energy away from more primary and perhaps more violent activities.

Censorship laws, such as that against the incitement to racial riot, are also of limited effectiveness in legally stopping the dissemination of racist material over the Internet. In an on-line article (http://www.ndirect.co.uk/ ~pjepson/index.html), Jepson discusses some of the problems that occur in the application of most such laws. Most significant for our present discussion is Jepson's point that many of these laws have only "national" application. Thus, what is considered "incitement to racial riot" in Germany may not apply in the United States. White supremacists easily can circumvent such a law by relocating their Internet sites to a provider outside Germany. This is what happened in the case of Ernst Zundel. Mirror sites were developed by supporters in other countries, allowing Zundel's material to be disseminated from outside his own national boundaries. Obviously, Europe has taken the right step in establishing commissions such as CRAX, made up of European Union members, to address this problem. Jepson suggests that instead of each individual country or regional union proposing its own set of antiracist laws, the United Nations should be approached so that uniform, "worldwide action" could be taken. However, given the uneven cross-national implementation of U.N. resolutions in the past on other issues of global concern, Jepson's suggested solution may also be of limited effectiveness.

Third, while many minority activists are well connected electronically, this does not mean that they follow an identical agenda or philosophy. This problem presents itself both at the level of the individual activist and that of the political organization. At the level of the individual antiracist activist, it seems that some of these so-called antiracist pages are set up by individuals whose skill is computers, not politics, and definitely not racial politics. Often it appears that their skill in creating "snappy" home pages outweighs careful, critical analysis. For example, The "Hate Page of the Week" includes a link to "the Black Panther coloring book" as an example of a racist Internet site. Excerpted and displayed on that page is a picture of a black teenage male with a gun held to a white policeman's head. The "Hate Page of the Week" has labeled this illustration racist and violent, without any discussion of why the illustration was chosen for inclusion. One can guess the web page creator's reasons: Liberals, especially whites, tend to have an immediately negative reaction to violence of any kind being directed against whites, especially white police officers. Apparently the web staff failed to adequately investigate why the Black Panthers utilized "counter-images" such as these during the 1960s. This was a time when African American communities were under siege daily by local, state, and national law enforcement agencies (this is not to say that they are not at present). Given the militarization of urban black communities, the call for armed "self-defense" against white police officers and other state agents of repression seemed appropriate to many blacks.

Finally, many of the pages established to fight white supremacy are linked in various ways to the extreme left. It is not surprising that many of their pages also call for action against major corporations. Given the U.S. government's history of repression against groups that were both antiracist and anticapitalist, one should not be surprised if the antiracist web pages come under attack by government forces—via surveillance or other means—because of their links to anticapitalist forces. Corn (1996) has asserted that the Department of Defense regularly monitors the Net and pays particular attention to "cyber-smart lefties."

NOTES

1. To aid my investigation into the cyber race war, I reviewed various newspapers, journal articles, and books pertaining to the racial struggle on the Internet. I also made electronic "visits" to various home pages, discussion lists, and electronically archived files originating in the United States, Canada, and Europe during the previous six months.

2. According to Brown in the *Star Tribune*, February 5, 1996: "More than a million Germans are now able to access these through Internet services. Last month Deutsche Telekom, the largest provider of Internet services in Germany, cut off all access to the computers of Web Communications, the company that rents space to Zundel. Since this is a large and respectable commercial concern, this also meant that the Deutsche Telekom subscribers lost access to another 1,500 web sites."

3. *Future Research*

Future research will entail the continued sampling of theoretically relevant sites in order to further develop, modify, and verify the above activities. This undertaking will be supplemented with the following activities: (a) content analyses of data obtained from Internet sites as well as from e-mail lists; (b) interview of Internet activists; and (c) ethnographic inquiry at Internet-generated antiracist events.

Future theoretical perspectives will focus on the following: (a) further analysis of the relationship between race-specific sites and multiracial sites; (b) assessment of the factors behind the expansion/contraction of the international network; and (c) assessment of the effectiveness of antiracist activity as it occurs via the Internet. Finally, I will explore the ways in which historical relationships between "real-world" political organizations affect the contours of the Internet struggle against racism.

REFERENCES

Barney, D. (1996). "White Separatists Leap on the 'Net." *Network World*. (January 8). News Section. P. 1.

Beckles, C. (1996). "Cyber-Sites: Internet Utilization by Racist and Anti-Racist Organizations." Paper presented at the annual conference of the Association of Black Sociologists, August 14–17, 1996, in Washington, D.C..

Besser, H. (1995). "From Internet to Information Superhighway." Pp. 59–70 in Brook, J., and Boal, I., eds., *Resisting the Virtual Life: The Culture and Politics of Information*. San Francisco: City Light Books.

Bray, H. (1996). "A Mixed Reception: Ethics Code Seeks to Ban Extremist Ideas from Internet." *The Boston Globe*. (January 11). Economy Section, p. 56.

Brook, J., and Boale, I. (1995). *Resisting the Virtual Life: The Culture and Politics of Information*. San Francisco: City Light Books.

Brown, T. (1995). Tony Brown Discusses "Black Lies, White Lies." The Charlie Rose Show. Transcript no. 1536–3. WNET Educational Broadcasting Company. Journal Graphics Transcripts.

Clough, M. (1996). Will Global War Erupt Along Internet? *Commercial Appeal*. (February 18). Viewpoint Section, p. 5.

Defife, S. (1995). "Virtual Communities: Giving Women a Place to Call Home." *Information Access Company Newsletter* 12 (p. 13). Future Systems, Inc.

Dennis, S. (1996). "European Commission Moves to Stamp Out Racism on Internet." *Newsbytes News Network*. Information Access Company.

Drew, J. (1995). "Media Activism and Radical Democracy." Pp. 71–84 in Brook, J., and Boal, I., eds., *Resisting the Virtual Life: The Culture and Politics of Information*. San Francisco: City Light Books.

Emerson, R. (1988). *Contemporary Field Research*. Prospect Heights, IL: Waveland Press.

Gandy, O. (1995). "It's Discrimination Stupid." Pp. 5–48 in Brook, J., and Boal, I., eds., *Resisting the Virtual Life: The Culture and Politics of Information*. San Francisco: City Light Books.

Gore, A. (1995). "Remarks Delivered at the Meeting of the International Telecommunications Union, Buenos Aires (March 21, 1994)." Pp. 59–70 in Brook, J., and Boal, I., eds., *Resisting the Virtual Life: The Culture and Politics of Information*. San Francisco: City Light Books.

Harris, R., and Battle, S. (1995). *The African American Resource Guide to the Internet*. Columbia, MD: On Demand Press.

Jones, V. (1995). "Cyber-diversity: African Diaspora Can Unite on the Net." *Commercial Appeal*. (December 17). Appeal Section, p. 1E.

Kleim, M. (1995). "On Tactics and Strategy for Usenet." Unpublished paper.

Louv, R. (1995). "Personal Decisions Ward Off Virtual Reality." *San Diego Union-Tribune*. (September 6). News Editorial, pp. 1–8.

Mann, B. (1995). *Politics on the Net*. Indianapolis, IN: Que.

Miller, L. "Women and Children First: Gender and the Settling of the Electronic Frontier". Pp. 59–70 in Brook, J., and Boal, I., eds., *Resisting the Virtual Life: The Culture and Politics of Information*. San Francisco: City Light Books.

Pethokoukis, J. (1995). "Will Internet Change Politics?" *Investor's Business Daily*. (January 9). National Issue, p. A1.

Schatzmann, J., and Strauss, A. (1973). *Field Research: Strategies for a Natural Sociology*. Englewood Cliffs, NJ: Prentice-Hall.

Sclove, R. "Making Technology Democratic." Pp. 85–104 in Brook, J., and Boal, I., eds., *Resisting the Virtual Life: The Culture and Politics of Information*. San Francisco: City Light Books.

Sheppard, N. (1995). "Hate Groups Find a Home in Cyberspace: White Nationalists Spread Message, Seek Recruits on the Net." *Austin American-Statesman*. (December 23). News, p. A1.

Shiller, H. "The Global Information Super Highway: Project for an Ungovernable World." Pp. 17–34 in Brook, J., and Boal, I., eds., *Resisting the Virtual Life: The Culture and Politics of Information*. San Francisco: City Light Books.

Strauss, A., and Corbin, J. (1990). *The Basics of Qualitative Research: Grounded Theory Procedures and Techniques*. London: Sage.

Times Wire Service. (1996). "AOL Added to German Probe of Racism on Internet." *Los Angeles Times*. (February 3). Business, p. D2.

Vallely, P. (1996). "Sex on the Net: A Very Modern Morality Tale." *The Independent*. (January 6). Saturday Story, p. 15.

twelve

Race, Ethnicity, and Nationality in the United States: A Comparative, Historical Perspective

PAUL WONG

In his introduction to the 1967 edition of W.E.B. DuBois's classic study *The Philadelphia Negro*, E. Digby Baltzell mentioned that not only had the book been out of print for almost half a century but it was virtually unobtainable even in some of the best research libraries. Baltzell stated: "Even at the University of Pennsylvania, under whose sponsorship the research was undertaken and the book published, although one copy has been preserved in the archives and one on microfilm, the sole copy listed in the catalogue and available for students in the library has been unaccountably missing from the shelves for several years" (Baltzell, 1967).

The Philadelphia Negro was first published in 1899. It was DuBois's view that the "color line" was the most important problem of the twentieth century. If one looks at the twentieth century in terms of the tumultuous race and ethnic relations during those hundred years—within and across national states in the world—one must affirm the validity of DuBois's prediction. Racial and ethnic problems in the United States and other advanced capitalist countries remain unsolved as we approach the end of this century. Furthermore, although many struggles to end colonization and racial oppression in the second half of the twentieth century have resulted in the formation of independent nation-states, racial and ethnic conflicts have continued to emerge in the erstwhile colonies, including a number of socialist countries that were formerly part of the Soviet bloc. It would not be alarmist, therefore, to contend that racial and ethnic issues will continue to be of paramount importance in the United States and in the international arena in the twenty-first century.

It is important, I think, to examine the history of scholarship on race relations and how it has changed over time. From DuBois's classic turn-of-the-century empirical study of Philadelphia to the development of general theories of assimilation and acculturation from the 1930s to the 1960s, the neo-Marxist perspectives in the 1970s and 1980s, and the racial formation perspective in the 1980s and 1990s, the field has experienced several paradigm shifts.

The Assimilation Paradigm

DuBois's book on the Negro community in Philadelphia was the first great empirical study on the Negro in American society. After laying out the plan of the book in chapters I and II, DuBois devoted the next two chapters to a historical analysis of the Negro in Philadelphia from 1638 to 1896. In Chapters V through XVI, he reported on his extensive social survey of various aspects of the life of African Americans in Philadelphia, using a methodology reminiscent of Charles Booth's survey of the poor in nineteenth-century London. DuBois was a meticulous empirical researcher. Theorizing was not a concern in his classic study. Instead, his interest was focused on possible social reforms and legislation that would be beneficial to African Americans. In Chapter XVI, entitled "The Contact of the Races," he dealt specifically with race relations including color prejudice and intermarriage; but he did not postulate any grand theory or hypothesis about the future of race relations except the view that the "color line" would be the major issue of the twentieth century. Also, perhaps because of the fact that *The Philadelphia Negro* focused on a local history and local community, it did not have the influence or impact of studies that address race relations on a national or even broader scale, or studies that emerged from a visible center of academia such as the Chicago school of sociology under the intellectual leadership of Robert E. Park.

From the 1930s to the early 1960s, the dominant paradigm in the field of race relations in the United States was assimilation. One of the most influential theories in the assimilation paradigm was Park's theory of race relations cycle (Park, 1950). Park postulated a natural evolution over time in the relationship between racial/ethnic groups, through the following stages: Contact leads to competition; competition leads to accommodation; and accommodation leads to assimilation. Though Park held that other variables such as customs regulations, immigration restrictions, and racial barriers have to be taken into account in this natural history, he predicted that these variables would not reverse the process, which would culminate in assimilation. In attempting to discover a "natural history," Park assumed that in the relations among different races, there is a cycle of events that tends everywhere to repeat itself (Ringer and Lawless, 1989, p. 125). Park was one of the first scholars to articulate an assimilation theory of race relations, a theory that was based largely on his observations of the American experience. Assimilation theories came under serious scrutiny in the late 1960s, which, in turn, led to the development of new theories of race relations, such as internal colonialism, which emerged in the late 1960s with the black, brown, red, and yellow power movements and which was subsequently eclipsed by racial formation theories of the 1980s. However, assimilation theories and the assimilation paradigm for explaining and predicting the development of race relations continue to hold perhaps the middle ground, between chauvinistic nativism and affirmative multiculturalism (Salins, 1997). In many respects, the political agenda of the assimilation paradigm is gradualism—that is, the view that assimilation of minority groups socially and economically into the dominant society would take place over several generations, largely as a result of natural processes of cultural diffusion rather than through affirmative race-conscious policies.

A number of questions may be raised concerning Park's claim of the generalizability of his assimilation theory:

Does the theory hold only for certain types of societies and certain historical contexts?

Does the theory hold only for the relationship between some racial/ethnic groups in a society and not for others?

What factors affect the pace of change from one stage to another, and how do these factors vary for different groups?

Are the stages reversible?

Could the stages be truncated in some racial/ethnic relations?

Have other major stages and outcomes been omitted from the theory?

In the context of the United States, for example, the relations between white settlers and American Indians started with contact, which led to competition, and in turn, to the annihilation of a number of Indian nations. In the case of African Americans, the first contact coincided with enslavement and racial subordination. For Puerto Ricans, contact led to colonization. For Chicanos in the Southwest, contact led to competition, and in turn, to conquest. In contrast, however, the relations between the earlier and later white settlers approximated Park's stages of natural history. For the so-called "middleman minorities"—the Chinese and Japanese—the pattern is one of partial assimilation coupled with periodic and systemic hostility as reflected in the Chinese exclusion movement in the late 1800s and the relocation of the Japanese to concentration camps during World War II.

By asking and answering these questions, we can see that Park's theory of assimilation may be useful in explaining or predicting the development of racial, ethnic, and nationality relations in highly circumscribed situations but has little validity as a general theory. In light of the complex historical, contextual, temporal, and situational factors involved in the development of race relations, one may also question the possibility of constructing grand theories versus interpretive, narrative approaches based on the researcher's intersubjective point of view.

Whereas Park was primarily concerned with macro-theorizing at the level of societal change, other scholars working within the assimilation paradigm dealt more closely with the individual and interpersonal levels of analysis. For example, in his theory of race relations cycle, Bogardus postulated that the final stage of interracial contact is marginality—that is, an incomplete assimilation for immigrant groups caught between the cultures of their country of origin and the country to which they have immigrated (Bogardus, 1930). Bogardus's theory was based mainly on his observations of two generations of Chinese, Japanese, and Filipino immigrants in the United States between the late nineteenth century and 1930. Bogardus's early research on social distance between various racial and ethnic groups may be of value in view of the emerging academic and policy concerns with multiracial, multiethnic relations in the twenty-first century.

The most influential book on assimilation theory, Gordon's *Assimilation in American Life* (1964), appeared just a few years before major paradigm shifts took place in theorizing about race and ethnic relations in the United States. Gordon built on earlier work, drawing new conceptual and empirical distinctions among different types of assimilation and how they fit into the linear sequence of stages of assimilation: Contact leads to cultural or behavioral assimilation; cultural or behavioral assimilation leads to structural assimilation; structural assimilation leads to marital assimilation; and marital assimilation leads to identificational assimilation.

For Gordon, cultural or behavioral assimilation is measured by the extent to which a minority group takes on the cultural and behavioral characteristics of the dominant group. Structural assimilation is reflected in the extensive entry of a minority group into the membership of clubs, organizations, and social institutions. Marital assimilation is synonymous with extensive exogamy between the minority and dominant group. Finally, identificational assimilation is the development of a sense of peoplehood based exclusively on that of the dominant or host society. In this sense, in reference to the United States, Gordon's identificational assimilation is indistinguishable from the "melting pot" notion of race relations based on conformity to the Anglo ideal. His idea of cultural pluralism pertains to the situation when minority groups preserve significant portions of their culture and communal life. In his sequence of assimilation processes, cultural pluralism would appear as a countertendency to the first stage, the cultural-behavioral stage of assimilation. Gordon also asserted that the sequence could end indefinitely, even with cultural or behavioral assimilation. However, once structural assimilation occurred, the subsequent stages would follow naturally.

Although Gordon limited his generalizations about assimilation to the historical experience of racial and ethnic groups in the United States, his theory also has been applied to studies of majority–minority relations in other societies (Wong, 1997). Gordon's theory may be regarded, in some respects, as the last major work on assimilation in the 1960s, before the reemergence of Marxist and neo-Marxist paradigms on race relations that paralleled the shift in the civil rights movement from an emphasis on desegregation to one on black power. However, though challenged by Marxist and neo-Marxist analysis in the 1970s and 1980s and by postmodern, poststructural analysis of race in the 1980s and 1990s, the resiliency of the assimilation paradigm cannot be underestimated. My contention is that assimilation is still the most dominant paradigm, particularly in academic studies of race relations as we head into the twenty-first century, because it is closely linked to the illusory American myth of socioeconomic mobility for all irrespective of race, ethnicity, and nationality. In other words, assimilation and the American myth of opportunity and socioeconomic mobility are inseparable in the mindset of Americans, including most scholars who study race relations. Positivists who are concerned with measurement would find the indicators of assimilation (e.g., extensive entry of a minority group into the memberships of clubs, organizations, and social institutions) confounded with the indicators of socioeconomic mobility. The coupling of assimilation and mobility in social scientific thinking is reflected, for example, in Steinberg's *Ethnic Myth,* in which the author attempted to debunk the causal connection between genetic and cultural differences among different racial and national origin groups and their educational as well as occupational achievement (Steinberg, 1989).

Gordon's theory was more conservative than Park's in that conflict was not explicitly included as a major factor in the assimilation process. It is not implied here that Park subscribed to a conflict paradigm. Park insisted that as a general social law, in the relations between races, competition and conflict lead inevitably to assimilation. In formulating a typology of relations between minority groups and the dominant group, Luis Wirth, in a classic article, offered a more general theory of race and ethnic relations in which assimilation was one of the end results of racial contact but not necessarily the only one (Wirth, 1945). Wirth's main propositions were as follows: Contact leads to striving for pluralism. If there is high tolerance for pluralism, then striving for incorporation, and finally, for assimilation, will follow. If there is low tolerance for pluralism, then racial/ethnic/nationalistic militancy will follow, resulting in secessionist tendencies or incorporation of the minority group into another nation-state.

Wirth regarded racial/ethnic relations in the United States as basically assimilationist, and drew examples from the experience of European minority groups near nation-state boundaries in explaining militant and secessionist tendencies in racial/ethnic relations. It should be noted that after the establishment of the USSR following the Bolshevik revolution, a number of non-Russian nations were absorbed into the Soviet Union. Wirth must have been aware of the persistent tensions in these border regions of the USSR. However, Wirth did not consider racial/ethnic situations in colonial plural societies or caste societies. Moreover, decolonization movements in the third world were still largely events of the future when Wirth was developing his typology, and he did not anticipate changes in majority–minority relations in postcolonial societies. He also did not recognize the need to explain the experience of minority racial groups in America in contrast to the experience of later European immigrants in the United States. Still, Wirth came closest among the theorists of the assimilation paradigm to identifying the contexts in which the assimilation process might be blocked by majority group intolerance, resulting in minority group resistance and separatist movements.

Theorizing on Race Outside of Academia: The Black Nation Thesis as a Different Paradigm

Although Luis Wirth drew attention to ethnic conflicts in Europe connected to nationalistic movements, nationalism and the national question in the United States did not receive much attention in academia in the 1930s and 1940s, which were otherwise two fertile decades in the cultivation of theoretical thinking about race relations. For example, in *The American Dilemma*, black nationalism was only touched upon on three of the almost fifteen hundred pages of the two-volume work. However, perhaps due partially to the influence of the Garveyites and later the black Muslims, considerable attention was given the black national question by communist and other leftist movements in the 1930s and 1940s. In the Communist Party of the United States of America (CPUSA), in the 1930s, the black national question was among the most important and frequently debated topics in party publications. The CPUSA polemics on this question were connected to major campaigns of the Party in the 1930s—that is, Organize the Unorganized in the basic industries such as steel, mining, and automobiles in the North, and organizing sharecroppers against white supremacy, as in the Scottsboro Boys Campaign in the South. In these efforts, the CPUSA had to attract black support on the basis of not only proletarian class interests but also their racial loyalty as well as nationalistic sentiments. These historical factors in the CPUSA's effort to recruit African Americans must also be viewed within the context of the international communist movement in the

1930s and 1940s under the leadership of Joseph Stalin. The Third Communist International (Comintern) had carried out serious debates on the national question, and as a result of the debates, major purges for incorrect policy positions on that question. By the early 1930s, Stalin's position on the national question had become the official line of the Comintern, guiding the movements for national and colonial liberation throughout the world. Stalin defined a nation as a "historically evolved, stable community of people with a common language (or several common languages), territory, economic life, and psychological make-up manifested in a community of culture" (Stalin, 1975).

The most systematic treatment of the black national question by the CPUSA is contained in Harry Haywood's book *Negro Liberation* (1948). Haywood stated: "The Negroes in the United States manifest all these attributes of nationhood listed in the concise and classic definition of Stalin. They are 'a nation within a nation.'"

It is important to point out the distinction between *nation* and *state* in Marxist-Leninist-Stalinist theory. A *nation* refers to a community of people with the four attributes identified previously. A nation may or may not be able to exercise self-determination, including self-governance through the exercise of sovereignty. In this sense, the black nation in the South was an oppressed nation—that is, lacking a sovereign state by means of which the people could govern itself.

The key to the conceptualization of the black national question is the identification of the location of areas in the black belt in the South as the historic homeland of the nation. In reframing the African American struggle in terms of nationhood rather than race, Haywood and the CPUSA could now address the double oppression (class and nationality) of the African American people in the context of the history of slavery, the Civil War, and Reconstruction. In this sense, the failure of Reconstruction was fundamentally a reflection of the lack of the right to self-determination of the African American people. The subsequent large-scale dispersal of the black race from the South to the North, as the new system of sharecropping further impoverished African American agricultural wage laborers, further masked the national, or territorial, aspect of the black struggle in the South.

Haywood maintained that "Negro labor, organically united with the militant and politically conscious section of white labor, is the only force which can rally and unite the scattered segments of the Negro people in its fight for freedom" (Haywood, 1948, p. 216). In his publications of the 1930s and 1940s, he condemned black reformist leaders for not fighting for the self-determination of the black nation in the South, and for having advocated black support of the U.S. war effort as a means of achieving desegregation and upward mobility, without having exposed the war's imperialist goals (Haywood, 1930, 1948; Foner and Shapiro, 1991).

A further complication to an understanding of the black nation thesis arose from a linguistic ambiguity: If certain areas in the South constituted the black nation, what would happen to whites and other nonblacks living there? The answer to this question is that if a nation-state were established in the South, it would most likely not be called "the Black Nation." All nation-states in the world contain more than one race of people as their inhabitants. The key problem to be solved is how different races are to live together within a nation-state and whether all races will enjoy freedom and equality.

Another difficulty in conceptualizing the African American struggle as a national liberation movement is the relative recency of the constitution of African Americans as a people and of its historic land base. In the more typical case, nations evolve over a much longer historical period and may appear to have inhabited a particular geographic area from time immemorial. In contrast, the African American people were forcibly removed from various tribes in Africa and enslaved in America.

By the 1940s, the CPUSA had shifted its strategic organizing from the domestic scene to the international front via the United Front Against War and Fascism. Organizing the African American people around national oppression took a back seat to mobilizing against the international fascist menace. In the post–World War II era, the black nation thesis never regained the political support that it had in the 1930s. The McCarthy anticommunist witch-hunt in the early 1950s had a lingering effect on the civil rights movement, from the mid-1950s to the late 1960s, as many of the movement's leaders attempted to avoid any connection with the communist movement. However, the black national question reemerged in the late 1960s, in leftist polemics in conjunction with the movement to build a new communist movement in the United States. In that context, Marxist theorists from each of the major racial minority groups—African Americans, American Indians, Asian Pacific Americans, and Chicanos/Latinos—articulated their analyses of the national question (October League, 1976; Revolutionary Union, n.d.). Two of the major themes in these analyses were the relationships between class and national oppression and between race and nation. The "national oppression" perspective on the minority racial groups in the United States never received a great deal of attention from scholars in academia. While there have been debates since the 1920s about the existence of the black nation in the South and more recently about the Chicano nation in the Southwest, it is surprising that the "national oppression" perspective has been largely neglected—not only by academic but also movement scholars—in examining the situation of Indian nations. Having lost the right to self-determination and being explicitly degraded in legal status as "domestic dependent nations" by Chief Justice Marshall in the second decade of the eighteenth century, about two hundred of these nations are still seeking federal recognition (Thornton, 1987; McCulloch and Wilkins, 1995).

Myrdal's *American Dilemma*:
From Assimilation to Racial Equality

In 1938, the Swedish social economist Gunnar Myrdal was invited by the Carnegie Foundation to come to the United States to conduct a study on the "American Negro problem." Myrdal assembled a team of American collaborators including Ralph Bunche, E. Franklin Frazier, Charles S. Johnson, Otto Klineberg, Arnold Rose, and Dorothy Swaine Thomas to carry out a monumental study, which became an international classic on the problem and prospects of race relations in the United States. To some extent, Myrdal's and his colleagues' work diverged from the dominant academic preoccupation with the question of assimilation. Instead, Myrdal's major concern was the prospect of freedom and equality for African Americans. On this issue Myrdal expressed boundless optimism. In the Preface to the first edition of his book, Myrdal italicized the statement that "not since Reconstruction has there been more reason to anticipate fundamental changes in American race relations, changes which will involve development toward the American ideal" (Wong, 1988, p. 164). In Myrdal's preface to the book's twentieth anniversary edition, he remarked (Myrdal, 1996, p. xxxiii):

> Since the national compromise worked out in the 1870s, the relative status of the Negro people had been rising but the pace of change had been exceedingly slow, and in some fields there had even been retreats. The most important conclusion of my study was, however, that an era of more than half a century during which there had been no fundamental change was approaching its close. . . . Or more positively, not since Reconstruction has there been more reason to anticipate fundamental changes in American race relations, changes which will involve a development toward American ideals."

Writing in the same volume in 1962, Arnold Rose—one of Myrdal's associates in the *American Dilemma* project, predicted that "the dynamic social forces creating inequality will . . . be practically eliminated in three decades" (Myrdal, 1996, p. liv).

The Myrdal project represented a partial paradigm shift in that it moved the hitherto academic focus in race relations studies from assimilation to the question of black/white inequality. Perhaps due to his background as an economist from one of the most developed, social democratic welfare states, Myrdal placed considerable emphasis—in a section of eleven chapters—on employment, income inequality, occupation, and poverty. There were separate sections on politics, justice, social inequality, and social stratification. Ten chapters in a section entitled "Leadership and Concerted Action" focused on leadership and organization to address the problems of inequality. Assimilation scarcely appeared in the two-volume work, and when it did, it was subsumed under "amalgamation"—two or more groups merged to form a larger, new group. This scenario contrasted with the conventional description of assimilation, in which one group assumes the identity of another. Yet Myrdal's fundamental assumptions that inequality could be overcome through education to end prejudicial attitudes, which in turn would end discrimination (behavior), meant that his approach was based on individual change rather than institutional and structural reform.

The Reemergence of Marxist and Neo-Marxist Paradigms

It is possible that the opening of new areas of civilian and military employment to blacks during and after World War II, and the initial black gains in educational as well as employment opportunities in the civil rights movement, might have lulled Myrdal and Rose into a false sense of the historical inevitability of racial equality in the United States (Wong, 1988, p. 164). However, a review of the previous several decades affirms the persistence of racial inequality. After the mid-1960s, Marxist perspectives on racial stratification emerged from a relative hiatus in the 1940s and 1950s, as both the old and new generations of Marxist scholars reintroduced structural explanations of racial inequality. In *Monopoly Capital*, Baran and Sweezy identified three sets of social forces and institutional mechanisms that have kept blacks at the bottom of the economy decade after decade (Baran and Sweezy, 1966, p. 263). They argued that private interests benefited from the continued existence of a segregated subproletariat. Employers benefited from divisions in the labor force that enabled them to play one group against another. Secondly, the authors pointed out that the existence of a pariah group at the bottom "acted as a kind of 'lightning rod' for the frustrations and hostilities of all the higher groups, the more so the nearer they were to the bottom" (pp. 265–266). Third, they asserted that as monopoly capitalism developed, the demand for unskilled and semiskilled labor declined both relatively and absolutely. They contended that this trend adversely affected blacks and condemned them to an inferior economic and social position.

Baran and Sweezy treated the situation of African Americans in terms of their class position and avoided the question of national oppression. In contrast to Baran and Sweezy, a number of scholars developed a neo-Marxist paradigm of "internal colonialism" to explain the situation of minority races in the United States (Blauner, 1972; Barrera, 1979). At the beginning, this paradigm owed its origin *politically* to the urban ghetto revolts led by organizations such as the Black Panther Party, and *ideologically* to third world neo-Marxist theorists, such as Franz Fanon (Fanon, 1968). In many respects, the internal colonialism paradigm may be regarded as a variant of the oppressed nation thesis, but the recognition of its affinity to the Marxist analysis of the national question only came later. Blauner gave the concept of internal colonialism a legitimate academic status in the late 1960s and early

1970s, although he had borrowed the term from the writings of the Black Panther Party at that time. The Black Panthers were, in turn, influenced by Malcolm X, Fanon, and other third world writers. Blauner also used the phrase "colonial analogy," which seems to indicate that he was not entirely convinced that the situation of minority races in America was truly "colonial." On the other hand, he also depicted the condition of the minority races in the United States as worse than that of the colonized masses in Asia and Africa:

> The oppressed masses of Asia and Africa had the relative "advantage" of being colonized in their own land. In the United States, the more total cultural domination, the alienation of most third world people from a land base, and the numerical minority factor have weakened the group integrity of the colonized and their possibilities for cultural and political self-determination. (Blauner, 1972, p. 74)

Blauner rejected the immigration/assimilation framework for analyzing the situation of racial minority groups in the United States. He stated:

> Colonization begins with a forced involuntary entry. Second, there is the impact on culture. The effects of colonization on the culture and social organization of the colonized people are more than the results of such "natural" processes as contact and acculturation. The colonizing power carries out a policy that constrains, transforms or destroys indigenous values, orientations and ways of life. Third, . . . the lives of the subordinate groups are administered by representatives of the dominant power." (p. 84)

Blauner recognized that the internal colonial model did not apply equally to the various racial minority peoples in America. The conquest of the Indian nations and the annexation of the Southwest followed the lines of classic colonialism. The Chinese experienced a mixture of free and forced entry in the nineteenth century. The Filipinos and Puerto Ricans were colonized in their homeland before immigration. African Americans were enslaved after forced entry. Despite the dissimilarities, Blauner noted that each racial minority group has undergone destructive, indeed cataclysmic experiences in America: Indians waged a three-hundred-year war and lost their true sovereignty; African Americans endured two hundred fifty years of slavery; Chinese experienced persecution under policies and politics of exclusion; and Japanese underwent imprisonment in concentration camps. In looking at the situation of minority racial groups from a third world, colonial perspective, Blauner and other scholars who adopted the internal colonialism perspective provided an alternative, structuralist paradigm to immigration/assimilation. As the black power movement and other minority political movements for self-determination declined by the late 1970s, the colonial analogy also lost its influence in academic studies of race relations.

Social Constructionism and Racial Formation Theory

In the social sciences, social constructionism was a reaction to the dominance of positivism and its epistemological assumptions. Applied to the field of race and ethnic studies, social constructionism questions essentialist definitions of race and ethnicity, especially those based on supposedly objective, biological criteria for racial classification. In this paradigm, the causal status of race as a variable is complex. Whereas positivist social science treats race only as an independent variable, social constructionists are concerned with the complex interplay of factors at the individual and institutional levels that lead to the formation of racial structures and imputations of racial meanings. In the United States, the historical and contemporary constructions of races and panethnicities have been the major subject matter of social constructionists in the field of race and ethnic studies. The usefulness of social constructionism in the analysis of race and ethnicity in other societies is just beginning to be recognized. For example, in the case of China, the formation of the Han people versus other ethnic groups and the meaning of "Chineseness," which had previously been taken for granted, is now being scrutinized by social scientists such as Fei Xiaotung (Yu, Rong, and Wong, 1998).

The most influential work in the 1980s and 1990s on the social construction of race was Omi and Winant's *Racial Formation in the United States* (1986, 1994). Omi and Winant's theoretical approach to the study of race was shaped by three related concerns: (1) to assess the significance of the emergence of new racial minority movements in the 1960s in their *rearticulation* of racial politics; (2) to locate race at the center of American political history, not in order to displace other important social relationships such as class and sex/gender, but to serve as a corrective to the reductionism characteristic of racial theory; and (3) to suggest a new, expanded model of the state and state activity that would place socially based movements, rather than traditionally defined, economically based interest groups, at the center of contemporary political processes (Omi and Winant, 1994, p. 4). They borrowed from postmodernism and poststructuralism in their perspective on the dynamic, shifting meanings of race and the changing as well as the decentering of the sites of struggles in racial politics. However, they also insisted that there is a center in the struggle against racial rule—that is, against the hegemony of the racialized state. Following Gramsci, they contended that hegemony was constituted by a combination of coercion and consent (Omi and Winant, 1994, p. 67).

One may argue that Omi and Winant were overly influenced by the black power movement and other racial minority movements of the 1960s and 1970s that asserted the primacy or even exclusivity of race as the sole criterion for unity or coalition building. Their intellectual and political motivation for placing race explicitly at the center of the struggle against hegemony emerged in reaction to both the neoconservative (e.g., Friedman, 1962; Murray, 1984) and neoliberal (e.g., William J. Wilson, 1987, [1978]) projects to liquidate race in theoretical and policy discourse. Omi and Winant therefore theoretically overcorrected for the tendency in social scientific theory to treat race as either a secondary factor or as one that could be subsumed under class. An example of this overcorrection is their concept of the racial state (Omi and Winant, 1994, pp. 77–91). Although I agree with them that "the (American) state from its very inception has been concerned with the politics of race" (Omi and Winant, p. 81), it would be reductionist to see the state as the instrument of racial rule. There are essentially three conceptions of the state: an instrument for the domination of one group (defined by class, race, gender or other categories) over others through coercion and/or consent; an arbiter between the dominant group and others; and an instrument to effectuate true equality among all groups. By characterizing the state as racial, they liquidated the class, gender, and other dimensions of state hegemony and undermined the possibility of social movements based on broader coalitions. They also negated the importance of the analysis of multiple subjectivities or subject positions—not only race but also nationality or national origin, class, gender, and other factors—in the construction of social meanings, identities, and social structures. The extension of Omi and Winant's work to address these problems remains an important, unfinished theoretical project in racial and ethnic studies. In Winant's recent examination of the relationship between race and class in the global hegemony of capitalism and in the formation of the "underclass" in *Racial Conditions*, he continued to assert the primacy of race over other factors (1994, pp. 111–129). Nevertheless, I think that he has modified the position that he and Omi took in *Racial Formation in the United States* (1986; 1994). This modification was evident when he stated that "in the contemporary United States, hegemony is determined by the articulation of *race and class* (italics added)" and "any counter-hegemonic initiative must be explicitly race-conscious in its approach to issues of class or fall victim to the same hegemonic strategies that have doomed so many other progressive political initiatives" (Winant, 1994, p. 33). At the same time, Winant pointed to the increasing significance of class and differential racialization along the lines of class in American society (Winant, 1994, p. 63). Moreover, he noted that the struggles of racially defined minorities—women, gays, and the exploited as well as impoverished—though they remain, in general, separate struggles, must confront a variegated but ultimately unified hegemonic order (Winant, p. 107). Winant also referred to the racial dimensions of hegemony rather than the racial state as he and Omi did in their earlier book. In the final analysis, however, Winant's hegemony is a black box whose contents have yet to be illuminated. Specifically, Winant did not convey a clear conception of who or what constitutes the hegemonic group or power elite in terms of class or other categories.

Trends in Current Research on Race, Ethnicity, and Nationality in the United States

In the transition from the twentieth century to the twenty-first, race and ethnicity are attracting more scholarly and public attention than ever before. Now we can echo DuBois's words about the central significance of the "color line" in American society. Some discernible current trends in research may be noted:

1. Research on race and ethnicity has become increasingly interdisciplinary. Besides the traditional fields of the social sciences and humanities, the new fields of communication, literary, and cultural studies have made important contributions in terms of theory, method, and substantive issues that otherwise might not be taken up in traditional scholarship. The establishment of interdisciplinary ethnic studies associations and ethnic studies departments in a broad spectrum of public as well as private colleges and universities between the 1960s and the 1990s has led to what might be described as the "marginalized institutionalization" of this field in academia. Academic institutions need ethnic studies for a number of possibly contradictory reasons—to enhance a public image of being enlightened, to ward off pressure from minority students and communities, to recruit minority faculty, to indicate acceptance of the field as legitimate, or in recognition that knowledge about ethnic groups is vital to students' social as well as career development. From world-class universities like Harvard and Berkeley to community colleges that serve predominantly local populations, ethnic studies has found a degree of acceptance as a field of specialization or as part of the general studies curriculum. However, there might well be negative repercussions, from the current attacks on affirmative action, bilingual education, and other policies that are designed to redress historical and contemporary gender, racial, ethnic, and national origin discrimination, on future support for ethnic studies. On the whole, ethnic studies still has only limited legitimacy in academia. This is evident in the difficulty that ethnic studies departments and programs have in securing permanent funding and personnel in most colleges both public and private.

2. From the 1960s to the 1970s, ethnic studies tended to focus on race. In the political movements of that period, the struggles of the minority races for equality were becoming less connected with those of their potential allies. The "decentering" of the social movements was evident both in praxis and in theoretical work. The "racial forma-

tion" paradigm, for example, looked at the state as "racialized" without examining its class nature and genderized aspects. The relative isolation of ethnic studies as a field has limited its effectiveness in developing wider political and academic support. However, in the last two decades, there has been significant growth in research on the intersections of race, class, and gender—especially on the additive and interactive patterns of these dimensions of stratification in terms of their origins and effects on democracy and equality in society. The broadening of the focus and linkages of ethnic studies with other fields such as women studies, labor studies, studies of the poor, and gay/lesbian studies may contribute to a widening of the democratic and progressive alliance in the academic and public arenas.

3. The scope of the field has expanded to multiracial, multiethnic issues since the late 1960s, contrasting with the emphasis on white–black relations and comparisons in previous decades. Until the late 1960s, the field of ethnic studies referred almost automatically to inequality and relations between blacks and whites. In empirical research, even at the national level, data were either unavailable for other racial groups, subsumed under the "other" category, or subsumed as nonwhite. Research on other nonwhite races was hampered by the unavailability of data and archives. This situation has changed significantly in the past three decades. Nevertheless, in research on more specialized topics, such as health and criminal justice, data are just becoming available for the analysis of nonwhite groups besides African Americans (Wong, 1998). In the theoretical realm, prior to the late 1960s, the immigration/assimilation paradigm dominated the academic field of ethnic studies. Outside of academia, the black nation thesis provided an alternative explanation of the historical and contemporary situation of blacks in America and a guide to political action, at least in the 1930s and 1940s. In the 1970s, internal colonialism theory went beyond black–white relations to include other nonwhite races within a matrix of "colonized" groups in American society. In the 1980s and 1990s, racial formation theory has been the most influential in addressing the multiple and ever-changing meanings of race at the micro (individual and interpersonal) level and the dynamics of changes in racial relations at the macro (institutional and societal) level. However, the overemphasis on race as the center of political struggle in racial formation theory still has to be redressed. Moreover, another theoretical issue that requires attention is the neglect of the political economy of race relations in the work of the racial formation theorists and others who have been influenced by postmodernism and poststructuralism.

The recent upsurge in interest in multiracial relations, especially in the relations among the minority races, is partly a consequence of the tremendous increase in the Asian and Chicano/Latino populations since the 1960s and, more immediately, the rise in tension in the urban areas among the minority races. Studies on Asian–Black, Hispanic–Black, and other minority group relations are beginning to appear (Wong, Lai, Nagasawa, and Lin, 1998). Conflict, cooperation, coalition building and other aspects of minority race relations are important frontiers of ethnic studies. Recent theoretical and empirical work has produced exciting results. For example, recognizing the multiracial and social class context in which assimilation takes place, some scholars have formulated a theory of segmented assimilation to explain the divergent paths that minority youths may follow as they grow up in cities in close contact with other races (Portes and Zhou, 1992, 1993). There is an urgent need to bring together scholars in Asian, African, Chicano/Latino, and Native American studies to discuss a collaborative and common agenda of theoretical and empirical research. The joint meeting of the Asian American Studies Association and Black Studies Association in 1996 in Oakland was one such effort.

Essentialist definitions tend to exaggerate categorical differences among the races and to nullify differences within each race. One trend of research since the 1970s has been the focus on explaining ethnic, national origin, and other differences within a race. Steinberg (1989), for example, debunked the cultural explanation of the differences in the educational and occupational mobility of Jews, Italians, Irish, and other white "ethnic" or national origin groups. A number of studies have been published retracing the social construction of the white race and debunking its supposedly biological origin (Alba, 1990; Roedinger, 1991; Waters, 1990; Winant, 1994). In the case of the minority races, the emphasis on ethnic solidarity has often suppressed differences within groups (Espiritu, 1992; Wong, Applewhite, and Daley, 1990). For Asians/Pacific Americans, differences based on gender, national origin, generation, class, timing, and circumstances of immigration, as well as other factors have only been given significant attention in the past ten years or so (Ong and Hee, 1994; Wong, Lai, Lin, and Nagasawa, 1998). One major set of studies on ethnic differences among Chicanos/Latinos was ironically provoked by William J. Wilson's attempt to apply his research on blacks and the underclass to Hispanics (Wilson, 1987). The critique of the validity of Wilson's concept of "underclass" for the analysis of various Chicano/Latino populations fundamentally reflected differences among these groups that previously were hidden beneath a patina of Hispanic panethnicity (Moore and Pinderhughes, 1993). Research on differences within racial and panethnic groups will continue to debunk the myths of homogeneity that tend to serve the interests of the more privileged segments of those populations.

Immigration and nationality have reemerged as major topics in ethnic studies in recent years. The changes in immigration laws since the 1960s have brought about major demographic changes in the composition of the racial and ethnic minority populations in the United States. The growth in numbers and diversity of the Asian/Pacific American and Chicano/Latino populations has reshaped the racial composition of a number of states and metropolitan areas. There has been a tendency for these groups to develop solidarity for social, economic, and political action along panethnic lines. However, nationality or national origin is still the most important factor among the immigrant groups in terms of identity formation, ethnic cohesion, and community development. In the 1930s and 1940s, the assimilation paradigm was developed mainly from the research on immigrants from a number of nations of southern and eastern Europe. The assimilation paradigm was incorrectly applied to nonwhite populations. Scholars researching the more recent, nonwhite immigrants have had to develop new paradigms that are valid in studying these populations (Lopez and Espiritu, 1990; Espiritu, 1992; Hing, 1993; Heer, 1996; Portes, 1996). The development of databases that include samples large enough for the analysis of different nationalities within a panethnic group and other research archives on national origin groups is also an urgent part of the current research agenda.

The studies of "whiteness" that deal with such diverse questions as "invisible" white power and privilege, "white trash" and poverty, white "ethnic options" and the making of Euro-Americans, white antiracism, and white "racial nationalism" have received significant attention in racial and ethnic studies since the 1970s (Alba, 1990; Roediger, 1991; Waters, 1990). These studies are important for several reasons. The knowledge and power gained in deconstructing the historical origins and contemporary manifestations of white privilege could well undermine the foundations of white racial hegemony. Second, research on white racial nationalism in terms of its ideology and social basis can shed important light on its linkage to fascistic tendencies in contemporary American culture and politics. Third, racism in the guise of advocating "color-blindness" and meritocracy, which draws support from a broad spectrum of the white population and a smaller portion of the racial minority population (including highly visible leaders like Linda Chavez, Wade Connerly, and Clarence Thomas), is clearly on the rise. Research is urgently needed on this new form of racism so akin to "friendly fascism" in its apparently nonviolent, civilized, sensible, and "nonracist" posture, but so devastating in its suppression of racial minorities, women, and other disadvantaged groups struggling to overcome structural discrimination. Fourth, white racial nationalism has been on the rise also in western Europe in the form of xenophobia against immigrants and minorities (Kushnick, 1995; Solomos, 1995). Comparative research on white racial nationalism on the

one hand and white antiracism on the other is important in building international coalitions against fascism and racism.

A Concluding Note

In many respects, the studies of race, ethnicity, and nationality in the United
States have been divorced from studies in other countries and from research
that approaches this subject from a comparative/historical perspective. Earlier efforts by, for example, Frazier (1957), Shibutani and Kwan (1965),
Schermerhorn (1970), and Lieberson (1975) have not, by and large, been followed by other comparative research on the United States and other capitalist, socialist, colonial, and postsocialist as well as postcolonial societies. The
persistence and increase in racial, ethnic, and national conflicts in recent
years on the one hand, and the shift in the character of these conflicts on the
other, have led to renewed interest in comparative studies (see Balibar and
Wallerstein, 1991; Bowser, 1995; Horowitz, 1985; Ringer and Lawless, 1989;
and Winant, 1994, pp. 111–169). The growing interest in diaspora studies
within ethnic studies in the United States has been due, in large part, to the
worldwide increase in immigrant and refugee populations. Another major
reason for this growth is that racial minority scholars, who have been largely
excluded from international area studies in previous decades, have sought to
rebuild linkages between the study of racial and ethnic groups in the United
States and research on the historic homelands of these groups (Hune, Kim,
Fugita, and Ling, 1991). In addition, in diaspora studies there is the opportunity to compare the situation and development of particular racial, ethnic, or
nationality groups in different cultural and political-economic contexts. In
the final analysis, it is the recognition of a number of danger signals in racial
and ethnic relations in recent years, not only in the United States but also in
other societies, that has led to the growing interest in comparative studies. In
the United States and a number of advanced capitalist countries in western
Europe, systematic attacks have been launched against laws and policies developed during the past several decades to redress racial inequality and injustice—attacks that are accompanied by the rise of a white racial nationalist,
protofascist consciousness (Bowser, 1995). In a number of postcolonial societies in Africa and Asia that were liberated from European and American
rule between the end of World War II and the 1970s, the incidence of ethnic
conflict and catastrophic violence has increased. These former "colonial
plural societies" (in the terminology of Furnivall, 1948, and Smith, 1965)
have experienced patterns of ethnic conflict associated with the rise of nativism and tribal, caste, and national chauvinism, as well as of religious fundamentalism. Arguably, these conflicts have their roots in the disruptive
colonial relations (which were, at the same time, racial relations) and the cultural, economic, and political segmentation that preceded the liberation of

these countries from imperialist rule (Horowitz, 1985, pp. 151–166, 205–209). Also, with the collapse of the USSR and Yugoslavia, ethnic conflicts have transformed a number of postsocialist countries into movements for national self-determination. The patterns of intergroup conflicts—which may be racial, ethnic, and/or nationalistic—in these postsocialist countries are reminiscent of the political and cultural breakdowns in a number of postcolonial societies, such as Indonesia, Zaire, and Afghanistan. Although the focus of this book is the United States, it is important to bear in mind the global significance of the issues of inequality and injustice connected with race, ethnicity, and nationality, as well as the need to address these issues in their interrelated domestic and international contexts.

REFERENCES

Alba, R. (1990). *Ethnic Identity: The Transformation of White America*. New Haven, CT: Yale University Press.

Balibar, E., and Wallerstein, I. (1991). *Race, Nation, and Class: Ambiguous Identities*. Trans. Turner, C. New York: Verso.

Baltzell, E. (1967). "Introduction." In DuBois, W.E.B., *The Philadelphia Negro*. New York: Schocken.

Baran, P., and Sweezy, P. (1966). *Monopoly Capital*. New York: Monthly Review Press.

Barrera, M. (1979). *Race and Class in the Southwest: A Theory of Racial Inequality*. Notre Dame, IN: University of Notre Dame Press.

Bogardus, E. S. (1930). "A Race Relations Cycle." *American Journal of Sociology* 35, no. 4, pp. 612–617.

Blauner, R. (1972). *Racial Oppression in America*. New York: Harper and Row.

Bowser, B. P. (1995). *Racism and Anti-Racism in World Perspective*. Thousand Oaks, CA: Sage.

DuBois, W.E.B. (1967). *The Philadelphia Negro: A Social Study*. New York: Schocken.

Espiritu, Y. L. (1992). *Asian American Panethnicity*. Philadelphia, PA: Temple University Press.

Fanon, F. (1968). *The Wretched of the Earth*. New York: Grove Press.

Foner, P., and Shapiro, H. (Editors). (1991). *American Communism and Black Americans: A Documentary History, 1930–1934*. Philadelphia: Temple University Press.

Frazier, E. F. (1957). *Race and Culture Contacts in the Modern World*. Boston: Beacon Press.

Friedman, M. (1962). *Capitalism and Freedom*. Chicago: University of Chicago Press.

Furnivall, J. S. (1956 [1948]). *Colonial Policy and Practice: A Comparative Study of Burma and Netherlands India*. New York: New York University Press.

Gordon, M. M. (1964). *Assimilation in American Life*. New York: Oxford University Press.

Haywood, H. (1930). "Against Bourgeois-Liberal Distortions of Leninism on the Negro Question in the United States." *The Communist* IX, August, pp. 694–712.
_____. (1948). *Negro Liberation*. New York: International Publishers.
Heer, D. M. (1996). *Immigration in America's Future: Social Science Findings and the Policy Debate*. Boulder: Westview.
Hing, B. O. (1993). *Making and Remaking Asian America Through Immigration Policy, 1850–1990*. Stanford: Stanford University Press.
Horowitz, D. L. (1985). *Ethnic Groups in Conflict*. Berkeley: University of California Press.
Hune, S., Kim, H., Fugita, S. S., and Ling, A. (1991). *Asian Americans: Comparative and Global Perspectives*. Pullman: Washington State University Press.
Kushnick, L. (1995). "Racism and Anti-Racism in Western Europe." Pp. 181–202 in Bowser, B. P., ed., *Racism and Anti-Racism in World Perspective*. Thousand Oaks, CA: Sage.
Lieberson, S. (1975). "A Societal Theory of Race and Ethnic Relations." In Laumann, E. O., ed., *Social Stratification: Research and Theory for the 1970s*. New York: Bobbs-Merrill.
Lopez, D., and Espiritu, Y. L. (1990). "Panethnicity in the United States: A Theoretical Framework." *Ethnic and Racial Studies* 13, no. 2, pp. 198–224.
McCulloch, A. M., and Wilkins, D. E. (1995). "'Constructing' Nations Within States: The Quest For Federal Recognition By the Catawba and Lumbee Tribes." *American Indian Quarterly* 19, no. 3 (Summer), pp. 361–387.
Moore, J., and Pinderhughes, R., ed. (1993). *In the Barrios: Latinos and the Underclass Debate*. New York: Russell Sage.
Murray, C. (1984). *Losing Ground: American Social Policy, 1950–1980*. New York: Basic Books.
Myrdal, G. (1944). *An American Dilemma: The Negro Problem and Modern Democracy*. New York: Harper and Row.
_____. (1996). *An American Dilemma: The Negro Problem and Modern Democracy*. 2 vols. New Brunswick, NJ: Transaction.
October League. (1975). *The Struggle for Black Liberation and Socialist Revolution*. Chicago: October League.
Omi, M., and Winant, H. (1986). *Racial Formation in the United States: From the 1960s to the 1980s*. New York: Routledge.
_____. (1994). *Racial Formation in the United States: From the 1960s to the 1990s*. New York: Routledge.
Ong, P., and Hee, S. J. (1994). "Economic Diversity." Pp. 31–56 in Ong, P., ed., *The State of Asian America: Economic Diversity, Issues and Policies*. Los Angeles: University of California, Asian Pacific American Public Policy Institute and Asian American Studies Center.
Park, R. E. (1950). *Race and Culture*. Glencoe, IL: Free Press.
Portes, A., ed. (1996). *The New Second Generation*. New York: Russell Sage.
Portes, A., and Zhou, M. (1992). "Gaining the Upper Hand: Economic Mobility Among Immigrant and Domestic Minorities." *Ethnic and Racial Studies* 15, no. 4, pp. 491–522.
_____. (1993). "The New Second Generation: Segmented Assimilation and Its Variants." In *Annals of the American Academy of Political and Social Sciences* 530, November, pp. 74–96.

Revolutionary Union. (n.d.). *Red Papers 5: National Liberation and Proletarian Revolution in the United States*. Chicago: Revolutionary Union.

Ringer, B. B., and Lawless, E. R. (1989). *Race-Ethnicity and Society*. New York: Routledge.

Roediger, D. R. (1991). *The Wages of Whiteness: Race and the Making of the American Working Class*. New York: Verso.

Rose, A. (1996). "Postscript: Twenty Years Later." Pp. xxxvii—liv in Myrdal, G., *An American Dilemma* (New Brunswick, NJ: Transaction).

Salins, P. D. (1997). *Assimilation American Style*. New York: Basic Books.

Schermerhorn, R. A. (1970). *Comparative Race Relations: A Framework for Theory and Research*. New York: Random House.

Shibutani, T., and Kwan, K. M. (1965). *Ethnic Stratification: A Comparative Approach*. New York: Macmillan.

Smith, M. G. (1965). *The Plural Society in the British West Indies*. Berkeley: University of California Press.

Solomos, J. (1995). "Racism and Anti-Racism in Great Britain: Historical Trends and Contemporary Issues." Pp.157–180 in Bowser, B. P., ed., *Racism and Anti-Racism in World Perspective*. Thousand Oaks, CA: Sage.

Stalin, J. (1975). *Marxism and the National Colonial Question*. San Francisco: Proletarian Publishers.

Steinberg, S. (1989). *The Ethnic Myth: Race, Ethnicity, and Class in America*. Boston: Beacon.

Thornton, R. (1987). *American Indian Holocaust and Survival: A Population History Since 1492*. Norman: University of Oklahoma Press.

Waters, M. C. (1990). *Ethnic Notions: Choosing Identities in America*. Berkeley: University of California Press.

Wilson, W. J. (1978). *The Declining Significance of Race: Blacks and Changing American Institutions*. Chicago: University of Chicago Press.

_____. (1987). *The Truly Disadvantaged: The Inner City, the Underclass, and Public Policy*. Chicago: University of Chicago Press.

Winant, H. (1994). *Racial Conditions: Politics, Theory, Comparisons*. Minneapolis: University of Minnesota Press.

Wirth, L. (1945). "The Problem of Minority Groups." In Linton, R., ed., *The Science of Man in the World Crisis*. New York: Columbia University Press.

Wong, P. (1988). "The Differential Impact of Employment and Income Security Policies on Minorities in the United States." Pp.164–183 in Sanders, D. S., and Fischer, J., eds., *Visions for the Future: Social Work and Pacific-Asian Perspectives*. Honolulu: University of Hawaii, School of Social Work.

Wong, P. (1997). "Race and Ethnic Studies in the United States: Toward the Twenty-First Century." Lecture presented at the Institute of Sociology and Anthropology, Beijing University, Beijing, China, June 9.

Wong, P. (1998). *Are Asian Americans Treated Fairly in Federal Criminal Sentencing?* A report submitted to the United States Sentencing Commission.

Wong, P., Applewhite, S., and Daley, J. M. (1990). "From Despotism to Pluralism: The Evolution of Voluntary Organizations in Chinese American Communities." *Ethnic Groups: An International Periodical of Ethnic Studies* 12, no. 2, pp. 215–233.

Wong, P., Lai, F., Nagasawa, R., and Lin, T. (1998). "Asian Americans as a Model Minority: Self-Perceptions and Perceptions By Other Racial Groups." *Sociological Perspectives* 41, no. 1, pp. 95–118.

Yu, C., Ma, R., and Wong, P. (1998). "Recent Development of Sociological/Anthropological Research on Minorities/Nationalities/Ethnic Groups in China." Working Paper of the Northwest Center for Comparative American Cultures and Race Relations, Washington State University, Pullman.

Index

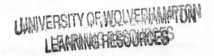